W9-ADO-773
enemies 144

PROBLEMS IN EUROPEAN HISTORY:
A DOCUMENTARY COLLECTION

The Ninth of Thermidor: The Fall of Robespierre

EDITED BY
RICHARD BIENVENU
University of Missouri

New York
OXFORD UNIVERSITY PRESS
London Toronto 1968

Library of Congress Catalogue Card Number: 68–22182
Printed in the United States of America

FOREWORD

Problems in European History: A Documentary Collection has arisen out of a collective teaching experience. The series seeks to overcome a shortcoming which the authors believe persists in college history instruction. Certainly the restricting confines of the traditional textbook have been expanded as numerous collections of "readings" have appeared. But the undergraduate still remains at a distance from the historian's workshop. A compilation of heavily edited "significant documents" does not make for the sense of contact with the past that the study of history ought to promote. And the predigested selections from contending historians, neatly arrayed on either side of "classic" controversies, does not get the student to probe the underlying evidence; in fact, these academic disputations often leave him bewildered.

The conviction that students learned little of the way in which historians actually worked prompted a group of young Harvard historians five years ago to develop a new approach. The course that resulted — Social Sciences 3: Problems in Modern European History — represented an attempt to focus intensively on a small number of problems. Each problem would involve careful analysis of a wide variety of original source material. The student could develop the skills and understanding of historical explanation. In learning to compare evidence, make and test hypotheses, and judge critically earlier accounts, he would encounter some of the problems of historical research as experienced by the working historian.

In Social Sciences 3 eight studies in historical analysis are presented in a year. Our intention here is to make these documentary collections available, not necessarily as a series except in their underlying aim, but as separate problems that can be studied individually in connection with courses in European history. Each book has been edited and introduced with that purpose in mind. Thus the student can wrestle with the problems inherent in historical writing and judgment while he studies intensively a segment of the history of the country or period being taught.

Social Sciences 3 has developed over the past four years through the efforts of our collaborators, who share in the creation of these books beyond what we can gratefully acknowledge. Individual problems were prepared or substantially recast by the respective authors, but each case study was discussed and scrutinized by the entire staff of Social Sciences 3. To all of them, to the Committee on General Education of Harvard College, which has generously given of its time and efforts, and to our students — whose criticisms and suggestions were a fundamental guideline — we extend our thanks.

Cambridge, Mass. RICHARD BIENVENU
August 1967 JOHN F. NAYLOR

PREFACE

The aims of this series have been set forth in our Foreword. The particular historiographical problems encountered in *The Ninth of Thermidor* are outlined in editorial comments throughout this volume. I am placing yet another introductory obstacle in the reader's path because I would like to discharge the pleasant duty of thanking the friends and collaborators who helped to collect, translate, and edit these sources.

The Ninth of Thermidor, like most of the volumes in this series, was not the work of one editor. It was revised from year to year in response to our experience in the classroom. The original version of this collection was planned and edited by Philip Dawson, who unfortunately could not collaborate on the present edition. I am grateful for the advice and comment that he generously gave. Fritz Ringer and Mack Walker directed an intermediate revision of the collection. Among those who translated many of the documents are Carol Helmstadter, Standish Meacham, Nancy Roelker, Robert Soucy, and Laurence Veysey. The final version draws heavily upon the efforts of these colleagues and I am in their debt. The shortcomings and faults that persist are, needless to say, my own doing.

I want also to acknowledge a debt of a different sort. The particular interpretation of the revolution from 1793 to 1794 that I present in the Introduction is based on the works of Georges

Lefebvre, George Rudé, Richard Cobb, and, above all, Albert Soboul. I hope that this acknowledgment will offset the absence of more specific indications in the Introduction, where footnotes were deliberately kept to a minimum.

Finally, a word of thanks goes to my former students at Harvard and Radcliffe for reactions and suggestions that were often both painfully frank and valuable.

Boulder, Colorado R. B.
January 1968

CONTENTS

The Ninth of Thermidor:
The Fall of Robespierre

INTRODUCTION

The Ninth of Thermidor was the last of the *grandes journées,* or Great Days, that mark the critical turning points of the French Revolution. The arrest of Robespierre and his allies on the ninth and their execution on the tenth of Thermidor (27-28 July 1794) was not, as the victors of Thermidor proclaimed, merely one more happy episode in the history of the revolution. When the Thermidoreans killed Robespierre, they killed the revolution.

The death of Robespierre was the beginning of a concerted attempt by moderates and reactionaries to wrest control of the government from the radical group in the National Convention known as the Mountain and to halt the revolution. The first objective of the Thermidorean reaction was the destruction of the Revolutionary Government, a system of institutions and policies whose vital center was the Committee of Public Safety and whose figurehead had been Robespierre.

The Great Crisis of the Revolution: Summer 1793

The Revolutionary Government that the events of Thermidor ultimately brought to an end had its origins in the great crisis that nearly destroyed the revolution—and France—during the spring and summer of 1793. This crisis, like most of the critical junctures of the revolution, was a compound of foreign invasion, mortally dangerous rebellions within France, and irreconcilable political divisions at the center of government. All of these threats were overcome, but from the onset of the crisis in the spring of 1793 to its end at the beginning of 1794, it was never certain that the revolutionaries would in fact save the new France they had created.

The crisis of 1793 came to a head when France suffered a series of military disasters in the war she had declared against Austria in March 1792. France did not unwittingly blunder into a disastrous foreign war. The decision to go to war was made at a time when the superficial consensus on the revolution had been virtually destroyed by the religious problem. The declaration of war was a serious miscalculation, but it was a decision urged by practically every political faction within France, each for its own reasons.

The loosely knit circle of deputies known as the Brissotins—their most prominent member was Jacques-Pierre Brissot—insisted that the war was the solution to the revolution's problems. A war against aristocratic Europe, they argued, would enable the true revolutionaries (they meant themselves) to assume power within the Legislative Assembly and then enact stronger repressive measures against the growing peril of internal counter-revolution.

The king and his supporters, on the other hand, were equally eager for war. Both Louis XVI and Marie Antoinette sought the war assiduously because they thought that the French armies, debilitated by the emigration of aristocratic officers, would be quickly defeated. In the resulting chaos the king could easily rally his faithful subjects around himself and recapture the prerogatives that the revolution had stolen from the monarchy. Thus it was that each side thought it was deceiving the other. The queen was describing the strategy of both sides when she wrote that the revolutionaries were fools not to see that they were playing the monarchy's game.

Robespierre was almost the only prominent revolutionary leader who opposed the policy of goading Austria into war. At the Jacobin club he fought against the war fever but succeeded only in weakening his influence there. In the bitter quarrel that divided the Society and laid the foundations for mutual hatred and suspicion between Robespierre's circle and the Brissotins, he argued that the real dangers facing the revolution originated at home, not across the frontiers. The revolution had to fight for its survival not at Coblenz—the center of *émigré* activity against the revolution—but in Paris against those who feigned acceptance of the revolution in order to destroy it. A foreign war would be disastrous because it would invest the king and his agents with power that they would turn against the new regime.

When the war began, it went very badly for the French, as Robespierre had predicted. The military reverses of the war led directly to the destruction of the monarchy and ultimately to the defeat of that portion of the revolutionary party which, having done the most to bring the war on, proved incapable of waging it successfully. As evidence accumulated of military ineptitude and royal collusion with the enemy, Robespierre vigorously attacked the instigators of the war. By the beginning of the summer of 1792 he had recaptured the leadership of the Jacobin club and aligned the club against the Legislative Assembly and the Brissotins who dominated it. Although the Brissotins were growing increasingly unpopular, they were not the first to pay for the blunder of starting the war. In the face of heightened anti-revolutionary reaction and growing suspicion of the king's treason, the two opposing revolutionary factions effected a momentary alliance against the crown.

General misery, fear of internal subversion, and suspicion of the king had created an explosive situation by the end of the summer. Late in July the commander of the invading armies, acting upon the instructions of the king and queen, issued a manifesto threatening to subject Paris to "military execution and total destruction" if the revolutionaries did the "least violence or least outrage to Their Majesties . . . ." A week after the publication of the duke of Brunswick's manifesto, the militant revolutionary masses in Paris planned and executed a concerted attack against the royal palace of the Tuileries. The royal family managed to find refuge with the Legislative Assembly, but the monarchy had fallen.

The causes leading to the "Second French Revolution" of August 10, 1792, are clear enough. The Parisian populace rightly suspected the king and queen of treating with the enemy. Even before the uprising the more militant Parisians had demanded the deposition of Louis XVI because, in the words of one Parisian *section,** the king was the "first link in the chain of counter-revolution." The goals of the uprising against the crown were outlined in the speeches that Robespierre made to the Jacobin club during the summer. Echoing and encouraging the masses, Robespierre declared that both the executive and legislative branches were rotten and had to be regenerated. The demands that he made before 10 August were met after that *grande journée:* Louis was dethroned and a National Convention, elected by universal suffrage, was convened for the purpose of giving France a new, republican constitution.

The August Revolution established the Republic but it also widened the split between Robespierre and the Brissotins. During July Robespierre had called for insurrection, while the Brissotins, once they were convinced that a new popular revolution was being prepared, tried to stop it. The mentality that this opposition to popular revolutionism revealed was the cause of the Brissotins' failure during the great crisis of 1793. Their inability to understand and use popular militancy explains why they were swept from the stage of the revolution some ten months after the foundation of the Republic.

The National Convention that met for the first time on 22 September 1792 had two tasks: to draw up a constitution and save the country from foreign invasion. Emerging as the dominant group in a heterogenous and fragmented assembly, the Brissotins

* During the revolution the municipality of Paris was reorganized into forty-eight *sections* or wards. Each *section* had its own assembly and sent delegates to the *commune* or municipal government. The *sections* became the focal points of popular revolutionary activism.

began to enjoy the power that they had sought in the first place when they helped to start the war. But with power and leadership came responsibility and accountability. During the spring of 1793 when the revolution was faced with its gravest threat, the Brissotins proved that they were not equal to the situation that they had done so much to create.

The Brissotins paid the price for their failure in June 1793 when a popular insurrection forced their expulsion from the Convention. As in virtually every instance of popular violence and insurrection in Paris, the *journée* of 2 June 1793 was prepared by bad news from the fronts that generated fear of imminent invasion. But the threat to the regime during the spring of 1793 was the gravest it had ever faced. For one thing, thanks largely to the bellicose leadership of the Brissotins, France was at war not merely with Austria and Prussia, but with all of Europe. Disaster followed disaster. In March came the news that Dumouriez, the most famous general of the French forces and the military darling of the Brissotins had gone over to the enemy when his troops refused to follow him in a treasonous attack on Paris. The magnitude of the crisis was vastly increased when a full scale civil war broke out in the Vendée, a region to the southwest of Paris. Finally, the fears of the Parisian populace were exacerbated by a severe economic crisis. The situation of the urban poor became desperate for they were caught between an ever swifter decline in the buying power of the government's paper money and a severe food shortage caused in part by the breakdown of communication in France.

Faced with these difficulties the Brissotins could not or would not take the measures required by the situation. Because they adamantly refused to relieve the situation of the poor by imposing price controls and assuring an adequate supply of grain, they hopelessly compromised themselves in the eyes of revolutionary Parisians who could not understand why the freedom of commerce should come before their right to eat. Quite naturally the populace began to blame both the food crisis and the military crisis on the group in power.

Robespierre, capitalizing on the fear, unrest, and hunger, sought to turn the hatred that the populace felt for the Brissotins to his own end. He wanted the political power that would enable him and his allies to save the revolution. Both at the Jacobin club and in the National Convention, where he had become the chief spokesman of the radical deputies known as the Mountain, he directed a relentless attack on the Brissotins. In April he began to speak of treason and treachery at the very center of government. The explosion he hoped for came at the end of May when the most active revolutionaries within Paris (the sans-culottes) rose up and overturned the municipal government. On the second of June they surrounded the National Convention and demanded that the Brissotins be purged. The Convention, cowed by the sight of eighty thousand armed sans-culottes, surrendered the proscribed deputies. From the *journée* of the Second of June to that of the Ninth of Thermidor the Convention was to be under the control of the Mountaineers, or *Montagnards*.

The purge of the Brissotins constituted a great turning point in the course of the revolution, but its effects were not immediately evident. For, although the Mountain had control of the Convention, it certainly did not have control of the situation. If anything, the situation worsened during the summer months and the crisis deepened. To the existing troubles were added rebellions in several great provincial cities, rebellions that in some instances were fomented by sympathizers of the purged Brissotins. At the end of the summer France lost an important seaport, Toulon, and half of her ships of the line when royalists within the city surrendered to the English fleet in the Mediterranean without firing a shot. During the course of the summer, moreover, the borders of France had been penetrated by enemy troops on the south, east, and north.

Forced to fend off invasion, repress extensive rebellion, and, at the same time, provide the urban populace with adequate food, the victorious Mountain found itself uncertain of the course it should take and was menaced by the possibility of another popular purge of the Convention. Throughout the summer the sans-culottes kept up a constant and dangerous pressure against a Convention that had used them but was slow to meet their demands. Despite the dark days of that summer, however, the purge of the Brissotins had indeed marked a turning of the tide. As long as the Brissotins remained in power no effective measures could be taken to alleviate the misery of the people; nor, indeed, could the war effort be measurably improved.

Robespierre and the men who became his colleagues on the Committee of Public Safety were able to lead France out of peril because they were political realists who could see the need for extraordinary measures and because they understood that no government could hope to stay in power without the support of the militant Parisian masses. These men were able to succeed where the Brissotins had failed because they could work with popular revolutionism and could, up to a point, accede to the demands of the sans-culottes. For what set the Brissotins apart from their victorious opponents was not political doctrine but the Jacobins'* more acute sense of political reality. In fact, it is very difficult to distinguish the political ideas of the Brissotins from those of the Jacobins. As Alfred Cobban points out, both groups were republicans who believed in popular sovereignty; both insisted on the sanctity of private property; both were, in theory, opposed to the intervention of the state in economic affairs; both were anti-clerical; and neither hesitated to resort to violence in political emergencies.

The difference between the two groups seems, in retrospect, to have been a difference in political intelligence and temperament, not in political doctrine. For several reasons the Brissotins were afflicted by a fatal antipathy toward what Carlyle called the nether sans-cullotic world. And their remoteness from the populace was so

* Throughout the remainder of this account "Jacobin club" and "the Mountain," "Jacobin" and "*Montagnard*" are used interchangeably. This is inaccurate but convenient. The deputies who belonged to the Mountain in the Convention were usually active members of the extra-parliamentary Jacobin club, but obviously not all the members of that club were deputies to the Convention. At the height of the revolution, the members of the Jacobin club in Paris were the staunchest supporters of *Montagnard* policy and constituted one of Robespierre's principal sources of strength.

great that the Brissotins were in effect anti-democratic. The Brissotins' antipathy toward popular revolution stemmed from their snobbishness, their arrogance, their arriviste quest for political power and social pre-eminence. This antipathy had the effect of blinding them to the needs and desires of the urban poor. Thus, while Robespierre and the Jacobins were theoretically opposed to state regulation of the economy, their democratic sentiments were nevertheless real enough, their commitment to the idea of popular sovereignty strong enough to make them willing to take whatever steps were necessary to save the revolution. What separated Brissotin from Jacobin, then, was social sympathy, not social thought. Most of the Brissotins were either men of some means or wanted to associate with people of means. They thought of themselves as destined by history itself to take charge of the revolution which was to end when they acquired power. Living in a style that was far removed from the habits of more austere and less socially pretentious revolutionary leaders like Robespierre, the Brissotins were driven —for emotional reasons—to a doctrinaire and inflexible defense of property and complete alienation from the popular movement. The revolution was eventually saved during the summer and fall of 1793 by men who had the intelligence and the necessary faith in real democracy to effect an alliance with the popular revolution.

Jacobin and Sans-culotte

The alliance between the Jacobins and the sans-culottes was an alliance between two quite separate movements or groups. Jacobism was, in most respects, not sans-culottism. The two allied forces differed in their social composition, had opposing economic interests, and incompatible ideas on government. As Albert Soboul argues so convincingly, the alliance between bourgeois men of government—the Jacobins or *Montagnards*—and the popular revolutionary movement was undermined by a fatal contradiction; once the overwhelming need for that alliance was over, once the revolution had been saved, the alliance broke down. When Robespierre, the most farsighted architect of that alliance was overthrown, the revolution itself ended.

The Jacobins were, above all, sons of the Enlightenment. Their political program and their political doctrine constitute an admirable epitome of eighteenth-century liberal thought. Although many of the men who were later to become Jacobins began their political careers as constitutional monarchists, the pressure of events forced them into a more and more extreme form of republicanism. Republicanism was, in fact, the only form of government compatible with the political goals of the Jacobins. They wanted what many of the *philosophes* and their middle-class supporters had been demanding for decades: a society free from political and civil distinction and privilege; a secular state that provided lay education; and a constitutional government in which the legislative branch was predominant. When the king's disavowal of the revolution destroyed the experiment in constitutional monarchy, the Jacobins became champions of popular sovereignty and a unicameral legislature.

The Jacobins drew their political ideals from the common storehouse of eighteenth-century enlightened thought. Their social and economic thought was a compound of the doctrines of the early "classical economists" and Rousseau's equalitarianism. The heart of Jacobin economic thought was a great and abiding respect for the sanctity of private property and an equally deep attachment to *laissez-faire*. Only the objective necessities imposed by the country's desperate economic and military situation in 1793 were for a time able to overcome Jacobin aversion to state control and interference in economic matters. At the very height of the revolution, when the Revolutionary Government was gradually exercising an unprecedented control over production, circulation, and prices, the Jacobins were careful to insist that they were in no way advocating permanent price control or measures against private ownership. During the fall of 1793, for example, a Jacobin club in the provinces thought it necessary to issue an address to the people condemning the "corrupt rich" who were spreading the slander that the Mountain wanted a "partition of lands." On the contrary announced the club, "the Convention assures you your property. . . ." *

The Jacobins' belief in private property and *laissez-faire* was tempered, however, by the spirit of Rousseau. Rousseau's views on property, the sincerely democratic tendencies of the Jacobins, and their own economic position all worked to give their economic views a certain egalitarian coloration. Rousseau and the Jacobins who followed his teaching held that private property and the independence that it produced were both necessary foundations for a just society. But they insisted that the right to property was not absolute and that gross inequalities in ownership were immoral. The kind of property that the Jacobins considered morally justifiable was the property of the independent producer, craftsman, farmer, or merchant. Extremes in property ownership were incompatible with their ideal because excessive wealth or poverty made it impossible to establish and maintain a just and viable state ruled by law. The only man who had the potential to become a virtuous citizen in the commonwealth envisaged by Rousseau and the Jacobins was the man who owned enough property to support himself in a moderate amount of comfort by his own labor. The rule of law, in their view, could not be accepted by the rich because they were too powerful or by the very poor because they were too miserable. When the Jacobins speak of the "poor man" as their social and civic ideal they mean a man who is satisfied with providing for his own needs and who does not lust after great wealth and luxury. On the whole, the Jacobin clubs preferred small property. The clubs in the provinces, for example, favored the small farm and insisted that the lands of *émigré* nobles be divided to encourage the independent farmer. The very rich were, for the Jacobins, objects of suspicion. Their ideal was aptly summarized by one of them when he said: "We must all be comfortably off, but there must be no more millionaires." †

* Quoted in Crane Brinton, *The Jacobins* (New York, 1930), p. 160.
† *Ibid., p.* 174.

The Jacobins carried their insistence on equality from the economic to the social realm. As Crane Brinton has shown in his study of the composition and thought of the Jacobins, equality is the keystone of Jacobin ideology.* For these men, social equality meant above all equality of opportunity, the career open to talents. In a more positive sense, the Jacobins sought to regulate man's unfortunate innate tendency to selfish aggression, domination, or egocentric assertions of pre-eminence. This aspect of the Jacobin ideal became especially prominent during the months immediately preceeding Thermidor when Jacobinism took extreme shapes. There are countless examples of attempts—which posterity has judged either ludicrous or frightening—to impose uniformity on externals such as manners, dress, and language. The Jacobin club at Nice, to take but one example, ordered the manager of a local theater to forbid "people to enter the theater before the regular opening of doors, for that is contrary to equality."

The men who belonged to the Jacobin clubs, like their economic principles, originated in the middle class. Jacobins were usually men of at least moderate property or they enjoyed a certain amount of economic security. Most of them were educated and many were members of one of the professions. It is difficult, however, to arrive at a more precise definition. For, even if modern scholarship has proved that the Jacobins were not the blood-thirsty and fanatical rabble luridly described in conservative demonology, it has also insisted that the Jacobins did not constitute a class in the sense that all Jacobins had the same economic interests, social status, and background. As Mr. Brinton has shown in his statistical study of the Jacobin clubs, the members were usually a typical cross-section of their communities; the very rich and very poor did not become Jacobins; and the Jacobin leaders were always men of wealth and standing—businessmen, lawyers, priests, and physicians.† In spite of our inability to determine the exact social composition of the

* The following examples of Jacobin equalitarianism are drawn from Chapter V of Brinton's *The Jacobins*.
† *Ibid.*, Chapter III.

Jacobins, it is nevertheless certain that both in membership and political ideas they were quite distinct from their sans-culotte allies of 1793–94.

The sans-culottes were for a long time either identified with the Jacobins or considered to represent Jacobinism in its most extreme or aberrant form. This confusion of the two groups had some basis in fact because at the height of the revolution they shared a common psychological state. Their differences, however, are significant. As the name suggests, the sans-culottes were men who were proud of the fact that they wore the plain trousers of an honest workman instead of the silk kneebreeches of an idle aristocrat. Their costume provides the starting point of a description: the sans-culottes were ordinary workers. Beyond this, however, it is best to define by exclusion. The sans-culottes were not the eighteenth-century prototypes of the industrial proletariat; they did not constitute a coherent economic class in the classical Marxist sense, because their membership tended to cut across class lines. The sans-culottes were not the extremely poor, nor were they the vagrants, criminals, pimps, and prostitutes who stagger drunkenly through the counter-revolutionary accounts of the revolution. On the other hand, the sans-culottes were not the professional men and the businessmen of the Jacobin clubs, men who did not have to work with their hands. Predominantly small shopkeepers, tradesmen, and artisans, they were, as Albert Soboul has put it, "a coalition of small master-craftsmen and [the] journeymen who worked and lived with them." *

The economic ideas of the sans-culottes differed from those of the Jacobins in one important respect: the sans-culottes approved and demanded price controls and they expected the government to assure an adequate supply of food and other necessities. In other respects, however, they were often content to follow their better-educated Jacobin allies. They shared with the Jacobins the social ideal of a community of independent producers in which the

* Albert Soboul, *The Parisian Sans-culottes and the French Revolution, 1793-1794*, tr. Gwynne Lewis (London, 1964), p. 50. I have translated *compagnons* into "journeymen."

state attempted to maintain a degree of equality. Their equalitarian tendency was, it is true, more pronounced; the sans-culottes wanted laws limiting the profits of manufacturers and merchants. A petition addressed to the National Convention by members of the Section des Sans-culottes late in 1793 epitomizes their ideal: "Let no one have more than one workshop, more than one store." This would, the petitioners concluded, "little by little cause the excessively great inequalities in fortune to disappear, and would increase the number of proprietors."

The sans-culottes learned their political theory from the Jacobins, but their political schooling took place in the streets of Paris. Insurrection, demonstrations, and the exercise of the most elemental kind of democratic politics in frequent *section* meetings all combined to transform the basic political ideas that the sans-culottes learned from the Jacobins. Unsophisticated men of action, the sans-culottes thought in concrete rather than abstract terms. Both Jacobin and sans-culotte were republicans and both believed in popular sovereignty. But the sans-culottes believed that they were literally sovereign, that their sovereignty was inalienable and imprescriptible. Sans-culotte democracy was direct democracy. Representatives, they argued, were the agents of the people and were at all times directly accountable to the sovereign people who continually exercised their sovereignty in the *section.* Representative bodies had to be kept under close surveillance lest they turn into an "aristocracy of deputies." Laws, the sans-culottes came to insist, were not valid until each part of the sovereign people had approved them. The sans-culottes considered themselves—the people —to be the source, the ark of legitimate political power. They meant to keep their power and exercise it through the most immediate political organ. This conception of direct democracy was of inestimable value in the struggle against the crown in 1792 and, later, against the Brissotin deputies. Shortly before the Tuileries palace was attacked, for example, the Section de Mauconseil (whose name was afterwards appropriately changed to Bon-Conseil) proclaimed that it could no longer recognize Louis XVI as king and was, consequently, withdrawing its allegiance. It invited the other *sections* to exercise their portion of sovereignty and follow Mauconseil's example. Jacobin leaders like Robespierre were able for a time to tolerate these conceptions because they had a use for the force that sans-culotte direct democracy made available. Once in power, however, the Jacobin men of government were to move decisively against the sans-culotte's exercise of his inalienable and imprescriptible rights of sovereignty.

An alliance between two such disparate groups would clearly not have been possible had Jacobin and sans-culotte not shared a common mentality: the revolutionary mentality of 1793–94. In the minds of revolutionary activists, the name *sans-culotte* was an honorable title designating the most zealous kind of citizen, the man willing to devote all his energies to the service of the revolution. In this sense, sans-culotte was a term that could be applied even to wealthy men if their political conduct and revolutionary zeal merited the appellation. To true republicans the term "wealthy *sans-culottes*" did not seem anomalous. There was, it is true, a certain vague sense of economic—or class—differentiation in the sans-culotte mentality, but this was overshadowed by the sans-culotte's conviction that his virtuous political activism made him morally superior. This amalgam is admirably caught in a sans-culotte document:

Response to the Insolent Question:
But What Is a Sans-culotte?

> A sans-culotte, you scoundrels? He is a person who always goes on foot, who has no millions—as you would all like to have—no chateaux, no valets to serve him, and who lives quite simply with his wife and children, if he has any, on the fifth or sixth story.
>
> He is useful for he knows how to work a field, to saw, file, cover a roof, make shoes, and shed the last drop of his blood for the safety of the Republic.
>
> At night he goes to the meeting of his *section* not powdered, perfumed, and booted in the hope of being noticed by all the

> *citoyennes* in the galeries, but rather to support good motions with all of his strength and pulverize the bad ones. . . .
>
> For the rest, a sans-culotte always has his sharp saber ready to cut off the ears of the malevolent. Sometimes he marches with his pike. But at the first sound of the drum he can be seen leaving for the Vendée, for the army of the Alps, or for the Army of the North.

This extreme moral earnestness and a sense of belonging to the revolutionary elite helped to bridge the differences separating the middle-class Jacobin and the sans-culotte artisan.

Formation of the Revolutionary Government

The victorious *Montagnard* faction survived because it was able to effect an alliance with the sans-culotte activists who had risen up on the second of June 1793. The Convention, however, did not rush to embrace sans-culotte policies immediately after the purge of the Brissotins. Instead the *Montagnards* temporized. They had used the violent and patriotic *sectionnaires,* but they were slow to implement the measures demanded by sans-culotte spokesmen. The bourgeois revolutionary leaders in the Convention did not consummate their alliance with the sans-culottes until events left them no choice.

After the *journée* of the second of June the *Montagnard* deputies were faced with two problems. They had, first of all, to save the Republic from invasion, civil war, and rebellion. At the same time they had to survive. Until the Mountain established its power securely, it was constantly in danger of being overwhelmed by a repetition of the June purge. Despite the urgency of the situation, however, the *Montagnards* were unable to agree on a course of action that could overcome the war crisis, halt internal disintegration, and remove the threat of popular insurrection in Paris.

For more than a month the Convention followed a policy of moderation. Instead of an all-out prosecution of the war, it sought a negotiated peace; instead of ruthless repression of rebellion and dissent, it tried to conciliate the enemies of the regime; instead of taking the emergency measures demanded by the sans-culottes, it procrastinated. This policy was the work of a group of *Montagnard* deputies who, along with the great revolutionary orator, Danton, served on the Committee of Public Safety until the middle of July. By then it became obvious that Dantonist moderation and conciliation were not adequate responses to the situation.

The single achievement of the Convention during June was the Constitution of 1793. Designed to appeal to as broad a spectrum as possible, the Constitution offered something for every class, something for friends as well as enemies of the revolution. Its extremely democratic provisions were designed to appeal to the sans-culottes, while its provisions for thorough decentralization were intended to placate the dissident federalists whose sympathies were with the Brissotins and against revolutionary Paris.

The "Constitution of '93," as it came to be known in the revolutionary tradition, embodies the most advanced political ideals of the revolution, but it was never implemented. The constitution was obviously not a solution to any of the country's perils. It did nothing, for example, to remove the threat of popular insurrection because it did not remove the causes of popular misery and fear. Shortly after the constitution was published, the sans-culotte reaction was uncompromisingly announced by Jacques Roux. Known as one of the *enragés*, or madmen, this ex-priest spoke for the poor of Paris when he harangued the bourgeois deputies of the Convention.

> The Constitutional Act is going to be presented to the sovereign for ratification. Does it proscribe speculation? No. Have you pronounced the death penalty for hoarders? No. Have you set limits to freedom of trade? No. . . . Well, we are telling you that you haven't yet done everything possible for the happiness of the people. Liberty is nothing but a vain illusion when one class of men can starve another and go unpunished. Equality is nothing but a vain illusion when the rich, because of their monopoly, exercise the right of life and death over

> their fellow men. The Republic is nothing but a vain illusion when from day to day the counter-revolution manipulates the price of food which three-quarters of the citizens can't reach without shedding tears. . . . Make another pronouncement, then. The sans-culottes will execute your decrees with their pikes.

The sans-culottes of Paris were, in other words, still hungry, angry, and afraid. They demanded merciless punishment of counter-revolutionaries and heroic repulsion of the invaders.

It was at the end of June that Jacques Roux intimated that the Convention could expect to survive only if it took energetic and drastic measures. During July a series of defeats on the frontier left no doubt that the Dantonist policy of moderation was bankrupt. The great forts that protected France on the north fell to the invaders—Condé on the tenth, Valenciennes on the twentieth. The French outpost to the east, Mayence, capitulated on the twenty-third. To the Parisians these defeats meant that nothing stood between the invading armies and their city. The people were, moreover, becoming increasingly convinced that France was being subverted from within by counter-revolutionary saboteurs, speculators, and assassins. These fears had been growing throughout the spring and summer. They reached a fever pitch when, on July 13, a young royalist girl named Charlotte Corday murdered the radical journalist Jean-Paul Marat.

Marat's death was the psychological turning point of the summer. For the sans-culottes, the assassination proved that the dangers of counter-revolution were terrifyingly real and immediate. After Marat's assassination their natural tendency to equate moderation or even indifference with counter-revolution became more pronounced. Henceforth, the Convention could ignore the people's demand for vigorous repression only if it were willing to risk the eruption of sans-culotte violence against real or suspected enemies of the revolution.

The men of the Convention did not want to take that risk. Indeed, even before moderation died with Marat, the Convention took a decisive step in a new direction. On the day that the fortress at

Condé fell, the Dantonists on the Committee of Public Safety failed to be re-elected. In their place the Convention named a group of men committed to victory over the invaders and the counter-revolution. Of the nine deputies elected on July 10, seven were to remain as members of the "Great" Committee of Public Safety that brought France safely through the crisis: Barère, Couthon, Hérault de Séchelles, Lindet, Prieur de la Marne, Saint-André, and Saint-Just. On 27 July they were joined by Robespierre, the one deputy who had the necessary influence at the Jacobin club and at the Commune to effect an alliance with the popular revolution.

From the middle of July a growing determination to govern and extirpate opposition appeared in all branches of the government. At the same time, the Convention shored up its precarious position by gradually accepting a series of sans-culotte measures. It was typical of the nature of the alliance between the popular revolution and the Convention that the bourgeois political leaders held back from the sans-culotte program as long as possible. Thus, the law providing the death penalty for hoarding (27 July), while it obviously satisfied the sans-culotte sense of justice, was far from the price controls which were needed by the poor and detested by the middle class.

The sans-culottes were not to be put off, however, and they kept threatening to use force. Reluctantly the Convention gave way. On August 23 the Convention issued a general summons to all Frenchmen: they were to consider themselves in the service of the country until the enemy had been driven from the soil of France. When the Convention decreed the *levée en masse* it was adopting a measure that the sans-culottes had been demanding since the military disasters of the spring. The sans-culotte idea of a national levy originated in the kind of military action the revolutionaries knew best—the urban uprising. Drawing from this rather limited military experience, the Parisian militants insisted that only a massive effort similar to the insurrections that overthrew the Bastille or captured the Tuileries could repulse the invaders. The leaders of the Convention, on the other hand, realized that a general conscription would have produced massive armies that would have neither arms nor food. Like so many sans-culotte ideas, the *levée en masse* had to be modified. The draft was limited to unmarried men or childless widowers between eighteen and twenty-five. The rest of the nation —men, women, children—were also to serve, but not as soldiers: "married men shall forge arms . . . ; women shall make clothes and tents and serve in hospitals; children will turn old linen into bandages, and old men will go to the public squares to arouse the courage of the warriors, preach the unity of the Republic and hatred of Kings."

The *levée* was evidence that the leaders of the revolution had begun to share the extreme sense of urgency that sans-culotte politics had always exhibited. It helped to satisfy the popular militants, but it was not enough. Inflation continued to destroy the ability of the poor to buy food. Bread and grain were scarce. Prices rose even higher. As the sans-culottes well knew, the law against hoarders was having no effect. It was clear that many of the revolution's undoubted enemies like Marie-Antoinette and the Brissotins had not yet paid the price of treason. The mood of Paris suggested that another uprising against the Convention was imminent, and the deputies in the Convention feared that they would suffer the fate of the Brissotins unless they somehow calmed the anger of the sans-culottes.

The expected outburst came on September 5 when a large crowd of sans-culottes marched from the Hôtel de Ville (City Hall), entered the Convention, and mingled with the deputies during the debates. The crowd did not attack the Convention, nor did it demand a purge. The signs that the demonstrators carried made it clear what the people wanted: "War on Tyrants," "War on Aristocrats," "War on Hoarders." The men of the Convention had learned the lesson of the second of June. They hurriedly pushed through a series of measures which, for the moment at least, satisfied the militant *sectionnaires* who had peaceably invaded the hall. The day ended without bloodshed. The price paid by the Convention for survival was not high. The measures enacted on September 4 were aimed not at property but at counter-revolution. From the sans-culotte point of view, the most important accomplishment of that day was the establishment of the "Revolutionary Army," a force of citizen-soldiers who were to circulate through the countryside forcing farmers to sell their produce so that the hungry townspeople might be fed. Those who resisted because of counter-revolutionary avarice or those who were guilty of conspiracy against the revolution were to be put to death on the portable guillotine that accompanied the army's columns. The Convention also decreed the arrest of citizens suspected of counter-revolutionary activity. Finally, to reduce the influence of the rich, it limited *section* meetings to two a week and arranged to pay citizens for attendance.

The decrees of September 5 were wrung from a Convention that had no choice. Yet, even by agreeing to the demands the Convention showed itself wiser than the Brissotins, for it finally admitted the necessity of an alliance with popular revolution. Once that step had been taken, it was impossible to resist continued sans-culotte pressure for the price controls that the poor needed. Fearing renewed violence, the Convention gradually gave ground during September. On September 11 the Convention set national maximum prices on grain, flour, and forage; later, on September 29, price controls were extended to cover a long list of "essential articles" ranging from basic foodstuffs to "soap, potash, and tobacco."

These essential concessions unified the sans-culottes behind the Committee of Public Safety, and made it possible for that body and its *Montagnard* supporters to utilize the great revolutionary energies of the popular revolution. The concessions also gave the Committee of Public Safety time to consolidate its position as the dominant force within the Revolutionary Government and time to organize France for victory. From the end of September to the beginning of the new year, the history of the revolution is largely the account of how the Committee of Public Safety simultaneously controlled the sans-culottes, fought down challenges from moderate and extremist elements in the Convention, and defeated the invaders and the rebels.

The Committee of Public Safety began to win a series of crucial military and political victories in October. At the beginning of the month the rebellious city of Lyon fell to the Convention's troops. Later in October the Committee's vigorous measures against the uprising in the Vendée started to take effect; by the end of the year the danger there had ended. The war against the invading armies also took a decisive turn, thanks largely to the Committee of Public Safety's unprecedented mobilization of the nation's resources and the intense *élan* that the revolutionaries at all levels began to display. The gigantic war effort included the training and equipping of the new armies provided by the *levée,* the establishment of government armament and munitions factories, and even the harnessing of scientific research for national defense. At the same time, the new ruthless—or heroic—mood mobilized the psychological—or spiritual—resources of the nation. At the front, the determination to win and punish the revolution's enemies was instilled in the troops by "Representatives on Mission." These were deputies sent to the armies with wide powers and instructions to watch the generals and punish officers for the least sign of treasonous timidity, or lack of initiative. By the year's end the invader had been thrown back at every frontier and France had a massive army in the field, ready to take the offensive. The revolution had been saved from invasion and rebellion.

At Paris the Committee of Public Safety fought and won battles on several fronts. It had to grapple with administrative chaos by providing the Revolutionary Government with effective organization. At the same time it had to find a permanent solution to the problem of disruptive and potentially fatal sans-culotte activism. Finally, it had to subdue its enemies to the left and right within the revolutionary regime. The Committee managed to find a solution to the first problem by improvising a highly centralized state apparatus under its own control.

The Committee of Public Safety won the first of its organizational victories at the beginning of October when the Convention declared that the government was to be "revolutionary until the

Peace." This decree was the legal foundation of the Committee's power, for it meant that the Constitution of 1793, still in abeyance, would not be implemented until the Committee had accomplished the task for which it had been established during the spring—that of saving the country. The "revolutionary" decree of October 10 also greatly increased the legal powers of the Committee by increasing its authority over local authorities, the various ministries of the government, and the generals. The Committee's power continued to grow during the fall because it was obvious to everyone that its policies were effective, that it was beginning to win the war. The final consolidation of power in the hands of the Committee was accomplished by the "Decree of 14 Frimaire" (4 December 1793). Sometimes known as the "Constitution of the Terror," the Frimaire decree effectively centered control of all ministries, commissions, and officials in the Committee of Public Safety. Only the police apparatus escaped its jurisdiction, for it remained under the control of another exceptional Committee emanating from the Convention, the Committee on General Security (*Comité de sûreté générale*). Aside from this one exception, the Committee of Public Safety became the focus of governmental activity. Institutions and agents that had formerly been relatively independent were made directly responsible to the Committee. The free-wheeling "representatives on mission" who had been carrying out their assignments in complete freedom—often with evil results—found that they were no longer independent "proconsuls." They were ordered to send regular reports to the Committee and with increasing frequency they were called back to Paris to account for their actions. Finally, the "Constitution of the Terror" struck a fatal blow at one of the greatest sources of weakness and disorder, for it either ended the independence of local authorities or subverted their power through the use of appointed officials from Paris, the "national agents."

The Law of 14 Frimaire was the final step in the consolidation of the legal position of the Committee of Public Safety, but the Committee's position depended on more than a reformed administrative framework. The Committee did not survive as the dominant power merely because it had defeated the invading foreigner and the counter-revolutionary rebels. The Committee was in fact forced to defend its policies and its control against friends as well as enemies of the revolution; it was successful in combating not only the external threat but also men, factions, and policies that the members of the Committee—and Robespierre above all—regarded as incompatible with the preservation of the revolution.

After the initial military victories of the fall, the only feasible policy, as Robespierre saw it, was that of steering a course between the extreme of uncontrolled terror and activism on the one hand and the extreme of excessive indulgence and anti-revolutionary moderation on the other. This was the course that Robespierre and the Committee maintained from the fall of 1793 to the spring of 1794 when it finally eliminated its enemies to the left and to the right. The Committee was able to overcome these threats because it had found a solution to the problem that had made the Revolutionary Government so unstable throughout 1793; it had discovered how to utilize *and* control sans-culotte activism.

The power of the Committee of Public Safety rested ultimately on the alliance with popular revolution that it consummated during September. The compromise was essential and it was, for a while, successful. But it was also doomed to fail because it was founded on misunderstanding and undermined by a contradiction. The two parties to this alliance had different notions about the nature of their partnership. For their part the sans-culottes thought that the Convention should follow popular initiative, or, at the very least, consult the people. If, by the end of September, they had succeeded in imposing part of their program, they did not mean to leave matters in the hands of the Revolutionary Government after that. The members of the Committee of Public Safety, on the other hand, had no intention of turning control of the revolution over to the sans-culottes. They meant to make and judge their own policies and were determined not to be forced to submit to constant sans-culotte intervention.

The sans-culottes did not understand that their views on government and what they wanted the Revolutionary Government to do were incompatible. They demanded a government that would repress counter-revolution and win the war, but failed to realize that such a government would have to be capable of making them obey, that such a government would have to destroy direct democracy as the sans-culottes practiced it. Robespierre, despite his sympathy for the militants and his willingness to accept many of their demands, saw this contradiction clearly. From earliest summer in 1793 to the Ninth of Thermidor, he remained constantly opposed to the practical implications of direct democracy. He never swerved from his belief that only a strong centralized government could save the revolution. Popular control was, in his mind, incompatible with an effective defense of the revolution and the country. As he announced at the Jacobin club shortly after the purge of the Brissotins, "all that the people can demand is that the Convention march in the direction of the Revolution. The Convention is doing that now. . . . The people *en masse* cannot govern themselves."

The Committee did not try to solve the problem of sans-culotte activism by a direct confrontation. It did not, in other words, attempt to destroy the sans-culotte as it was to destroy "factions" of Hébert and Danton. Instead, the Committee neutralized the danger of repeated sans-culotte interventions by channeling militant activity into legal (and, hence, controllable) forms, and by slowly bringing the political organs of the sans-culottes under its own jurisdiction. Throughout the fall and winter, the Committee of Public Safety whittled away at the militants' independence of action.

The Committee first struck at the hub of sans-culotte activity when it forbade nightly *section* meetings. Similarly, the central government began to extend its control over the *comités de surveillance* (vigilance or watch committees) which, because they were responsible for turning in lists of suspects, wielded a great deal of power in their neighborhoods. Staffed by the most militant members of the *sections*, the vigilance committees were an essential part of the sans-culotte political machinery. Eventually they were drawn away from the influence of their own *sections* and brought under the direct control of the Committee on General Security. By these and other measures, and as a natural result of the Revolutionary Government's growing hold on everything, the popular revolution was subjugated. In many cases the militant sans-culotte who walked with his pike had become something of a tamed government employee, used to taking orders and less and less inclined to exercise his sovereignty spontaneously.

When the Committee of Public Safety successfully domesticated the revolutionary animal, it had removed the one force that could have seriously challenged its position. At the same time, however, it destroyed the ability of the revolution to maintain its momentum. For, by extending its control over the popular revolution, the Committee had disciplined and exhausted the great source of revolutionary energy. The zeal of the sans-culottes did not, it is true, diminish. But the militant revolutionaries had learned to take orders from the central government. The extent of the government's control became evident during the spring of 1794 when the Committee moved against Hébert and other extreme leftist agitators whom the sans-culottes had always considered their friends and spokesmen. The sans-culottes were confused and demoralized by Hébert's trial and execution, but they did not go into the streets because they had come to accept the leadership of the men at the center of the government. The Committee of Public Safety had taught the militants to obey the government. On the Ninth of Thermidor Robespierre and his friends were destroyed partly because the sans-culottes had learned their lessons well.

I

THE THEORY OF THE TERROR

Introduction

The documents in this section introduce the problem of the terror. Two kinds of historical sources illustrate different but complementary approaches. In the first set of texts, men who were themselves deeply involved in the revolution offer explanations of the origins, nature, and purpose of the terror. The remainder of the section consists of several of the principal tables and maps from Donald Greer's statistical study of the terror, as well as Greer's *précis* of the three major interpretations of the terror.

There are several basic problems which the reader might keep in mind while studying these sources. One that immediately suggests itself is a comparison of the explanations advanced by the terrorists and revolutionaries with those offered by modern historians. Such a comparison will involve several questions. For example, do any of the historians agree substantially with the explanations given by Robespierre, Levasseur, Thibaudeau, or Fouché? Further, are historians like Aulard, Mathiez, and Lefebvre content to ask the same questions raised by the men of the revolution? In other words, do modern historians go beyond the categories of analysis that the revolutionaries use? Finally, how can one account for the different conclusions reached by the last named? Fouché's account of the terror and his apology for the role that he played should be read in the light of his biographical sketch which appears at the end of this volume.

Interpretative problems of a different kind are presented by the statistical tables. It was Greer's intention to test the three major historical viewpoints on the terror by the statistical evidence. What questions must be asked of the data to substantiate or undermine the views of Taine, Aulard, or Mathiez? Aulard's thesis of circumstance, to take one example, can be tested by correlating the statistical data from the "Calendar of the Terror" with the chronology of revolutionary wars—both internal and external.

One should also pose this fundamental question: Can any of the explanations be proved or disproved by statistical evidence alone? Greer holds that the figures lead to one incontrovertible conclusion. The terror was above all political; it was aimed at crushing rebellion and counter-revolutionary opposition. The social incidence of the terror, according to Greer, cannot be reconciled with Mathiez's contention that the terror was an instrument of class war. Even a superficial examination of the tables will show, Greer argues, that the terror was not socially selective. It claimed victims from every social class and was merciless toward the enemies of the revolution, whether they were peasants or aristocrats. But is it enough to know that the overwhelming majority of those executed in the Vendean war were either peasants or workingmen? In a "Note on Statistics and Conservative Historiography," * Barrington Moore, Jr., insists that it is not. The social composition of two armies provides no basis for a judgment about the nature of the war they are waging. In this instance, must the historian of the terror be willing to admit that statistical evidence, apparently objective and definitive, has its limits and can easily lead to the wrong conclusions?

The longest document in this chapter—Robespierre's speech of 17 Pluviôse, Year II (5 February 1794)—requires special comment. Described as "one of the most notable utterances in the his-

* Barrington Moore, Jr., *The Social Origins of Dictatorship and Democracy* (Boston, 1966), pp. 517-18.

tory of democracy,"* this speech is also of fundamental importance for understanding both the terror and the policy the Committee of Public Safety was to follow during 1794. Robespierre's conception of the principles underlying democratic government under normal conditions are set forth in the first part of the speech. He then describes what principles must guide a democratic government when it is fighting for its life. Of particular importance are Robespierre's definitions of "virtue," "terror," "justice," and, above all, his conception of the "people."

It has been argued that by Pluviôse, Robespierre and his colleagues on the Committee of Public Safety had arrived at a view of the purpose and aims of the terror which made it inevitable that repression would be intensified. The "thesis of circumstance," consequently, is entirely inadequate as an explanation of the terror during 1794. Given Robespierre's definition of political opposition, can the terror be seen as a defensive reaction? Or has Robespierre established the theory for an offensive program of intimidation and, *in extremis,* extermination that would end when only the "virtuous" remained?

Robespierre's equation of virtue with correct policy, or vice with opposition, was to appear ever more menacing to nearly all the members of the Convention after Pluviôse. In this speech, however, he singles out two "factions" for special condemnation and shows why the Committee of Public Safety believed that both of the factions were anti-revolutionary. The Committee had come to believe that the extremists who had been conducting an increasingly rabid anti-Christian campaign (the Hébertists) and the moderates who had been calling for a relaxation of the terror and peace abroad (the Dantonists) were somehow involved in a terrible anti-revolutionary conspiracy. The speech of 17 Pluviôse served notice that the Revolutionary Government was determined to remain above the factions.

* R. R. Palmer, *Twelve Who Ruled* (Princeton, N. J., 1941), p. 275.

National Convention

17 Pluviôse, Year II [5 February 1794]

ROBESPIERRE:

Citizen-representatives of the people.

Some time ago we set forth the principles of our foreign policy; today we come to expound the principles of our internal policy.

After having proceeded haphazardly for a long time, swept along by the movement of opposing factions, the representatives of the French people have finally demonstrated a character and a government. A sudden change in the nation's fortune announced to Europe the regeneration that had been effected in the national representation. But, up to the very moment when I am speaking, it must be agreed that we have been guided, amid such stormy circumstances, by the love of good and by the awareness of our country's needs rather than by an exact theory and by precise rules of conduct, which we did not have even leisure enough to lay out.

It is time to mark clearly the goal of the revolution, and the end we want to reach; it is time for us to take account both of the obstacles that still keep us from it, and of the means we ought to adopt to attain it: a simple and important idea which seems never to have been noticed. Eh! how could a lax and corrupt government have dared realize it? A king, a haughty senate, a Caesar, a Cromwell are obliged above all to cover their plans with a religious veil, to compromise with all the vices, to humor all the parties, to crush the party of the honest folk, to oppress or deceive the people, in order to reach the goal of their perfidious ambition. If we had not had a greater task to fulfill, if we had been concerned here only with the interests of a faction or of a new aristocracy, we could have believed, like certain writers still more ignorant than they are depraved, that the plan of the French revolution was written out in full in the books of Tacitus and Machiavelli, and we could have sought the duties of the people's representatives in the histories of Augustus, Tiberius, or Vespasian, or even in that of certain French legislators; because, except for a few nuances of perfidy or cruelty, all tyrants are alike.

For ourselves, we come today to make the world privy to your political secrets, so that all our country's friends can rally to the voice of

Robespierre read this speech in the name of the Committee of Public Safety. It was entitled *On the Principles of Moral Policy that Ought to Guide the National Convention in the Internal Administration of the Republic*. See *Archives Parlementaires,* LXXXIV, 330-37.

reason and the public interest; so that the French nation and its representatives will be respected in all the countries of the world where the knowledge of their real principles can penetrate; so that the intriguers who seek always to replace other intriguers will be judged by sure and easy rules.

We must take far-sighted precautions to return the destiny of liberty into the hands of the truth, which is eternal, rather than into those of men, who are transitory, so that if the government forgets the interests of the people, or if it lapses into the hands of corrupt individuals, according to the natural course of things, the light of recognized principles will illuminate their treachery, and so that every new faction will discover death in the mere thought of crime.

Happy the people who can arrive at that point! Because, whatever new outrages are prepared against them, what resources are presented by an order of things in which the public reason is the guarantee of liberty!

What is the goal toward which we are heading? The peaceful enjoyment of liberty and equality; the reign of that eternal justice whose laws have been inscribed, not in marble and stone, but in the hearts of all men, even in that of the slave who forgets them and in that of the tyrant who denies them.

We seek an order of things in which all the base and cruel passions are enchained, all the beneficient and generous passions are awakened by the laws; where ambition becomes the desire to merit glory and to serve our country; where distinctions are born only of equality itself; where the citizen is subject to the magistrate, the magistrate to the people, and the people to justice; where our country assures the well-being of each individual, and where each individual proudly enjoys our country's prosperity and glory; where every soul grows greater through the continual flow of republican sentiments, and by the need of deserving the esteem of a great people; where the arts are the adornments of the liberty which ennobles them and commerce the source of public wealth rather than solely the monstrous opulence of a few families.

In our land we want to substitute morality for egotism, integrity for formal codes of honor, principles for customs, a sense of duty for one of mere propriety, the rule of reason for the tyranny of fashion, scorn of vice for scorn of the unlucky, self-respect for insolence, grandeur of soul for vanity, love of glory for the love of money, good people in place of good society. We wish to substitute merit for intrigue, genius for wit, truth for glamor, the charm of happiness for sensuous boredom, the greatness of man for the pettiness of the great, a people who are magnanimous, powerful, and happy, in place of a kindly, frivolous, and miserable people—which is to say all the virtues and all the miracles of the republic in place of all the vices and all the absurdities of the monarchy.

We want, in a word, to fulfill nature's desires, accomplish the destiny of humanity, keep the promises of philosophy, absolve providence from the long reign of crime and tyranny. Let France, formerly illustrious among the enslaved lands, eclipsing the glory of all the free peoples who have existed, become the model for the nations, the terror of oppressors, the consolation of the oppressed, the ornament of the world—and let us, in sealing our work with our blood, see at least the early dawn of universal bliss—that is our ambition, that is our goal.

What kind of government can realize these wonders? Only a democratic or republican government—these two words are synonyms, despite the abuses in common speech, because an aristocracy is no closer than a monarchy to being a republic. Democracy is not a state in which the people, continually meeting, regulate for themselves all public affairs, still less is it a state in which a tiny fraction of the people, acting by isolated, hasty, and contradictory measures, decide the fate of the whole society. Such a government has never existed, and it could exist only to lead the people back into despotism.

Democracy is a state in which the sovereign people, guided by laws which are of their own making, do for themselves all that they can do well, and by their delegates do all that they cannot do for themselves.

It is therefore in the principles of democratic government that you should seek the rules of your political conduct.

But, in order to lay the foundations of democracy among us and to consolidate it, in order to arrive at the peaceful reign of constitutional laws, we must finish the war of liberty against tyranny and safely cross through the storms of the revolution: that is the goal of the revolutionary system which you have put in order. You should therefore still base your conduct upon the stormy circumstances in which the republic finds itself; and the plan of your administration should be the result of the spirit of revolutionary government, combined with the general principles of democracy.

Now, what is the fundamental principle of popular or democratic government, that is to say, the essential mainspring which sustains it and makes it move? It is virtue. I speak of the public virtue which worked so many wonders in Greece and Rome and which ought to produce even more astonishing things in republican France—that virtue which is nothing other than the love of the nation and its laws.

But as the essence of the republic or of democracy is equality, it follows that love of country necessarily embraces the love of equality.

It is still true that that sublime sentiment supposes the preference of public interest to all particular interests, whence it follows that love of country implies or produces all the virtues; There is no other force, for what are they but the strength of soul which makes men capable of these sacrifices? And how, for example, can the slave of avarice or ambition be made to sacrifice his idol for the good of the country?

Not only is virtue the soul of democracy, but virtue can only exist within that form of government. Under a monarchy I know of only one individual who can love his country—and who, for this, does not even need virtue—the monarch. The reason for this is that among all the people of his state, the monarch alone has a fatherland. Is he not the sovereign, at least in fact? Does he not stand in place of the people? And what is the fatherland if it is not the land where one is a citizen and a participant in the sovereign power?

As a consequence of the same principle, within aristocratic states the word *patrie* means nothing except to the patrician families who have invaded sovereignty.

It is only under a democracy that the state is the fatherland of all the individuals who compose it and can count as many active defenders of its cause as it has citizens. There lies the source of the superiority of free peoples above all others. If Athens and Sparta triumphed over the tyrants of Asia and the Swiss over the tyrants of Spain and Austria, one can seek no other cause.

But the French are the first people of the world who have established real democracy, by calling all men to equality and full rights of citizenship; and there, in my judgment, is the true reason why all the tyrants in league against the Republic will be vanquished.

There are important consequences to be drawn immediately from the principles we have just explained.

Since the soul of the Republic is virtue, equality, and since your goal is to found, to consolidate the Republic, it follows that the first rule of your political conduct ought to be to relate all your efforts to maintaining equality and developing virtue; because the first care of the legislator ought to be to fortify the principle of the government. Thus everything that tends to excite love of country, to purify morals, to elevate souls, to direct the passions of the human heart toward the public interest, ought to be adopted or established by you. Everything which tends to concentrate them in the abjection of selfishness, to awaken enjoyment for petty things and scorn for great ones, ought to be rejected or curbed by you. Within the scheme of the French revolution, that which is immoral is impolitic, that which is corrupting is counter-revolutionary. Weakness, vice, and prejudices are the road to royalty. Dragged too often, perhaps, by the weight of our former customs, as much as by the imperceptible bent of human frailty, toward false ideas and faint-hearted sentiments, we have less cause to guard ourselves against too much energy than against too much weakness. The greatest peril, perhaps, that we have to avoid is not that of zealous fervor, but rather of weariness in doing good works and of timidity in displaying our own courage. Maintain, then, the sacred power of the republican government, instead of letting it decline. I do not need to say that I have no wish here to justify any excess. The most sacred principles can indeed be abused. It is up to the wisdom of the government to pay heed to circumstances, to seize the right moments, to choose the proper means; because the manner of preparing great things is an essential part of the talent for performing them, just as wisdom is itself an element of virtue.

We do not intend to cast the French Republic in the Spartan mold; we wish to give it neither the austerity nor the corruption of a monastic cloister. We have come to present to you in all its purity the moral and political principle of popular government. Thus you have a compass which can guide you amid the storms of all the passions and the whirlwinds of intrigue which surround you. You have the touchstone by which you can test all your laws, all the proposals which are made to you. In comparing them unceasingly with that principle, you can from now on avoid the usual perils which threaten large assemblies, the danger of surprises and of hasty, incoherent, and contradictory measures. You can give to all your operations the cohesion, the unity, the wisdom and the dignity that ought to distinguish the representatives of the first people of the world.

The obvious consequences of the principle of democracy do not require detailed description; it is the simple and fruitful principle itself which deserves to be expounded.

Republican virtue can be considered as it relates to the people and as it relates to the government. It is necessary in both. When the government alone is deprived of it, there remains a resource in the virtue of the people; but when the people themselves are corrupt, liberty is already lost.

Happily virtue is natural to the people, despite aristocratic prejudices to the contrary. A nation is truly corrupt when, having gradually lost its character and its liberty, it passes from democracy to aristocracy or to monarchy; this is the death of the body politic through decrepitude. When after four hundred years of glory avarice finally drove from Sparta its morality together with the laws of Lycurgus, Agis died in vain trying to bring them back! * Demosthenes thundered in vain against Philip of Macedon, Philip found more eloquent advocates than Demosthenes among the degenerate inhabitants of Athens. There was still as large a population in Athens as in the times of Miltiades and Aristides, but there were no longer any true Athenians.† And what did it matter that Brutus killed a tyrant? Tyranny still lived in every heart, and Rome existed only in Brutus.

But, when, by prodigious efforts of courage and reason, a people breaks the chains of despotism in order to make of them trophies to liberty; when, by the force of its moral character, it leaves, as it were, the arms of death in order to recapture the vigor of youth; when it is in turn sensitive and proud, intrepid and docile—such a people can be stopped neither by impregnable ramparts nor by the countless armies of tyrants ranged against it; it halts only before the image of the law. If such a people does not move rapidly forward to the height of its destiny, it can only be the fault of those who govern it.

Moreover one could say, in a sense, that in order to love justice and equality the people have no need of a great degree of virtue; it suffices if they love themselves.

But the magistrate is obliged to sacrifice his interest to the interest of the people, and his pride in power to equality. The law must speak with authority especially to those who are its instruments. The government must weigh heavily upon its parts in order to hold them all in harmony. If there exists a representative body, a highest authority constituted by the people, it is up to it to inspect and ceaselessly control all the public functionaries. But who will curb the legislature itself, if

* [Agis IV, king of Sparta 244-240 B.C., tried to bring back traditional customs and the laws of Lycurgus, of several hundred years before, under which Sparta had been the austere garrison-state of so much renown. Agis also sought to temper the power of the oligarchy which dominated Sparta in his own day, but he was imprisoned and murdered. Editor's notes will be indicated by brackets.]

† [Demosthenes (384?-322 B.C.) unsuccessfully opposed the Macedonian conquest of Greece led by Philip, father of Alexander the Great. On Alexander's death he tried to raise a general Greek revolt but was forced to flee, and took poison. Miltiades was the Greek commander in the Battle of Marathon (490 B.C.); Aristides served as a general at the Battle of Salamis (480 B.C.) and was instrumental in organizing the Athenian confederacy (478 B.C.).]

not its own sense of virtue? The higher this source of public order is elevated in position, the purer it should be; the representative body must begin, then, by submitting all the private passions within it to the general passion for the public welfare. Fortunate are the representatives when their glory and even their interests, as much as their duties, attach them to the cause of liberty!

We deduce from all this a great truth—that the characteristic of popular government is to be trustful towards the people and severe towards itself.

Here the development of our theory would reach its limit, if you had only to steer the ship of the Republic through calm waters. But the tempest ranges, and the state of the revolution in which you find yourselves imposes upon you another task.

This great purity of the French revolution's fundamental elements, the very sublimity of its objective, is precisely what creates our strength and our weakness: our strength, because it gives us the victory of truth over deception and the rights of public interest over private interests; our weakness, because it rallies against us all men who are vicious, all those who in their hearts plan to despoil the people, and all those who have despoiled them and want impunity, and those who reject liberty as a personal calamity, and those who have embraced the revolution as a livelihood and the Republic as if it were an object of prey. Hence the defection of so many ambitious or greedy men who since the beginning have abandoned us along the way, because they had not begun the voyage in order to reach the same goal. One could say that the two contrary geniuses that have been depicted competing for control of the realm of nature, are fighting in this great epoch of human history to shape irrevocably the destiny of the world, and that France is the theater of this mighty struggle. Without, all the tyrants encircle you; within, all the friends of tyranny conspire—they will conspire until crime has been robbed of hope. We must smother the internal and external enemies of the Republic or perish with them. Now, in this situation, the first maxim of your policy ought to be to lead the people by reason and the people's enemies by terror.

If the mainspring of popular government in peacetime is virtue, amid revolution it is at the same time [both] virtue and *terror*: virtue, without which terror is fatal; terror, without which virtue is impotent. Terror is nothing but prompt, severe, inflexible justice; it is therefore an emanation of virtue. It is less a special principle than a consequence of the general principle of democracy applied to our country's most pressing needs.

It has been said that terror was the mainspring of despotic government. Does your government, then, resemble a despotism? Yes, as the sword which glitters in the hands of liberty's heroes resembles the one with which tyranny's lackeys are armed. Let the despot govern his brutalized subjects by terror; he is right to do this, as a despot. Subdue liberty's enemies by terror, and you will be right, as founders of the Republic. The government of the revolution is the despotism of liberty against tyranny. Is force made only to protect crime? And is it not to strike the heads of the proud that lightning is destined?

Nature imposes upon every physical and moral being the law of providing for its own preservation. Crime slaughters innocence in order to reign, and innocence in the hands of crime fights with all its strength.

Let tyranny reign for a single day, and on the morrow not one patriot will be left. How long will the despots' fury be called justice, and the people's justice barbarism or rebellion? How tender one is to the oppressors and how inexorable against the oppressed! And how natural—whoever has no hatred for crime cannot love virtue.

Yet one or the other must succumb. Indulgence for the royalists, some people cry out. Mercy for the scoundrels! No—mercy for innocence, mercy for the weak, mercy for the unfortunate, mercy for humanity!

Social protection is due only to peaceful citizens; there are no citizens in the Republic but the republicans. The royalists, the conspirators are, in its eyes, only strangers or, rather, enemies. Is not the terrible war, which liberty sustains against tyranny, indivisible? Are not the enemies within the allies of those without? The murderers who tear our country apart internally; the intriguers who purchase the consciences of the people's agents; the traitors who sell them; the mercenary libelers subsidized to dishonor the popular cause, to kill public virtue, to stir up the fires of civil discord, and to prepare political counter-revolution by means of moral counter-revolution—are all these men less to blame or less dangerous than the tyrants whom they serve? All those who interpose their parricidal gentleness to protect the wicked from the avenging blade of national justice are like those who would throw themselves between the tyrants' henchmen and our soldiers' bayonets. All the outbursts of their false sensitivity seem to me only longing sighs for England and Austria.

Well! For whom, then, would they be moved to pity? Would it be for two hundred thousand heroes, the elite of the nation, cut down by the iron of liberty's enemies or by the daggers of royalist or federalist assassins? No, those are only plebeians, patriots; in order to be entitled to their tender interest, one must be at least the widow of a general who has betrayed our country twenty times. To obtain their indulgence, one must almost prove that he has sacrificed ten thousand Frenchmen, as a Roman general, in order to obtain his triumph, was supposed to have killed, I believe, ten thousand enemies. They listen composedly to the recital of the horrors committed by the tyrants against the defenders of liberty—our women horribly mutilated, our children murdered at their mothers' breasts, our prisoners undergoing horrible torments for their moving, sublime heroism. The too slow punishment of a few monsters who have fattened on the purest blood of our country is termed by them a horrible butchery.

They suffer patiently the misery of generous citizens who have sacrificed their brothers, children, husbands to the finest of causes, while they lavish their most generous consolations upon conspirators' wives. It is accepted that such women can seduce justice with impunity, pleading (against liberty) the cause of their near relations and their accomplices. They have been made almost a privileged corporation, creditor and pensioner of the people.

With what simple good-heartedness are we still the dupes of words! How aristocracy and moderatism still govern us by the murderous maxims they have given us!

Aristocracy defends itself better by its intrigues than patriotism does by its services. Some people would like to govern revolutions by the quibbles of the law courts and treat conspiracies against the Republic like legal proceedings against private persons. Tyranny kills; liberty argues. And the code made by the conspirators themselves is the law by which they are judged.

When it is a matter of the national safety, the testimony of the whole world cannot compensate for the proof of actual witnesses, nor obviousness itself for documentary evidence.

Slowness of judgments is equal to impunity. Uncertainty of punishment encourages all the guilty. Yet there are complaints of the severity of justice, of the detention of enemies of the Republic. Examples are sought in the history of tyrants because our enemies do not wish to select them from the history of peoples nor derive them from the spirit of threatened liberty. In Rome, when the consul discovered a plot and simultaneously smothered it by putting to death the accomplices of Catiline, he was accused of having violated the legal forms. And by whom? By the ambitious Caesar, who wanted to swell his faction with the horde of conspirators, by Piso, Clodius, and all the evil citizens who themselves feared the virtue of a true Roman and the severity of the laws.

To punish the oppressors of humanity is clemency; to pardon them is barbarity. The rigor of tyrants has only rigor for a principle; the rigor of the republican government comes from charity.

Therefore, woe to those who would dare to turn against the people the terror which ought to be felt only by its enemies! Woe to those who, confusing the inevitable errors of civic conduct with the calculated errors of perfidy, or with conspirators' criminal attempts, leave the dangerous schemer to pursue the peaceful citizen! Perish the scoundrel who ventures to abuse the sacred name of liberty, or the redoubtable arms which liberty has entrusted to him, in order to bring mourning or death into patriots' hearts! This abuse has existed, one cannot doubt it. It has been exaggerated, no doubt, by the aristocracy. But if in all the Republic there existed only one virtuous man persecuted by the enemies of liberty, the government's duty would be to seek him out vigorously and give him a dazzling revenge.

But must one conclude from these persecutions, brought upon the patriots by the hypocritical zeal of the counter-revolutionaries, that one must give freedom to the counter-revolutionaries and renounce severity? These new crimes of the aristocracy only show the need for severity. What proves the audacity of our enemies, if not the weakness with which they have been pursued? That is due, in large part, to the slack doctrine that has been preached lately * in order to reassure them. If you listen to those counsels, your enemies will reach their goal and will receive from your own hands the ultimate prize of their evil crimes.

How frivolous it would be to regard a few victories achieved by patriotism as the end of all our dangers. Glance over our true situation. You will become aware that vigilance and energy are more necessary for you than ever. An unresponding ill-will everywhere opposes the operations of the government. The inevitable influence of foreign courts is no less active for being more hidden, and no less baneful. One senses that crime, frightened, has only covered its tracks with greater skill.

The internal enemies of the French people are divided into two factions, like two corps of an army. They march under the banners of different colors and by diverse routes, but they march toward the same goal. That goal is the disruption of the popular government, the ruin of

* [By Camille Desmoulins and other friends of Danton.]

the Convention—which is to say, the triumph of tyranny. One of these two factions pushes us toward weakness, the other toward excess. The one wants to change liberty into a frenzied nymph, the other into a prostitute.

The minor intriguers, and often even some good but misled citizens, are ranged in one or the other of these parties. But the chiefs belong to the cause of royalty or aristocracy and always unite against the patriots. The rascals, even when they make war upon each other, hate each other much less than they detest the well-meaning folk. Our country is their prey; they fight each other in order to divide it. But they form a league against those who are defending it.

One group has been given the name of moderates. There is perhaps more wit than accuracy in the term *ultra-revolutionaries* by which the others have been called. That name, which cannot be applied in a single case to the men of good faith whose zeal and ignorance can carry them beyond the sound policy of the revolution, does not precisely characterize the perfidious men whom tyranny hires in order, by a false and deadly digilence, to compromise the sacred principles of our revolution.

The false revolutionary is even more often, perhaps, short of rather than in excess of the revolution. He is moderate; he is insanely patriotic, according to the circumstances. What he will think tomorrow is set for him today by the committees of Prussia, England, Austria, even by those of Muscovy. He opposes energetic measures and exaggerates their import when he has been unable to impede them. He is severe toward innocence but indulgent toward crime, accusing even the guilty who are not rich enough to purchase his silence nor important enough to merit his zeal, but carefully refraining from being compromised to the point of defending slandered courage; now and then discovering plots that have already been discovered, ripping the masks off traitors who are already unmasked and even decapitated, but extolling living and still influential traitors; always eager to embrace the opinion of the moment and not less alert never to enlighten it, and above all never to clash with it; always quick to adopt bold measures, provided they have many drawbacks; slandering those who speak only of the advantages, or better, adding all the amendments which can render the measures harmful; speaking the truth sparingly, and just so much as he must in order to acquire the right to lie with impunity; exuding good drop by drop and pouring out evil in torrents; full of fire for the grand resolutions which signify nothing; worse than indifferent to those which can honor the people's cause and save our country; giving much attention to the forms of patriotism; very much attached, like the devout whose enemy he declares himself to be, to formal observances—he would prefer to wear out a hundred red caps than to do one good deed.

What difference can you find between the false revolutionaries and your moderates? They are servants employed by the same master, or, if you wish, accomplices who feign a quarrel in order better to hide their crimes. Judge them not by the different words they use but by the identity of the results. He who attacks the National Convention by his senseless speeches, and he who deceives it in order to compromise it, are they not in agreement? He who, by unjust rigors forces patriotism to tremble for itself, invokes amnesty in favor of aristocracy and treason. Such a man, who was calling France to the conquest of the world, had no other goal than to call the tyrants to the conquest of France. The foreign hypocrite who for five years has been proclaiming Paris the capital of the globe only expresses, in another jargon, the anathemas of the vile federalists who dedicated Paris to destruction. To preach atheism is only a way of absolving superstition and accusing philosophy; and the war declared against divinity is only a diversion in royalty's favor.

What other method remains for combatting liberty? Will one, on the example of the first champions of the aristocracy, go about praising the delights of servitude and the benefits of the monarchy, the supernatural genius and the incomparable virtues of kings?

Will one go about proclaiming the vanity of the rights of man and the principles of eternal justice?

Will one go about exhuming the nobility and the clergy or calling for the imprescriptible rights of the high bourgeoisie to their double inheritance?

No. It is much more convenient to don the mask of patriotism in order to disfigure, by insolent parodies, the sublime drama of the revolution, in order to compromise the cause of liberty by a hypocritical moderation or by studied extravagance.

And so the aristocracy establishes itself in popular societies; counterrevolutionary pride hides its plots and its daggers beneath rags; fanaticism smashes its own altars; royalism sings victory hymns to the Republic; the nobility, overwhelmed with memories, tenderly embraces equality in order to smother it; tyranny, tainted with the blood of the defenders of liberty, scatters flowers on their tomb. If all hearts are not changed, how many countenances are masked! How many traitors meddle in our affairs only to ruin them!

Do you wish to test these people? Ask of them, in place of oaths and declamations, real services.

Is action needed? They orate. Is deliberation required? Then they clamor for action. Have the times become peaceful? They obstruct all useful change. Are times stormy? Then they speak of reforming everything, in order to throw everything into confusion. Do you want to keep sedition in check? Then they remind you of Caesar's clemency. Do you want to deliver patriots from persecution? Then they propose to you as a model the firmness of Brutus. They discover that so-and-so was a noble when he served the Republic; they no longer remember this as soon as he has betrayed it. Is peace appropriate? Then they display the rewards of victory. Has war become necessary? They praise the delights of peace. Must our territory be defended? They wish to go and punish the tyrants beyond the mountains and seas. Is it necessary to recapture our own fortresses? They want to take the churches by assault and ascend to heaven. They forget the Austrians in order to make war on the devout. Do we need the faithful support of our allies? They declaim against all the governments of the world and suggest that you put on trial the great Mogul himself. Do the people come to the capital to give thanks to the gods for their victories? They intone lugubrious chants over our previous reverses. Is it a matter of winning new victories? In our midst they sow hatreds, divisions, persecutions, and discouragement. Must we make the sovereignty of the people a reality and concentrate their strength by a strong, respected government? They discover that the principles of government injure popular sovereignty. Must we call for the rights of the people oppressed by the government? They talk only of respect for the laws and of obedience owed to constituted authority.

They have found an admirable expedient for promoting the efforts of the republican government: it is to disorganize it, to degrade it completely, to make war on the patriots who have joined in our successes.

Do you seek the means for provisioning your armies? Are you busy wresting from greed and fear the supplies of food that they have caused to be hidden away? They groan patriotically over the public misery and announce a famine. The desire to foresee evil is for them always a reason for magnifying it. In the north they have killed the hens and deprived us of eggs on the pretext that the hens eat grain. In the south it was a question of destroying the mulberry trees and the orange trees, on the pretext that silk is a luxury article and oranges are superfluous.

You could never have imagined some of the excesses committed by hypocritical counter-revolutionaries in order to blight the cause of the revolution. Would you believe that in the regions where superstition has held the greatest sway, the counter-revolutionaries are not content with burdening religious observances under all the forms that could render them odious, but have spread terror among the people by sowing the rumor that all children under ten and all old men over seventy are going to be killed? This rumor was spread particularly through the former province of Brittany and in the *départements* of the Rhine and the Moselle. It is one of the crimes imputed to [Schneider] the former public prosecutor of the criminal court of Strasbourg. That man's tyrannical follies make everything that has been said of Caligula and Heliogabalus credible; one can scarcely believe it, despite the evidence. He pushed his delirium to the point of commandeering women for his own use—we are told that he even employed that method in selecting a wife. Whence came this sudden swarm of foreigners, priests, nobles, intriguers of all kinds, which at the same instant spread over the length and breadth of the Republic, seeking to execute, in the name of philosophy, a plan of counter-revolution which has only been stopped by the force of public reason? Execrable conception, worthy of the genius of foreign courts leagued against liberty, and of the corruption of all the internal enemies of the Republic!

Thus among the continual miracles worked by the virtue of a great people, intrigue still mingles the baseness of its criminal plots, baseness directed by the tyrants and quickly incorporated into their ridiculous manifestos, in order to keep the ignorant peoples in the mire of shame and the chains of servitude.

Eh! what effects do the heinous crimes of its enemies have upon liberty? Is the sun, veiled by a passing cloud, any less the star which animates nature? Does the impure scum on the beach make the Ocean any less mighty?

In deceitful hands all the remedies for our ills turn into poisons. Everything you can do, everything you can say, they will turn against you, even the truths which we come here to present this very day.

Thus, for example, after having disseminated everywhere the germs of civil war by a violent attack against religious prejudices, these individuals will seek to fortify fanaticism and aristocracy against the very measures, in favor of freedom of religion, that sound policy has prescribed to you. If you had left free play to the conspiracy, it would have produced, sooner or later, a terrible and universal reaction; but if you stop it, they will still seek to turn this to their account by urging that you protect the priests and the moderates. You must not even be surprised if the authors of this strategy are the very priests who have most boldly confessed that they were charlatans.

If the patriots, carried away by a pure but thoughtless zeal, have somewhere been made the dupes of their intrigues, they will throw all the blame upon the patriots; because the principal point of their Machiavellian doctrine is to ruin the Republic, by ruining the republicans, as one conquers a country by overthrowing the army which defends it. One can thereby appreciate one of their favorite principles, which is that one must count men as nothing—a maxim of royal origin, which means that one must abandon to them all the friends of liberty.

It is to be noticed that the destiny of men who seek only the public good is to be made the victims of those who seek to advance themselves, and this comes from two causes: first, that the intriguers attack using the vices of the old regime; second, that the patriots defend themselves only with the virtues of the new.

Such an internal situation ought to seem to you worthy of all your attention, above all if you reflect that at the same time you have the tyrants of Europe to combat, a million and two hundred thousand men under arms to maintain, and that the government is obliged continually to repair, with energy and vigilance, all the injuries which the innumerable multitude of our enemies has prepared for us during the course of five years.

What is the remedy for all these evils? We know no other than the development of that general motive force of the Republic—virtue.

Democracy perishes by two kinds of excess: either the aristocracy of those who govern, or else popular scorn for the authorities whom the people themselves have established, scorn which makes each clique, each individual take unto himself the public power and bring the people through excessive disorders, to annihilation or to the power of one man.

The double task of the moderates and the false revolutionaries is to toss us back and forth perpetually between these two perils.

But the people's representatives can avoid them both, because government is always the master at being just and wise; and, when it has that character, it is sure of the confidence of the people.

It is indeed true that the goal of all our enemies is to dissolve the Convention. It is true that the tyrant of Great Britain and his allies promise their parliament and subjects that they will deprive you of your energy and of the public confidence which you have merited; that is the first instruction for all their agents.

But it is a truth which ought to be regarded as commonplace in politics that a great body invested with the confidence of a great people can be lost only through its own failings. Your enemies know this; therefore do not doubt that they are applying themselves above all to awaken in your midst all the passions which can further their sinister designs.

What can they do against the national representation if they do not succeed in beguiling it into impolitic acts which can furnish the excuse for their criminal declamations? They are therefore necessarily obliged to desire two kinds of agents, those who seek to degrade it by their speeches, and those, in its very bosom, who do their utmost to deceive it in order to compromise its glory and the interests of the Republic.

In order to attack this Convention with success, it was useful to begin civil war against the representatives in the *départements* which had justified your confidence, and against the Committee of Public Safety; and so they have been attacked by men who seemed to be fighting among themselves.

What better could they do than to paralyze the government of the Convention and to smash its mainsprings at the moment which is to decide the destiny of the Republic and of the tyrants?

Far from us is the idea that there yet exists in our midst a single man weakling enough to wish to serve the tyrants' cause! But farther from us still is the crime, for which we would not be pardoned, of deceiving the National Convention and betraying the French people by a culpable silence! For this is the good fortune of a free people, that truth, which is the scourge of despots, is always its strength and safety. Now it is true that there still exists a danger for our liberty, perhaps the only serious danger which remains for it to undergo. That danger is a plan which has existed for rallying all the enemies of the Republic by reviving the spirit of faction; for persecuting patriots, disheartening them, ruining the faithful agents of the republican government, rendering inadequate the most essential parts of our public service. Some have wished to deceive the Convention about men and about things; they have sought to put it on the wrong track about the causes of abuses which they have at the same time exaggerated, so as to make them irremediable; they have studiously filled it with false terrors, in order to lead it astray or paralyze it; they seek to divide it, above all to divide the representatives sent out to the *départements* and the Committee of Public Safety. They have sought to influence the former to contradict the measures of the central authority, in order to bring disorder and confusion; they have sought to embitter them upon their return, in order to make them the unknowing instruments of a cabal. The foreigners profit from all private passions, even from abused patriotism.

They first decided on going straight to their goal by slandering the Committee of Public Safety; they flattered themselves aloud that it would succumb under the weight of its laborious duties. Victory and the good fortune of the French people defended it. Since that time they have decided on praising it while paralyzing it and destroying the fruit of its labors. All those vague declamations against necessary agents of the Committee; all those plans for disorganization, disguised under the name of reforms, already rejected by the Convention, and reproduced today with a strange affectation; this eagerness to extol the intriguers whom the Committee of Public Safety was obliged to remove; this terror inspired in good citizens; this indulgence with which one flatters the conspirators—this entire scheme of imposture and intrigue, whose principal author is a man [Fabre d'Églantine] whom you have driven from your bosom, is directed against the National Convention and tends to give reality to the vows of all the enemies of France.

It is since the time when this scheme was made public and made real by public actions, that aristocracy and royalism have again begun to raise their insolent heads and patriotism has again been persecuted in a part of the Republic, that the national authority has experienced resistance of a sort which the intriguers had not lately displayed. Even if these indirect attacks had served only to divide the attention and energy of those who have to carry the immense burden which is your charge, and to distract them too often from the great measures of public safety, to occupy themselves with thwarting dangerous intrigues,—even so, they could still be considered as a division useful to our enemies.

But let us reassure ourselves. Here is the sanctuary of truth; here reside the founders of the Republic, the avengers of humanity and the destroyers of tyrants.

Here, to destroy an abuse it suffices to point out its existence. It suffices for us to appeal, in the name of our country, from counsels of self-love or from the weaknesses of individuals, to the virtue and the glory of the National Convention.

We are beginning a solemn debate upon all the objects of its anxiety, and everything that can influence the progress of the revolution. We adjure it not to permit any particular hidden interest to usurp ascendancy here over the general will of the assembly and the indestructible power of reason.

We will limit ourselves today to proposing that by your formal approval you sanction the moral and political truths upon which your internal administration and the stability of the Republic ought to be founded, as you have already sanctioned the principles of your conduct toward foreign peoples. Thereby you will rally all good citizens, you will take hope away from the conspirators; you will assure your progress, and you will confound the kings' intrigues and slanders; you will honor your cause and your character in the eyes of all peoples.

Give the French people this new gage of your zeal to protect patriotism, of your inflexible justice for the guilty, and of your devotion to the people's cause. Order that the principles of political morality which we just expounded will be proclaimed, in your name, within and without the Republic.

LEVASSEUR, THIBAUDEAU, AND FOUCHÉ: ON TERROR

Memoirs of René Levasseur

We have arrived at the middle of the era of the terror whose painful crises have caused so many Frenchmen to curse the revolution. Let us admit first that whoever was to blame, the blood shed during this period covered our glorious revolution with an indelible stain. Let us admit that this hateful abyss which swallowed up all the parties in turn has, by stirring up a general panic, prepared the way for the reign of military despotism.

It must be repeated, however, that no one wanted to push the revolution down these sinister paths and even the most bloodthirsty man, were he even a Collot d'Herbois or a Fouquier-Tinville, would have recoiled from the hideous tableau of so much suffering had it been presented to him as the consequence of his acts. Doubtless a few fanatics, at whose head one must place Saint-Just, had calculated that it was necessary to shed blood in order to establish liberty. Doubtless these fierce republicans wished to strike terror into the hearts of the two opposing factions by the aspect of the scaffold where their members were dragged. But they never imagined that they would arrive at a state of things, even as a transitional phase, in which not even the most obscure position in society would protect a man from political vengeance.

Danton was the first who dared to show us that anarchy was a

Mémoires de René Levasseur, ex-conventionnel (Paris, 1831), III, 1-4. There is a notice on Levasseur in the Biographical Appendix.

weapon and that popular disorders were an indispensable source of power. Danton was also the first to recoil from his own work when he saw excesses that had in a way become permanent on the verge of swallowing up the whole social order. Camille Desmoulins, who had dared to take the comically ferocious title of district attorney of the lamppost, was seized with horror at the sight of judicial murders whose end was impossible to foresee. And Robespierre himself felt his head turn when he contemplated the revolutionary movement wound its tightest.

As for us, obscure mountaineers who without ever pretending to manipulate the machinery of state had devoted our lives to the Republic, we could not look upon the transitory results of our energetic measures and the opposition that they aroused without shuddering. Seized by the liveliest sorrow when we perceived the new obstacles placed in the way of the foundation of the Republic and the repeated outrages that humanity had to undergo, we consoled ourselves with this single thought: we had sought the public interest by ridding ourselves of personal sentiment and we had applied ourselves to studying the condition of France promptly to remedy her ills and cauterize her recent sores and her old wounds at the same time. Convinced that we were surrounded by treachery, we did not dare to stop the somber energy of the Committee of Public Safety violently because we feared that we had nothing to put in its place.

We waited in silence for a propitious moment in which we could make the necessary changes and establish a better order of things. But in the midst of this frightful conflagration we never doubted the Republic. The welfare of France was the goal that had to be attained and, keeping it constantly before our eyes, we never despaired of reaching it. . . . The regime of terror weighed heavily upon us, but we would have wished to put an end to it without losing any revolutionary energy, without disavowing anything in our past.

Memoirs of Antoine-Claire Thibaudeau

The enemies of the revolution have traced the terror back to the first lynching that followed the storming of the Bastille. They are right in their own way because to them that constitutes the whole revolution. In fact, a nation does not break its chains without spreading dread

Mémoires sur la Convention et le Directoire (Paris, 1824), pp. 43-47, 50-51. See the Biographical Appendix for a notice on Thibaudeau.

among those who keep it enchained. Public rejoicing saddens them and the triumph of liberty freezes their blood. Like popular revolutions, despotism also has its terror. Under a despotism the multitude trembles; in a revolution only a few. Terror changes its course and its goals as the people are more or less irritated by the plots of their enemies. If it were possible for a revolution to occur without harming the interests of some people or for the individuals who were injured to offer no resistance, there would be no terror. It originates, then, only in the conflict of interests. . . .

But the terror as it is understood in France subjected the whole nation to its bloody scepter. It began on May 31 and ended on 9 Thermidor. . . . In a despotic state the ruler, the courtiers, and certain classes and individuals are at least unaffected by the terror they inspire. They are like gods who hurl thunderbolts without fear of being struck. In France under the reign of terror no one was exempt; it hovered over everyone's head, striking them down indiscriminately; it was as arbitrary and swift as Death's scythe. The Convention, as well as the people, supplied its own contingent. Danton, Camille Desmoulins, and the officers of the commune of Paris perished on the same scaffold to which they had dragged the Gironde. The people impartially applauded the death of both executioners and victims. Marat, who seemed to be unsurpassable in ferocity and whose execrable features so horribly symbolized the terror, would not have escaped had not the dagger of a courageous woman led him to the Pantheon. And Robespierre finally, the high-priest of the bloody fury, was reserved as its last victim.

Those who attribute to certain persons the invention of a so-called *system of terror* overestimate human perversity. Had the terror been presented suddenly and in all its horror, there is not a man, however barbarous, who would not have recoiled aghast. Nothing was further from a system than the terror. Despite its rapidity, its development was progressive. Men were dragged into it little by little and followed it without knowing where it was going. They went further and further because they did not dare draw back and because they could see no way out. Camille Desmoulins and Danton, the one famous for the boldness of his ideas and the wit of his pamphlets, the other for his athletic appearance and popular eloquence, perished because they talked of moderation. And Robespierre, when he was attacked by men much more occupied with their own safety than that of France, was preparing to blame them for the crimes of the terror.

The terror was introduced bit by bit because of the opposition of the revolution's internal and foreign enemies. They brought into being an exaggerated kind of patriotism. This began in the upper classes with hot and violent speeches and ended in the lower classes with atrocious acts. When the Third Estate abolished privileges, it took the place of the aristocracy in the eyes of the people, and when the people completed the war against the defenders of its own rights, it sought out obscure victims in its own ranks in order to feed the terror, just as slaves break their chains, exterminate their tyrants and their liberators and then fall upon one another, drunk with blood and blinded by their victories. It seemed then that there was no way to escape prison or the scaffold but by bringing others there. Some people denounced and proscribed for hatred and vengeance, but the greatest number believed that they were performing a praiseworthy act and serving well their fatherland. . . .

The terror was more deadly for the friends of liberty than for its enemies. The latter had emigrated because of false points of honor, or because they hated the revolution or because they wished to save themselves. The former, secure in their good conscience and patriotism, remained faithful to the soil of the country that was devouring them. In this great holocaust fewer priests and nobles perished than plebeians. . . . Patriots who could not be accused as royalists or aristocrats were proscribed for federalism and moderatism. The greater part of those citizens and officials who disapproved of the fatal day of May 31 paid for this generous resolution with their heads. When the *émigrés* saw the prisons, where the terror heaped together all its victims pell-mell and mixed all classes, aristocratic pride still persisted in preserving distinctions. Even on the scaffold the royalist was often less worried about death than about the humiliation of perishing along with patriots with whom he could not bring himself to live.

Memoirs of Joseph Fouché

My first introduction into the Government was in the committee of public instruction, where I connected myself with Condorcet, and through him with Vergniaud. A circumstance relating to one of the most important crises of my life must here be mentioned. By a singular chance, I had been acquainted with Maximilian Robespierre at the time I was professor of philosophy in the town of Arras, and had even

The Memoirs of Joseph Fouché, Duke of Otranto (London, 1825), I, 12-16. The French edition appeared in 1824. See the Biographical Appendix.

afforded him pecuniary assistance to enable him to settle in Paris, when he was appointed deputy to the National Assembly. When we again met at the Convention, we, at first, saw each other frequently; but the difference of our opinions, and, perhaps, the still greater dissimilarity of our characters, soon caused a separation.

One day, at the conclusion of a dinner given at my house, Robespierre began to declaim with much violence against the Girondins, particularly abusing Vergniaud, who was present. I was much attached to Vergniaud, who was a great orator, and a man of unaffected manners. I went round to him, and advancing towards Robespierre, said to him, "Such violence may assuredly enlist the passions on your side, but will never obtain for you esteem and confidence." Robespierre, offended, left the room, and it will shortly be seen how far this malignant man carried his animosity against me.

I had, however, no share in the political system of the Gironde party, of which Vergniaud was the reputed head. I conceived that the effect of this system would be to disunite France, by raising the greater portion of it in circles (*zones*) and provinces, against Paris. In this I foresaw great danger, being convinced that there was no safety for the state but in the unity and indivisibility of the body politic. This was what induced me to enter a faction whose excesses I inwardly detested, and whose violences marked the progress of the revolution. What horrors waited on the names of Morality and Justice! But, it must be admitted, we were not sailing in peaceful seas.

The revolution was at its height; we were without rudder, without government, ruled only by one assembly, a species of monstrous dictatorship, the offspring of confusion, and which alternately presented a counterpart of the anarchy of Athens and the despotism of the Ottomans.

It is here, then, that the revolution and the counter-revolution are politically at issue. Is the question to be decided by the jurisprudence which regulates the decisions of criminal tribunals, or the correctional police? The Convention, notwithstanding its atrocities, excesses, and its furious decrees, or, perhaps, by those very decrees, saved the country beyond its integral limits. This is an incontestible fact, and for that reason, I do not deny my participation in its labours. Each of its members, when accused before the tribunal of history, may confine himself to the limits of Scipio's defence, and say with that great man, "I have saved the republic—let us repair to the capitol to thank the gods!"

There was, however, one vote which is unjustifiable; I will even own, without a blush, that it sometimes awakens remorse within me. But I call the God of Truth to witness, that it was far less against the monarch that I aimed the blow (for he was good and just) than against the kingly office, at that time incompatible with the new order of things. I will also add, for concealment is no longer of avail, that it then appeared to me, as to so many others, that we could not inspire the representatives, and the mass of the people, with an energy sufficient to surmount the difficulties of the crisis, but by abandoning every thing like moderation, breaking through all restraint, and indulging the extremity of revolutionary excess. Such was the reason of state which appeared to us to require this frightful sacrifice. In politics, even atrocity itself may sometimes produce a salutary effect.

The world would not now call us to account, if the tree of liberty, having taken strong and firm root, had resisted the axe wielded even by those who had planted it with their own hands. That Brutus was more happy in erecting the noble edifice which he besprinkled with his children's blood, I can readily conceive; it was far more easy for him to have placed the fasces of the monarchy in the hands of the aristocracy already organized. The representatives of 1793, by sacrificing the representative of royalty, the father of the monarchy, for the purpose of founding a republic, had no choice in the means of accomplishing their object. The level of equality was already so violently established in the nation, that the authority was necessarily entrusted to a floating democracy: it could only work upon a moving sand. After having condemned myself as judge and accused, let me, at least, be allowed to avail myself, in the exercise of my conventional duties, of some extenuating circumstances. Being despatched upon a mission into the department, forced to employ the language of the times, and to yield to the fatality of circumstances, I found myself compelled to put in execution the law against suspected persons. This law ordered the imprisonment, *en masse,* of priests and nobles. The following is what I wrote, the following is what I dared to publish, in a proclamation issued by me, on the 25th of August, 1793:—

"The law wills that suspected persons should be removed from social intercourse; this law is commanded by the interests of the state; but, to take for the basis of your opinions vague accusations, proceeding from the vilest passions, would be to favour a tyranny as repugnant to my own heart as it is to natural equity. The sword must not be wielded at hazard. The law decrees severe punishments, and not proscriptions, as immoral as they are barbarous."

It required at that time some courage to mitigate as much as was in one's power the rigour of the conventional decrees. I was not so fortunate in my missions as collective commissioner (*commissariat collectif*), because the power of decision was not entrusted to myself alone. Throughout my missions, the actions which may be considered as deserving of censure will be found far less than the every-day phrases, expressed in the language of the times, and which in a period of greater tranquillity still inspire a kind of dread; besides, this language was, so to speak, official and peculiar. Let not also my situation at this period be mistaken. I was the delegate of a violent assembly, and I have already proved that I eluded or softened down several of its severe measures. In other respects, these pretended pro-consulates reduced the commissioned deputy to be nothing more than a man-machine, the wandering commissary of the committees of Public Safety and General Security. I was never a member of these government committees; therefore, I never held, during the reign of terror, the helm of power; on the contrary, as will shortly be seen, I was myself a sufferer by it. This will prove how much my responsibility was confined.

A Statistical Analysis of the Terror

The interpretation of the Terror has involved three major theories which may be briefly described as the philosophic or sociologic, the political, and the economic. The first of these is that of Taine and his numerous following; the second was the life-work of Aulard; the third, though elaborated by Jaurès, is more closely associated with the names of the two leading scholars of recent years in the revolutionary field, Albert Mathiez and Georges Lefebvre, who combine it with some of Aulard's conclusions. Since our first purpose is to test the validity of these theories in the light of statistics we must have clearly before us their principal tenets.

To Taine and his school the Terror was a political philosophy written in blood. The philosophy was that of Rousseau, and the Terror was an interlude of Jacobin paranoia induced by the virus of the *Social Contract*—a crime committed collectively by the dregs of society which this poisonous leaven had brought to the top for a brief reign of destruction. Viewed in this light, the Terror was a class war of

Reprinted by permission of the publishers from Donald Greer, *The Incidence of the Terror During the French Revolution* (Cambridge, Mass.: Harvard University Press). The text is from Greer's Introduction, pp. 5-12. Tables are adapted from those on pp. 164-5 and 152.

a sort, for if its motivation was primarily philosophic it resolved itself into a struggle between the socially fit and the socially unfit. The Jacobin drawn by Taine or Augustin Cochin, his most scholarly disciple, was intellectually an automaton energized by the ideas of Rousseau and Mably; but he was also a social delinquent, at best a small town failure, unstable visionary, clever rogue, or charlatan; at worst—the majority—a cutthroat, vagabond, or jailbird. The vicious and the indigent, then, were aligned against the virtuous and the respectable in an attempt to invert the social edifice of centuries. The correlation of baseness and indigence on one hand, of stability and talent on the other, had produced an aristocracy of "notables"; the chief purpose of the Terror was to destroy this élite. "It is," said Taine, "the notables who are chiefly aimed at and who, in their possessions as well as their persons, have suffered most." [2]

But in order to reconcile his theory with the broad facts of the social incidence of the Terror, which had been published by Granier de Cassagnac and Berriat-Saint-Prix, Taine was obliged to shape his definition of "notables" like a cone, constantly widening its base as he pushed it deeper and deeper into the social order. Naturally, the nobility, the clergy, and the upper bourgeoisie came first; but their bones made only a small beginning of the pile heaped up by the Terror. The "half notables," land-owning peasants, prosperous shopkeepers, artisans who had risen a degree above their companions, were added. Still the pile was too small. To make up the deficit, Taine tossed in what was left of society, reserving only "those who had nothing . . . , those who live from day to day, the wretched, the poor, the vagabonds and the famished," [3] a residue which apparently would qualify for Jacobin membership. At this point, however, he was in danger of being trapped in a tacit admission that the Terror was not selective, a conclusion quite incompatible with his theory. He escaped only by expressing the conviction that in default of ladies and gentlemen of the upper classes, "the principal swath consists of the élite of the people," [4] well-to-do peasants, shopkeepers, and artisans.

A definition so inclusive is a shield against criticism. Taine's "notables" comprise almost everyone except the rabble left over to make up the Jacobins. In general, however, his position is that the Terror was aimed at all that was best in French society whether found in the nobility, clergy, bourgeoisie, or laboring classes, and that it struck hard-

[2] Taine, H., *The French Revolution* (Eng. trans.), III, 304.
[3] *Ibid.*, III, 330. [4] *Ibid.*, III, 330.

est towards the base of the cone, taking the more aspiring and industrious plebeians.

Taine ignored the circumstantial environment; Aulard attributed unique importance to it. The Terror, he contended, was a national reflex, comprehensible only when related to the foreign war and the counter-revolution. Treason, desertion, and defeat on the frontiers in the spring of 1793, synchronizing with sedition and civil war within the country, brought France to the brink of catastrophe. The situation grew worse during the summer as the Austrians advanced into France, the Vendéens won victory after victory, and the great commercial and maritime cities—Lyon, Marseille, Toulon, and Bordeaux—rebelled. To save France from dismemberment and the Revolution from extinction, the leaders of the Mountain "resigned themselves to violent measures," [5] and created a "dictatorship of national defense," [6] or, in Marat's words, a "tyranny of liberty."

Aulard drew up a striking account of the provocative circumstances and the correlative terrorist laws and policies,[7] but he carried it only as far as the end of 1793. In the spring of 1794 France was no longer in immediate danger from either her foreign or internal enemies. The Austrian, Prussian, English, Spanish, and Piedmontese armies had been driven back and were held at bay on the frontiers; the Vendée was a smouldering ruin; Lyon, Marseille, Toulon, and Bordeaux had been captured and terribly punished; and even the sporadic insurrections which had occurred almost everywhere in 1793 seemed to be at an end. Why, then, was the Terror continued into the spring and summer of 1794? To assure victory. The spring campaign was imminent. To win, France needed "une volonté une." But a year of violent repression had failed to mold a unanimous loyalty to the Republic. Open rebellion had been suppressed, the opposition had been smothered; but "the truth is that even under the Terror the enemies of the regime never disarmed. They only changed their methods." [8] Silent but implacable, they secretly hoped for the victory of foreign powers and the overthrow of the Republic. The iron laws and sanguinary policies directed against them had to be continued in order to prevent another attack from the rear.

The corollary of this explanation is that the Terror followed in the

[5] Aulard, A., *The French Revolution* (Eng. trans.), II, 292.
[6] Aulard, A., *Taine historien de la Révolution française*, 217.
[7] *Ibid.*, 168-77, 213-16.
[8] Mathiez, A., *Annales historiques de la Révolution française* (1926), III, 193.

wake of civil war, insurrection, or any sort of anti-revolutionary opposition. It struck down the enemies of the Republic whoever and wherever they were. It was socially indiscriminate but politically perspicacious. Its victims belonged to the classes which hated the Revolution or lived in the regions where rebellion was most serious. "The severity of repressive measures in the provinces," wrote Mathiez, "was in direct proportion to the danger of revolt." [9]

The pervasive economic interpretation of history has been applied to the French Revolution with illuminating results, and if we are content to regard the Terror as neither the flux of a vicious political philosophy nor the defense of a nation in dire straits, we may be able to agree with the materialists. Their explanation of the origins of the Terror is that the pressure of the *sans-culottes* forced the Convention to adopt the policies whose lurid significance colors the period. The reluctant deputies, *Montagnards* as well as others, were swept along the course of terrorism by a ground swell of popular agitation caused by the chronic food shortage and soaring prices, traceable in turn to the war, the blockade, and the inflation. The fears and desires of the people were first articulated by radical spokesmen of the Parisian populace, the *Enragés* led by Jacques Roux, who formulated the program of the Terror months before the Convention adopted it. Eventually the demands of the *Enragés* had to be granted; but they were conceded one at a time, partly as bribes for lower class support, partly under the menace of violence.

Mathiez analysed in minute detail the interrelations of food supply, prices, and popular agitation on the one hand and the responses of the Government on the other.[10] His conclusion is that the Terror came from below. Most of the important political and all the great economic measures of the period were wrung from an unwilling or hesitant Convention, often after all the expedients known to politicians—vague promises, irrelevant alternatives, stillborn laws—had been tried and had failed. The Revolutionary Tribunal of Paris was instituted during the riots of March 9 and 10. The first *maximum* (limitation of prices for grain) was the price paid by the Mountain for the *sans-culotte* army used against the Gironde on June 2. The law against hoarding (*accaparement*) and the creation of state granaries were manœuvres calculated to soothe the agitators and to avoid the general *maximum* (limitation of prices for all commodities). And finally, the major ter-

[9] Mathiez, A., *The French Revolution* (Eng. trans.), 400.
[10] Mathiez, A., *La vie chère et le mouvement social sous la Terreur*, Paris, 1927, *passim*.

roristic acts of September, 1793—the law of suspects, the reorganization of the Revolutionary Tribunal, the creation of a revolutionary army, the forced loan of a billion francs, and the general *maximum*—were voted when the *Hébertistes,* who had supplanted the *Enragés,* threatened to overthrow the Government.

So much for the economic origins of the Terror. The materialistic explanation of the succeeding stages is more intricate. The economic program adopted in the autumn of 1793 committed the Government to terrorism. Requisitioning and the *maximum* on grain alienated the peasants; capital levies and the general *maximum* disaffected the middle classes. There remained the workingmen of the towns and the agricultural laborers who would support the dictatorship of the Committees as long as it assured them of the necessities of life at tangible prices—in other words so long as it maintained the *maximum.* And the *maximum* was maintainable only by means of intimidation. The circle is obvious, as are its implications of class war.

Perhaps the history of the First Republic would have had a different ending if the attempt to balance wages and prices had succeeded. But the *maximum* failed, and its failure left the Revolutionary Government standing on quicksand. Robespierre and his friends alone appeared to understand the imperative necessity of creating another bond to attach the *sans-culottes* to the Republic. More than that, they looked beyond the exigencies of the moment to realize that great differences in wealth would make a farce of democracy.[11] Saint-Just drafted the famous Ventôse laws providing for the expropriation of suspects and the distribution of their property among the poor—laws which were intended not merely as another expedient but as the inception of a social revolution, the first clause of the moral and social code upon which their authors hoped to found a democratic republic without extremes of wealth or poverty.[12] In order to achieve these changes, more sweeping than the overthrow of the throne or the aristocracy, it was more than ever necessary to continue and even to accelerate the Terror. Local revolutionary tribunals and commissions were suppressed, revolutionary justice was concentrated in Paris, and the law of 22 Prairial (June 10, 1794) made the Revolutionary Tribunal a perfect instrument of class warfare. But the *Robespierristes* encountered the opposition of their colleagues in the Committees of

[11] Mathiez, A., "La Terreur instrument de la politique sociale des Robespierristes." *Girondins et Montagnards,* ch. 5.
[12] *Ibid.* For a critique of the Ventôse laws v. Lefebvre, G., *Questions agraires au temps de la Terreur,* Introduction.

Public Safety and General Security, who though willing enough to perpetuate the Terror were not ready to use it in the interest of social revolution. Robespierre and his friends were overthrown, and the Democratic Republic flickered out. The Revolution then became what it had from the first threatened to become—the realization of the narrow and selfish aims of the property-owning classes, the triumph of the bourgeoisie. The ideal of equalitarian democracy was replaced by the more concrete and attainable end of a capitalistic state.

One need not, it is true, seal these theories in hermetic compartments. Possibly none of the three is exclusively true or completely false. Each has a very strong argument and in certain aspects, at least, can be supported by evidence which it is difficult to reject entirely. The real explanation of the Terror perhaps lies in a fusion of some parts of all three interpretations. No complete synthesis has been attempted, nor will our statistics in themselves help us to make one. They will, however, enable us to test these theories; if some emerge badly damaged, perhaps fragments will remain that will fit into another pattern.

Table 1. The Terror in Paris

Indictments For	*Number for Seine (Paris)*	*Per cent of Total Indictments*
Emigration	66	2½%
Intelligence with the Enemy	292	11%
Sedition	114	4½%
Federalism	56	2%
Treason	95	3½%
Conspiracy	676	25½%
Trees of Liberty	7	
Counter-Revolutionary Opinions	988	37½%
Refractory Clergy	29	1%
Concealment of Refractory Clergy	5	
Hoarding (*Accaparement*)	11	½%
Traffic in Assignats	36	1%
Corruption	100	4%
False Witness	3	
Counterfeiting	0	
Miscellaneous	161	6%
TOTALS	2639	100%

Note: All numbers in this and the following tables are indictments *followed* by executions.

Table II. Geographic Variations of the Social Incidence

Départements or Regions	*Nobles*		*Upper Middle Class*		*Lower Middle Class*		*Clergy*		*Working Class*		*Peasants*		*No Status Given*		*Total*
France (exclusive of Paris)	412	4%	1218	11%	1131	10%	674	6%	3896	34%	3867	34%	163	1%	11441
Vendéen War Region (1)	112	2%	230	3%	244	3%	160	2%	2991	41%	3518	48%	50	1%	7305
Doubs, Lozère and Aveyron	1		12	6%	10	5%	35	18%	34	17%	103	52%	3	2%	198
Rhône (Lyon)	151	8%	449	24%	611	32%	136	7%	471	25%	49	3%	13	1%	1880
Southern Federalist Centers (2)	85	17%	175	35%	70	14%	68	14%	53	10%	26	5%	24	5%	501
Quiet Départements (3)	16	13%	13	11%	6	5%	29	23%	32	26%	14	11%	13	11%	123
Paris	666	25%	746	28%	357	14%	246	9%	493	19%	94	4%	37	1%	2639

Note: The left columns are indictments followed by executions. The percentages in the right columns are of the total numbers of indictments (executions) for the month.

1 All the *départements* of the West plus the Orne and the Manche.

2 The Gironde, the Haute-Garonne, the Hérault, and the Gard.

3 Twenty-seven départements in which fewer than 10 executions took place.

Table III. The Calendar of the Terror

Date	Nobles		Upper Middle Class		Lower Middle Class		Clergy		Working Class		Peasants		No Status Given		Total
1793															
March	1	4%			3	14%			9	41%	9	41%			22
April	9	5%	20	10%	34	16%	4	2%	80	38%	57	26%	6	3%	210
May	6	10%	10	17%	6	10%	3	5%	19	33%	10	17%	4	8%	58
June	7	19%	8	8%	8	8%	7	7%	21	21%	46	47%	2	2%	99
July	7	19%	9	25%	6	16%	5	14%	6	16%			3	9%	36
August	4	19%	4	19%	2	9%	4	19%	2	10%	4	19%	1	5%	22
September	5	7%	9	12%	5	7%	7	10%	33	46%	11	15%	2	3%	72
October	16	9%	46	26%	19	11%	24	13%	34	19%	30	17%	10	5%	179
November	38	8%	133	27%	88	18%	31	6%	113	23%	81	17%	7	1%	491
December	113	3%	293	9%	380	11%	75	2%	1228	37%	1251	37%	25	1%	3365
1794															
January	75	2%	182	5%	242	7%	108	3%	1409	40%	1481	42%	20	1%	3517
February	57	7%	113	14%	102	13%	82	11%	250	31%	175	22%	13	2%	792
March	73	12%	125	21%	61	10%	70	12%	123	21%	130	22%	7	2%	589
April	111	10%	165	15%	80	7%	90	8%	309	28%	315	29%	29	2%	1099
May	124	16%	186	24%	113	14%	54	7%	172	22%	107	14%	24	3%	780
June	160	14%	277	24%	168	14%	123	11%	321	28%	95	8%	13	1%	1157
July	341	24%	349	25%	165	12%	204	15%	214	15%	100	7%	24	2%	1397
August	10	12%	8	9%	1	1%	17	20%	19	22%	27	31%	4	5%	86
No Date Given	1	1%	27	24%	5	5%	12	11%	27	25%	32	29%	6	5%	110
TOTALS	1158	8¼%	1964	14%	1488	10½%	920	6½%	4389	31¼%	3961	28%	200	1½%	14080

Note: The left columns are indictments followed by executions. The percentages in the right columns are of the total numbers of indictments (executions) for the month.

1. Tuileries
2. Champs-Elysées
3. République
4. Butte-des-Moulins
5. Piques
6. Lepeletier
7. Mont-Blanc
8. Muséum
9. Gardes-Françaises
10. Halle-au-Blé
11. Contrat-Social
12. Guillaume-Tell
13. Brutus
14. Bonne-Nouvelle
15. Amis-de-la-Patrie
16. Bon-Conseil
17. Marchés
18. Lombards
19. Arcis
20. Faubourg-Montmartre
21. Poissonnière
22. Bondy
23. Temple
24. Popincourt
25. Montreuil
26. Quinze-Vingts
27. Gravilliers
28. Faubourg-du-Nord
29. Réunion
30. Homme-Armé
31. Droits-de-l'Homme
32. Fidelité
33. Indivisibilité
34. Arsenal
35. Fraternité
36. Cité
37. Pont-Neuf
38. Invalides
39. Fontaine-de-Grenelle
40. Unité
41. Théatre-Français
42. Bonnet-de-la-Liberté
43. Luxembourg
44. Thermes
45. Panthéon-Français
46. Observatoire
47. Jardin-des-Plantes (later Sans-Culottes)

Place de la Révolution
National Convention
Jacobin Club
Palais Royal
Tuileries Gardens
Tuileries Palace
Louvre
Pont Neuf
Cordeliers Club
Palais de Justice
Notre Dame
Île de la Cité
Hôtel de Ville
Place de Grève
Place de la Bastille
Luxembourg Palace
Mètres
0 300 600

***Sections* of Paris 1793-1794**

Adapted from *The Crowd in the French Revolution*, by George Rudé, published by Oxford University Press, 1959. Reprinted by permission of the publisher.

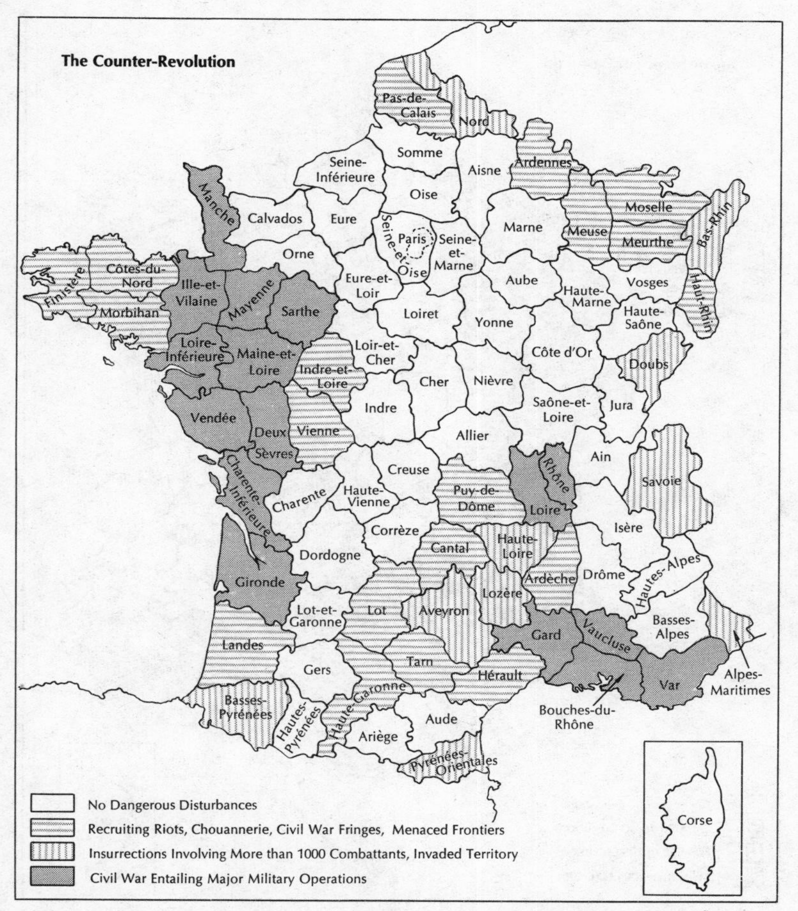
The Counter-Revolution
Pas-de-Calais
Nord
Somme
Aisne
Ardennes
Seine-Inférieure
Oise
Manche
Calvados
Eure
Seine-et-Oise
Paris
Seine-et-Marne
Marne
Meuse
Moselle
Meurthe
Bas-Rhin
Finistère
Côtes-du-Nord
Orne
Ille-et-Vilaine
Mayenne
Sarthe
Eure-et-Loir
Aube
Haute-Marne
Vosges
Haut-Rhin
Morbihan
Loiret
Yonne
Haute-Saône
Loire-Inférieure
Maine-et-Loire
Loir-et-Cher
Indre-et-Loire
Côte d'Or
Doubs
Cher
Nièvre
Vendée
Indre
Saône-et-Loire
Jura
Deux Sèvres
Vienne
Allier
Ain
Rhône
Charente-Inférieure
Creuse
Savoie
Charente
Haute-Vienne
Puy-de-Dôme
Loire
Corrèze
Isère
Cantal
Haute-Loire
Dordogne
Hautes-Alpes
Gironde
Ardèche
Drôme
Lozère
Lot-et-Garonne
Lot
Aveyron
Gard
Vaucluse
Basses-Alpes
Landes
Tarn
Gers
Hérault
Var
Alpes-Maritimes
Haute-Garonne
Basses-Pyrénées
Hautes-Pyrénées
Aude
Bouches-du-Rhône
Ariège
Pyrénées-Orientales
Corse
No Dangerous Disturbances
Recruiting Riots, Chouannerie, Civil War Fringes, Menaced Frontiers
Insurrections Involving More than 1000 Combattants, Invaded Territory
Civil War Entailing Major Military Operations

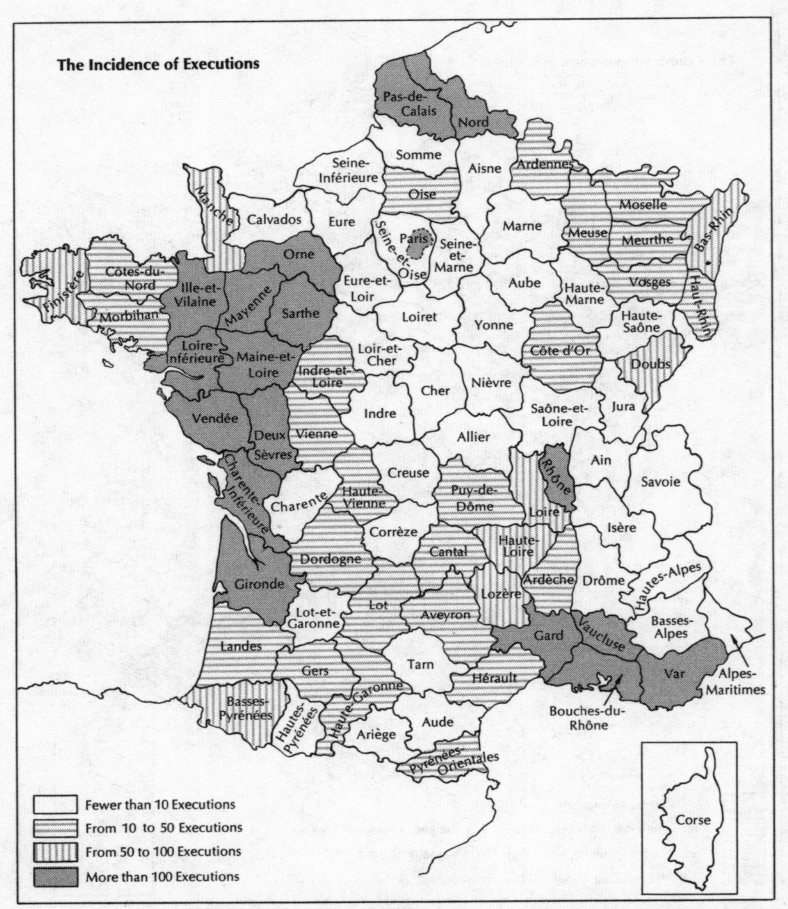

Adapted from *The Incidence of the Terror,* by Donald Greer, published by Harvard University Press, 1935. Reprinted by permission of the publisher

II
THE GREAT TERROR

Introduction

Robespierre's speech of 17 Pluviôse announced that the Committee of Public Safety would tolerate neither counter-revolutionary moderation nor divisive extremism. This section of the documents covers the period during which the Committee eliminated the threats from the left and the right. It struck at the Hébertists in mid-March and moved against the Dantonists early in April. These great—and bloody—political victories prepared the way for the "Great Terror," a period of intense repression that followed the passage of the Law of 22 Prairial (10 June 1794).

The "Reports by Agents of the Ministry of the Interior," provide the historian with a rare and invaluable opportunity to recreate the mood of revolutionary Paris. From the candid remarks of Parisians, always sociable and voluble even during the terror, one can learn what problems really concerned the "little people," and, above all, how the city reacted to the great struggle between the Committee and the factions. The reports shed some light on the effect that Hébert's execution had on the people. It seems safe to conclude that the agents did not fabricate reports of popular rejoicing; yet, despite the agents' natural eagerness to report popular approval of the government's policy, they nevertheless provide evidence that some patriots reacted differently to the events of Germinal.

Hébert was a demagogue posing as champion of the poor. His execution confused and unsettled the sans-culottes, but he was not mourned by the deputies of the Convention. The arrest of Danton, Desmoulins, and their friends—prominent members of the Convention and popular revolutionary heroes—was another matter: in Germinal the terror entered the Convention itself. The excerpt from the session of 11 Germinal introduces the men of the Convention in debate and suggests how they will react to the Committee's growing ruthlessness and power.

The Law of 22 Prairial confirmed the fears that had haunted many deputies after Danton's death. Introduced by one of Robespierre's closest associates on the Committee of Public Safety, the law provided for a reorganization of the Revolutionary Tribunal in the interest of increased efficiency. Despite the fact that the factions had been eliminated, despite the great military victories of the spring, the terror was to be intensified, not relaxed. Historians have not been able to agree on the origins and significance of the law. To some it is evidence that Robespierre and the rest of the Committee had finally succumbed to a kind of insanity. The revolution, they point out, was secure. There was no need for the sickening increase in executions after 22 Prairial. Other historians contend that the state of mind exhibited by many revolutionaries is sufficient explanation for the law. It is not necessary to suppose that Robespierre and the Committee had become bloodthirsty monsters. The excerpt from the meeting at the Jacobin Club on 6 Prairial will enable the reader to sample the emotional exaltation and fear that characterize the "Great Terror." The "two precious men" referred to are Collot d'Herbois and Robespierre. On 3 Prairial a man named Admirat had fired at and missed Collot d'Herbois, and on the following day a girl named Cécile Renault was arrested at Robespierre's lodgings when she insisted on an interview. She had been carrying two knives, and everyone assumed that she intended to play Charlotte Corday to Robespierre's Marat.

Excerpts from Couthon's prefatory remarks on 22 Prairial, as well as portions of the text of the law itself will help to explain how the terrorists viewed the situation. The debates that followed Couthon's speech indicate that the possible implications of the law were not lost on some deputies.

REPORTS BY AGENTS OF THE MINISTRY OF THE INTERIOR

17 Pluviôse, Year II [5 February 1794]

Report by Pourvoyeur

A number of patriots are complaining that the Égalité palace still serves as a haunt for aristocrats and counter-revolutionaries, that this place of prostitution is frequented only by them. Notably at Roberts's restaurant one encounters these individuals who affect to be dressed as sans-culottes but who are nothing else than counter-revolutionaries who attempt to provoke the patriots.

One also encounters these same individuals at the Café Valois; the café no longer displays this name since a patriot got it removed, but nothing has been put in place of the proscribed name, although they've been told to call it the Café Marat. It seems, say the patriots, that they are just waiting for the counter-revolution to put back the old name: Café Valois.

It is astonishing that more investigations aren't made into this impure place; also it should no longer have the name Égalité since it is the scene of every kind of crime.

In a group composed of good republicans they were saying that there ought to be a maximum on all fortunes, without, however, having the agrarian law, but people should not be allowed to augment their fortunes beyond an income which would give a certain comfort. That a citizen who is well off might marry a girl who has nothing while a girl who has a fortune might marry a citizen who has none, and that lack of a fortune should no longer be a reason for discord in marriages. It is just, the people say, that those who have more should give to others.

The people were pleased to see the former countess of Marbeuf and her worthy companion [Joseph Payen] condemned by the Revolutionary Tribunal. They were saying the guillotine is too good for them.

The butchers have no meat at all at fourteen *sous* or even fifteen *sous,* but they do have it at twenty-five to twenty-seven *sous.* The

Between the end of August 1793 and April 1794 hundreds of reports were written by agents of the Ministry of the Interior. Officially designated as Local Commissioner-Observer for the Department of Paris, each agent turned in a report every morning at the Ministry. During the day the reports were summarized in a *précis* entitled "Extract of the Situation in Paris." Copies of this document were sent to the Committee of Public Safety, the Committee on General Security, and the Minister of the Interior. The reports given here were published in *Paris pendant la Terreur. Rapports des agents secrets du Ministre de l'Interieur,* Pierre Caron, ed. (1940-64), III, 345-6, 349-53, 366-7, 371-3, 377-99, 381-7; VI, 1-5, 10, 13, 19, 21, 32-4, 51, 74-6, 95-6, 115-7, 189, 220-21, 225-6.

people ask them where they can find meat from one minute to the next at this price.

A number of citizens expressed their astonishment at seeing a very large number of volunteers in the capital walking around in the streets, in the public squares and in the garden of the former Tuileries, accompanied by women of ill repute. They were saying that, if someone doesn't pay close attention to this, when it comes time to rejoin their regiments these young people will soon be unable to bear arms because they will have contracted all possible diseases, and that on arriving at the garrison they will have to go into the hospitals. Most of these volunteers wear short jackets and carry a stick in hand.

They say that several battalions of volunteers from Arras and Cherbourg are going to arrive in Paris. People are very worried about their fate. They think it would be good not to let them stay with their families, and to make them leave as soon as possible. Many citizens say that they are being brought here to be judged.

The grocers continue to give the citizens garbage; their brandy is abominable, the vinegar is worthless as is the oil; the best of it is not fit to be eaten on salad.

18 Pluviôse, Year II [6 February 1794]

Report by Bacon

The Café des Arts, Rue Saint-André-des-Arts, ought to be watched. It contains only Jews who sell each other ingots of silver; they even do commerce in silver and gold.

According to information I have received the restauranteur Robert, on the Égalité gardens, near the former Café Valois, receives men in his restaurant who, although wearing jackets and breeches in the Carmagnole style, hold the most counter-revoluntionary ideas. I suggest that the people's magistrates have this place watched.

In one of my reports I denounced the silver merchants who are very numerous and who, by means of a special language they have adopted, buy gold and silver without people realizing that that is what they are doing. The code at that time was "yellow linen" meaning a [gold] *louis* and "white linen" meaning a *louis* in [silver] crowns. This code caused several of them to be arrested, according to what has been told me, since they were caught in their own snares. Well! I have learned that they changed the code three days ago, and here is the new code. When they see each other they ask "what price did you get for the lemon?" (which means a *louis*). "Such and such an amount." "How much is one-sixteenth of a bushel of beans worth today?" (which means a *louis* in crowns). "Such and such an amount." I say here that this is the only way of recognizing these speculators and silver merchants.

I denounce Desjardins, according to what has been told me (and I declare that I have never seen him), who is staying at 10 or 11 Passage des Petits-Pères. He is a small dark man who is an agent for the brokers. In approaching him in order to sell gold, in order to be up to date, you must always talk of "the lemon" and "the sixteenth of a bushel of beans." One will certainly get information which could be useful.

I am at this minute about to get the address of another silver merchant who, they tell me, is very rich.

Report by Béraud

Never has there been a revolution as terrible as ours, they were saying in a group at the Café Corraza, Égalité gardens. If it were only the guilty who fell under the law's blade, if it were only the evil-minded who were hidden away in the prisons, it would be mild, but the harsh measures which are taken at every instant make it so bitter that people can't help grumbling. Whose fault is it? It is the fault of those who, neglecting to attend their *section* meetings, have let schemers take over, who having had scarcely enough to subsist on before their rise now make a show of patriotism that is more like tyranny than like the virtues they should profess. If there is cause to complain of the revolutionary committees, what can be said of the Committee on General Security, which seems to close its eyes to barbarousness? "Do you believe," said an old man, "that if this committee restrained their audacity, there would be so many unjust imprisonments? No—you would see three thousand or four thousand or five thousand fathers returned to their children; for I do not let the small number given in the newspapers fool me; and the Republic which seems to be covered with mourning cloth would become the haven of happiness."

"New obstacles, new atrocities," they were saying at the Café de la République. "Would you believe that in certain *sections* they no longer want to give certificates of civic conduct to those who, having only twelve hundred *livres* in income from investments, and several children, ask for certificates in order to get jobs? Really, if this continues, they will smash, break, and reform everything, everything will fall into confusion and chaos, and everyone will have to get by as best he can."

"Then don't you see," answered one individual, "that Madame Aristocracy, whom you see wearing a red bonnet in your assemblies, who bangs with her foot, shouts, and calls you a scoundrel if you are rich or if you talk sense, wants to set up a new kind of monopoly, to create a shortage of men for the official positions in order to keep educated men out of them? Her plan was prepared long ago and you have only to go to the administration in the Massiac mansion, into the offices for the sale of the émigrés property near the city hall, etc., etc.; you will see many of these creatures who can scarcely scribble their own names. Thus consider how everything will go if we let them get too much control."

Report by Charmont

Half of Paris went without meat today. Vegetables have reached a fantastic price. Many women grumble loudly. "Will this last for long?" they were saying. "All that is needed to finish us is to send off the second levy [to the army], then we'd surely die of hunger. At least," they were saying, "if everything were not so expensive there are many things we would be able to afford; but one can't come close to paying for anything and that is very hard." Three of the most necessary articles can be obtained only with coupons; to obtain these coupons one must go to his *section,* and that means losing considerable time and raises the price of the merchandise still more. They say that in the Saint-Marceau suburb there is such misery as to arouse compassion in the commissioners charged with seeing that these unhappy people have what they need, and their needs are very great, for three-fourths of them lack everything.

The citizens are reassured by the resolution adopted by the Jacobin society against the departure of the second levy; because for almost a month, ill-will has rumored it everywhere, even in the *départements,* to the point that in the Yonne *département* families were in a state of despair. "We're going," they were saying, "yesterday the first, today the second, tomorrow the third, and finally everybody." This kind of talk was still heard yesterday in several cafés. But today it is very different; everyone is satisfied; there is hope of conquering our enemies since they have scarcely touched the first levy and it is still complete; this was the feeling in the groups.

On the other hand, people are very surprised that General Jourdan has been replaced by Pichegru, since a large number of the sans-culottes were counting on him to deliver the North from the scoundrels who are still there. "But at least," people tell us, "our hopes have not been let down. We have the conqueror of the Rhine." It is hoped that he will not do as Custine and Houchard did, that he will not say he doesn't know the map as those two scoundrels said they didn't know the country.

Robespierre's report to the Convention pleased the public very much; he can rest assured that this speech has won him the public esteem, for he is being praised to the skies. I don't think there is anyone in Paris at present who doesn't praise him; everyone offers him thanks for his intellect and his talents and his love for our country.

It is being asked again that the Convention decree that coins bearing the royal face be withdrawn from circulation, after a fixed date. Another citizen was saying that we ought to force the citizens to take their gold and silver money to the mint to be exchanged for assignats and that corporal punishment be inflicted on offenders. By that means in a short while we should no longer have the vexation of having to look at that assassin of the people who has finally been put to death.

News is spreading that the army of the Rhine is retreating, that it has abandoned Worms and is falling back on Landau, that the generals are doing their best to carry off all the provisions and supplies and everything which they can take with them from the Palatinate. "That needs to be confirmed," another citizen was saying, "it is true that they are sending everything they can back to France, but it is not true that the army has been forced to retreat."

Citizens have been arrested tonight at several gates [of Paris] bringing in bread, linens, and oil which were only for the use of people living in the environs of Paris.

Report by Latour-Lamontagne

Several vague rumors seem to make people fear that the public tranquillity is going to be disturbed. People are talking about nocturnal meetings in several places, about a plan to petition the National Convention for the expulsion of several deputies. A few people claim there will be a great shake-up on this subject. However they don't have any precise information about this; it is a few placards directed against certain deputies, and the assembly held at the [former] archiepiscopal palace which has given rise to most of these rumors and which ill will is glad to exaggerate. The people are very tranquil and their confidence in their representatives protects them from all uneasiness.

They have complained for a long time about an abuse which it seems the police have finally recognized today. In order to further move the sensibilities of passers by and to get more alms, begging women go about the streets with three or four children hanging from their necks, the greater number of whom don't belong to them but have been kidnapped from their real parents. Four of these unfortunates, accused of this horrible offense, were brought before the committee of the Mountain *section* this morning. The people were extremely satisfied to see that care is being taken to repress severely such disorders.

I have just left a group in the Revolution [formerly Luxembourg] Garden where I just heard it said that within a week we will have a 31st of May.

19 Pluviôse, Year II [7 February 1794]

Report by Charmont

"Tomorrow will be a very difficult day to get through," said several women who were talking together. "Tomorrow we will have no meat at all, the butcher shops will be closed at eight o'clock. The butchers tell you that you can have only a pound and a half of meat at a time regardless of the size of your family—too bad, they just don't have any more." They approve of the Convention's decree on the subject; it is time that they put down these leeches who practically bleed the people.

They say that the grocers are going to be supplied with sugar and that one will be able to get it with a coupon from his *section.* Already all the women are preaching this everywhere. They say "You see, these grocers were loafers, and still are. Since the municipality sent for it on its account, the grocers could just as well have done as much, as if it were the municipality that is bringing it." They claim that we could have everything with ease if we were willing to pay what was necessary.

Listened to thirty conversations, everyone says his bit; it's all the fear of being worse off than one is. . . .

Report by Latour-Lamontagne

The political horizon seems to grow darker from day to day thanks to the perfidious maneuvers of those enemies of the people, of those vile agents of Pitt, who by fabricating and spreading more and more disastrous news hope to discourage the people, to misguide them and to lead them into movements subversive of the holy laws protecting liberty.

After having announced the capture of Maubeuge, they now announce that the enemy has captured the important fortified place of Cambrai, and that the Republic has henceforth only feeble barriers to oppose to this devastating torrent. In order to cast terror into people's minds under the pretense of alarmed patriotism and pained humanity, they announce with a mysterious air that plots are being hatched against the public tranquility; they hint at restlessness in the prisons and seem to fear that the sad days of September will be repeated; they still speak of a second levy as if it were ready to march and were absolutely necessary to fill the gaps in our armies made by enemy bullets, and they even go so far as to say that our forces in the North are too inferior to those of Cobourg to expect any success, and add that it is this too sincere confession made by General Jourdan which led to his dismissal; finally they turn in every direction to instill into the people a feeling of terror which they can turn to the advantage of the counter-revolution.

Those are the perfidious men whom those to whom the people have entrusted part of their authority should constantly keep a sharp eye on. A citizen in a group was saying "They lock up a multitude of supposedly suspect persons, among whom nevertheless it is incontestable there are a great many patriots, and they allow to circulate undisturbed in Paris a mass of men who perhaps have no civil existence, whom one meets everywhere preaching disorder and sounding alarm. Why don't the revolutionary committees, especially constituted to maintain public order, give priority to these preachers of anarchy over the women and old men who have often done no other wrong than to have belonged to a proscribed caste?" "If I were a member of a committee," said another, "I should wish, despite a certain Prudhomme who said in his last issue [of *Révolutions de Paris*] that there could be no republic where there was not entirely free speech and free press, I should wish, I say, that within a week, in the territory where I exercised my powers, no remarks could be heard that could aid malevolence and the aristocracy." . . .

One hears on every side complaints against the revolutionary committees, which are accused of tyranny and embezzlement. They complain also against the popular societies [in the *sections*], which are suspected of a tendency to federalism and whose dissolution, already urged by a vigorous resolution of the Jacobins, seems generally desired. . . .

This evening at the Jacobin club Brichet moved that the society and the galleries all together ask the Convention for the complete annihilation of the right. Robespierre wisely spoke against this proposal, which he called counter-revolutionary, and asked for Brichet's expulsion. Robespierre's speech was much applauded.

Report by Monic

The police commissioners in the Maison-Commune *section* should have a look at the prostitutes in Vannerie and Tannerie streets. Those women are bothered so little, although very close to the Maison-Commune [city hall], that they carry on their commerce in broad daylight, greatly scandalizing the good citizens.

Patrols are very rare at night in the neighborhood of the Convention and the former Palais-Royal [known during the revolution as the Palais-Égalité]. It would nevertheless be necessary for public peace and the citizens' safety that the commandants in those *sections* give orders for more frequent patrols, above all from ten o'clock in the evening until one o'clock in the morning. It is during those three hours that rascals of all kinds pour out of the houses of debauchery and gambling. If an honest citizen on his way home has the misfortune to find himself in their hands he is often robbed because, the patrols being very rare, the scoundrels have complete freedom to commit their brigandage without having to fear being taken by surprise or arrested.

Report by Pourvoyeur

In all the groups today they were talking about the food supply. They said it was astonishing that there was nothing in Paris, that everything was lacking, meat was impossible to get as well as other kinds of food; vegetables, there aren't any; beans are twenty *sous* for a sixteenth of a bushel; it is only bread that is not scarce but it is bad, especially in certain places. Some citizens are saying that they have gotten news from a *départment* in Burgundy and that the estate managers and peasants there are saying "When they send us bread, we'll send our produce to Paris; but since we have no bread we have to eat our eggs, potatoes, and beans, etc."

In one group they were talking about Camille Desmoulins. They said he had always been a patriot from the beginning of the revolution; that he had proven himself well, above all at the stormiest moments; that people talk about him as much as about even Marat; that if he has made mistakes it was only an error of the moment, not made through lack of patriotism and that it would really be unjust to forget what he has done since and for the revolution.

They say it is not surprising that food supplies are getting more expensive, since speculation in silver is still going on. In order to recognize these individuals one must ask them, for silver, how much an ell of white linen is worth, then they answer "forty *sous*" which means forty *livres*. For gold, it is "How much is grey linen worth?" They say "fifty *sous*" which similarly means fifty *livres* for a twenty-four-*livre* gold piece. And there isn't a day when this doesn't increase with events. Those individuals are often found in the cafés around the Égalité palace; they place themselves in the little rooms at the backs of the shops.

The groups were quiet; Paris is as calm as possible, especially at a moment when the people are experiencing vexations from the merchants of all kinds, and when they no longer want to sell any merchandise.

The Committee of Public Safety gets the people's admiration. It is astonishing, they say, with what activity and genius it directs operations, in both internal and foreign affairs, with the greatest wisdom imaginable. And so this committee is astonishing the whole universe.

20 Pluviôse, Year II [8 February 1794]

Report by Bacon

In my report ten days ago, I spoke of the dogs who by their noise were preventing the people from being educated in the Temple of Reason; I also said that sentinels must be posted to foil people with bad intentions. Well! Today at the former church of Bonne-Nouvelle there were sentinels everywhere, and the dogs were chased away. The greatest calm reigned. Here is what happened.

The church I just mentioned was full of people and there were many young people of both sexes. One citizen had a number of citizens, the oldest being nine or ten, recite the Declaration of Rights and several articles of the republican constitution. These young people were applauded several times and on all sides they cried "Vive la République! Vive la Convention! Vive la Montagne!" Another citizen then occupied the pulpit of truth. There he read a little discourse filled with morality, patriotism, and philanthropy, the main lines of which bore on fanaticism, the crimes of kings, the horror of federalism, and love of liberty. This discourse, gracefully read (and the orator had a sonorous and powerful voice), produced, I might say here, a fine effect, and I noticed that it stirred the souls of the listeners. This passage was much applauded: "What thanks we should offer to the holy Mountain, to the National Convention, and to the Committee of Public Safety for having brought about the insurrection of the 31st of May, which saved our country and killed federalism. Without this holy uprising the brigands with their crosses, their rosaries, their banners, and their saints, would have arrived in Paris. Brave Parisians, where would we have been?" ("The Convention forever!") This passage also was vigorously applauded: "And you, brave English sans-culottes, we shall give you liberty; for soon you will no longer have lords nor clergy nor King George the Ninny, nor Pitt, that most pitiful of all men. We will hold out our arms to you." (Everyone cried "It won't be long!") But it was this sentence which received universal applause lasting for more than two minutes: "No peace with Kings! They must be entirely destroyed; the man in his cottage must receive the rewards due to his virtues." (Bravo! Vive, vive et vive la République!")

Lefèvre, the opera singer, sang patriotic songs and the *Marseillaise*. A charming voice, a melodious tone, and great emotion made tears flow, and, while weeping, people cried "Vive la République!" At the church they sold more than four hundred copies of a printed discourse on public education by Jault, a member of the Commune of Paris. People were grabbing for it. Then they planted the tree of liberty which the young citizens had carried around the *section*. There were a great many people there. The young republicans, in planting the tree of liberty, promised to spill their last drop of blood to defend it.

I have gone into all these details because I think they will give pleasure to the friends of the revolution.

At the former church of Saint-Laurent, citizens read decrees of the Convention and republican instructions to the people. They sang very revolutionary songs. There were a great many people in the temple of Philosophy; but at least three-fourths of the women were wearing short dresses, round bonnets, no powder, I mean like country citizens. Above all there were young people. The young women applauded several times, laughing, at a song on the abolition of religion. Here is the last chorus of a verse that received great applause: "That Eucharist which drew such praises / We have used to make plain wafers." I observed that at the word "wafers" the old women moved their legs, the old men in wigs quickly took a pinch of snuff, smiling falsely; and the effect of the snuff was so violent that it resembled a cannon shot. This other chorus of a verse was much applauded: "The true religion / Is to love our Constitution." Other songs about the crimes of kings earned vigorous applause. . . .

The general assembly of the Arsenal *section* was very numerous, for there were more than seven hundred persons at it. Many women in the galleries. Orders sent by the Committee of Public Safety, concerning saltpeter, were read. Certificates of civic conduct were attended to, and also the question of a larger and more wholesome meeting place. (Good public spirit.) . . .

The general assembly of the Lombards *section* was extremely numerous; and often they lost precious time in useless debates because many members had drunk heavily at dinner. They read the orders of the Committee of Public Safety relative to saltpeter. . . . (Good public spirit).

The general assembly of the Cité *section* was very numerous. They concerned themselves only with saltpeter, with regard to which they adopted revolutionary orders.

The general assembly of the Maison-Commune *section* was very attractive. Beginning at five o'clock in the afternoon, young citizens of both sexes were presented to the assembly with martial music. They were received appropriately. Some recited verses on martyrs for liberty; others recited the Declaration of Rights; others recited articles of the Constitution; others, finally, sang patriotic songs. There was a considerable crowd in the church. Never was a spectacle more moving. The women, weeping tears of joy, cried "Vive la République!" The men, the children, the women, the girls, went in turns to the platform and sang songs as they came to their minds. These songs all revolved around the crimes of kings, the happiness of liberty and equality. This fine spectacle did not end until eleven o'clock; and as the people left they shouted "Vive la Convention!"

Having learned, in a café on the boulevard, that the general assembly of the Temple *section* would be stormy, I presented myself there at six thirty. I placed myself in a corner of the women's gallery to ascertain the public mentality. After ten minutes, the battalion commandant, a pimply man, arrived with five men; all six were drunk, and unrecognizable as men (I note that I was only in a public gallery). The commandant, on seeing me, asked me "What are you doing there?" "I am here waiting for a friend," I replied, "to go to our *section*." Pushing me, and ordering two lugs to hold me by the collar, he told them "Hold that man, he's a stool-pigeon." In fact they were talking about a man arrested in the assembly. A citizen from the Jacobin society, who was in a public gallery, had already been arrested. While the battalion commander was about to talk with the assembly about another citizen and me, women were saying to me "Citizen, be patient; for some time everyone's mind has been troubled." Other citizens, seeing me stay near the door, said: "Citizen, nobody in the world enters the galleries any more; the *section* is exposed to the plots of schemers and scoundrels, but we'll make ourselves known."

A moment later, some citizens disagreed and from my observations I saw only men resembling lions furious at having missed their prey. I found the mind of the citizens of the Temple *section* very different, alas! from the republican mentality of the Maison Commune *section*. . . .

I think, from what I have heard, that the cause of these aberrations in certain *sections* comes from the schemes of certain men who have arrived from the Vendée and who are perhaps the chiefs of the brigands.

Paris appeared peaceful to me.

1 Germinal, Year II [21 March 1794]

Report by Bacon

In a very large group near the Place de la Commune the talk was about the affair of Hébert and his accomplices. There were people who said: "We won't believe that he's guilty until we see the conviction papers with our own eyes—in spite of our great confidence in the Committee of Public Safety." Some women also said that there were many citizens from the Bonne-Nouvelle *section* (Hébert's *section*) implicated in this affair. . . .

In a crowd under the arcades of the Place de la Fabrication des armes some workers were talking about the Convention for which he [*sic*] has the greatest respect. Then they spoke about a newspaper published by a sapper who was trying to take the place of Hébert's paper. "It is quite astonishing," they said, "that this paper which will finally corrupt the public with its swearing isn't stopped." "Let us not lose sight of the fact," said a fairly elderly citizen, "that to be a true patriot, one must love virtue and probity." ("That's very true," people shouted.) In the same group it was said that the white-coated Austrians who walked about in gangs to cut the throats of patriots were no longer seen in the streets since the scoundrels, Vincent and the others, were locked up.

I saw the little people. Well! Would you believe it? Hébert still has a considerable following among such citizens. Let the magistrates be aware of that!

In the rue [des] Nonnains d'Hyères several women who spoke ill of the constituted authorities were arrested.

I made the rounds of different cabarets frequented by workers. No one spoke of anything but Hébert's interrogation. "As for myself," said a worker, "I'd rather go to work than go get an arm broken at the

Palais [de justice] to see Monsieur le Père Duchesne. Let that guy take care of himself—he's in the judges' hands." Others replied: "We feel the same way you do."

Paris seemed quiet to me.

Report by Béraud

All of the groups in the Jardin National talked only about the food supply and the scarcity was attributed to Hébert and his clique. Some of his partisans who wanted to come to his defense were regarded as scoundrels and one of them was knocked about. . . .

Everywhere people insisted that the Bonne Nouvelle *section* was involved in Hébert's plot. It was said in this regard that a number of its inhabitants had been imprisoned and that in a little while at least three-quarters of the *section* would also be arrested. "Bravo!" said the sans-culottes of the Porte Saint-Denis, "we've got bad blood and it must be drawn. . . ."

Public opinion is in general good, few agitators, some partisans of Hébert, but the sans-culottes are hounding them.

Report by Dugas

. . . The meeting at the Jacobins was interesting only for Robespierre's speech. The orator painted our present situation in the most somber colors. "We are caught," he said, "between two factions that wish to destroy the Revolution. The first faction is known and it will soon be crushed. But if the National Convention does not take the strongest measures to exterminate the other as soon as possible it will be risking its own existence and, consequently, that of the people's liberty. This second faction, whose ramifications extend from Paris even into the *départements* and the armies and whose principles are based on a perfidious moderation, is prepared to cause the defeat of our armies, deprive us of food supplies, bring fire and the sword to all of France and spread the horrors of civil war over the face of the land. . . ."

Report by Leharivel

The Jacobin meeting offered nothing extraordinary or new. The fears inspired by Robespierre in his speech on the aftermath of the fearful plot that had just been unmasked didn't please everyone. Regarding this it was said: "What do we have to fear since the conspirators have been arrested and now that, according to the assertion of citizen Couthon himself, we have unraveled all the threads of the conspiracy? Anyway, isn't the confidence of the people in the Convention established in a firm and lasting fashion? Let's not worry, then, and calmly await the events that will and must benefit the Republic." The citizens and citizenesses who heard these just reflections applauded them wholeheartedly.

Report by Pourvoyeur

. . . There were a lot of people at the doors of the Tribunal at three in the morning. Never has so great a desire to hear the guilty interrogated been shown. Several people said: "I've never seen anyone guillotined, but I'll go to see these with pleasure, especially Hébert and Chaumette, those scoundrels who tricked us with their false patriotism. . . ."

In a very large group it was said that it was essential for the Convention to remain at its post, that it had become more necessary for us than ever, and that the people should rise *en masse* to make this request unanimously. In the same group someone praised Robespierre's virtues: "He has never changed," they said. "He was the implacable enemy of the monarchy and he has the virtues of a true republican. His fortune has not been known to increase since the beginning of the revolution, his habits are proper and his intentions pure and for the welfare of the people."

It was feared that the party of these scoundrels might try something. People saw many very suspect characters, especially those who had hooks and large sticks and roamed around crowds and in all parts of the city. They appeared to want to provoke all of the citizens.

2 Germinal, Year II [22 March 1794]

Report by Hanriot

The Mountain *section,* having received the list of the members who were to compose the commune when it was renewed, appointed Citizen Isabeau as commissioner to gather information on six of these individuals. Acting upon the information that it received from its commissioner, the *section* rejected two of them. One of them, although a good patriot, had been a lawyer. Moreover, despite his patriotism he was still a formalist and always used circumlocutions and rarely came to the point. . . .

The patriots are still impatiently awaiting the law of the new maximum that had been announced for the first of Germinal. Some grumbling arose, but a notice posted at the Palais-Royal by order of citizen

Lullier, national agent for the district, appeased them a little. "Troubling circumstances," it said, "have deferred the posting of the new law until the third of this month when it will fix the price of articles of prime necessity."

The indictment against the conspirators, circulated throughout Paris, has saddened all of its readers. Citizens and patriots complain bitterly that the French nation, ever since the beginning of the Revolution, has always been fooled by those in whom it had the greatest confidence. It was unanimously agreed that patriots had no protectors other than the National Convention, the Jacobin club, and the two committees of Public Safety and General Security, and everywhere they were very highly praised. Suspicion of those who affected to wear and even to exaggerate the supposed republican costume is every day increasing. "Let's not trust them," it was said yesterday in the vicinity of the Palais. "Especially those little red ribbons worn in the buttonhole. From afar they are taken for the former Knights of Saint-Louis and that flatters their vanity. . . ."

Report by Latour-Lamontagne

In a group at the Place de la Révolution some citizens were talking about the way in which the Tribunal was proceeding in the trial of the accused Hébert, etc. "They are hardly allowed," it was said, "the liberty to defend themselves. The president speaks to them harshly: 'It's yes or no that I require of you,' he is constantly telling them. 'There's no question here of phrases, etc.' " Another citizen added: "The people, as angered as they are by the conspirators, are pained to see the Tribunal follow a course so opposed to the demands of humanity and justice." Here the orator was interrupted by the murmurs of several sans-culottes. One of them cried: "These are the first complaints that I've heard made against the Tribunal and it is quite singular that people have waited so long to complain about it. The one who finds the Tribunal so rigorous now—would he perhaps applaud its severity were the entire Convention and the Jacobins put in the place of Hébert and his accomplices?" This reply was loudly applauded and the individual who had deserved the attack lost no time disappearing. . . .

3 Germinal, Year II [23 March 1794]

Report by Boucheseiche

. . . People are waiting for the first poster on the *maximum* that the national agent had promised. It hasn't been put up. This delay is worrying the people and from this stem great dissertations on public functionaries who are always making and breaking promises. There was a lot of talk about food supplies. The scarcity was blamed on the accused and it was hoped that after their judgment we would no longer lack anything. . . .

The public promenades and the boulevards are filled with people *dressed in their Sunday best.* This is a proof that fanaticism and superstition still have a prodigious number of partisans in Paris.*

4 Germinal, Year II [24 March 1794]

Report by Bacon

The Père Duchesne and consorts were guillotined to cries of "Vive la République." Wherever they passed hats were lifted into the air and people shouted: "Vive la République! *ça va, ça ira.*† An immense throng had collected to see this execution. Joy and pleasure were evident on every face. After the execution everyone talked about the conspirators. It was said: "They died like gutless cowards.** Others said: "We thought that Hébert would have shown more courage, but he died like a J[ean] F[outre].†† The Brissotins went to the guillotine more bravely." Many citizens in the crowd sang couplets on the scoundrels and others recited quatrains. . . .

In a group near the Porte Bernard it was said that the casters had been forbidden to make molds for Marat's bust. This astonished no one.

Report by Charmont

The villains were judged and punished today to the great satisfaction of all of the people. The cortege seemed more like a festival than an execution. Most of the condemned seemed very tranquil. Hébert was the most unmanned of the group.

It was rumored in different groups that Hébert had denounced some

* [March 23, 1794, fell on a Sunday.]
† [The *Ça ira* was a popular and rather bloodthirsty revolutionary song.]
**[The French "*couyons*" is considerably stronger.]
†† [An even harsher and, till recently, unprintable term for "coward."]

forty deputies who were also accomplices in his affair. It was high time, people said, that this conspiracy was discovered because it was asserted in several *départements* that Paris had been put to fire and sword. Letters received from fifty leagues away announced the coming of a great upheaval in Paris where there was great fear for the safety of the Convention. What is certain is that the plot is unmasked and there is nothing more to fear. . . .

The *maximum* is on the order of the day and diverse opinions on this law are being expressed. Some people assert that the law will have bad effects in the *départements* and that it will never be enforced as strictly as desired. Others retort, on the other hand, that only a bad citizen would inveigh against this law and asserted that the law was the despair of all of the Republic's enemies. . . .

5 Germinal, Year II [25 March 1794]

Report by Boucheseiche

. . . The first poster on the *maximum,* awaited impatiently, was put up during the afternoon and attracted everyone's attention. No one reading it failed to say that this *maximum* was very advantageous for the country people and the merchants. The article on meat prices was especially commented upon. Many people said that the *maximum* had been set at sixteen to eighteen *sols* in order to prevent sans-culottes from eating meat. It was observed that if the object of the law was to diminish the amount consumed it would be better to fix the quantity that each family could have per *décade,* or establish supplementary prices like those for bread. Only the rich would then bear the cost of the rise in price. . . .

Report by Charmont

The *maximum* began to appear today. Crowds began to gather where it had been posted. Everywhere I saw [*sic*] the same words, everywhere people said: "Oh! Now we'll be able to buy anything because the prices are those the merchants want." Others said, "Oh well, whatever the price, at least we'll get something," and everywhere people left without saying a word.

The Hébert affair is still being discussed. Many talk about . . . the great things that Hébert revealed, among other things that he denounced Marat. And many others even say that the Marat *section* had already decided to veil his busts, asserting everywhere that he was quite lucky to have been assassinated because he would have been guillotined like all the others. It was also bandied about that more than two thousand citizens had been denounced in the affair and that during the course of the month all of them would pass through the Little Window. There are even some newspapers that dare to publish such things.

Report by Soulet

Yesterday they arrested the dandies who said that the cavalry should be jumped just when the execution was being carried out. They were brought to the vigilance committee of the Tuileries *section.*

In all of the public places aristocrats and moderates rejoice over this execution and affect a great deal of patriotism. Patriots also rejoice, but they are all keeping an eye on one another.

Report by Rolin

. . . Malicious men are taking advantage of the betrayal of one in whom we had the highest confidence. They have the extreme impudence to try (in crowds and public places) to fill the people with distrust and this can only deprive our magistrates and perhaps even the National Convention of the trust that we have placed in them and which they have merited in the highest degree. I have kept them under surveillance to the utmost of my ability. I believe that it would be good to show men like these no indulgence whatsoever. Several of them repeated these words with an aristocratic smile: "They'll all disappear," adding derisively, "those scoundrels." If I had been less hemmed in and shoved about by the crowd, I probably could have had a few of them locked up. . . ."

9 Germinal, Year II [29 March 1794]

Report by Latour-Lamontagne

"I don't know where all of this is going to end," a citizen said at the Café de la République. "People complained about the revolutionary committees and managed to make them suspect. The Revolutionary Army was criticized and now it is dissolved. It seems that people have it in for everything that bears the adjective 'revolutionary.' " Then this man, fearing perhaps that he had said too much, withdrew precipitously. Another person said: "I recognize him. I've often seen him on horseback, following the general [Ronsin] of the Revolutionary Army."

10 Germinal, Year II [30 March 1794]

Report by Pourvoyeur

In a very large group several people were talking about the revolution. Someone complained that the end of the conspirators was yet to come and that people thought that simply because the source of aristocracy had been destroyed the intriguers would no longer dare to show themselves." Several patriots replied: "Let well enough alone. The Committee of Public Safety is watching over us and we should be grateful for that." "Anyway," it was observed, "how long do you think we've had a real revolution? You can't start counting before the 31st of May and I think that there's nothing to complain about. A lot of things have been done since then and if things keep going as they have our revolution will be over in eighteen months." All of the deputies who had served the Republic well were discussed, notably Robespierre, who was praised. But a patriot observed, he said [*sic*] that although Robespierre had rendered services to his country, if he happened to change it would be the duty of a republican to forget what he had done and from then on consider only his crime and demand that the law strike him down.

Again it was pointed out that moderates did us more harm than aristocrats, that the latter could be recognized by unmistakeable signs while the others knew how to hide themselves, and, moreover, are more dangerous than the real aristocrats.

11 Germinal, Year II [31 March 1794]

Report by Grivel

Events in Paris. The rumor spread that sixteen of the best-known members of the Convention were arrested last night by order of the Committee of Public Safety and the Committee on General Security sitting jointly. Spreading with great speed, this news created a tremendous sensation. People were astonished and shocked to learn that deputies who had always been in the vanguard of the patriots during the affair of August 10 and at the establishment of the Republic and the revolutionary government, men such as Danton, Legendre, Bourdon (de l'Oise), Camille Desmoulins, Thuriot, etc., were among the prisoners. People lamented but no one dared to judge.

The Agents Assessed

Béraud and Latour-Montagne
Good observers, have made many reports beneficial to the Republic concerning complaints made by the indigent, fathers of families, defenders of the *patrie*. Have often given advance warning against the perfidious intentions of the malicious and on several occasions have accurately grasped the state of public opinion.

Béraud, in addition, fit for anything, writes with ease and quite well.

Bacon
Good observer, ordinarily reporting what has happened in several popular societies or general assemblies. Senses well the mind of the most needy class of the people and has made important denunciations, either against speculators or against the enemies of the Republic.

Pourvoyeur
Poor observer, gives no or very little information useful to the public welfare.

Charmont
Without knowing how to write well, explains fairly well what is said and done in crowds.

Among the papers of the Ministry of the Interior there is a confidential assessment of several of the observers. It was drawn up at the end of Germinal, Year II. For a complete text of this report, as well as biographical information on the agents, see Caron's General Introduction to *Paris pendant la Terreur,* I, i-lx.

National Convention

11 Germinal, Year II [31 March 1794]

Tallien presiding:

DELMAS: I ask for the floor for a point of order. The members of Convention who are also members of the committees have been busy

Le Moniteur universel, XX, 94-6.

there until two or three in the morning. I demand that they be invited to appear in the Convention at once.

The proposition is adopted.

LEGENDRE: Citizens: four members of this assembly were arrested last night. I know that Danton is one of them. I don't know the names of the others. What do their names matter if they are guilty? But citizens, I am here to request that the arrested members be brought to the bar of the Convention where you will hear them and where they will be accused or absolved by you.

Citizens, I am but the fruit of liberty's genius. I am merely its creature and I will develop the proposition I am now making with the greatest simplicity. My education was not the work of men, but nature's. Don't expect anything from me but the explosion of an emotion.

Citizens, I declare, I believe that Danton is as pure as I am and I don't think that anyone could reproach me for any deed that would wound the most scrupulous probity . . . (*Murmuring interrupts the orator.*)

CLAUZEL: President, maintain freedom of speech.

THE PRESIDENT: Yes, I will maintain freedom of speech. Yes, everyone can freely say what he thinks. We are all here to save liberty. (*Applause.*) . . .

LEGENDRE: I will apostrophize no member of the committees of Public Safety and General Security. But I have the right to fear that personal hatred and individual passion will wrench from liberty men who have rendered her the greatest, the most useful services. . . .

The enemy was then [1792] at the gates of Paris. Danton came and his ideas saved the country.

I insist that I can not believe him guilty. . . . I repeat that I find him as pure as I am. He has been behind bars since last night. No doubt they fear that his replies will destroy the accusations made against him. I demand, consequently, that before you hear any report the prisoners be brought and heard. . . .

FAYAU: I oppose the motion made by Legendre. It seems to me that the Convention can not have two sets of weights and measures. Citizens, I heard it said around me that this was murdering one another. I would observe, first of all, with the just indignation that such words inspire in me, which would never have come from the mouth of a friend of liberty, that it is national justice that is in operation now and that if we have anything to lament it is the sight of such a large number of traitors.

Remember, moreover, that already they are guilty in the eyes of your committees of Public Safety and General Security which, invested with your confidence, had them arrested. . . .

I demand, therefore, that the National Convention not admit the prisoners to the bar but that it hear the report of its committees.

THE PRESIDENT: Robespierre has the floor.

ROBESPIERRE: . . . It is easy to perceive . . . that this is a matter of great interest, that it is a question of knowing whether a few men should come before the country today. . . . Why was this motion, rejected when it was proposed by Danton for Bazire, Chabot, and Fabre d'Églantine, received just a moment ago by a portion of the members of this assembly? Why? Because today it is a matter of knowing whether the interests of a few ambitious hypocrites shall come before the interests of the French people. (*Applause.*) . . .

Legendre appears not to know the names of those who were arrested. The whole Convention knows them. His friend Lacroix is among the prisoners. Why does he pretend not to know this? Because he knows that one can not decently defend Lacroix. He speaks of Danton because he no doubt thinks that privilege is attached to this name. No, we won't have any of that, no privileges. No, we won't have any idols! (*Applause at several points.*) . . .

Citizens, this is the moment to speak the truth. I do not recognize anything in all that has been said but the sinister presage of the decadence of principle. Who, in fact, are these men who sacrifice the interests of the country to personal liaisons, to fear, perhaps? Who, at the moment when liberty is triumphant, dare to try to destroy it within these walls? They want to make you fear an abuse of power, of this national power that you have exercised and which does not reside only in a few men. What have you done that you have not done freely, that has not saved the Republic, that has not been approved by all of France? They want to make you fear that the people are perishing as the victims of these committees which have obtained the public confidence, which emanated from the National Convention. . . . It is feared that the prisoners are being oppressed; they therefore suspect the administrators of national justice, men who have obtained the confidence of the National Convention. They distrust the Convention that has given them this confidence, they distrust public opinion which has sanctioned it! I say that whoever trembles now is guilty, for the innocent will never fear public vigilance. (*Applause.*) . . .

. . .

BARÈRE: . . . The word dictatorship has been used and it has rung in my ear for the last quarter of an hour. It is essential to destroy such an idea. I see that the friends of the prisoners are the only ones who tremble for liberty's sake. The only dictatorship I know is the one of a man who assumes all masks; now that of audacity, now that of suppleness. . . .

What! Would there be a dictatorship in the committees which are removable every month, every minute! The day when they will stop defending liberty, when they will cease to protect our borders, when they will neglect to combat the factions that are liberty's enemies, on that day they will be denounced from this rostrum, and I myself, a member of this committee, will be the first to support these denunciations. . . .

I demand that Legendre's motion be tabled.

Saint-Just, reporter for the Committee of Public Safety, enters the hall and goes to the rostrum.

Legendre's proposition is tabled.

The reporter gets the floor. A profound silence reigns in the assembly. . . .

Memoirs of Joseph Barras

It is too true that the Terror, rendered necessary by the manoeuvres of the aristocrats and the monarchs, was at that time unfortunately turned against the citizens. The first victims were the representatives of the people themselves. Their state of division and dread afforded the Governmental committees a pretext for preserving their cruel domination. The National Convention, on all sides appealed to to save liberty, not only neglected to secure to the citizens the possession of their heads: it suffered to be taken, and even offered, those of its members. When once the committees shall have begun to indulge in reciprocal threats, the dissension born of their own danger will rally the Convention against its oppressors. . . .

In the meantime, the sentiment felt at the oppression endured by the Convention was beginning to find an outlet in private conversations, and even in the public writings of a few men less timid than the others. Camille Desmoulins was publishing his *Vieux Cordelier,* and Phélip-

Memoirs of Barras, G. D. Duruy, ed., translated by C. E. Roche (London, 1895), I, 192-6.

peaux his declamations against the bad management of the Vendean war, which was the reason that it continually rose from its ashes.

As I was leaving the Convention one day in the company of Danton, Courtois, Fréron, and Panis, we met in the Cour du Carrousel several deputies who were members of the secret committees. Danton, going towards them, said to them, "You should read the memoirs of Phélippeaux.[1] They will supply you with the means of putting an end to this Vendean war which you have perpetrated with the view of rendering your powers necessary." Vadier, Amar, Voulland, and Barère charged Danton with having caused these memoirs to be printed and circulated; Danton merely replied, "I am not called upon to vindicate myself." Thereupon an angry discussion ensued, degenerating into personalities. Danton threatened the members of the Committee that he would take the floor in the National Convention, and charge them with malversations and tyranny. The others withdrew without replying, but bearing him no good-will. I said to Danton, "Let us at once return to the National Convention; take the floor; you may rest assured of our support, but do not let us wait until to-morrow, for there is a likelihood of your being arrested to-night." "They would not dare to," was Danton's contemptuous rejoinder; then, addressing himself to me, he said, "Come and help us to eat a pullet." I declined. Brune, the friend, and up to that time the inseparable aide-de-camp, of Danton was present. I remarked to Brune, "Guard Danton carefully, for he threatened where he should have struck." . . .

Suddenly, at nine o'clock in the morning of the 11th Germinal, I hear of Danton's arrest. I at once proceed to his residence in the Passage du Commerce, where I had dined two days earlier; on my arrival there the news of his arrest is confirmed to me: it had taken place at five o'clock that morning. He had been torn from his bed and cast into the Luxembourg prison, where he was in close confinement. I hasten to the National Convention; it was scarcely eleven o'clock. Its members were wending their steps thither, the greater part of them not having the faintest suspicion of this most extraordinary arrest—extraordinary even at a time when those occurring daily were becoming more and

[1] The manuscript here bears a marginal note written in pencil by Prieur de la Côte-d'Or: "Phélippeaux was in the wrong. The Committee had taken energetic and proper measures for the destruction of La Vendée, resulting in the decisive event of the sudden capture of Châtillon, Mortagne, and Chollet, and in consequence of this success the Vendean army moved to the north of the Loire, where it was almost annihilated. Phélippeaux was a bungler, vainglorious, and thoughtless. Danton's imprudent words were the cause of his ruin; but, there was in this affair a misunderstanding on both sides. [Duruy's note.]

more extraordinary. Some few of the members had heard rumours to which they attached no faith, and asked me questions as to what I seemed to have learnt; in the midst of all this enter the members of the Committee of Public Safety, Saint-Just bringing up the rear. He at once ascends into the tribune, and reads out the most singular and monstrous indictment ever dreamt of. Phlegmatic, and in his sententious tone, he recites this incredible theme, holding the manuscript in a hand that remains motionless, while the other makes but one gesture, inexorable and from which there is no appeal—a gesture like unto the very knife of the guillotine. I received a copy of this report, together with a mass of other printed documents such as are usually distributed among the members of legislative bodies. As I write I have before me this copy, bearing the imprint of the National Printing Office; it is dated Year II. of the Republic, and is entitled: *Report addressed to the National Convention, in the name of the Committees of General Security and Public Safety, on the conspiracy hatched for some years past by criminal factions for the purpose of absorbing the French Revolution by a change of dynasty. Printed by order of the National Convention at its sitting of the 11th Germinal.* The reading of this report by Saint-Just, even after a lapse of thirty years, overwhelms me with astonishment and chokes me just as much as on the day when I first heard it. . . .

Jacobin Club

6 Prairial, Year II [25 May 1794]

Voulland presiding:

During this interesting session the entire Society, all the citizens in the galleries, received with compassion and ecstatically applauded two of the most ardent defenders of the rights of the people, two men whom the British government had marked for a place between Marat and Lepelletier. The God of free men watched over them. Providence was their shield: they escaped the blows of the assassins and shared, in advance, the honors that the French nation has designated for martyrs for liberty, without the people having to shed tears over their funeral urns.

When they entered the meeting hall all eyes were fixed on these precious men, all hearts soared at once. . . .

COLLOT: In the midst of this emotion which, at once sweet and

Le Moniteur universel, XX, 577-9.

strong, had profoundly touched me, I have learned this truth: whoever has run dangers for his country receives new strength from the fraternal interest that republican hearts show to him. . . .

It was not yesterday, citizens, that we knew that assassinations had been planned by the tyrants; it was not yesterday that we knew that the inventiveness of tyrants was limited to criminal deeds. We knew that the execrable Pitt subsidized all of the crimes. We knew that he was obstinately going ahead with the plan to dissolve the National Convention by multiplied murders. We knew that in this majestic Convention whose courage and ceaselessly energetic attitude oppressed and tormented him for the sole reason that the labors of the Convention insured the happiness of all men worthy of enjoying liberty; we knew, I say, that in the midst of this representative body of a free, strong, and powerful people there was not one friend of virtue whose head had not been proscribed by these odious English and Austrian ministers, the slaves of tyrants.

All of the courageous men who make up this Society doubtless share this proscription. Already several virtuous men, defenders of the people's cause, have been struck down by assassins' blows. Their memory will live eternally in our hearts and their shades are awaiting us. . . .

The allied tyrants are accumulating crimes. They are amassing them. They abound in cruelties. They have not one thought that is not an outrage to nature and humanity. What can we conclude from this, citizens, but that the tyrants are approaching their destruction. . . . They murder because they no longer have any resources and means with which to fight us.

Each of our victories casts them into new consternation. The genius of liberty menaces them, crushes them. They shudder, they try to forget, they plunge into and bathe themselves in crime to turn aside the idea of their destruction. . . . Well, . . . let them brew poisons, let them distribute daggers, let them plan ambushes! We will nevertheless march toward our goal with the same ardor. Poisons, daggers, and ambushes will not delay for a minute the success of liberty.

Do they imagine then that they can frighten us? Don't they know that when a patriot falls beneath their blows it is on his tomb that we once more swear vengeance for their crime and proclaim the eternity of liberty? . . .

They will not kill the deathless sentiment of liberty embedded in our hearts. They will not kill the people as a whole which, virtuous and strong, has voted their destruction. . . .

All the citizens rise in ecstasy crying: Vive la république! . . .

LEGENDRE: The hand of crime is raised to strike liberty. But nature's God had not allowed crime to succeed. . . .

Legendre invites patriots to redouble their vigilance and activity and not to allow the representatives of the people to go out alone, for their existence is very useful to the Republic. He announces that he himself will be on guard and that he is ready to offer his body to the murderers' steel when it is aimed at the representatives that the tyrants wish to steal from France. . . .

Dumas takes the floor to make known the details of assassinations planned for several representatives. He announces that the citizen Voulland, now president of the Society, had almost become one of these victims.

After elaborating on the already-known particulars of Collot d'Herbois's assassination, he speaks about the new one attempted against Robespierre by a twenty-year-old girl.

He then presents observations on the proposition made to give the representatives of the people a bodyguard; he declares that he will never allow it even if it had the name of Guard of Friendship and that they are guarded well enough since they know that the people are keeping all of the conspirators and traitors under surveillance.

COUTHON: We should not be astonished to see tyranny fight liberty. But it is necessary to go back to the source of the assassinations and discover their cause. The foreigner's faction has its hot-beds of activity in Paris. . . . It operates with the help of immoral beings, of atheists, corrupters, and assassins. The conspiracies have been discovered. The foreigner has seen this and he has trembled. To create a diversion he has ordered the assassins into action. . . .

Someone spoke of giving us guards. I would like to believe that his proposition stemmed from a pure intention. But I will say that only despots want to have guards and that we were not made to be likened to them. We don't need guards to defend us. It is virtue, the confidence of the people, and Providence that watch over our days. We also have enough friends here to come to our aid. It would be an insult to our friends, to the people, and to Providence to believe that we could have better guards.

We must redouble our vigilance and remember that most of the men who surround us and who wish to appear as the most ardent patriots are often our cruelest enemies. But let them not be deceived: they are known, their bad faith is out in the open. One sometimes meets, beneath these masks of patriotism, that abominable foreigner's faction which subsidizes assassinations and crimes, a faction directed by the British cabinet, the author of the most atrocious crime.

I would request that the Society, without making a formal motion, declare in a spontaneous movement that it regards this frightful government as guilty of *lèse-humanité*. (Yes, Yes, *simultaneously cry all the members and all of the citizens present, rising in a spontaneous movement.*) . . .

Legendre protests that he did not have any bad intention in inviting good patriots not to allow the representatives whose lives were menaced to go out alone. He affirms that yesterday when a citizen told him that it was necessary to give a bodyguard to the committees of Public Safety and General Security he replied that this measure was counter-revolutionary and that such a thought had never entered his mind.

"I have a wife and a child," *he said.* "Well! I'm not any less determined to sacrifice myself for my country. I have never been guided by any interest other than the hope of working for the happiness of my fellow citizens. I have been unfortunately fooled by the scoundrels who hid behind the mask of patriotism, but this is an error of my mind and not of my heart." (*Applause.*)

National Convention

22 Prairial, Year II [10 June 1794]

COUTHON: In the name of the Committee of Public Safety: All of our ideas concerning the different parts of government need to be reformed. They are all of them nothing but prejudices created by perfidy and the interests of despotism, or rather a bizarre mixture of imposture and truth, the inevitable effect of the transactions by which reason extorted them from despotism.

These false or obscure notions have in large part survived the revolution itself. . . .

The judicial system offers us a particularly striking example of this: it was as favorable toward crime as it was oppressive toward innocence. . . .

The rights of the Republic have been even less respected in the prosecution of crimes against liberty than have the rights of civil order and of the weak in the prosecution of ordinary offenses. . . .

Le Moniteur universel, XX, 694-700.

What especially favored the conspiracy of the Indulgents was the skill with which they confused the most disparate things, that is the measures taken by the Republic to smother conspiracies with the ordinary functions of the court for civil offenses committed during tranquil times. . . .

Ordinary offenses directly wound individuals alone; society is only indirectly hurt. And, since they do not expose the public safety to imminent danger, and because justice is weighing individual interests, it is possible to allow delays, a certain luxury of procedure and even a kind of partiality toward the accused. . . .

The crimes of conspirators, on the other hand, directly threaten the existence of society or its liberty, which is the same thing.

The lives of scoundrels are in this case balanced with those of the people. In this case any delay is culpable, any indulgent or superfluous formality is a public danger.

The period necessary for punishing the fatherland's enemies should be only the time it takes to recognize them. It is a matter less of punishing them than of annihilating them.

A revolution like ours is nothing but a rapid succession of conspiracies because it is a war of tyranny against liberty, of crime against virtue. It is not a question of making a few examples, but of exterminating the implacable satellites of tyranny, or of perishing with the Republic. Indulgence toward them is atrocious, clemency is parricide. . . .

The Republic, attacked in its infancy by enemies as perfidious as they are numerous, must strike them with the speed of lightning while taking the precautions necessary for saving slandered patriots. . . .

The natural defenders and necessary friends of accused patriots are patriotic jurymen. Conspirators should have none. How much would we husband the blood of good citizens, how much misfortune would we spare the fatherland if we were able to leave the rut of routine, follow the principles of reason and apply them to our political situation. . . .

Here is the draft of the decree that I have been appointed to present to you.

"The National Convention, after hearing the report of the Committee of Public Safety, decrees: . . .

"IV. The Revolutionary Tribunal is instituted to punish the enemies of the people.

"V. The enemies of the people are those who seek to destroy public liberty, either by force or by cunning.

"VI. Deemed enemies of the people are those who have instigated the re-establishment of royalty or who have sought to denigrate or dissolve the National Convention and the revolutionary and republican government of which it is the center;

"Those who have betrayed the Republic when they were in command of places and armies or in any other military function, carried on correspondence with the enemies of the Republic, or worked to disrupt the provisioning or service of the armies;

"Those who have sought to impede the provisioning of Paris or to cause scarcity within the Republic;

"Those who have supported the plans of the enemies of France, either by favoring the sheltering and impunity of conspirators and the aristocracy, by persecuting and slandering patriotism, by corrupting the representatives of the people, by abusing the principles of the revolution, the laws or measures of the government by false and perfidious applications;

"Those who have deceived the people or the people's representatives in order to lead them into undertakings contrary to the interests of liberty;

"Those who have sought to inspire discouragement in order to favor the enterprises of the tyrants in league against the Republic;

"Those who have spread false news in order to divide or disturb the people;

"Those who have sought to mislead public opinion and to prevent the instruction of the people, to deprave morals and corrupt the public conscience, and impair the energy and purity of revolutionary and republican principles, or to stop their progress, either by counter-revolutionary or insidious writings, or by any other machination. . . .

"Those who, charged with public office, abuse their offices in order to serve the enemies of the revolution, harass patriots, or oppress the people. . . .

"VII. The penalty provided for all offenses coming under the jurisdiction of the Revolutionary Tribunal is death. . . .

"XVI. The law provides slandered patriots with patriotic jurymen for defenders. It accords none for conspirators. . . ."

RUAMPS: This decree is important. I demand that it be printed and that we postpone discussion. If it is adopted without a postponement I will blow my brains out.

LECOINTRE DE VERSAILLES: I support the indefinite postponement that has been demanded.

BARÈRE: Doubtless it is not an indefinite postponement that is being demanded.

SEVERAL VOICES: No, no!

BARÈRE: When a law that completely favors patriots is proposed, and which insures the prompt punishment of conspirators, legislators can have but a unanimous will. I demand at least that the postponement not exceed three days.

LECOINTRE DE VERSAILLES: We're only demanding a two-day postponement.

ROBESPIERRE: There is no circumstance so delicate, there is no situation so embarrassing in which defenders of liberty can be placed that can force them to hide the truth. I will say, therefore, that although the right to demand a postponement is incontestable (even though it is perhaps being covered with specious motives), it nevertheless compromises the safety of the fatherland.

Two strongly pronounced opinions manifest themselves in the Republic, citizens. One is that which tends to punish the crimes committed against liberty in a severe manner. It is the opinion of those who are horrified by the culpable obstinacy with which the old conspiracies are revived. . . .

The other is that cowardly and criminal opinion of the aristocracy which, since the beginning of the revolution, has not ceased to demand, either directly or indirectly, an amnesty for conspirators and the fatherland's enemies.

For two months you have been asking the Committee of Public Safety for a law more sweeping than the one which it is presenting to you today. For two months the National Convention has been under the assassin's blade; and the moment when liberty seems about to enjoy a striking triumph is the moment when the enemies of the fatherland conspire with even more audacity. . . . The entire Republic has been denouncing the new conspiracies and that numberless multitude of foreign agents which abound on her surface: it is in these circumstances that the Committee of Public Safety presents you with the draft which you have just heard read. . . .

I submit that there is no one here who is not capable of deciding about this law as easily as he decided about so many others of greater importance which were adopted with enthusiasm by the National Convention. Why am I making these observations?

Is it to prevent postponement? No. I have merely wished to pay homage to the truth, to warn the Convention of the dangers it is facing. For, and be assured of this, citizens, whenever a line of demarcation is established, whenever a division occurs, then there is something that affects the safety of the country. It is not natural that there should be a separation between men equally smitten with love for the public weal. (*Applause.*) It is not natural that there should arise a sort of coalition against a government that has devoted itself to the salvation of the fatherland. Citizens, they are trying to divide you (No, no! *come cries from everywhere in the hall,* they will not divide us!) Citizens, they wish to frighten you. Well, let them remember that it was we who defended a part of this assembly against the daggers that villainy and false zeal wished to sharpen for you. We have exposed ourselves to individual assassins in order to prosecute public assassins. We would gladly die, but only that the Convention and the fatherland be saved! (*Lively applause.*) We will brave the perfidious insinuations by which they seek to stigmatize the measures that the public interest prescribes as excessively severe. This severity is terrible only for conspirators, only for the enemies of liberty. (*Applause.*)

BOURDON DE L'OISE: In the discussion that has arisen there is a point on which everyone can agree. In his speech Robespierre told us that there aren't enough jurymen. Well, since none of us wants to slow the march of national justice nor expose public liberty, let us vote on the proposition: let us adopt the list that the Committee of Public Safety has presented to us in order to complete the number of judges and jurymen and postpone the rest.

ROBESPIERRE: I demand that the draft be discussed article by article on the spot. . . . I demand that, without pausing for the proposition for postponement, the Convention discuss, until nine o'clock in the evening, if necessary, the draft of the law that has been submitted to it. (*Lively applause.*)

Robespierre's proposition is adopted.

*Couthon reads the first five articles. They are adopted without discussion. . . .**

COUTHON: The powers of the Committee have expired. I have been commissioned to ask you for its renewal.

The Convention continues the powers of the Committee of Public Safety. . . .

National Convention

23 Prairial

BOURDON DE L'OISE: Despite the bitterness that was mixed into the discussion that took place yesterday on a decree concerning the Revolutionary Tribunal, it is still necessary to return to principles. I do not believe that the National Convention, by restricting the right of bring-

* [The *Moniteur* goes on to record that the rest of the draft was accepted with one slight amendment.]

Le Moniteur universel, XX, 694-700.

ing citizens before the Revolutionary Tribunal to the Convention, the committees of Public Safety and General Security, and the Public Prosecutor, and by derogating all previous laws that did not agree with the present decree, the Convention, I say, did not intend that the power of the committees be extended over the members of the Convention without a preliminary decree. (No, no! *cry voices from everywhere.*) I am pausing for these happy murmurs. They announce that liberty is deathless. Let us decree that the committees will, as in the past, make provisional arrests, but that the representatives of the people can not be brought before the Revolutionary Tribunal until after the Convention issues an indictment against them. . . .

DELBRET: Bourdon doesn't have the right to distrust the intentions of the committees.

BOURDON DE L'OISE: It is astonishing that after hearing the murmurs by which homage was rendered to principles it could be said that I have abused the committees. The object of my proposition was that the committees would continue to make provisional arrests . . . , but that the Convention would express formally in a decree that it alone has the right to send one of its members to the Revolutionary Tribunal. Our laws can not be too carefully written when public liberty depends on their wording. I insist that my proposition be put to a vote. . . .

MERLIN DE DOUAI: I call for the previous question with a preamble. (*Murmurs.*) The Convention can not deprive itself of the right it has that none of its members can be brought before the Revolutionary Tribunal unless it has given its assent. This right is inalienable. The jury that should decide whether there is a true bill against a representative of the people is the Convention. This is how I request that the previous question be justified.

Merlin de Douai presents the draft of his proposition.

BOURDON DE L'OISE: I demand that Merlin draw up his proposition, that the draft be read on the spot to the Convention. . . .

Merlin de Douai presents the draft of his proposition.

It is adopted. . . .

National Convention

24 Prairial

Second speech, delivered by Carrier, on the decree passed at the session of the 22nd on the organization of the Revolutionary Tribunal. Listed

Table Chronologique du Moniteur, No. 266.

among the crimes for which one could be prosecuted was that of depraving morals. Charles Delacroix called for a less vague and more specific description of crimes than this. Accepted. Mallarmé asked what was meant by the words: "The law provides defenders for unfairly accused patriots by giving them patriotic jurors." Duhem, Charlier, and Legendre found this article quite clear and asked that it be accepted. Adopted. Couthon protested passionately against the reflections that had just been made and against those made the day before, and especially condemned giving any consideration to the amendment that had been proposed, an amendment which he regarded as harmful to the Committee of Public Safety. He was quite positive in believing that it accused the committees of the Convention of wanting to usurp power, while actually they abhorred the idea of any domination other than that of the people. He moved that the Convention vote upon all the proposals against the law and, with the just disdain that they merited, strike them down. Bourdon (de l'Oise), indicted by Couthon during the course of the debate, asked what would happen to liberty if one were regarded and treated as a counter-revolutionary when one, out of love of liberty, expressed one's doubts about a certain measure, however ill-founded these doubts might be! "Let the members of the committees know," he said, "that if they are proud to be patriots, so are we!" He finished by saying that he esteemed Couthon, the Committee, and the unshakeable Mountain which had saved liberty.

Robespierre replied: "It is not by speeches, which, under the guise of agreement and patriotism, continually attempt to divide the national representation, that these actions can be justified. They give sustenance to the likes of those who supported Chabot, Hébert, Danton, and Lacroix, factions which remained organized. The Convention needs all its wisdom, all its energy, to perceive and strike down their heirs, heirs which have gone too long without punishment. Not to do so would be to outrage the fatherland, assassinate the people, and suffer these intruguers, more miserable than their predecessors because they are more hypocritical, to infiltrate a section of the Mountain and make themselves the leaders of a party." *Bourdon cried out that it had never been his intention to become a leader of a party. Robespierre continued. Bourdon complained of being clearly designated a scoundrel and defied Robespierre to prove it.* "I have not named Bourdon," *Robespierre interrupted.* "Misfortune to him who names himself! but if he wants to recognize himself in the general portrait that I have just drawn, it is not in my power to prevent him." *He continued his attack against intriguers and recalled that the same day that the law under attack had been passed, certain persons confronted several patriots after the session and insulted them, accusing them of being among the twenty thousand spies that served the committees of Public Safety and General Security, and finally came to blows with them. Thus, concluded the speaker, did some people want so badly, and at such a heavy price, to debase and disturb the national representation. He finished by asking the Convention to aid the committees, agencies which were nothing without its support. Loud applause. Charles Delacroix declared that he had had no intention of casting suspicion upon the motives of the Committees. Couthon replied that the Committee of Public Safety was far from thinking so. Merlin (de Douai), editor of the* Considérant *wanted to justify himself. Robespierre declared that his observations had nothing to do with him; those concerned would be named. Tallien, designated by Robespierre as one of those who had insulted and struck patriots in an attempt to incite a floor revolt, accused Robespierre of inexactness and wished to set the record straight: five individuals had attempted to leave, the deputies told them what they thought of them, they replied in kind, the representatives had them arrested.*

ROBESPIERRE: That is false. But one thing is true: Tallien was one of those who spoke continually, fearfully, and publicly of the guillotine, regarding it as something which had its eye on them for debasing and troubling the national convention.

TALLIEN: It was not at all a question of twenty thousand spies.

ROBESPIERRE: Three hundred witnesses heard him. Citizens, you can judge what those who try to defend a crime with a lie are capable of; it is easy in this case to distinguish between the assassins and the victims.

BILLAUD-VARENNE: Tallien's impudence is extreme; he lies to the assembly with incredible audacity. Those whom he attacks are excellent Jacobins, like the one named Jarry; but citizens, we will hold ourselves united; conspirators will perish and the fatherland will be saved. *Applause.*

III
THE CONSPIRATORS AND THE ISOLATION OF ROBESPIERRE

Introduction

This and the following section bring us to the eve of 9 Thermidor. The events leading to Robespierre's arrest are too intricate and complex to be fully exposed in a mere sampling of documents. We can, however, establish the main outlines of the struggle by a careful reading of the sources presented here. The disintegrating relationship between Robespierre and the other members of the Committee of Public Safety, the quarrel between that Committee and the older but less powerful Committee on General Security, and the tangled web of conspiracies against Robespierre—all of these causes should emerge from the evidence.

The selections from the memoirs of Fouché and Barras serve to introduce the anti-Robespierrist conspirators. Memoirs like these are among the least trustworthy of historical sources. Even when authors do not intentionally lie or omit incriminating evidence, memoirs inevitably distort the truth. Only a great deal of critical analysis and extensive comparison with other accounts can establish the veracity of a particular memoir. In the present instances, however, even the inexperienced reader will be put on his guard by the air of self-importance exhibited by the memoirs of Barras and Fouché. Their description of the defeated Robespierre is obviously an attempt to vilify their enemy. Barras's appraisal of

Fouché should be compared with the latter's account of his actions and motives in the weeks before Thermidor.

A number of rather loosely related texts follow the memoirs. They will perhaps enable the reader to form an impression of the weeks known as the "Great Terror." The reports on the decisions of the Revolutionary Tribunal are included to illustrate the Tribunal's activities. Examples of the *fournées* are included. The practice of trying and executing prisoners whose cases were unrelated in batches—or *fournées*—became a common feature during this period. The patriotic exaltation, fraternal enthusiasm, and collective paranoia that the Jacobin club manifested at its meeting of 6 Prairial resulted in the mass trial of 29 Prairial. The report on the Revolutionary Tribunal for that date notes that the condemned wore the red gown of the parricide.

Robespierre's speech at the Jacobin club on 21 Messidor (9 July) is of interest because it was the occasion of one of his rare appearances in public during the last six weeks of his life. From 18 June to 26 July (8 Thermidor), Robespierre did not speak in the Convention, and, what is more unusual, delivered only a few addresses at the Jacobin club. The speech of 21 Messidor was his first appearance at the club's tribune in a month. It should be compared with the great address on the Principles of Moral Policy (17 Pluviôse). Has Robespierre added anything to his definition of virtue? Is there any change in his views concerning political opposition? Does the speech indicate what policy Robespierre himself will follow after his month-long withdrawal from politics?

Memoirs of Joseph Barras

The Committee of Public Safety became in the course of events the executive power, dictatorially intrusted with the direction of the war as well as political matters. To the Committee of General Security befell the attribute sufficiently designated by its name—power of life and death over the citizens, whose liberty was at its mercy; prison gates flew open at its will. The National Convention paid dearly for thus delegating its powers; a great assembly which makes concessions of such magnitude must sooner or later become their victim. The slightest usurpation of its authority, when once tolerated, is soon to lead to many others.

. . . At the time of the judicial murder of Danton, a murder preceded and unfortunately followed by many others, the Convention was truly tyrannised over by the committees of the Government, which had, in the words of that great Republican, "decimated and cut it down periodically," as in the case of a forest. The audacity of the committees was such that, on the 22nd Prairial, Couthon proposed in their name a law depriving persons arraigned before the Revolutionary Tribunal of defending counsel.

The Convention was indignant, but did not dare to reject this proposition. Robespierre, who had been looked upon as disposed, from policy at least, to incline towards some little moderation, had himself come forward in a frenzied outburst to defend this ferocious law, and had secured its adoption. The influence my missions to the south had invested me with still clung to me on the benches of the National Convention, where I received the support of the esteem granted to a character which did not bow before the storm. I openly and loudly censured the committees. Merlin de Thionville spoke in the same sense, and together we inspired fear.

I led an isolated life, belonging to no coterie and avoiding dinners; my conduct, which gave no hold upon my person, imposed upon people, and by the very fact pointed to me as one of the leaders of the opposition. We sought to come to an understanding as to the best means of putting a curb on the excesses of the committees of the Government, and assisting the National Convention to recover its proper standing. We inaugurated a series of meetings, by day at Doyen's, the eating-house keeper in the Champs-Elysées, and by night in a cabinet of the Café Corazza. This simple coffee-house keeper, of Italian origin, was at the same time a diplomatic personage; he possessed letters-patent from

Memoirs of Barras, I, 204-13.

the Pope, empowering him to make stipulations in the interests of the pontifical throne. Corazza was devoted to me.

In our group was Courtois, the deputy, an active and shrewd man, who since the death of Danton had become the relentless and personal enemy of his murderers; affable, and with insinuating ways, Courtois was on good terms with the several parties; he had taken upon himself to prepare his colleagues for the attack we were proposing to make on the committees, and was fulfilling his task to perfection.

Although I sat with the Montagne, as did also Merlin de Thionville and Courtois himself, we were far from feeling as certain of that party of the Convention as of the rest of it. The reason for this was simple enough. The Montagnards had bowed to the will of the committees, at the time of the attack on Danton, with a docility which had settled the fate of the victim. Several even had taken an active part in bringing about this dire result, owing to the feeling of jealousy that men of mediocrity generally exhibit towards those who are superior to them. Compromised by this their line of action, the members of the National Convention knew not how to part company with the Committee of Public Safety; they found themselves in the false position of not knowing how to join issue or how to work in harmony with it. In order to convince each and every one of them of the possibility of acting definitively on the offensive, all sorts of negotiations were necessary; their success was slow, but still we gained adherents. Daily fresh deputies recruited by Courtois would say confidentially to me, "You may depend on us."

I no longer left my house unless armed. The nucleus of our assemblage comprised nine members. Merlin de Thionville and I, defying the committees, threatened to cut off the head of the first myrmidon attempting to arrest us, and that his head should be shown to the people, who, like ourselves, abhorred tyranny. This hostile attitude had its due effect on our adversaries. The committees, estranged from Robespierre because they were *the majority,* deemed it advisable to enter into an alliance with him in order to compass our destruction, and with that end in view made a final attempt.

Robespierre, believing that he was stronger than all of them together, rejected the proposed alliance; thereupon the committees themselves saw that there was no other way out of the dilemma than to create a diversion, and unite with the National Convention in an attack on Robespierre, Couthon, and Saint-Just. The plan was submitted to several members of the National Convention; those allowed to hear of it resolved on concentrating upon these three individuals the charges which were, in the first instance, to have been formulated against the whole of the members of the committees collectively; this prudent resolution isolated therefrom the triumvirate, rendered it vulnerable, and afforded the best chances of success towards giving back to the Convention its standing. We agreed to this transaction, although it necessarily compromised the Convention, and preserved the power of men who, to my way of thinking, were as guilty as Robespierre—men who up to that very time had been his accomplices in deeds of cruelty, and to-day his enemies only on the question of the division of power, in other words, of the quarry.

But all our resolutions were still far from the day when they should be carried out; and it is when an event is about to happen that uncertainty worries most those who have experienced the greatest trouble in coming to a decision. Rendered uneasy, above all things, at the consequences of the energy of some of the deputies with whom it was necessary to unite, and anxious as to the issue of the struggle, the committees bethought themselves of sending on mission near the armies those members of the Convention whose determination of character they stood in awe of. Carnot, meeting me in the Rue des Petits-Champs as I was walking along with one of my friends who is still living, came up to me and said, "Citizen colleague, the Committee of Public Safety has you in its mind for the fulfillment of an important mission—to wit, that you should at once join the Army of the Rhine, where your firmness and civism will serve to reconcile many interests, and will put an end to unhappy dissensions which have broken out in its midst." "I will not join the Army of the Rhine," was my reply to Carnot; "the post of honor is in the Convention, and I will not abandon it."

I am far from suspecting Carnot of any evil intention in this desire to send me away to the army. Carnot, intent on his miliary occupations, yet not quite so exclusively as he has since pretended, ever had his eyes in the direction of the frontier which it was necessary to defend; such was the thought upper-most in his mind. It was nevertheless easy to detect the influence of the committees in his proposition. It was likewise rejected by several of my colleagues. We were all agreed that we should remain on the very battlefield where the intestine war was being waged—a war that had become even more fraught with perils than that waged by the coalition itself.

Robespierre's silence, and his disdainful ignoring of Fréron and myself on the day of the visit I have referred to previously, had left a doubt in my mind as to whether he had taken sufficient notice of me to know me again. On the day following the one on which I declined

Carnot's proposal to go again on mission, I was afforded the opportunity of seeing for the first time that I did in some measure occupy a space in the memory of Robespierre, for, coming towards me, he turned, as if repentant of his former coldness, and calling me by my name with an air of good-will which constituted for him so great an effort that it was almost tantamount to a convulsion, he said to me, "You have, I learn, felt the necessity of remaining with the Convention; it is time it should shake off the oppression of the factious majority of the committees." Not grasping the significance of Robespierre's utterance, nor dersirous of coming in view of it to any conclusion in his favour, but merely with the hope of beginning the fight wherein, everybody being brought face to face, it would become necessary to conquer or die, I answered Robespierre thus: "Well then, ascend the tribune and unmask the conspirators." "The day is not far distant when I shall attack them," replied Robespierre. In what way did he contemplate his attack, and where would he make it? Was it in the body of the Jacobins, where he wielded so potent an influence, or in the bosom of the Convention, where his influence was none the less genuine? In the Convention this influence had until now been due to his position as member of the Committee of Pubiic Safety, and to the predominancy with which his popularity invested him even in the bosom of this Committee, which, still remaining superior to all executive powers, had become the sole executive power, the one impelling the National Convention to action. But the scene was about to change; the members of the Committee were divided against themselves, and Robespierre no longer attended its sittings. If the power imparted to them by the presence of this colossus of popularity was to be diminished by his withdrawal from their midst, the influence that Robespierre in turn had derived from the solidarity of power could not but diminish in a like ratio. But the public not having yet been taken into confidence in regard to the weakness of the dissentients, Robespierre, with a view of getting the start of all others, was circulating and causing to be bruited about by his adherents his strong and indignant disapproval of a proposition which he attributed to the members of the Committee of Public Safety, of wishing to adjourn the sittings of the Convention; and he alleged this reason as one of those on account of which he had not appeared at the sittings of the Committee of Public Safety for a month past. But even admitting that he no longer participated in its acts of authority, was Robespierre, the accuser of his colleagues, any the less wicked than they? Did he not enjoy in Paris a preponderance inspiring as many fears as the powers of all the committees together?

In the midst of all these complicated enmities Saint-Just drew up a report on the position of the Republic, and of Paris in particular, asking that the Committee of Public Safety should allay all alarms, and, in order to accomplish this, that it should no longer conceal anything from the public, as it had done heretofore. The propositions of Saint-Just were rejected. The order was issued on the 1st Messidor, by the Committee of Public Safety, to detach 18,000 men from the Army Sambre-et-Meuse for the purposes of a secret operation; but the order was revoked, as it was argued that its execution would compel the army to abandon its positions and retire under the walls of Givet. Prieur de la Marne and Jeanbon Sant-André being away on missions, the Committee found itself reduced to a membership of five. . . .

Accustomed as he was to impose his wishes and see them carried out without discussion, Robespierre was astounded and as if stupified. He had already encountered opposition on the part of Billaud, a phlegmatic yet irritable individual who never spoke except sententiously and insultingly; on the part of Collot, a sort of boor of unparalleled violence, whose popular eloquence from the tribune of the Jacobins and from that of the Convention feared not to measure itself with that of Robespierre; on the part of Carnot, who laid no claim to oratory, but whose military object of securing France's independence gave additional strength to his character; on the part of Prieur de la Côte-d'Or, associated with Carnot, his former comrade in the Engineers; on the part of Lindet, whose love of labour made him one with those who laboured; on the part of Barère, whose activity and loquacity could not but be of service to his colleagues, since they constituted the majority, for Barère was ever with the majority. This group, brought together by the common danger, was assuredly a motive of alarm for Robespierre. His too well known character of implacable revenge, moreover, did not allow those whom he threatened to entertain any hope of their own safety otherwise than through his defeat, not to say his death. At a time when the Convention was already in a high state of alarm he had circulated a list of five or six deputies. It was rumoured that Robespierre intended to have them arrested as a little treat to himself, alleging their immorality as the motive of this proposed act of severity. Robespierre, informed of what was being imputed to him, asserted that such an idea was foreign to him, and, desirous of hurling it back at its authors, he maintained that it had originated with the majority of the Committee, which, he alleged, had pushed its cruelty so far as to seek to include thirty-two deputies in its latest proscription list. . . .

Memoirs of Joseph Fouché

. . . One man alone in the convention appeared to enjoy an inexpugnable popularity: this was Robespierre, a man full of pride and cunning; an envious, malignant, and vindictive being, who was never satiated with the blood of his colleagues; and who, by his capacity, steadiness, the clearness of his head, and the obstinacy of his character, surmounted circumstances the most appalling. Availing himself of his preponderance in the committee of public safety, he openly aspired, not only to the tyranny of the decemviri, but to the despotism of the dictatorship of Marius and Sylla. One step more would have given him the masterdom of the revolution, which it was his audacious ambition to govern at his will; but thirty victims more were to be sacrificed, and he marked them in the convention. He well knew that I understood him; and I, therefore, was honoured by being inscribed upon his tablets at the head of those doomed to destruction. I was still on a mission, when he accused me of oppressing the patriots and tampering with the aristocracy. Being recalled to Paris, I dared to call upon him from the tribune, to make good his accusation. He caused me to be expelled from the Jacobins, of whom he was the high-priest; this was for me equivalent to a decree of proscription. I did not trifle in contending for my head, nor in long and secret deliberations with such of my colleagues as were threatened with my own fate. I merely said to them, among others to Legendre, Tallien, Dubois-Crancé, Daunou, and Chénier: "You are on the list, you are on the list as well as myself; I am certain of it!" Tallien, Barras, Bourdon de l'Oise, and Dubois-Crancé evinced some energy. Tallien contended for two lives, of which one was then dearer to him than his own: he therefore resolved upon assassinating the future dictator, even in the convention itself. But what a hazardous chance was this! Robespierre's popularity would have survived him, and we should have been immolated to his manes. I therefore dissuaded Tallien from an isolated enterprise, which would have destroyed the man, but preserved his system. Convinced that other means must be resorted to, I went straight to those who shared with Robespierre the government of terror, and whom I knew to be envious or fearful of his immense popularity. I revealed to Collot d'Herbois, to Carnot, to Billaud-Varennes, the designs of the modern Appius; and I presented to each of them separately, so lively and so true a picture of the danger of their situation, I urged them with so much ability and success, that I insinuated into their breasts more

Memoirs of Fouché, I, 17-22.

than mistrust,—the courage of henceforth opposing the Tyrant in any further decimating of the convention. "Count the votes," said I to them, "in your committee, and you will see, that when you are determined he will be reduced to the powerless minority of a Couthon and a Saint-Just. Refuse him your votes, and reduce him to stand alone by your *vis inertiœ*."

But what contrivances, what expedients were necessary to avoid exasperating the Jacobin club, the Seides, and the partisans of Robespierre! Sure of having succeeded, I had the courage to defy him, on the 20th Prairial (June 8, 1794), a day, on which, actuated with the ridiculous idea of solemnly acknowledging the existence of the Supreme Being, he dared to proclaim himself both his *will* and *agent,* in presence of all the people assembled at the Tuileries. As he was ascending the steps of his lofty tribune, whence he was to proclaim his manifesto in favour of God, I predicted to him aloud (twenty of my colleagues heard it,) that his fall was near. Five days after, in full committee, he demanded my head and that of eight of my friends, reserving to himself the destruction of twenty more at a later period. How great was his astonishment, and what was his rage, upon finding amongst the members of the committee an invincible opposition to his sanguinary designs against the national representation! It has already been too much mutilated, said they to him, and it is high time to put a stop to a proscription, which at last will include ourselves.

Finding himself in a minority, he withdrew, choked with rage and disappointment, swearing never to set foot again in the committee, so long as his will should be opposed. He immediately sent for Saint-Just, who was with the army, rallied Couthon under his sanguinary banner, and by his influence over the revolutionary tribunal, still made the convention and all those who were operated on by fear, to tremble. Being confident of the support of the Jacobin club, of Hanriot, the commander of the national guard, and of all the revolutionary committees of the capital, he flattered himself that he had still adherents fully sufficient to carry him through. By thus keeping himself at a distance from the seat of power, he was desirous of throwing upon his adversaries the general execration, of making them appear as the sole perpetrators of so many murders, and of delivering them up to the vengeance of a people which now began to murmur at the shedding of so much blood. But cowardly, mistrustful, and timid, he was incapable of action, and permitted five weeks to pass away between this secret secession, and the crisis which was silently approaching.

I did not overlook his situation; and seeing him reduced to a single faction, I secretly urged such of his enemies as still adhered to the committee, at least to remove the artillery from Paris, who were all devoted to Robespierre and the commune, and to deprive Hanriot of his command, or at least to suspend him. The first measure I obtained, thanks to the firmness of Carnot, who alleged the necessity of sending reinforcements of artillery to the army. As to depriving Hanriot of his command, that appeared too hazardous; Hanriot remained, and was near losing all, or rather, to speak the truth, it was he who on the 9th Thermidor (the 27th July) ruined the cause of Robespierre, the triumph of which was for a short time in his power. But what could be expected from a *ci-devant* drunken and stupid footman.

Memoirs of Joseph Barras

. . . [Fouché] had certainly been at all times an ultra-Revolutionist, and had shown what he was made of in his support of the system of terror, but he had not exactly hit the idea of Robespierre, or rather he had become his rival, and had given him offence by going even farther than he did. Fouché's position was therefore not one to afford him opposite his enemy a frank and clearly-defined character enabling him to attack him openly. Robespierre had told Fouché that his face was the expression of crime. Fouché, far from replying, took it as a matter of course; expelled from the Jacobins, he had not been able to return to the fold; he no longer dared show himself even in the Convention, but busied himself actively and with a will with intrigues and machinations of the lowest kind. I sent him hither and thither to inform our friends of what we knew of the intentions of Robespierre, Saint-Just, and Couthon. His personal dread of the triumvirs served but to increase in his eyes the idea of their hostile plans. Everything that he already dreaded most sincerely was artfully exaggerated by him when seeking to stimulate those whom he sought to induce to make up their minds to action. Rising at early morn, he would run round till night calling on deputies of all shades of opinions, saying to each and every one, "You perish to-morrow if he does not." To those who mourned Danton, and who were threatened with the resentment of his executioners, Fouché was wont to say, "We may, if we see fit, be avenged to-morrow, and to-morrow only will we be safe." Such was the terror produced by Robespierre, that a member of the National Convention

Memoirs of Barras, I, 224-6; 229-30.

who thought the gaze of the dictator was fixed upon him just as he was putting his hand to his forehead in musing fashion, quickly withdrew it, saying, "He will suppose that I am thinking of something." In order to instil fresh courage into minds so stricken with fright more than one speech was required to place the question before each and every one in such a way that he should see his own interests in it. Hence it cannot be denied that Fouché, gathering together by his clever intriguing all sentiments against Robespierre, was a genuine resource in the midst of the elements extant ready to make a decisive move against the oppressors of the Convention.

Robespierre accused Fouché of having dishonoured the Revolution by exaggerating all measures and erecting atheism as a doctrine. "No, Fouché," he said to him in the hall of the Jacobins, "death is not an eternal sleep." Besides, to use his own expression, he believed he "held" him in his power in the matter of honesty, as Fouché had been charged with not having been any too strictly faithful on the occasion of his mission to Lyon, where, outstripping his epoch in those early days, he was believed to have enjoyed a foretaste of that corrupt century. Reports, possibly mendacious, had reached Robespierre, according to which Fouché is said to have, in the midst of the demolition of the dwellings in the town doomed to endure his cruelty, behaved somewhat like the incendiaries who carry on their business by the light of the flames. It is that which caused Robespierre to assume so lofty a manner against Fouché, because Fouché was supposed to have begun "to make money" at a time when no one in the Republic had so far dreamt of doing such a thing, either because of the Terror, which was not disposed to indulgence towards thieves, or because of a sentiment of genuine honesty which dominated men whose sole thought was the defence of the Republic. . . .

. . . Robespierre had told the Committee, previous to leaving it, that "the impunity enjoyed by Fouché was one of 'his' grievances." He had pursued this theme among the Jacobins, and caused him to be expelled from their club. It will be seen that Fouché's position was fully, in those days, one of the most in jeopardy. I have told previously how Fouché and Tallien had separately paid a visit of deference and respect to Robespierre; how each of them, just like Fréron and myself, had met with no other reception than an obstinate silence—a refusal to give any explanation or word which this very silence did not plainly express. Matters were growing worse apace; no longer was there any possibility of a reconciliation, even under the mask of mutual deceit. Not only had hostilities been declared, but a war to the knife proclaimed. In spite of all Fouché's prudence, a letter written in his own hand had been intercepted, containing particularly the following line addressed to a colleague in the Convention: "Ere a fortnight has rolled over us either Maximilien or we shall have ceased to exist." Hence the quarrel could end only by the destruction of one side or the other; nothing was left but to conquer or die.

Even at a time when he was brought face to face with the necessity of defending himself it was not in Fouché to do so above-board. Indirect means, those of ceaseless and underground intrigue, in which he had served his apprenticeship at the Oratory, he was familiar with; and just as everything comes handy in a household, so in a conspiracy, which is itself but an intrigue more serious than others, skill and manœuvring constitute the necessary elements; and it will be seen that Fouché was to be, if not by his courage, at least by his doings, a useful co-operator in what was about to take place. He has, in later days, boasted that he dealt mortal blows to Robespierre; the fact is that, in order to flee from his wrath and, if he could have done so, from his relentless memory, Fouché no longer appeared at the National Convention nor slept at home; it was at night alone that, under various disguises, he would go the rounds of such of his colleagues as were busily engaged in preparing means of defence against Robespierre, and Fouché brought and carried from one to the other every particular as to what was taking place, and went on the errands it was requisite should be dexterously done in order to cement the alliances we were forming pending the moment, impossible to positively determine, when the decisive blow was to be struck. . . .

Jacobin Club

26 Prairial, Year II [14 June 1794]

Raisson declared that he would refuse to communicate further with Tallien until the grave charges which had been made against him had been withdrawn.

Rousselin was denounced as the leading oppressor of the patriots of Troyes.

Report by Dumas on the demands made by the nurses of the national children's home; he exposed the frightful abuses which reigned at this

Table Chronologique du Moniteur, No. 271.

institution. Couthon demanded punishment for its administrators and their replacement. Decreed that they be denounced to the committees of the Convention.

Couthon saw the shades of Danton, Hébert, and Chaumette walking among patriots, and the faction of the foreigner agitating everywhere, citing what happened at the session of the 24th as an example: "There exist certain evil persons in the heart of the Convention who are trying to divide the representatives of the people by painting the committees of Public Safety and Security with the frightful features of Sulla and Nero. There are those who deliberate in secret and prepare proscription lists. . . . The Convention and the committees abhor crime and wish to see it severely punished. Those who are pure have nothing to fear, but those who tremble have themselves made the judgment." He announced the arrest of another Admirat who had found it strange that Robespierre continued to live.

National Convention

2 Messidor (20 June)

Report by Barère on *section* committees assigned to distribute relief. Decreed that those who have failed to carry out the decree of this subject pronounced 10 Messidor last be sent before tribunals for punishment. As for those who have used the funds sent by the relief commission for other purposes, they shall be declared to have misused public funds and judged by the Revolutionary Tribunal.

The Convention tabled a motion, presented by Couthon, prescribing means to ascertain in each commune the size of the harvest, and sent a proposal of Dubois-Dubay about imprisoned peasants to the committees of Public Safety and Security.

Table Chronologique du Moniteur, No. 273.

Revolutionary Tribunal

29 Prairial [17 June]

Fifty-four condemned to death, among them: Admirat, the assassin of Collot-d'Herbois; the daughter of Renault and her family, charged with wanting to assassinate Robespierre, Sombreuil, ex-governor of les In-

Ibid., No. 275.

valides, and his son; Rohan-Rochefort, Laval-Montmorency, Sartine, ex-master of ceremonies, his wife and mother-in-law Sainte-Amaranthe; the ex-prince Saint-Maurice; Cardec, fiscal agent; Jauge, banker; Pottier-de-Lille, printer; Burlandeux and Ozanne, ex-peace officers; Michonis, Marino, Froidure, Soulès and Dangé, ex-chiefs of police, etc., as accomplices in a foreign conspiracy. They were taken to the guillotine dressed in red gowns.

The same day. Seven condemned to death. Two acquitted.

1st of Messidor. Seventeen condemned to death. Three acquitted.

National Convention

5 Messidor [23 June]

Report by Couthon on the assassination of Malignon, a national agent, by the inhabitants of the commune of Cruzières-Saint-André. Decreed that his name be inscribed on a column of the Pantheon, that his widow and children receive a pension of three hundred livres each, that the individuals arrested and suspected of being either the authors or accomplices of the assassination be taken to the Revolutionary Tribunal and judged there without delay, etc. The name of the commune is suppressed and replaced with that of the Commune of Claisse, the name of the river which waters the territory.

Table Chronologique du Moniteur, No. 276.

Revolutionary Tribunal

2 Messidor [20 June]

Thirty-eight condemned to death. Two acquitted.

Jacobin Club

6 Messidor [24 June]

Dumas announced that Gaudet and Salles have paid with their heads for their crimes against the Republic. Observations by Couthon on the attitude of certain journalists: he invited good citizens to keep a close surveillance over enemies of the Republic, and over journals which second them in their adroit perfidies.

Ibid., No. 279.

National Convention

11 Messidor [29 June]

Report by Barère on the battle of Fleurus of 8 Messidor, which lasted twelve hours, and in which generals Jourdan, Dubois, Marceau, Lefebvre, and Kléber distinguished themselves. The enemy army was commanded by Beaulieu, Cobourg, etc. "Eight to ten thousand slaves were strewn over the field of battle. All the *reds* have been killed; no mercy, no indulgence was allowed these brigands; not one Englishman reached by republicans continues to breathe. Never was a combat more terrible, more stubborn, more bloody. A single prisoner, is the result of this great day." Official reports on the subject. The news was received with enthusiasm. Decreed that the armies of the North, of the Ardennes, and of the Moselle have not ceased to be worthy of their fatherland and that they will be reunited under the name of the Army of Sambre-et-Meuse.

Table chronologique du Moniteur, No. 282.

Revolutionary Tribunal

8 Messidor [26 June]

Forty-eight condemned to death, among whom was Osselin, ex-deputy of the Convention.

Ibid., No. 286.

National Convention

14 Messidor [2 July]

Mallarmé was indignant to see sitting with the Mountain a vile slanderer named Philip, who was not an official deputy and who had published a diatribe against him in which he accused him of being a Brissotin, a Girondin. He demanded that this audacious person be taken to the Committee on General Security. Decreed.

Jacobin Club

13 Messidor [1 July]

Speech by Robespierre against the enemies of the fatherland who accuse the defenders of the Republic of injustice and cruelty against conspirators. From London, he is denounced to the French army as a dictator, painted as an assassin of honest men. They say that in France assassination plots are fabricated in order to provide him with a military guard. In Paris, the same libels have been repeated: society is said to tremble. There has been found in the papers of the secretary of Camille Desmoulins a document which repeats Louvet's accusation that France is on the verge of a dictatorship. They say that the Revolutionary Tribunal has been organized to devour patriots and members of the Convention; Robespierre is depicted as a tyrant and an oppressor; but truth is his only asylum against crime, his defense in his conscience. He protests that all these tyrants and their varlets can do nothing to impair his courage, and he declares that if he is forced to renounce part of those functions with which he is charged, the function of representative of the people will still be his and that he will continue to wage a war to the death against all tyrants and conspirators.

Table chronologique du Moniteur, No. 287.

National Convention

17 Messidor [5 July]

Bézard presented a report dealing with four peasants of the commune of Gizac, condemned to death by the local district tribunal, for having killed Montclard, their former lord, in an insurrection that he himself had provoked. The report recounted his vexatious acts and his crimes, attested to by a large number of witnesses, and demanded that the death sentences be annulled and that the four peasants be set free. Decreed.

Ibid., No. 289.

National Convention

19 Messidor [7 July]

Le Carpentier, representative of the people, writes the Convention that at Coutances a day of celebration has just taken place, presided over by the patriotism of republicans and embellished by the terror that is felt by aristocrats and federalists; they are not wrong to be afraid, for the list of political prisoners shows that twenty of their kind have been taken to the Revolutionary Tribunal. Religious troubles have occurred at Carentan and Mortain. The troublemakers have been interrogated and sent, like the others, to the avenging tribunal of the law. The following will occupy Le Carpentier during the rest of his mission: further celebrations will be held to honor republicans and death will continue to be meted out to enemies of the fatherland.

Sans-culottes who constitute the popular society of Castillon and who have been looking for Pétion and Buzot write that they have found their bodies, hideously disfigured, half devoured: their scattered limbs have become the prey of hungry dogs and their bloody hearts food for ferocious beasts.

Table chronologique du Moniteur, No. 290.

National Convention

21 Messidor [9 July]

Report by Barère on the petitions presented against Joseph Lebon, representative of the people from the *département* of Pas-de-Calais. He was reproached for his somewhat rough manners and his excessive severity; but he had completely beaten the aristocrats, compromised the malicious, and had been especially effective in punishing counter-revolutionaries and traitors. The vigorous measures that he had taken had saved a Cambrai rife with treasons. This service seemed a decisive factor for the Committee of Public Safety and it proposed to deny the aristocracy a triumph. Barère proposed, consequently, that the denunciations against Lebon be rebuffed. Adopted unanimously.

Ibid., No. 282.

Revolutionary Tribunal

18 Messidor [6 July]

Thirty condemned to death, among whom were twenty-two former members of the Parlement of Toulouse. Nine acquitted.

Letter to the Committee of Public Safety

25 Messidor [13 July]

Citizen-representatives:

[Two paragraphs omitted.]

In the evening, towards nine o'clock, while I was at the house of a friend, someone called on me to deliver a message which had been left for me at the registry. As a result, I repaired to a local inn. Here around a table, the conversation dealt with the factions of Hébert, Danton, and Ronsin. Deschamps unburdened himself to me all at once with the greatest confidence; he assured me that, although the leading Hébertists, etc., were guillotined, it was a party that would seek to rise again, that the committees of Public Safety and General Security, however, would know perfectly well how to confound them, that the moment had not yet come to strike, and that tested patriots were upset at seeing certain people mimicking patriotism, heedless of the Republic's well-being, and solely to satisfy their private hatreds. Up to this point you will doubtless detect only the language of a man who loves his country; but now note what follows. The conversation turned to the Jacobins. I told him that the Society would refuse to stray, that it was there that Couthon, Robespierre, and Collot d'Herbois spoke with the greatest confidence against those who wished to attack the conduct of the Committee members, whether it be by fawning upon them, by idolizing them, or by slandering them in order to halt the good deeds of the revolutionary government. Ho!—Deschamps says to me—don't think that the Jacobin Society contains only tested patriots; there are more than a few among its ranks who are men of no account, readers of gazettes, men little capable of offering resistance at a critical moment in the clash of factions. I observed that the newspapers had mentioned the adoption of many new members by the

This letter from the National Agent for the District of Boulogne to the Committee of Public Safety was published in *Revue historique,* CXVII (1915), 70-80, 85-7.

Society, but that it appeared it had only been debated for a long time. Deschamps told me that that was done on purpose and that I knew why. I replied that, being distant from the events, we couldn't always see things as clearly as if we were in Paris, and, besides, we were assured that the Jacobins supported the Convention as their rallying point, just as they did the committees of Public Safety and on General Security. Note that Pillon, Deschamps's colleague, said nothing more than "yes" and "no" to all this. All at once I now heard that last-named launch into a lament over Robespierre, calling him unfortunate and saying that the Committee itself had an enemy in its bosom. I was thunderstruck. I could not resist telling him that his remarks seemed indiscreet to me, that he ought to be careful about expressing himself in such a way, and that these remarks could compromise the public good if uttered to someone whose patriotism was doubtful. Deschamps responded that he knew me, that he could size men up rapidly, and that he saw well that he could trust me. I invited him then to name the traitorous member of the Committee. Very well! he said, it is Carnot. Yes, Carnot. He is a filthy beggar who spends the night at the Committee's office in order to be able to open all the packages. Ho! And there are a good many others, he said . . . Legendre is surrounded. Tallien is a tramp; Bourdon de l'Oise is no better.

You can judge, citizen-representatives, what my position was. An individual whom I did not know, who doubtless did not know me any better, announces himself as being privy to the government's secrets and blithely reveals them in his conversation! I leave it to your wisdom to pronounce on this case. These remarks chagrined me greatly as soon as I had heard them. I could not brusquely leave the room without depriving myself of the means of being a party to the conversation. The rest of the conversation focussed on the subject of individuals who scheme within the government for their own benefit and create further factions with their debauchery. Deschamps viewed these immoral human beings with contempt and assured me that the government would know how to nip their plots in the bud one day and bring them to justice. Here the conversation ended. I took leave of the two commissioners and I returned to my friend's house in order to take a bit of food. I consulted at once with three of my friends who happened to be there. Their surprise was extreme. After much talking, it was decided that I should report all this to the committees of Public Safety and General Security. I did not do so at once because I wanted a favorable occasion. I knew that Hector Barère would be passing within our walls. He is now at Boulogne. I will confide to his hands a faithful narrative of the conversation. I expect that he will make such use of it as the wisdom and prudence of a republican will dictate. I declare on my honor, on my word as a French citizen, that I speak the whole truth.

Boulogne, the 25th Messidor, 2nd Year of the Republic.

Quignon the Elder

Revolutionary Tribunal

21 Messidor [9 July]

Sixty condemned to death, among whom were Duplain, journalist; Ornano, lieutenant in the former government of Bayonne; Nicolai, son of the president; Geoffroy-d'Assay, former general treasurer of finances; Moreau, architect of the city; ex-Marshal Chambot-d'Arbouville, and his wife; Faquet, ex-valet of the household of the aunt of Capet, etc., for having provoked a revolt in prison; Sainte-Marie, age fourteen and a half years, convicted of also being an enemy of the people, sentenced to twenty years imprisonment in a house of correction. Two acquitted.

Table chronologique du Moniteur, No. 295.

Jacobin Club

23 Messidor [11 July]

A member announced that the Commune-Affranchie has been regenerated, that it is now in step and that it is to the friends of Chalier that this happy change is due. He had proof of it by a letter sent by this commune to the Convention. Demas considered it prudent to suspend judgment as to the state of mind of the generality of the inhabitants of this rebel city and to continue to exercise the most active surveillance over developments there. Robespierre said that he had known Chalier at the time when many patriotic representatives were being persecuted: it was he who was the first to uncover the perfidy of Roland and who denounced him. Since that time, Robespierre had known Chalier only by the acts of heroism which have immortalized him. His friends, their services and their persecutions are also well known to him. The

Ibid., No. 296.

speaker recalled the escape of de Précy and other conspirators, favored by Dubois-Crancé, and swore to avenge Chalier, Gaillard, and all such victims of the infamous aristocracy. Couthon had the name of Dubois-Crancé struck from the list of members of the Society. Upon the request of Robespierre, Fouché will be invited to come and defend himself against the reproaches that have been made against him. Robespierre the younger loudly complained about the silence and torpor that had taken hold of the Society; patriots were being tormented and Jacobins failed to take up their defense! Certain people want to divide them; some have even tried to separate him from his brother, but in vain: so much does he believe in morality and in terror for scoundrels that he seeks no greater glory than to share the same tomb. He invited all patriots to rally to the side of the friends of liberty and to defend them with the greatest energy. Couthon declared that he wished to share the blows of any daggers directed against Robespierre and that charges that the Committee of Public Safety seeks domination must be combatted.

National Convention

24 Messidor [12 July]

Report by Berlier on the question of whether all attacks upon defenders of the fatherland should be forbidden during their terms of service. The speaker decided in the negative: democracy would be severely wounded if one could say: citizens are liable before one law, soldiers before another. Adopted.

National Convention

25 Messidor [13 July]

The Jacobins have just celebrated the fifth anniversary of the revolution. The speaker retraced its causes, its effects, sketched a picture of those factions which wanted to annihilate the liberty of the people, federalize the departments, corrupt the public conscience, and divide, dissolve, or devour the national representation. He also expressed society's vow to overthrow thrones everywhere and annihilate all the oppressors of the world.

Revolutionary Tribunal

22 Messidor [10 July]

Forty-four condemned to death, among whom were Caradeuc de la Châlotais, ex-speaker of the former *parlement* of Rennes; Pariseau and Tournon, journalists; Leclerc-de-Buffon, son of the former count of the same name, etc., as accomplices in a prison conspiracy. Eleven acquitted.

Table chronologique du Moniteur, No. 297.

National Convention

28 Messidor [16 July]

Report by Barère on the *section* celebrations and civic feasts which, for some days, have multiplied with a rapidity which does not seem to him natural. It is a new intrigue ordered by the testamentary executors of the legacy of Hébert and Chaumette. Fraternity does not consist of meals in the streets; there can be nothing in common between the opulent egoist, who sighs for inequality and kings, and the sans-culotte, full of candor, who loves only the Republic and equality. In other times and with other men, the Convention would have needed to pass a decree forbidding such meals and such flaunting of equality, but with free Frenchmen, the intention of the legislator is enough: it is in the morality of republicans, it is in the revolutionary tribunal of public opinion that the National Convention confides. This is how the proscription of these allegedly fraternal banquets will be brought about. Decreed that the report be published and sent to the *départements* and to the armies.

Table chronologique du Moniteur, No. 299.

Jacobin Club

21 Messidor [9 July]

ROBESPIERRE:

All the particular injustices which you have denounced merit your serious attention. The first duty of a patriot is to help the oppressed;

Le Moniteur universel, XXI, 239-41.

whoever fails to fulfill this duty does not have even the sentiment of patriotism. Of all the virtues which have served as a foundation for the revolution, the most beautiful and the most genuine is the most neglected. There is nothing more common than beautiful but insignificant speeches, nothing more rare than the generous defense of the oppressed when there is no profit to be gained from it; nothing so common as circumspect behavior where aristocrats are concerned and nothing so rare as a sincere humanity towards good citizens in distress.

Of all the decrees which have saved the Republic, the most sublime, the only one which has rooted out corruption and delivered the people from tyranny, is that one which makes probity and virtue the order of the day. If this decree were carried out, liberty would be perfectly established and we would no longer need to keep the popular tribunes; but some men who have only the mask of virtue place great hindrances in the way of carrying out laws of the same virtue; they wish to use this mask as a means of arriving at power.

There are very few generous men who love virtue for its own sake and ardently desire the happiness of the people. All the scoundrels have abused the law which has saved liberty and the French people. They have pretended not to know what that supreme law which the Convention made the order of the day was, that is to say the duty to confound hypocrites, to aid the unhappy and oppressed, and to fight tyrants: they have omitted those great duties and have used them as an instrument to torment the people and to lead patriots astray.

There exists in the Republic a revolutionary committee; you will perhaps think that it fancied it ought to annihilate the aristocracy? Not at all; it believed that it was necessary to arrest all the citizens who, on a holiday, were found drunk. Thanks to this *happy* application of the law, all the counter-revolutionaries remained undisturbed and comletely safe, while the artisans and the good citizens who had by chance given themselves over to a spirit of gaiety, were pitilessly imprisoned.

Doubtless we are more the enemies of every kind of vice than these wicked and hypocritical inquisitors; we know that drunkenness is an illness of which men must be cured, but we also know how to tell the false patriots who persecute the people while showing indulgence for the aristocrats.

The league of all the factions has the same system everywhere; if there is among them any appearance of virtue, it is only a deceptive mask; the scoundrels who assume this mask never exact real obedience to the laws of the Republic; they see the nobles as only peaceful agriculturalists and good husbands and they do not ask whether they are friends of justice and the people.

The decree which makes virtue the order of the day is rich in ramifications. We had anticipated that it would be abused but at the same time we had thought that this decree, aimed against the oppressors, would impose on public officials the duty to exercise virtue and never to stray from the obligations they owe the fatherland; but those obligations do not force them in the least to be weighed down with severe inquisitions into the actions of good citizens at the expense of taking their attention from the crimes of wicked men; these wicked men who no longer attract the officials' attention are those very same ones who oppress humanity and are the real tyrants. If the public officials had made these reflections, they would have found few guilty people to be punished, for the people are good and the class of wicked men is the smallest class.

It is in vain that Roland vaunts his virtues to me and presents to me the picture of his private life; without examining either this fastidious apology or the scandalous story of the private life of a Barbaroux, I ask a man: What have you done for the prosperity of your country? What works have you undertaken to deliver the French people from the odious yoke of servitude? If he answers my question satisfactorily, then I believe him virtuous.

Necker was a veritable tyrant in his own family; do not be surprised; a man who lacks public virtues cannot have private virtues. This virtue of Necker and Roland, which intriguers have pretended resulted from the decree of which I spoke to you just a minute ago, is diametrically opposed to heroism and humanity. If I wished to follow the perfidious system of those men who don't know virtue at all, you would see good men oppressed and intriguers raising their haughty heads. Our enemies say in their secret assemblies:

"Act so that there will be nothing but scoundrels; let us persecute the patriots and let us not cease to support those who, like Hébert wish to destroy secretely the liberty of France, as well as those who by their moderate position wish to lead her back into slavery: let us persecute all those who aspire to the liberty of the human race."

These monsters consign, by consequence, every man whose austere habits and stern probity they fear to opprobrium and torment.

The duty of the government is to remedy this abuse. To achieve this aim we must have a great deal of unity, wisdom, and action. Whoever wishes to plot against the government is a traitor, and I denounce here all those who have made themselves guilty of this crime. They want to slander the revolutionary government in order to dissolve it. They want to dishonor the Revolutionary Tribunal so that the conspirators may breathe in peace; the most infamous artifices are invented in order to persecute energetic patriots and to save their mortal enemies.

There is only one remedy to so many evils, and it consists in the execution of the laws of nature, which require that every man be just, and in virtue, which is the fundamental basis of all society. We might as well go back into the woods as dispute among ourselves honors, reputation, and riches; nothing can result from this struggle but tyrants and slaves. After fifty years of tumult, troubles, and carnage, the result would be the establishment of a new despot.

It is natural to go to sleep after victory; our enemies, who know this well, do not fail to make efforts to turn our attention away from their crimes. The real victory is that which the friends of liberty win over faction: it is that victory which is called among the people peace, justice, and happiness. A nation is not honored for having cast down tyrants or enslaved peoples; this was the fate of the Romans and of several other nations; our destiny, which is much more sublime, is to found the empire of wisdom, justice, and virtue on earth.

We can only attain this goal by wise institutions which can be built on the ruin of the incorrigible enemies of liberty. See what happens to every effort of patriotism contrary to virtue; the factions redouble their ruses in the same measure that we show our energy; and if this same energy begins to slacken, they will profit from it to summon up new forces; they will fight for every inch of ground and will give the conspirators time to rally. They try constantly to cause division and to give themselves out as partisans; if we do not take care, there will soon be factions formed in great enough numbers to fight against liberty and to slaughter liberty's friends.

In presenting these reflections to you, I denounce the efforts of our enemies without foretelling their success; I know that everything which is criminal is going to disappear from the earth, but it is nonetheless true that crime has made, from the beginnings of time down to our own day, the unhappiness of the world.

We would have to be extremely frivolous to be lulled into a sense of security where these plots are concerned and to lose this ardent courage, which leads us to denounce the conspirators, even for one moment; it is not to demand any other severe measure against the guilty ones that I am speaking here; what difference does their life or their death make to me as long as the people and the Convention are enlightened!

My aim is to warn all the citizens against the traps which are laid for them, and to extinguish the new torch of discord which our enemies are trying to light in the Convention. What we see every day, what we cannot hide from ourselves, is the fact that they wish to degrade and destroy the Convention by a system of deathly ideas; they try to persuade every member that the Committee of Public Safety has proscribed him.

This plot exists; but since we are aware of it, all good citizens must rally to smother it. It is here that at all times the patriotic deputies have met to make virtue triumph: if the rostrum of the Jacobins has become mute for some time, it is not because they have nothing more to say; but the profound silence which reigns there is the effect of a lethargic sleep which keeps them from perceiving the dangers which threaten the fatherland. But there *are* those who want to make the Convention tremble, to prejudice it against the Revolutionary Tribunal, and to re-establish the system of Danton and Camille Desmoulins; they have sowed the seeds of division everywhere; they have substituted distrust for openness, the selfish motives of weak souls for the generous sentiments of the founders of the Republic: one must always come back to those principles; public virtue and supreme justice are the two sovereign laws to which all those who are charged with the interests of the fatherland must bow.

There is only one path for a people who cannot by itself constantly penetrate into the secret places of intrigue; that is to protect its rights and to act in such a way that courage will not fail in the face of treachery; it is to compare all that which has only the appearance of justice with justice itself. All that leads to a dangerous end is dictated by treachery.

There is a sentiment engraved on the hearts of all patriots which is the touchstone by which to recognize their friends: when a man is quiet at the moment when he should speak, he is suspect; when he covers himself with secrecy or shows energy for a few minutes, which disappears as quickly; when he contents himself with vain tirades against tyrants without occupying himself with the public morals and the happiness of his brother citizens, he is suspect.

When one sees men sacrificing aristocrats only for form, one must look severely into their characters.

When one hears commonplaces against Pitt and the enemies of

humankind cited and when one sees the same men surreptitiously attacking the revolutionary government; when one sees men who are sometimes moderate and sometimes excessive, always declaiming and always opposed to putting into effect what they propose, it is time to be on guard against conspiracies.

The revolution would end in a simple manner and without being disturbed by the factions, if all men were uniformly friends of the fatherland and of the laws.

But we are far distant from having reached this point; I call men of probity to witness; let them declare whether, when they want to defend a patriot riddled with wounds from the aristocracy, and a soft-spoken compromising aristocrat presents himself, there are not many men who will group themselves around this aristocrat and try to support him.

But the groans of an oppressed patriot—is it not more difficult for these to make themselves heard among certain people than the hypocritical complaints of the aristocracy?

Let us conclude that the republican government is not yet well enough established, and that there are factions which thwart its efforts. The revolutionary government has two objects: the protection of patriotism and the destruction of the aristocracy. As long as there are factions opposing it, it will never be able to achieve this goal. To establish liberty on unshakable foundations will be for it an impossible thing as long as each individual is able to say to himself: if the aristocracy triumphs today, I am lost. There will always be a strong reaction against intrigues in the breast of the people, and there will perhaps result from that too many internal discords.

But the scoundrels will not triumph, for it is impossible that men who have espoused the profound system of liberty and justice should ever consent to allow to such vile enemies a triumph which would be at once the shame and the loss of all humanity. Either these cowardly conspirators must renounce their infamous plots or they will wring our lives from us. I know that they will try to do this—they are continually trying every day—but the genius of the fatherland watches over patriots.

I would have liked to give more order and precision to these reflections, but I have followed the feelings of my soul. I seek to stifle the seeds of division and to prevent the formation of two parties in the Convention; I invite all members to be on guard against the perfidious insinuations of certain people, who, fearing for themselves, wish to make their fears shared. As long as terror persists among the representatives, they will be incapable of fulfilling their glorious mission. Let them rally to eternal justice, let them foil the plots by their surveillance, so that the fruit of our victories may be liberty, peace, happiness, and virtue, and so that our brothers, after having spilt their blood to win so many advantages for us, may themselves be assured that their families will enjoy the immortal fruit which their generous devotion should guarantee them.

National Convention

29 Messidor [17 July]

Veau presented a short summary of recent correspondence. The national belief of Frenchmen in the existence of the Supreme Being and in the immortality of the soul is universally expressed. Adherence of several popular societies to the principles and virtues of the Convention. . . .

Decree, based on the report of Berlier, regulating the mode of procedure whenever the competence of the Tribunal of the Family is contested, and when it is a question of the sale and liquidation of individual property.

Report by d'Oudot on the question of whether the surveillance and revolutionary committees are competent to make seizures of merchandise and foodstuffs upon the pretext that they had not been declared in conformity with the law of 12 Germinal.

Table chronologique du Moniteur, No. 301.

National Convention

30 Messidor [18 July]

Barère complained that the valor of our armies barely leaves the Committee enough time to publish the news of their continual victories. Those of the Moselle and the Rhine made the Prussians flee before them as far as twenty leagues. Newstadt, Spires, Platzberg, Kerveiller and Tripstadt are the fruit of their courage. In Belgium, the advantageous positions of Montagne-de-Fer and the abbey of Florival have been taken. Louvain and Malines are now under our control. Acclamations, prolonged applause.

Commune of Paris, General Council

27 Messidor [15 July]

A national agent called the Council's attention to the fraternal banquets which have been taking place for some days: he does not know if they are good, but Danton several times proposed banquets of this kind. He does not know if they are useful, but at Marseille, aristocrats seek to use them to seduce friends of liberty. These meals are the signal for a perfidious reconciliation, the precursors of the counter-revolution. The speaker invited the people not to allow themselves to be tricked by these banquets which carry only the name of fraternity; such banquets can exist along with principles of equality only when the aristocracy in its entirety has been sent to its grave. He declared, finally, that he was opposed to any rigorous measures to put an end to these banquets, because it sufficed to indicate the trap that awaited good patriots, for them to shun it. The Council concurred with this opinion and voted down the motions calling for repressive measures.

Table chronologique du Moniteur, No. 302.

Jacobin Club

26 Messidor [14 July]

A citizen complained about the oppression taking place in the commune of Troyes. He denounced the members of a commission, called the Twenty-Four, organized by Rousselin, which, in concert with him, has created a thousand vexations. Among the grievances mentioned, he cited a revolutionary tax of one million seven-hundred thousand livres, levied by Danton and Rousselin, against which no one dared to complain and of which Rousselin and Gachet, the mayor, have themselves used eighteen thousand livres. Couthon considered the speech of the previous speaker quite proper in its exposure of the continuing existence of the system of Hébert and Danton and their followers, scoundrels who exasperated the people with their atheism and their taxes. He invited the previous speaker to give testimony before the Committee of Public Safety.

Fouché, of Nantes, wrote the Society begging it to suspend its judgment until the committees of Public Safety and General Security have made their report on his public and private conduct. Robespierre de-

Ibid., No. 303.

clared that the individual Fouché interested him not at all: "It is less for his past crimes that he denounced him than for the fact that he was preparing others and that he regarded him as the chief of a conspiracy that had to be stopped. He was indignant that he had failed to appear before the Society. He is a vile and miserable impostor whose action attests to his crimes. His conduct is the same as that of Brissot and scoundrels like him. But virtue will never be sacrificed to baseness, nor liberty to men whose hands are dirtied by rapine and crime."

A citizen of the Commune-Affranchie made several very grave charges against Fouché; the Society voted to have them taken before the Committee of Public Safety and, on the motion of a member, pronounced Fouché's exclusion.

Jacobin Club

1 Thermidor [19 July]

Deputy Gauthier, desirous of responding to the denunciations made against him and occupied with drafting his justification, invited the Society by letter to suspend its judgment until he had been heard. Gauthier's denouncer demanded that he take the podium now or be stricken from the membership. Gouly denounced the previous speaker as a slanderer and as an instrument of an intrigue which is active throughout the *département* of Indre; he demanded that he come with him to the Committee on General Security and explain himself. Adopted.

Gouillard, from the district of Béthune, juror on the Revolutionary Tribunal, asked the Society to decide whether it was going to purge him. Robespierre the younger asked that decisions on purges be suspended for citizens recently arrived from the *départements,* on whom there was no positive information. Dumas supported this view; he announced that on that very day the Revolutionary Tribunal had allowed a man to go free who, after having emigrated five times for the purpose of carrying millions worth of gold to the former princes of Artois and Condé, had had the audacity to take a position as secretary of the tribunal which had formerly condemned him and had also found the means to be admitted into the Society. Robespierre's proposal was adopted.

A citizen from the department of Jura denounced representative Prost for having caused several vexations and persecutions. Robes-

Table chronologique du Moniteur, No. 306.

pierre declared that Prost did not have the character of a conspirator or a leader of a party. Nothing was easier, he said, than rendering justice to oppressed citizens and not finding the guilty ones among their representatives. Patriots must take precautions against the wickedness of enemies who wish to fill the Convention with their own uneasiness in order to conspire against it with impunity.

National Convention

2 Thermidor [20 July]

Barère announced the capture of Namur and everywhere the flight of the Prussian army. After reading several official letters from general Jourdan and representatives Hentz and Goujon, condemning the tyrants of Europe, Barère asked the legislators and the armies not to relax their efforts in the middle of success, attributing a great share of the recent triumph to that most terrible and most beneficial institution, the revolutionary government. He spoke of coming political storms which seemed to have been forming now for several days. The committees have taken measures which cannot be divulged; they propose the following provisional decrees: (1) that all citizens ordered arrested who have escaped arrest, and all public officials who have been suspended or replaced must leave Paris within three days and return to their original domiciles within two weeks; if they delay in obeying these orders they will be declared *émigrés* and punished as such; (2) that all commissioners, under pain of dismissal, return to their last domiciles and justify their return before their municipal authorities, without delay. Adopted unanimously.

Table chronologique du Moniteur, No. 303.

Jacobin Club

3 Thermidor [21 July]

Denunciation by two citizens of Tours against the person named Sénard, sent as agent of the Committee on General Security to this commune, and guilty of more than twenty crimes against the people; they asked for defenders. Couthon supported their position and asked that the denunciation be taken to the government. He invited citizens to maintain their surveillance, to denounce all conspirators, traitors,

Ibid., No. 309.

and good-for-nothings, and to see that they are delivered to the proper authorities. Robespierre the younger complained of a universal system of oppression, but said that it only provoked the courage of republicans to greater combat. Couthon asked his colleagues to present their reflections to the Convention, a Convention which would not permit itself to be subjugated by four or five scoundrels. He declared that up until the moment that the daggers entered his weak body, he would continue to fight all scoundrels and traitors. His proposition was adopted. . . .

Sijas accused Pille, commissioner in charge of army affairs, with having trampled the decrees of the Convention beneath his feet instead of implementing them. He invited all citizens to be on guard against the establishment of a military government.

IV
ROBESPIERRE'S CHALLENGE

Introduction

Robespierre's last speech is reprinted in its entirety in this section. It is a long, tedious, and often turgid piece of oratory, but it must be carefully analyzed because it was Robespierre's reply to the conspiracies which were being organized against him. The speech also announced to his colleagues on the Committee whether he would accept Barère's efforts to smooth over the differences that divided the Committee.

Robespierre's quarrel with certain members of the Committee on General Security centered on the intricate Théot affair, which he describes in some detail. Shortly before 8 Thermidor a joint meeting of the two committees had been held to arrange a *modus vivendi* between the two bodies, whose powers and jurisdictions tended to overlap in certain areas. At that meeting, Robespierre refused to effect a reconciliation with his opponents on the Committee on General Security. Voulland's letter to local officials in his constituency attempts to discount rumors of an impending rupture. Voulland offers as evidence of harmony the speech that Barère had given on 7 Thermidor in the name of the two committees. It should be obvious that Voulland wrote his letter before he had heard Robespierre's speech.

This speech indicates, then, what strategy Robespierre will follow. It is also of critical importance for the information it gives us on Robespierre's frame of mind. It has been suggested that Robespierre's mental condition was in large part responsible for his defeat on 9 Thermidor. The jarring and disconnected outbursts that occur at several points in the speech, as well as Robespierre's description of his role, should help to establish whether Robespierre was indeed in the grip of an emotional crisis.

In the debate that followed the speech, Robespierre committed what some historians consider to have been the greatest tactical mistake of his career. Was Robespierre's self-righteous and uncompromising refusal to answer the question put to him by several deputies a fatal blunder? The significance of the Convention's immediate reaction to the speech will be more apparent if one realizes that the printing and distribution of major addresses was a matter of course.

The reception accorded to Robespierre when he repeated his speech at the Jacobin club that evening may help to explain why Robespierre failed to anticipate the attack that was to be made on the 9th.

National Convention

7 Thermidor, Year II [25 July 1794]

DUBOIS-CRANCÉ: Citizens, you have made virtue and probity the order of the day, and also justice and truth. For nine months my soul has been filled with bitterness; for nine months, I have been foully slandered but I have not yet been denounced as a traitor. I have come to divest myself of my sorrow in the breast of the Convention. If I am a traitor, my head must fall, but if I have served my country usefully, the Convention will recognize it. I speak in the presence of this Society which I esteem, and to the establishment of which I have also contributed. My public life has been known for five years. For fifteen months I have been away on various missions. I have given great aid to the destruction of federalism in Lyon. Having been sent to Brest to form the brigades, I commandeered 51,000 men from that area who fought against the enemy; and it was at that moment that I was anathematized! On the road which I traveled people regarded me as a traitor, as a man worthy of the scaffold! A man who had been constantly at the breach against the aristocrats, however innocent he may be, is filled with sorrow when he is the butt of such cruel reproaches.

They say that I let the rebels escape from Lyon, that I was not at all opposed to it; that is false. I call upon all those of my colleagues who were with me or in the neighborhood, in the *départements* of Rhône-et-Loire and of the Isère, and all those who know the facts.

I ask them to say if it is not an established fact that the rebels left by the Porte-de-Vaize? If it is, how did the column to which I was attached—not as a general for that was a title which they gave me to make me ridiculous; every column had a general and there was moreover a general-in-chief; I was attached to the column only as a representative of the people—I ask how could this column have permitted the exit of the rebels when it was guarding the Croix-Rousse gate and that of Ste-Claire, and when between these gates and that by which the rebels left there lies the river Saône and sheer mountains, and when in order to go from one to the other, one must go five leagues: If it was five leagues from the gate where I was to the one by which the rebels left, how can I be accused of not having guarded it? It was my very accusers who were at the Porte-de-Vaize. Nevertheless, I do not accuse anyone; I believe that everyone did his duty, for the rebels were cut to pieces; how can they be brought to life again today? They could only

Le Moniteur universel, XXI, 301-2 (Edition of 8 Thermidor).

have escaped by balloon; and the fact is that there has not been any question of them since.

But there is more; if I had been with the column at the Porte-de-Vaize I would not be guilty, for that column did its duty. As soon as it learned of the flight of the enemy, it proceeded along the Saône to destroy it. But why accuse me? On October 2 the Committee of Public Safety ordered that I should be recalled into the breast of the Convention. On the 6th my removal was known. On the 7th I left my column to come join my colleagues. Removed on the 6th and no longer with my column, why make me responsible for an event which only happened three days later, for since the enemy did not leave until the 9th, when I had already been without my powers for three days? There are two material alibis.

Never was there a conspiracy as extensive as that of Lyon, and never was there one as promptly, as completely crushed, as witness the Vendée and the Chouans. As for my last mission, I saved Brittany from civil war; for the 51,000 men whom I brought from there might have been enlisted into their party by the Chouans; they would have fought on the frontier, and you would perhaps have needed an army to combat them.

They say that a slandered patriot is a public calamity. Has any one seen me waver in five years? I ask my colleagues. Robespierre has made a mistake; he denounced me as a traitor who permitted the rebels to escape from Lyon. I do not accuse anyone. But since I have demonstrated that I have not dishonored the fatherland, give me the liberty of thought, the public esteem for which I have fought since that time; Robespierre himself will soon recognize his error.

Since no one has raised his voice against me, I ask that the assembly declare that the quarrel is finished and that I have not dishonored the Republic.

It is moved that the matter be referred to the committees of Public Safety and of General Security.

DUBOIS-CRANCÉ: Although the people who have denounced me are members of these committees, I rely too much on the justice of these two committees not to support the referral myself. But I ask them to make the report immediately, even tomorrow; the information is there and I am ready.

It is moved that the report be made in three days.

These proposals are decreed.

Voulland's Correspondence

Paris, this 8th Thermidor of the Year II of
the One and Indivisible Republic

Voulland, citizen of the commune of Uzès, representative of the People to the National Convention
To his fellow-citizens, the Administrators of the district of Uzès

Several days ago, brothers and friends, you were so kind as to write me that you had decided to carry on a weekly correspondence with me to keep me informed about everything important that happens in your district. I recognize in this step the zeal which has constantly animated you—inspired by the purest patriotism—and I can only wish to second it with all my feeble means. I shall do my best. You know the important matters with which I am charged and to which I give myself entirely, with the activity and devotion I owe to the confidence of the Convention and of my fellow-citizens. I shall consecrate to you with pleasure all the time I can spare . . . from the many important tasks of the Convention, and if our correspondence can prove beneficial to the public good and to the greater advantage of our *département* and our district, you and I will certainly have deserved well of our fellow-citizens, in whose happiness we shall find the only possible happiness for ourselves.

At the moment you are perhaps not without some slight concern because of certain rumors people have chosen to spread with a great fuss, to make people believe what they really don't believe themselves but what they ardently desire, namely, that the two committees of the Government are not in agreement. I assure you of the contrary. It was believed that the horizon surrounding the two committees was misty. This mist that the evil-doers wished to make visible and to endow with some substance was seen only by them. They have taken great pains to present it as a dark cloud containing the thunder of an inevitable rupture. This storm, which existed only in the eyes and hearts of those who desired it—for reasons known to them—has been broken up and dissipated even before it was formed.

As evidence of what I say, I refer you to the report Barère gave yesterday in the name of the two committees jointly. I will not go into detail, either about his theme or the facts that motivated it, I will limit myself to assuring you that he was heard with the greatest interest and applauded with the most sincere enthusiasm. I will say no more of it today. As soon as it is printed, which I expect will be to-

Annales historiques de la Révolution française, IV (1927), 66-77.

morrow, I shall hasten to send you some copies, and if the circumstances require it I shall share with you any reflections it may inspire in me.

Our foreign enemies have certainly acted in concert with their vile agents here at home, but the energy of the Convention—whose great majority is still pure and can never be corrupted nor carried away—has nothing to fear from the terrors with which [the conspirators] wished to strike it down. The Mountain is not shaken; it is still well guarded and well defended. Therefore, rest assured, if anyone has tried to frighten you, you can resume your usual sense of security with confidence.

Besides, our victories are continuing, and the despots' satellites cannot make up their minds to face the troops of the Republic, which are in possession of the important town of Antwerp. The enemy—who well knew that they were incapable of fighting over it for long had the good sense to evacuate it very suddenly when they found that we intended to take it. There is a citadel essential to anyone who would control the city. This news will not be known in the Convention until two o'clock; in the *départements* not until tomorrow. I thought it would please you to know it twenty-four hours in advance. I give you my word that it is true.

I learned with great satisfaction that our dear fellow-citizen Sorbier had been acquitted by the revolutionary tribunal of Nîmes. Lantheyrès d'Alais was also, and I am equally delighted. Try to keep me informed of what goes on in that community. It is with regret that I see there domestic divisions whose development it is very important to check. Two distinct parties seem to be forming there and they will come to a show down if it is not possible to reconcile them. The Committee on General Security is besieged with conflicting demands, for and against Lantheyrès and Rovère. Let us avoid giving the enemy the spectacle of a tragic division in our ranks, which would only please them and lend them weapons to attack us.

I would not mention my father-in-law if I did not know that the steps justice and humanity inspired you to take in his behalf must have determined his fate.

I am waiting to hear the outcome with the impatience so natural to filial piety, which is a Republican virtue. I hope it will be as we all desire; whatever duty it demands of me I shall fulfill—I am a Republican.

> A true Republican has as father and son only virtue, the gods, the Law, and his Country.

My father-in-law is not an enemy of the revolution, however. I believe that he will soon be restored to liberty, the first-fruit of the revolution.

Adieu, brothers and friends, I embrace you all from the bottom of my heart.

Salut et Fraternité

Voulland

National Convention

8 Thermidor, Year II [26 July 1794]

ROBESPIERRE:

Citizens, let others present to you flattering pictures; I come to speak to you useful truths. I come not to realize the ridiculous alarms spread by perifidy, but to extinguish, if possible, the firebrands of discord, by the sole force of truth. I am about to defend before you your outraged authority and violated liberty. I will also defend myself. You will not be surprised; you resemble not the tyrants you combat against; your ears are not offended by the cries of outraged innocence; and well you know that this cause is no stranger to you.

The Revolutions which up to this time have changed the face of empires, have had for their object a change of dynasty, or the transfer of power from the hands of a single chief to those of several chiefs. The French Revolution is the first that shall have been founded on the theory of the rights of humanity, and on the principles of justice. Other Revolutions required only ambition; ours requires virtue. Ignorance and brute force have absorbed all former Revolutions in a new Despotism; ours, having emanated from justice, can repose but in the bosom of justice. The Republic insensibly led by the force of circumstances, and by the struggle of the friends of liberty against ever-reviving conspiracies, has glided along, as it were, through the midst of all the factions; but it found their power organized around it, and every means of influence in their hands; accordingly has it been incessantly persecuted, from its birth, in the person of every upright man that fought in its defence. The reason is this: to conserve the advan-

This translation is reprinted from a pamphlet entitled *The Last Discourse of Maximillian Robespierre* (London, 1867). The speech was "translated by the late James Bronterre O'Brien, B.A., while incarcerated in Lancaster Castle (for alleged political offences), during the year 1840-41." O'Brien's rhetorical embellishments are retained.

tages of their position, the chiefs of the factions and their agents have been forced to hide themselves beneath the form of the Republic. Thus Précy at Lyon, and Brissot at Paris, were crying "*Vive la République!*" whilst plotting its destruction. The same of all the conspirators; they have all adopted, even with more than ordinary forwardness and apparent zeal, all the formulas, all the rallying words of Patriotism. The Austrian, whose craft or profession it was to combat the Revolution—the partisan of Orleans, whose game it was to play the patriot—were to be met on the same line; neither the one nor the other could be distinguished from the genuine Republican. They did not combat our principles, but they corrupted them; they did not blaspheme against the Revolution, but they sought to dishonour it under the guise of serving it. They declaimed against the tyrants, and conspired for the tyranny; they glorified the Republic, and calumniated the Republicans. The friends of Liberty seek to overthrow the power of tyrants by the force of truth; the tyrants seek to destroy the defenders of Liberty by calumny; they give the name of tyranny to the ascendancy of even the principles of truth itself. Let but this system once prevail, and Liberty is no more! There is then nothing legitimate but perfidy, nothing criminal but virtue; for it is in the very nature of things that one or the other influence must exist wherever men are gathered together—the influence of tyranny or that of reason. Whenever the latter is proscribed as a crime, tyranny reigns; wheresoever good citizens are condemned to silence, the wicked must needs be in the ascendant, and the reigning Government was necessarily a Government of villains.

Here I have need to open and disburden my heart: you, too, have need to hear the truth. Believe not that I have come here to enter any accusation: a more pressing care engrosses me—and, besides, 'tis not for me to take charge of other men's duties. Indeed, we are beset by so many and such imminent dangers, that the business of accusation is now but of secondary importance in my eyes. I have come here in order, if possible, to dissipate cruel errors; I come to stifle the horrid fermentations of discord with which it is sought to fire this temple of Liberty and the entire Republic. I come to unveil abuses which menace the country with ruin, and which your probity alone can repress. If I say ought of the persecutions directed against myself, you will not, I hope, make it a crime. You have nothing in common with the tyrants who pursue me; the cries of oppressed innocence are not foreign to your hearts; you do not make a sport of justice and humanity, and you are well aware that the machinations I allude to are not irrelevant to your cause and to that of the country. Now, what foundation is there for this odious system of terror and calumnies? To whom ought we to be objects of dread? Is it to the enemies or to the friends of the Republic? Is it for knaves and tyrants to fear us, or is it for honest men and patriots? What, *we,* objects of terror to patriots? *We,* who have rescued them from the hands of every faction that conspired against them!—*we,* who day after day are contesting and wrestling, as it were, for every inch of ground with the deep-designing hypocrites who still dare to oppress them!—*we,* who are in hot pursuit of the miscreants that seek to prolong their calamities by involving them and us in endless deceits and inextricable mazes of imposture!—*we,* objects of terror to the National Convention? And what, pray, are we without the Convention? And who is it that defended the National Convention at the peril of his life? Who devoted himself for its conservation, when execrable factions were conspiring its ruin, in the face of France? Who devoted himself for its glory when the vile agents of tyranny were preaching Atheism and immorality in its name—when so many others were culpably silent on the misdeeds of their accomplices, and seemed only to await the signal of carnage to imbrue their hands with the blood of the people's Representatives—when virtue herself stood mute, appalled at the horrible ascendancy of crime? And for whom did the conspirators destine their first blows? Against whom did Simon conspire in the Luxembourg? Who were the victims marked out for sacrifice by Chaumette and Ronsin? To what place was the troop of assassins to march, after opening the prisons? Is there no poignard for us in the cargoes which England is consigning to her accomplices in France and Paris? It is at *us* the assassin's dagger is aimed, yet *we* it is who are painted as objects of terror. And what, pray, are those great acts of severity we are reproached with? Who, and of what character, were the victims?—Hébert, Ronsin, Chabot, Danton, Delacroix, Fabre d'Églantine, and some few of their accomplices. Is it with *their* punishment we are reproached? Why, not a man would dare to defend them. But if we have only denounced monsters whose death has saved the Convention and the Republic, who can feel alarm at our principles—who can accuse us by anticipation of injustice and cruelty, if it be not those who resemble them? No, we have not been too severe. I call to witness the Republic which respires! I call to witness the National Representation, environed, as it is, with the respect due to the representation of a great people! I call to witness the patriots who are once more groaning in the dungeons which the miscreants have opened for them! I call to witness the fresh and repeated crimes of the enemies of our liberty, and the guilty perseverance of the tyrants in league against us! Talk of our rigour, indeed, while the country is at this moment reproaching us with our weakness!

Is it we who have plunged the patriots into dungeons, and carried terror into all ranks and conditions? No! it is the monsters we have accused. Is it we who, conniving at the crimes of the aristocracy, and protecting known traitors, have declared war against peaceable citizens —erected into crimes what were only incurable prejudices, or matters of indifference, in order to find crimes and culprits everywhere, and thus render the Revolution odious to the very people who made it? No! it is the monsters we have accused. Is it we who, raking up old and long-abandoned opinions (the fruit of tyrannic influences), have waved the axe of the Revolution over the heads of the great majority of the National Convention, and in the popular societies have demanded the heads of *six hundred representatives* of the people? No! it is the monsters we have accused. Can it be forgotten that we it was who threw ourselves into the breach between them and their perfidious adversaries, at a time when . . . . [Here occurs a gap or break in Robespierre's Manuscript, which leaves the sentence imperfect.]

You know the march of our enemies. They first attacked the National Convention in mass; that project failed. They next attacked the Committee of Public Safety in mass; that, too, has failed. Their plan now is to attack us one by one, in detail—to isolate us from one another, the more easily to overwhelm us. In this way they have for some time waged war against certain of the members of the Committee of Public Safety. Indeed, they would fain appear to attack only one member of it—the individual now before you. But, however they may vary their tactics, they always march towards the same end. That the tyrants of Europe should dare to proscribe a Representative of the French People is unquestionably the excess of insolence; but that Frenchmen calling themselves Republicans should labour to carry into execution the death-sentence pronounced by the tyrants, is the excess of scandal and opprobium. Is it true that odious lists have been hawked about, in which are noted down for victims a certain number of members of the Convention—lists which they pretend to be the work of the Committee of Public Safety, and to have been prepared by me in particular; for they refer the authorship to me? Is it true that our enemies have dared to invent sittings of the Committee which have never been held—to imagine rigorous resolves and warrants which have never existed, and attestations no less chimerical and false? Is it true they have tried to persuade a certain number of irreproachable members of this House that their destruction was resolved upon—to persuade all who by some error had paid an inevitable tribute to the fatality of circumstances and to human weakness, that they were devoted to the doom of conspirators? Is it true that this game of imposture has been played with so much art and audacity, that a great number were actually afraid to pass the night in their own homes? Yes! the facts are authenticated, and the proofs of these two manœuvres are in the hands of the Committee of Public Safety. And you, too, Deputies who have just returned from mission in the Departments—you could disclose many similar facts. And you, Deputies who have just arrived to take the place of ex-members—you can tell us of the intrigues set on foot to deceive you, to sour and prejudice you, and that with a view to drag you into the fatal coalition of the conspirators. What was the language used—what were the acts done in those mysterious coteries, at those nocturnal cabals, at those repasts where perfidy distributed to the guests the poisons of hatred and calumny? What wished they for—the authors of these machinations? What did they desire? Was it the safety of the country—the dignity and unity of the National Convention? Who were they? What facts are there to justify the horrible idea they sought to convey of us—the horrible impression they sought to leave behind? What other persons have been accused by the Committees, besides the Chaumettes, the Héberts, the Dantons, the Chabots, the Delacroixs? Is it, then, the memory of conspirators they would defend? Is it the death of conspirators they would avenge? If they accuse us of having denounced some traitors, let them also accuse the Convention, which authorized their accusation; let them accuse Justice, which has smitten the traitors; let them accuse the people, who have applauded their punishment. Which is the more likely party to harbour guilty designs against the National Representation—the man who prosecutes its enemies, or the man who protects them? And how long is it since the punishment of crime began to terrify virtue?

Such is, however, the basis of those projects of Dictatorship, and treasonable designs against the National Representation, imputed, in the first instance, to the Committee of Public Safety in general, and subsequently to myself alone. By what fatality has this grave accusation been suddenly transferred to a single member of the Committee? Strange project, indeed! for a man to engage the National Representation to murder itself in detail with its own hands, in order to pave the way for himself to absolute power. I leave other people to perceive the ridiculous side of these inculpations; for myself I can see only their atrocity. Monsters! who would thus rob me of the esteem of the National Convention—the most glorious reward that mortal ever reaped from his labours—a reward, too, which I have neither usurped or inveigled, but which I have been forced to conquer. I call upon you, monsters! to render account to public opinion of your frightful perseverance in following up your own bloody project—*your project to massacre all the friends of their country.* To appear an object of terror in the eyes of those we revere and love is, for a man of feeling and probity, the most frightful of tortures. To make such a man undergo it, is the most enormous of crimes. But let me call down the full weight of your indignation on the atrocious manœuvres resorted to, to prop up these extravagant calumnies.

Everywhere acts of oppression and tyranny had been multiplied to extend the system of terror and calumny; impure agents were prodigal of unjust arrestations; destructive projects of finance menaced every moderate fortune, and brought despair upon a countless multitude of families attached to the Revolution. The nobles and the priests were terrified by concerted motions; the payments due to the creditors of the state, and to public functionaries, were suspended; a resolution was surprised from the Committee of Public Safety, which renewed the prosecution (long since abandoned) against the members of the Committee of the 10th August, under the pretence of compelling them to tender their accounts. Within the Convention itself, it was pretended that the Mountain was menaced, because certain members sitting in that part of the hall thought themselves in danger; and in order to interest the entire National Convention in the same cause, the affair of the seventy-three imprisoned (Girondins) Deputies was, on a sudden revived; and mark! —*all these events were industriously imputed to me, who was an absolute stranger to them!* The conspirators gave out that I wished to immolate the Mountain; *they* gave out that I wished to destroy the other half of the Convention as well. On the right side of the House they painted me as the persecutor of the sixty-two Deputies in custody! On the opposite side, they accused me of defending them, and said that I supported the Marais. That was the expression of my calumniators. Let me remark, that the most potent argument employed by the Hébertist faction to prove me a *Moderate,* was the opposition I had given to the proscription of a great part of the National Convention, and more particularly my opinion on the proposition for putting the *sixty-two* Deputies on their trial without a previous report.

Ah! indeed, when at the risk of offending public opinion, and when consulting only the sacred interests of my Country, I saved from a hasty and fatal decision men whose opinions would have sent me to the scaffold, had their opinions triumphed—when, upon other occasions, I had exposed myself to all the furies of a hypocritical faction, to insist upon having the principles of strict justice carried out in favour of men who had never shewn the like forbearance towards me—I was far, indeed, from supposing that the country would deem itself under any obligation to me for such conduct; mean, indeed, is the opinion I should have formed of a country in which such conduct would be thought remarkable, or in which pompous and laudatory names would be given to what an honest man regards only as indispensable duties. But still farther was I from supposing that the day would come when I should be accused of being the executioner of the very men in whose behalf I had fulfilled those duties, and of being the enemy of the National Convention, which I had served with devotion; least of all did I imagine that I should be at one and the same time accused of wishing to defend the Convention, and of wishing to murder it! But, be the consequences what they may, nothing shall ever change my principles or my sentiments. As to the Deputies under arrest, I declare that, so far from having participated in the decree concerning them, I considered it, to say the least, extraordinary under the circumstances; I declare that they have never for an instant formed the subject of my thoughts since I discharged, in their behalf, the full tribute of duty which my heart dictated, by opposing the proposition for sending them to the Revolutionary Tribunal. The rest is a tissue of atrocious impostures. As to the Convention, my first duty, as my first bias, is an unbounded respect for it, as being the Representative of the Nation. Without wishing to absolve crime, without wishing to justify in themselves the disastrous errors of several members, without wishing to tarnish the glory of the energetic defenders of liberty, nor to weaken the illusion of a name sacred in the annals of the Revolution, I declare that every Representative of the people, whose heart is pure, ought to resume the confidence and dignity which befits him. I know but two parties, that of *good,* and that of *bad,* citizens. I believe patriotism not to be an affair of party, but an affair of the heart; that it consists neither in insolence, nor in that flighty impetuosity which respects neither principles, nor good sense, nor morality; much less that it consists in devotedness to the interests of a faction. My heart seared by the experience of so many treasons, I believe more and more in the necessity, the permanent necessity, of invoking Probity, and every generous sentiment, to the relief of the Republic—but Probity before all. I feel that wherever an honest man is to be met with, wheresoever he be seated, we ought to extend to him the hand of fellowship, and press him to our heart. I believe in certain fatalities in the Revolution which have nothing in common with criminal designs; I believe in the detestable influence of intrigue, and, above all, in the sinister power of calumny. I see the world peopled with dupes and knaves; but the knaves, though a small minority, cause all the evils. 'Tis the knaves, and the knaves only, that ought to be punished for the crimes and calamities of the world. I will not, therefore, impute the treasons of Brissot, or the Gironde, to the honest men of that party, whom they sometimes deceived. I will not impute those of Hébert to the citizens, whose sincere patriotism was at times betrayed beyond the bounds of reason. The real conspirators would not be conspirators if they had not the art of dissembling with sufficient address, to usurp for some time the confidence of honest men. But there are certain signs by which one may distinguish dupes from accomplices, and error from crime. How then is this distinction to be made? Good sense and justice will make it. Ah! how necessary are good sense and justice in human affairs! Perverse men call us men of blood, because we have made war on the oppressors of the world; therefore, to be humane in their eyes, we must join their sacrilegious league, to massacre the people, and ruin the country!—Shall we do so?

For the rest, if there be privileged conspirators—if there be certain inviolable enemies of the Republic, I consent to impose on myself an eternal silence; in respect of them I have discharged my own duty; I wish not to charge myself with the duties of others. A more pressing care agitates me at this moment. The grand question with me is to save public morals, and the Conservative principles of Liberty; it is to snatch from oppression all the generous friends of the country. For these are the parties accused of treasonable designs against the National Representation! And where are they to find support, if not with you—after having combated all your enemies, after having devoted themselves to the fury of all the factions, in order to defend both your existence and your dignity, where should they seek, or expect to find, an asylum, if not in the bosom of this assembly?—"But they aspire," it is said, "to supreme power, they already exercise it, &c., &c."—So the National Convention does not exist then!—the French people, too, is annihilated! —Stupid calumniators!—Perceive ye not that your ridiculous declamations are an insult not to a mere individual, but to an invincible nation, which subdues and punishes kings? For myself, I should feel an invincible repugnance to defend myself, personally, before you, against the meanest of all the tyrannies, were you not convinced that *you* are the veritable objects of the attacks of all the enemies of the Republic. For what am I, forsooth, to merit their persecutions, if they did not enter into the general system of their conspiracy against the National Convention? Have you not remarked that, to isolate you from the nation, they have published to the world that you were Dictators, reigning by terror, and disavowed by the tacit vows of the French. Have they not called our armies *"Conventional hordes,"* and the French Revolution, *"Jacobinism"*?—And whilst they affect to give to a feeble individual, exposed to the outrageous hatred of all the factions, a gigantic and ridiculous importance, what other end can they have in view but to divide us, and to degrade you, by denying your very existence, like the impious wretch who denies the existence of the Divinity he dreads. Nevertheless, this word *Dictatorship* has magical effects; it sears Liberty; it cheapens the Government; it uproots the Republic; it degrades all our revolutionary institutions, by presenting them as the work of a single man; it renders odious the National justice which it presents, as instituted by the ambition of a single man; it directs to a single point all the rancours, and all the poignards, of fanaticism and aristocracy.

What a terrible use have the enemies of the Republic made of the bare name of a Roman magistracy! And if their erudition is so fatal to us, what may we not expect from their treasures and their intrigues! I speak not of their armies; but let me be permitted to return to the Duke of York and to his Royalist scribes the patents of that ridiculous dignity which they were the first to despatch to me. But it is carring insolence too far, for Kings, who are not sure of conserving their own crowns, to arrogate to themselves the right of distributing them to others; I can conceive how a frivolous prince—how that unclean and sacred species of animals, which still goes by the name of Kings, may find delight in their littleness, and honour in their ignomy; I can conceive how that son of George, for example, may feel regret for the French sceptre he so vehemently coveted, and I sincerely pity that modern Tantalus; I will even own, to the shame, not of my country, but of the traitors she has punished, that I have known unworthy Delegates of the people, who would have exchanged that glorious title for that of *"Valet de Chambre"* to George or Orleans, but that a Representative of the people, who feels the dignity of that character, that a French citizen conscious of his rank and worthy of the name, could stoop so low as to covet the guilty and despicable grandeurs he has helped to sweep away—that he should submit to civic degradation to descend to the infamy of the throne, this is what will appear probable only to those perverse beings who have not even the right to believe in virtue! Virtue, did I say? Virtue is no doubt a natural passion, but what can those venal souls know of it, which have never expanded themselves but to mean and ferocious passions; miserable intriguers who never associated patriotism with any moral idea, who marched in the revolution in the train of some important and ambitious personage—of, mayhap, some despised prince, just as our lacqueys of old used to dance attendance on their masters. Nevertheless, it exists; that tender, imperious, irresistible passion, at once the torment and delight of magnanimous souls! that profound horror of tyranny, that compassionating zeal for the oppressed; that sacred love of country, that sublimest, holiest love of humanity, without which a great revolution is but a splendid crime which destroys another crime; yes, it exists! that generous ambition to found on the earth the first republic of the world! that egoism of non-degraded men which finds a celestial pleasure in the calm of a pure conscience, and in the ravishing spectacle of public happiness! you, men of pure purposes, feel it at this moment burning in your souls; I feel it in mine. But how should our vile calumniators divine it; how can the man blind from his birth have the idea of light? Nature has refused them a soul, so that, after all, they have some right to doubt not only its immorality, but its very existence.

They call me TYRANT! Oh, if I were a tyrant they would grovel at my feet; I would have only to gorge them with gold, and give them a license to commit all manner of crime, and they would bow to me in gratitude! Were I a tyrant, the Kings we have vanquished, so far from denouncing me as they do now (what a tender interest they take in our liberty!) would proffer me their guilty support, and we should soon come to terms. But is it to me they look? Why, what are those Kings expecting just now in their distress, but the succour of a faction protected by them, and which is actually at this moment selling to them the glory and liberty of our country? How do men arrive at tyranny? How else but by the aid of traitor-knaves. Yes, by the agency of knaves it is that men become tyrants. But whither speed those who combat them? To the tomb and immortality! Who is the tyrant that befriends me; what is the faction I belong to? Name it! 'Tis to yourselves: to you and you only do I belong. Which is the faction, that from the beginning of the Revolution, has overthrown all factions, and made so many accredited traitors disappear from the stage? 'Tis *you*—'tis the *people*—'tis our principles. Behold the faction to which alone I am devoted, and against which all crimes are in league.

Believe me, 'tis you—'tis the country—'tis the friends of liberty that this persecution strikes at; if; therefore, I continue to defend myself, consider that I am defending you. Think, oh! think, how many others have sunk under dark oppression! who will ever again dare to serve his country, when I am still obliged to answer such calumnies? They instance as proofs of my ambitious designs, what are but the natural, unavoidable effects of civism and Liberty, to wit, my popularity and influence. Yes, the moral influence of the old Athletes of the revolution, is, nowadays, assimulated to tyranny by those calumniators! Wretches who thus calumniate the power of truth, you are, yourselves, the basest of all tyrants! What aim ye at; what is your purpose, ye slanderers, who want truth to be without force, and to fall powerless from the lips of the Representatives of the French People? Undoubtedly, truth has its power, it has its wrath, its despotism; it has its touching, animating, terrible accents, which vibrate with force, and which reverberate with force in pure hearts, as in guilty consciences, and which it is no more given to falsehood to imitate, than it was to Salmoneus to imitate the thunder of heaven. But do not accuse me for it. Accuse nature of it, accuse the French people who fear and love it. There are two great powers on earth, that of reason and that of tyranny. Wherever the one reigns the other is banished. Those, therefore, who denounce as a crime the moral force of reason, can only want to bring back tyranny. And if you will not suffer the defenders of principles to obtain any influence in this arduous struggle of liberty against intrigue, must you not manifestly desire the victory to be on the side of the intriguers. If those representatives of the people who defend the public cause must not obtain the people's esteem without suffering for it, what else will be the consequence of such a system but *to render it impossible for the people to have any faithful servants at all?* to proscribe the Republic, and re-establish Despotism? And what tyranny more odious, more abhorrent, than that which punishes the people in the persons of their defenders? For, if ever a thing was held free and sacred in this world, beyond all things else—the thing freest and most sacred of all, even under the reign of Despotism—is not that thing friendship? But you make it a crime in me to have the people's friendship! Is it that you are jealous of it? That would be some excuse; but even that you have not, for you set no value on the people's friendship, your regards are only for gold and the perishable riches which tyrants lavish on those who serve them. And do ye not serve them who corrupt public morals, and protect all crimes: for does not the guarantee of conspirators lie in the oblivion of principles, and corruption; whilst that of the defenders lies altogether in the public conscience? Yes, ye serve the tyrants! ye, who ever above, or below the truth, alternately preach, at one time, the perfidious moderation of the aristocracy; at another, the outrageous fury of false democrats. Ye, too, serve them, obstinate predicators of Atheism and vice! Yes, ye seek to destroy the National

Representation, all who degrade it by your conduct, or factionize it by your intrigues. Which is the more culpable, he who strikes at its safety by violence, or at its justice by seduction and perfidy? To deceive the Representation is to betray it; to impel it to acts contrary to its intentions and principles, is to tend to its destruction; for its power is founded only in virtue and the national confidence. We, on the contrary, cherish the Representation; we, who after having battled for its physical safety, are at this moment defending its glory and its principles. Is it thus your would-be-tyrants go to work; is it by this road they march to despotism? But what cruel derision to erect into despots citizens who are continually under the ban of proscription! And what else are they who have remained faithful to the interests of the country? The Republic has triumphed! its defenders never! Whatever the country has gained, we, its defenders, have gained nothing. What, for example, am I that they should accuse me? A slave of liberty—a living martyr of the Republic, not less the victim than the enemy of crime! There is not a knave that does not openly insult me; actions the most indifferent, the most legitimate, when done by others, are crimes in me! nay, the instant a man makes my acquaintance he is calumniated! Other men are forgiven their misdeeds; my zeal is made an unpardonable crime! What sustains me? My conscience. Take away my conscience, and I am the most miserable of men. I have not even the rights of a common citizen; citizen, did I say, when I am not even suffered to discharge my duties as a Representative of the people.

Now is the time for me to let the truth appear, and to lay bare the veritable sores of the Republic. The public affairs are again proceeding in a perfidious and alarming train. The combined system of the Héberts and Fabre d'Églantine is, nowadays, pursued with unheard-of audacity; the counter-revolutionists are protected; those who dishonour the Revolution with the forms of Hébertism are openly protected; the others with more reserve; Patriotism and Probity are proscribed by both factions alike. It is sought to destroy the Revolutionary Government in order to immolate the country to the caitiffs who are tearing it to pieces; and to that odious end the agents of the caitiffs are marching by two different routes. By one faction (Dantonists) the revolutionary institutions are openly calumniated; by the other (Hébertists) it is sought to render them odious by excesses. For example, peaceable, unobtrusive men, and men of no account, are tormented; patriots are every day plunged into dungeons without cause, whilst the aristocracy is favoured by every means, direct and indirect. This, forsooth, they call *indulgence, humanity!* But is that the sort of Revolutionary Government we intended, when we instituted it; is that the sort of Government? No! the Revolutionary Government, rightly understood, is the rapid and unerring march of justice; it is the thunderbolt of retribution launched by the hand of liberty against crime; but never did we intend it to subserve the aristocracy, or to be an instrument of despotism in the hands of knaves; much less to render crime independent of all laws, human and divine. Without the Revolutionary Government, the Republic cannot be established, for factions will smother it in its cradle; but, on the other hand, if it falls into perfidious hands, it becomes itself the instrument of the counter-revolution. At present the plan is to de-naturalize it, in order to destroy it, and both the men who calumniate it and those who compromise it are the same parties. I will not attempt to develop all the causes of these abuses, but I will point out to you a single cause, which will suffice to explain all the disastrous consequences referred to. It is the excessive perversity of the subaltern agents of a respectable authority composed of members of this House (Committee of General Security). There are on that committee individuals whose civic virtues one cannot but cherish and respect. Still that is but an additional reason for abolishing an abuse which has sprung up unknown to them, and which they will be the first to war against when they understand its effects. In vain would a fatal policy pretend to encompass the agents I speak of with a sort of superstitious sanctity. I can have no reverence for knaves; much less can I adopt the old royal maxim *"it is useful to employ them."* The arms of liberty ought not to be touched but with pure hands. Let us, then, instead of tinkering and patching one vice with another, proceed at once to purify the National Surveillance, by purging the whole of the Police Department. Let us not fear truth. Truth is a stumbling-block only to corrupt governments; it is the bulwark of ours. For myself, I shudder when I think that notorious enemies of the Revolution—that quondam professors of Royalism—that ex-nobles, aye, even emigrants, have, all on a sudden, become revolutionists, and metamorphosed themselves into clerks of the Committee of General Security, with a view to revenge themselves on the friends of the country, for their loss of caste, and for the successes of the Republic! Yet, that such cases have actually occurred I entertain not the slightest doubt. Not that such gentry have not apparently earned for themselves some titles to patriotism, by occasionally arresting some noted aristocrat; but what care our foreign enemies to sacrifice a few French traitors, provided, by so doing, they may more easily immolate the patroits, and subvert the Republic.

To those powerful motives which had long since determined me to denounce these men—though unavailingly, let me add another, which has relation to the plot I had begun to develop. We have received information that they are paid by the enemies of the Revolution to dishonour the Revolutionary Government itself, and to throw the odium of their own acts on such of the Representatives of the People as the tyrants have vowed the destruction of. For instance, when the victims of their perversity complain, they excuse themselves by saying—*"It is Robespierre's will and pleasure, we cannot dispense with him."* The infamous disciples of Hébert held the same language in former times when I denounced them; they called themselves my friends, but they afterwards declared me convicted of *Moderatism*. The same species of counter-revolutionists it is that still persecute patriotism. How long will the honour of citizens and the dignity of the National Convention be at the mercy of such men? But the trait I have just instanced is but a branch of a more extended system of persecution, of which I am the object. By way of backing up their accusation of Dictatorship (made the order of the day by the tyrants), the conspirators have set to work to throw upon my shoulders all their own iniquities, all the untowardness of fortune, and all the severities commanded by the safety of the country. To the nobles they said, *" 'Tis he alone who has proscribed you!!!"* At the same time they said to the patriots, *"He wishes to save the nobles!"* To the priests they said, *" 'Tis only he that persecutes you, but for him you would be at peace and triumphant!"* To the fanatics they said, *" 'Tis he that pulls down religion."* And to the persecuted patriots, *" 'Twas he ordered it, or would not prevent it."* Thus have they saddled me with every complaint and grievance, the cause of which I had tried in vain to remove, saying—"Your fate depends on him *alone*." Nay, men have been stationed in the public places, whose business was to propagate, day by day, this perfidious system. Some of them took their station in the place where the sittings of the Revolutionary Tribunal are held; others in the places of public execution, when enemies of the country were about to expiate their crimes. *"Look,"* said they, *"at these unhappy wretches, do you know who brought them here? why Robespierre, to be sure!"* They have been at particular pains to prove that the Revolutionary Tribunal was a *tribunal of blood created by me alone* (and of which I was complete master), with a view to massacre every honest man, and even the knaves too; for the object was to raise up against me enemies of every class and kind. This cry was echoed in all the prisons; this plan of proscription was executed simultaneously in all the departments by the emissaries of tyranny! This is not all. They lately proposed certain finance projects, which appeared to me calculated to ruin citizens of small fortune; I had often in vain called the attention of the Committee of Public Safety to this subject. Well, would you believe it? they have spread the report that these finance projects were my work! and in order to accredit that report, they gave out that there was a Commission of Finance on the Committee of Public Safety, and that I was its President! But as the main purpose was to ruin me in the good opinion of the National Convention, they pretended that I alone had dared to think that it comprised in its body some members unworthy of it; and they told each deputy on his return from his mission into the departments, that I alone had provoked and was the sole cause of his recall; in fact, I was accused by certain very active and insinuating persons, of all the good and of all the evil that had befallen—of the good, to excite the bad against me; of the evil, to excite the good against me. They reported to my colleagues both everything I had said, and especially what I had not said. They carefully set aside all suspicion that they themselves had had any share in any of the acts complained of. Oh, no! 'twas I that had done all, exacted all, commanded all; for you must not forget my title of Dictator! When they had brewed this tempest of hatred, vengeances, terror, and irritated self-love, "Now," said they, "is the time for its explosion." Those whose consciences gave them reason to dread me, flattered themselves openly that my destruction—now certain—was about to assure them their safety and triumph. Whilst English and German journals were announcing my arrestation, it was cried about the streets of Paris by the hawkers and newsvendors. My colleagues here present know the rest much better than I; they know all the manœuvres employed about them to prepare the success of a romance which would seem a new edition of that of Louvet. Several could render an account of unexpected visits made to them, to dispose them to proscribe me. In fine, I have been assured that, *by way of a feeler,* the National Convention, generally, was forewarned that an act of accusation was about to be preferred against me; the minds of the members have been sounded on this subject; and every thing proves that the probity of the National Convention has forced the calumniators to abandon, or, at least, adjourn their crime. But who were these calumniators? Let me first apprise you, by way of answer to the question, that in a Royalist manifesto, found among the papers of a known conspirator, who has already suffered the penalty due to his crimes, and which appears to be the text of all the calumnies, renewed at this moment, we read in proper terms this conclusion, addressed to all descriptions of the people's enemies—*"If that crafty demagogue (Robespierre) was cut off—if he had paid with his head for his ambi-*

tious manœuvres, the nation would be free; every man might then reveal and publish his thoughts, and Paris would be spared that multitude of assassinations (vulgarly known by the false name of judgments) of the Revolutionary Tribunal." I may add, that this passage is the analysis of the proclamations manufactured by the coalesced Princes and Foreign journals in the pay of the Kings, who in this way seem every day to give the signal or word of order to all the Conspirators of the Interior. I shall cite but this passage from one of the most accredited of those writers. I may reply, then, that the authors of this plan of calumny are primarily the Duke of York, Mr. Pitt, and all the tyrants armed against us. Who are the secondary authors? Ah! I dare not name them in this present time and place; I cannot come to the resolution to rend entirely the veil which covers this profound mystery of iniquities; but what I can affirm positively is, that amongst the authors of this plot are the agents of that system of corruption and extravagance so often denounced to you, and the most potent of all the means invented by foreign influence to destroy the Republic, are the impure apostles of Atheism and of immorality, of which it is the basis.

'Tis a very remarkable circumstance that your decree of the 18th Floréal, which gave strength and durability to the tottering bases of public morality, was the signal for a paroxism of fury on the part of the enemies of the Republic; from that epoch it is that date the assassinations, and the new calumnies, more criminal than the assassinations; the tyrants felt that they had a decisive defeat to repair; the solemn proclamation of your veritable principles destroyed in a single day the fruits of several years of intrigues. The tyrants were on the point of triumphing; the French people were placed between famine and Atheism more odious than famine. The people can support hunger, but not crime; the people can sacrifice all except its virtues. Tyranny had not yet outraged human nature so far as to make it ashamed of morality, and to deem depravity a duty; this outrage of outrages was reserved by the vilest of conspirators of the French people in its glory and in its power. Tyranny had but demanded from men their possessions and their lives; these conspirators claimed from us our very consciences. With one hand they presented to us all evils, and with the other snatched from us all hope. Atheism, escorted by all crimes, was spreading over the people mourning and despair; and on the National Representation suspicious contempt and opprobium. A just indignation, compressed by terror, was darkly fermenting in all hearts; an eruption terrible, inevitable, was heaving in the entrails of the volcano, whilst petty philosophers were stupidly playing the game of folly on its summit, with consummate villains for their playmates. Such was the situation of the Republic, that whether the people consented to endure tyranny or should violently shake off the yoke, Liberty was equally lost; for by its reaction it would have given a death-blow to the Republic, and by their patience the people would have rendered themselves unworthy of it. Wherefore of all the prodigies of our Revolution, that which will most astonish posterity is, that we were able to escape this two-edged danger! Immortal thanks to you be rendered! you have saved the country; your decree of the 18th Floréal is itself a revolution; with one and the same blow you smote Atheism and Sacerdotal Despotism, you have anticipated by half-a-century the day of doom for tyrants. You have re-knit and re-wedded to the cause of the Revolution all pure and generous hearts; you have presented it to the world in all the lustre of its celestial beauty. Oh! day for ever blessed! when the whole of the French people arose, as one man, to render to the author of nature the only homage worthy of him! what an affecting congregation of every object that can enchant the regards and hearts of men! Honoured old age! Generous ardour of the children of the country! Pure and simple joy of the youthful citizens! Delicious tears of mothers melting with tender affection! Divine charms of innocence and beauty! Majesty of a great people made happy by the sole sentiment of its force, its glory, and its virtue! Being of Beings! did the day of Creation itself—the day the world issued from thy all-powerful hands, shine with a light more agreeable in thy sight than that day on which, bursting the yoke of crime and error, this nation appeared in thy sight in an attitude worthy thy regards, and its own destinies?

That day had left upon France a profound impression of calm, of happiness, of wisdom, and of goodness. In sight of this sublime reunion of the first people in the world, who would have believed that crime still existed on the Earth? But when the people, in whose presence all private cries disappear, have returned to their domestic fire-sides, the intriguers re-appear on the stage, and the play of charlatans re-commences. It is since that epoch we have seen them agitate and exert themselves with increased audacity, and seek vengeance on all those who had disconcerted the most dangerous of complots. Will it be believed that, in the very midst of public rejoicing, there were men to respond by bursts of fury to the touching acclamations of the people? Will it be believed that the President of the National Convention, while speaking to the assembled people, was insulted by them, and that those men were Representatives of the people? This single trait explains all that has occurred since. The first essay made by the evil-disposed was to try to degrade the great principles you had proclaimed, and to efface the thrilling remembrance of the national fête. Such was the end or purport of the character, and of the solemnity, given to what has been called the *Affair of Catherine Théot.* Malevolence knew well how to turn to account the political conspiracy concealed under the name of some imbecile devotees, and, accordingly, did the conspirators present to public attention only mystic farce, and an inexhaustible subject of indecent or puerile sarcasms. While Paris, and all France, were made to ring with the name of the *Mother of God!* the real conspirators escaped. At the same moment were hatched, and seen to break forth (as if from a shell), a multitude of disgusting pamphlets worthy of *Père Duchêne*, the end of which was to degrade the National Convention, and the Revolutionary Tribunal, to renew religious dissentions, and to open a system of persecution as atrocious, as impolitic, against weak or credulous minds, imbued with some superstitious remembrances. In fact, a great number of peacable citizens, and even known patriots, have been arrested on account of this affair, while the really guilty parties are still conspiring at large; for the plan is to save the guilty, to torment the people, and to multiply the discontented. What means have not been tried, what has been left undone, to arrive at this end? Open predictions of Atheism, sudden acts of violence against religious worship—exactions committed under forms the most indecent—persecutions directed against the people under the pretext of superstition—a system of famine, first through forestalling and monopoly, afterwards by exciting war against all licit commerce and under the pretext of monopoly—the incarceration of patriots—all tended to this end. At the same time the National Treasury suspended payments—the small creditors of the state were reduced to despair by Machiavellian projects; violence and craft were employed to make them subscribe engagements disastrous to their interests, and that in the name of law itself, which disavows the manœuvre. Every occasion to harrass a citizen was seized with avidity, and all vexations were disguised, according to custom, under pretences of the public good. The conspirators were serving the aristocracy, but, at the same time, they disturbed and alarmed it on purpose to swell the number of the disaffected, and to drive the aristocracy to some act of despair against the Revolutionary government. They published that Hérault de Séchelles, Danton, Hébert, &c., were victims of the Committee of Public Safety, and that they must be avenged by the destruction of that Committee. They wished to tamper with the chiefs of the armed force; they persecuted the magistrates of the Commune; and they spoke of recalling Pache to the functions of Mayor. Whilst representatives of the people were openly holding this language—whilst they were persuading their colleagues that they could find no safety but in the destruction of the members of the Committee—whilst jurors of the Revolutionary Tribunal, who had caballed scandalously in favour of the conspirators accused by the Convention, were proclaiming everywhere that it was time to resist oppression, and that there were twenty-nine thousand patriots determined to overthrow the existing Government—whilst all this was going on, here is the language which was being held by the foreign journals, which, at every time of a crisis, have always faithfully announced every plot when just on the eve of its execution, and whose authors would seem to have relations with the conspirators. *"There must, necessarily, be an outbreak for the criminals; in consequence, they have congregated in Paris, at this moment, from all parts of the Republic, the miscreants who were making a desert of it in the times of Hébert and Chaumette"*—meaning those whom you have ordered by your decree to be sent before the Revolutionary Tribunal. They have rendered the Revolutionary government odious in order to prepare its destruction. After having gathered together all its orders, and thrown all the blame of them on the shoulders of those whose destruction they seek, through a dark and universal system of calumny, they were to abolish the Revolutionary Tribunal, or compose it of conspirators; invite the aristocracy to their side; proffer impunity to all the enemies of the country, and exhibit to the people its most zealous defenders as the authors of all the past calamities. *"If we succeed,"* said the conspirators, *"it will be necessary to present, by way of contrast to the present state of things, an extreme indulgence."* This expression comprises the entire conspiracy. What were the crimes laid to the charge of Danton, Fabre, and Desmoulins?—Preaching indulgence for the enemies of the country, and conspiring to assure to them an amnesty fatal to liberty. Now, what would you say if the authors of the complot, I have just spoken of, were of the very party which led Danton, Fabre, and Desmoulins, to the Scaffold? What was the conduct of the first conspirators? Hébert, Ronsin, and Chaumette made it their study to render the Revolutionary government intolerable and ridiculous, whilst Camille Desmoulins attacked it in his satirical writings, and Fabre and Danton were intriguing to defend him. One faction calumniated, whilst the other was preparing pretexts for the calumny. The same system is openly continued at this hour. By what fatality is it that those, who formerly disclaimed against Hébert, are now defending his accomplices? How is it that those who declared themselves the enemies of Danton have become his imitators? How comes it that those who, whilom, were vehement accusers of certain members of the Convention, are found banded to-day, in league with those members, against the patriots whom it is sought to destroy? Base and cowardly miscreants!—not satisfied with taking my life then, they would send me to the tomb covered with ignominy!—and, to satiate them, I must leave behind me in the world only the memory of a tyrant! With what perfidy they have abused my honest confidence!—with what seeming sincerity did they adopt the principles of all good citizens!—with what simplicity of nature, and caressing eagerness, did they tender me their false friendship! But mark the change. All on a sudden their visages are covered with dark clouds; a ferocious joy shown in their eyes! it was the moment when they believed all their measures well taken to overpower and crush me. Disappointed for the moment, they again caress me anew to-day; their language is become more complaisant than ever—more the language of homage than ever before! Three days ago they were ready to denounce me as a Catiline; to-day they give me credit for all the virtues of Cato! Ah! a little more time was wanted to perfect their guilty machinations. How atrocious their purpose!—but how contemptible their means! Judge of them by a single trait. I was momentarily charged, in the absence of one of my colleagues, with the surveillance of an Office of General Police, recently and feebly organized, in the Committee of Public Safety. My brief administration has been limited to about thirty resolves, which I caused to be taken, either to set at liberty patriots suffering persecution, or to make sure of some enemies of the Revolution. Well! will it be believed that this word, General Police, has served as the sole pretext for throwing on my head the responsibility of all the operations of the Committee of General Security, the responsibility of the errors of all the constituted authorities, and of the crimes of all my enemies to boot? There has hardly, perhaps, been one individual arrested, hardly a single citizen vexed or harassed in any way, to whom they have not said of me, *"Behold the author of your calamities; you would be happy and free if he* (Robespierre) *were no more!"* How could I recount or divine all the species of impostures which have been clandestinely insinuated both in the National Convention and elsewhere, in order to render me an object of odium or terror? I will confine myself to the statement of one bare fact; it is that, for now upwards of six weeks, the action and the force of calumny, coupled with my state of utter impotence to effect good, and prevent evil, has forced me to abandon, absolutely and entirely, my functions of member of the Committee of Public Safety; and I swear that, even in that act, I have consulted only my reason, and the good of my country. I prefer my rank or quality of representation of the people to that of member of the Committee of Public Safety; and I place my quality of *man* and *French Citizen* before all.

Well, whatever be the upshot, there is, at least, six weeks that my dictatorship has expired, and during which I have no species of influence whatever on the government. Now, has patriotism been more protected?—the factions more timid?—the country more prosperous and happy? I wish it were so. But my influence on the government! That influence has, at all times, been limited to pleading my country's cause before the Representatives of the Nation, and the Tribunal of Public Reason. I have been permitted to combat the factions which menaced you. I have sought to uproot the system of corruption and disorder they had established, and which I regard as the sole obstacle to the consolidation of the Republic, for I still consider that it can rest securely only on the eternal bases of morality. But all parties were in league against me, and against those who held the same principles; after having vanquished the disdain, the contumelies, and the contradictions, of several of them, I proposed, for your open adoption, the great principles engraven in your hearts, and which have scattered to the winds the complots of the counter-revolutionary Atheists. You consecrated them by your sanction. But it is the fate of principles to be proclaimed by honest men, and applied or thwarted by wicked men. On the very eve of the Festival in honour of the Supreme Being, it was sought to postpone it under a frivolous pretext. Since then, your enemies, and mine, have never ceased to cast ridicule and odium on everything appertaining to religious ideas, and to favour everything that might resuscitate the doctrine of the conspirators you have punished. Only the other day, they began to sweep away the traces of all the monuments made to commemorate certain grand epochs of the Revolution. Those in commemoration of the moral revolution, which avenged you of calumny, and which founded the Republic, are the only ones that have been destroyed. In several of my colleagues I have seen no inclination to observe fixed principles—no disposition to keep the path of justice, or pursue the course marked out between the two sunken rocks, which the enemies of the country have placed in our career. If I must dissemble these truths, bring me the hemlock (of Socrates); my reason, not my heart, is on the point of doubting (the possibility of) that virtuous Republic, of which I had sketched to myself the plan.

Methinks I divine the veritable end of this strange imputation of Dictatorship, I call to mind that Brissot and Roland had already filled Europe with it, at a time when they exercised a power almost without bounds. In what hands are at present our armies, our finances, and the internal administration of the Republic. *In those of the Coalition which persecutes me.* All the friends of principles are without influence. But it is not enough for my enemies to have forced into retirement, through despair of doing good, a man whose surveillance incommoded them, but they must also bereave him of life; his bare existence is an object of terror to them, and they had meditated in darkness, unknown to their colleagues, the project of snatching from him the right of defending the people, by snatching his life. Oh! if my life will satisfy them, I will abandon it to them without regret, I have had experience of the past, I forsee the future. What friend of humanity can wish to survive the moment when he is no longer permitted to serve it or his country and defend oppressed innocence! Why seek to dwell in an order of things where intrigues eternally triumph over truth, where justice is a lie, where the vilest passions or the most ridiculous fears occupy in men's hearts the place of sacred interests of humanity? How endure the torture of seeing that horrible succession of traitors more or less expert in concealing their hideous souls under the veil of virtue, and even of friendship, but who will all leave to posterity the puzzle of deciding which of the enemies of my country was the basest and most atrocious. Seeing the multitude of vices which the torrent of the revolution has rolled up, pell-mell with civic virtues, I have sometimes feared, I confess, being sullied in the eyes of posterity by impure contact with the perverse men who introduced themselves amongst the sincere friends of humanity, and I glory in seeing the fury of the Verres and Catilines of my country draw a deep line of demarcation between themselves and all upright men. I have seen in history all the defenders of liberty, in past ages, overwhelmed by calumny; but their oppressors are dead also! The good and the wicked disappear from the earth, but in very different conditions. Frenchmen! suffer not your enemies to dare to abase your souls, and to enervate your virtues by their desolating doctrine! No, Chaumette, no! *Death is not an eternal sleep!*—Citizens efface from the tombs that maxim engraven by sacrilegious hands, which throws a funeral crape over nature, which disheartens oppressed innocence, and which insults death. Rather engrave upon them this maxim, "Death is the commencement of Immortality."

I promised some time ago to leave behind a will or testament, which should ever after strike terror into the oppressors of mankind. I am now about to publish it from this moment, with the independence which befits the situation I am placed in: *I bequeath to them dread truth and death!*

Representatives of the French people, it is time to resume the pride and loftiness of character which befits you. You are not made to be ruled, but to rule the depositaries of your confidence; the homage they owe you consists not in those vain adulations, in those flattering recitals, lavished on Kings by ambitious ministers, but in telling you the truth, and above all in profound respect for your principles. You have been told that all goes well with the Republic—I deny it. Why did those who, *the day before yesterday,* predicted to you so many and such frightful tempests, behold *yesterday* only a few light transient clouds? Why do those who lately said to you *"I declare to you we are marching over Volcanoes,"* believe to-day that we are marching only on roses? Yesterday they believed in conspiracies; to-day they do not!—Now I declare that I believe in one at this moment.

Those who tell you that the founding of a Republic is so easy an enterprise deceive you, or rather they can deceive nobody. Where are the sage Institutions, where is the plan of regeneration to justify that ambitious language? Have they been wholly and solely occupied with that grand object? What say I? Why have they not sought to proscribe the very man who had prepared them? They praise us to-day, because they think themselves weaker than we; they will accordingly proscribe us again tomorrow should they become the stronger party. In four days, say they, all injustices will be repaired, all wrongs redressed; why then have they been committed with impunity for months? And how are all the authors of our evils to be corrected or cashiered in four days? You are much complimented on your victories, and that with an academic flippancy which would lead one to suppose that they cost our soldiers neither blood nor labour; related in less pompous language they would appear greater. It is not by rhetorical phrases, nor even by the exploits of war, that we shall subdue all Europe; but by the wisdom of our laws, by the majesty of our deliberations, and by the grandeur of our character. What has there been done to turn our military successes to the profit of our principles, to prevent the dangers of victory, or to assure to us its fruits? I warn you to look sharp to Belgium—I warn you that your decree against the English has been constantly violated; and that England, so maltreated by our harangues, is spared by our arms: I warn you that the philanthropic comedies by Dumouriez in Belgium are repeated at the present time; that we are amusing ourselves in planting sterile trees of Liberty in an enemy's country, instead of reaping the fruits of victory, and that the vanquished slaves are favoured at the expense of the victorious Republic. Our enemies retreat, it is true, but it is only to leave us to our intestine divisions. Look, pray, to the end of the Campaign, fear the factions of the interior; fear intrigues favoured by distance and absence in a foreign territory. Division has been sown amongst the generals; the military aristocracy is protected; the faithful generals are persecuted; the military administration is enveloped with a suspicious authority; your decrees have been violated in order to shake off the yoke of a necessary surveillance. These truths are well worth the epigrams you have heard. (*Alluding to Barère's report.*)

Our internal situation is still more critical. A reasonable system of finance is to be created; that which reigns now is mean, prodigal, shifting, intermeddling, devouring, and, in point of fact, absolutely independent of your supreme surveillance. Then, our external relations are absolutely neglected; almost all our agents employed in foreign states, after being decried for their incivism, have openly betrayed the Republic with an audacity unpunished to this hour.

The Revolutionary government merits all your attention. Let it be destroyed to-day, and to-morrow liberty is no more. We must not calumniate it, but restore it to its principle; we must simplify it, diminish the innumerable multitude of its agents—above all, purify them. We must render security to the people, but not to its enemies. Our business is not to impede the march of justice by new forms; the penal law must necessarily have some degree of vagueness; because the actual character of the reigning conspirators being dissimulation and hypocrisy, the justice of the country must be able to seize them under all forms. A single mode of conspiring being left unpunished would render it illusory, and compromise the safety of the country. The guarantee of patriotism lies, therefore, not in the *tardiness* nor in the weakness of the National Justice, but in the principles and integrity of those to whom it is confided, in the good faith of the government, in the frank protection it affords to patriots, and in the energy with which it crushes the aristocracy; in the public spirit, in certain moral and political institutions which, without obstructing the march of justice, offer a safeguard to all good citizens and compress the wicked by their influence on public opinion and on the direction of the revolutionary movement. *The institutions I allude to shall be proposed to you as soon as the conspiracies now impending will permit the friends of liberty to breathe freely.*

Let us guide the revolutionary movement by sage maxims firmly maintained; let us punish severely those who abuse revolutionary principles to the annoyance and persecution of our fellow-citizens. Let us be well convinced that every one of our agents charged with the national surveillance shall, disengaged from all party spirit, resolutely co-operate with us for the triumph of patriotism and the punishment of the guilty. Thus will everything return to order; thus will all march forward to the veritable end of revolutionary institutions, and the terror impressed on crime will be the best guarantee for innocence. But if we have reason to believe that men of vast influence secretly desire the destruction of the revolutionary government—that they incline to indulgence rather than to justice; if they employ corrupt agents; if they calumniate to-day the only authority that imposes on the enemies of liberty, and retract their words to-morrow in order to intrigue *de novo,* as before; if, instead of rendering liberty to the patriots, they render it, without distinction, to conspirators—then all the intriguers league together to calumniate the patriots, and the patriots are oppressed. It is to all these causes we are to impute the abuses I complain of, and not to the revolutionary government; for there is no government which would not be insupportable under the same conditions. The revolutionary government has saved the country: we must save this government itself from all the sunken rocks which environ it. It would be most perverse reasoning to conclude that it ought to be destroyed, simply because the enemies of the public good have first paralysed, and now labour to corrupt it. 'Tis a strange mode of protecting the patriots, to set counter-revolutionists at liberty, and make knaves triumph! 'Tis the terror of crime that makes the security of innocence.

For the rest, I am far from imputing the abuses to the majority of those to whom you have given your confidence. The majority is itself paralysed and betrayed; intrigue and foreign influence triumph! There is concealment, there is dissimulation, there is deception; *there is, therefore, a conspiracy!* The parties were audacious; they meditated a grand act of oppression; they surrounded themselves with an armed force, to crush public opinion after having exasperated it; they now seek to seduce the public functionaries, whose fidelity they dread, and they incessantly persecute the friends of liberty. *There exists, therefore, a conspiracy!* They suddenly become supple, and even flattering; they spread dark and dangerous insinuations against Paris; they seek to lull public opinion asleep; they calumniate the people; they erect civic solicitude, or the natural apprehensions of patriotism, into a crime; they do not send away the deserters, the prisoners of war, the counter-revolutionists of all sorts, who are congregated in Paris; and they are sending away the cannoniers, they are disarming the citizens, they are intriguing in the army; in short, they are trying to seize and take possession of everything. *There is, therefore, a conspiracy!* Within the last few days, they sought to throw you on a false scent touching the conspiracy; to-day they deny it, and 'tis even a crime to believe in it. One day they sound the note of alarm, the next they encourage you to repose and security! The same alternation of hopes and fears is repeated anew, and so the game goes on. *There you have the veritable conspiracy! It stands confessed!*

The counter-revolution reigns in the Finance department. It bears altogether on a system of counter-revolutionary innovation, disguised under the exterior of patriotism. It has for its end to foment stock-jobbing, to shake public credit by dishonouring French loyalty, to favour the rich creditors of the state, to ruin and drive to despair the poor ones, to multiply the discontented, *to despoil the people of the National property,* and to bring about by insensible degrees the ruin of the public fortune.

Who are the supreme Administrators of our Finances? Brissotins, Feuillants, Aristocrats, and notorious knaves; they are your Cambons, Mallarmés, Ramels—the companions and successors of Chabot, Fabre d'Églantine, and Julien (de Toulouse). To palliate their pernicious designs, they have taken it into their heads, of late, to secure the adhesion of the Committee of Public Safety to their acts, because they are pretty sure that this Committee, distracted by the multiplicity and magnitude of its labours, would adopt in confidence (without examination), as has sometimes happened, all the projects of Cambon. 'Tis a new stratagem hit upon, to multiply the number of the enemies of the Committee, whose destruction is the principal aim of all the conspiracies. The National Treasury, directed by a counter-revolutionary hypocrite named Lhermina, seconds their designs to a nicety by the plan it has adopted, by throwing impediments in the way of all urgent demands and disbursements, under pretext of a scrupulous adherence to forms, of not paying anybody, except aristocrats, and of tormenting and harassing the less easy class of citizens by refusals, by delays, and oftentimes by odious provocations.

The counter-revolution is in every department of our political economy. The conspirators have precipitated us, in despite of ourselves, into violent measures, which only their own crimes have rendered necessary, and reduced the Republic to the most frightful state of scarcity and famine—a famine which would have starved it to death, but for the concurrence of events the most providential and unexpected. This system was the work of Foreign influence, which proposed it, through the venal intermediary of the Chabots, Lulliers, Héberts, and so many other miscreants. Believe me, we need every effort of genius to restore the Republic to that mild and natural regime which alone can ensure abundance; and this work is not yet begun. Just call to mind all the crimes lavished to realize the *Famine-compact,* engendered by the infernal genius of England. To save us from that scourge, we absolutely needed two miracles, equally unexpected. The first was the safe return of our Convoy, sold to England (by traitors) before its departure from America, and which the Cabinet of London counted as a sure prize; and the abundant and premature harvest spontaneously given us by nature: the other was the sublime patience of the people, who have endured starvation itself to conserve its liberty. There still remains for us to surmount the deficiency of hands, of horses, and vehicles (which will delay the harvesting of the crops, and the culture of the soil), and all the manœvres set on foot last year by our enemies, and which they will not fail to renew.

The counter-revolutionists have flocked here in crowds to join their accomplices, and defend their patrons by dint of intrigues and crimes. They count upon the counter-revolutionary prisoners, on the gentry of the Vendée, and on the deserters and prisoners of war who, according to all accounts, have been for some time escaping in crowds to repair to Paris, as I have already repeatedly denounced in vain to the Committee of Public Safety; finally, they count upon the aristocracy, which is secretly conspiring around us and in the midst of us. Their plan of proceeding will be this:—*They will get up violent discussions in the National Convention; the traitors hitherto concealed under hypocritical outward appearances will fling off the mask; the conspirators will accuse their accusers, and make a lavish use of all the stratagens formerly put in practice by Brissot to smother the voice of truth. If they cannot master the Convention by this means, they will divide it into two parties; and thus a vast field will be opened to calumny and intrigue. If they master it (though but for a moment), they will accuse of despotism and of resistance to the national authority those who will combat with energy their criminal league; the cries of oppressed innocence—the manly accents of outraged liberty—will be denounced as evidences of a dangerous influence or of personal ambition; you will fancy yourselves brought once more under the knife of the old conspirators. The people will be indignant; they will be called "a faction," and the real guilty faction will continue to goad and exasperate them. It will strive to sever the Convention from the people; in fine, by dint of a combination of treasonable projects, they hope to involve the Republic in disorders, in the midst of which they will bring in the aristocracy, with all their accomplices, to massacre the patriots, and re-establish the old Tyranny!* There is *part the first* of their plan of conspiracy. And to whom must these calamities be imputed? To ourselves; to our own base weakness and indulgence for crime, and to our culpable abandonment of the principles proclaimed by ourselves. Let us not deceive ourselves. To found an immense Republic on the basis of reason and equality—to bind together by an enduring chain all the parts of this immense empire—is not an enterprise which levity or fickleness can consummate: it is the masterpiece of virtue and human reason, and as such requires a master-hand. 'Tis in the very nature of a great revolution to vomit forth factions of all sorts. How are you to repress them, but by constantly keeping all the passions in subjection to justice? You have no other guarantee for liberty than the rigid observance of the principles and universal morality you have proclaimed. If reason does not reign, crime and ambition must reign. Without it, victory is but a means of ambition, and a danger to liberty itself,—a fatal pretext, of which intrigue makes use to lull patriotism to sleep on the brink of a precipice. Without it, what signifies victory itself? Of what use or value is victory at all? It only serves to arm ambition, lull patriotism to sleep, awaken pride, and to dig with glittering hands the tomb of the Republic. What boots it that our armies chase before them the armed satellites of Kings, if we recede before the vices which destroy public liberty? What boots it to conquer Kings, if we are vanquished by the vices which bring back King-craft and Tyranny? Then what steps have we taken of late to make head against them? We have proclaimed great prizes! What is there that has been left undone to protect them amongst us? What have we done for some time past to destroy them? Nothing! Do they not raise their heads in insolent contempt of us, and menace virtue with impunity? Nothing, I repeat; for the government has receded before the factions, and those factions find protectors among the very depositories of the public authority. Let us expect, therefore, all manner of evils, since we abandon to them the reigns of empire. In the career we have entered upon, to halt before its termination is to perish; and we have shamefully retrograded! You have ordained the punishment of some miscreants, the authors of our calamities; they dare to resist the justice of the nation, and we sacrifice to them the destinies of the country and of humanity! Let us, therefore, expect all the scourges and tribulations that those restless, because unpunished, factions can draw down upon us. In the midst of so many fiery passions, and in so vast an empire, the tyrants, whose armies I see fugitive, but not enveloped, not exterminated, are retiring to leave you a prey to your intestine dissensions, which they kindle themselves, and to an army of criminal agents whom you cannot even perceive. Let but the reins of the government slacken a moment in your hands, and you will see them seized by military despotism; and you will see the chiefs of the rival factions overthrow the degraded National Representation. An age of civil war and calamities will desolate our country, and we shall perish for not having availed ourselves of a favourite moment marked in the history of man to found the temple of Liberty. We shall abandon our country to an age of calamities, and instead of blessings, the maledictions of posterity will attach to our memory, which might and ought to be dear to the human race! We shall not even have the merit of having undertaken great things from virtuous motives; we shall be confounded with the unworthy delegates of the people, who have dishonoured the National Representation, and we shall participate in their crimes for having suffered them to go unpunished. Immortality lay open before us—we shall perish with ignominy; The good citizens will perish; the wicked will perish likewise; for would an outraged and victorious people suffer them to enjoy in peace the fruits of their crimes? Would not the tyrants themselves break these vile instruments? What justice have we done to the oppressors of the people? What patriots have we avenged? Oppressed, though they have been, by the most odious abuses of the National Authority? Alas! where are the patriots that have even been able to make heard with impunity the voice of oppressed innocence? Have not the men of guilt established this frightful principle, that to denounce a faithless representative, is to conspire against the National Representation? The only answer of the oppressor to the oppressed men's complaints, is incarceration and fresh outrages! Are the departments, however, where these crimes have been committed, ignorant of them, because we forget, or neglect them? And do not the complaints which we refuse to hear reverberate with augmented force in the constrained hearts of the unhappy citizens? It is so easy and so sweet to be just! Why devote ourselves to the opprobrium of culprits by tolerating them? But can we stand still, if we would? Will not the abuses, if tolerated, go on increasing? Will not the culprits if left unpunished, hurry on from crimes to crimes? Are we willing to share in so much infamy, and doom ourselves to the fearful lot of oppressors of the people? What claims or titles have they to oppose to even the meanest tyrants? One faction would pardon another faction; the miscreants would soon avenge the world by cutting each other's throat, and if they escaped man's justice, or their own fury, would they escape eternal justice, which they have outraged by the most horrible of all offences?

For myself, whose existence appears to the enemies of my country an obstacle to their odious projects, I willingly consent to make them the sacrifice of it, if their frightful empire is still to endure. Oh! who could desire any longer to behold that horrible succession of traitors more or less adroit in concealing their hideous souls under a mask of virtue, up to the very moment their crime seemed ripe for execution—and who will all leave to posterity the puzzle to decide which of the enemies of my country was the most base and atrocious? Were it to be proposed here to pronounce an amnesty in favour of the perfidious deputies, and to put every representative's crimes under the safe-guard of a decree, red blushes of shame would cover the face of every man of us; but to throw upon the shoulders of faithful representatives, the responsibility of denouncing the crimes, and, nevertheless to afterwards abandon those faithful representatives to the rage of an insolent league, for daring to do their duty! is not that a still more revolting disorder? *It is more than protecting crime, it is immolating virtue to it!*

Seeing the multitude of vices which the torrent of the revolution has rolled along pell-mell with the virtues of civism, I have sometimes shuddered with the fear of being sullied in the eyes of posterity, by the impure vicinage of those perverse men who have mixed themselves up, in our ranks, with the sincere champions of humanity. But the defeat of rival factions has, as it were, emancipated all the vices. They fancy they have no more to do now, than to divide the country amongst them, as so much booty, instead of rendering it free and prosperous; and I thank them in that their fury against all who oppose their projects, has drawn a deep line of demarcation between them, and all honest men. But the Verres and Catilines of France, already think themselves advanced far in the career of crime, to expose on *the tribune of harangues,* the head of their accuser. Well! I promised not long ago, to leave to my fellow-citizens a testament of dread import for the oppressors of the people. In fulfilment of that promise, *I bequeath to them* (the oppressors) *from this moment, opprobrium, and death!* I feel it is easy for the leagued tyrants of the world to overwhelm a single man; but I know also what are the duties of a man who can die in defending the cause of the human race. I have seen in history all the defenders of liberty overwhelmed by fortune or calumny; but soon after their oppressors and their assassins perished likewise. The good and the wicked, the tyrants and the friends of liberty, disappear alike from the earth, but on very different conditions. Frenchmen! suffer not your enemies to try to abase your souls and to enervate your virtues by a fatal doctrine. No! Chaumette, no! Fouché—death is not an eternal sleep! Citizens efface from the tombs that impious maxim, which casts a funeral crape over nature, and which insults death; rather engrave upon them this, *"Death is the commencement of Immortality."*

People! remember that if, in the Republic, justice does not reign with an absolute power, and if this word does not signify the love of equality, and of countries, liberty is but an empty sound! People! whom thy tyrants fear, whom they flatter, and whom they despise; thou, acknowledged to be sovereign, art always treated as slaves! bear in mind that, wherever justice does not reign, it is the passions of your magistrates (that *do reign*), and that the people has changed its chains, but not its destinies! Remember that there exists in thy bosom a leagued horde of knaves, which struggles against public virtue—which has more influence than thyself over thy own affairs—which dreads thee, and flatters thee, in mass, but proscribes thee, in detail, in the person of every public man faithful to thy interests, in the person of all good citizens! Call to mind that, far from sacrificing this handful of knaves to thy happiness, thy enemies wish to sacrifice thee to this handful of knaves, the authors of all our evils, and the sole obstacles to public prosperity!

Know that every man who will stand up to defend your cause, and public morals, will be overwhelmed with wanton insults, and proscribed by the knaves; know that every friend of Liberty will be ever placed between a duty and a calumny; that those who cannot be accused of having betrayed thee, will be accused of ambition; that the influence of probity and of principles will be compared to the force of tyranny, and to the violence of factions; that thy confidence and thy esteem will be titles, or warrants, of proscription for thy friends; that the cries of oppressed patriotism will be called cries of sedition; and that, not daring to attack thyself in mass, thou wilt be proscribed, in detail, in the persons of all good citizens, until men of ambition have organized their tyranny! Such is the empire of the tyrants armed against us, such is the influence of their league with all the men of corruption ever forward to serve them. Thus, then, the villains would impose it as law upon us, to betray the people, under pain of being dubbed Dictators. Shall we subscribe to this law? No! let us defend the people, at the risk of losing its esteem; let the villains speed to the scaffold by the road of crime, and we (if it must be) by that of virtue!

Shall we say that all is well? Shall we continue to praise, by habit or by practice, what is bad? Yes! if we would destroy our country! Shall we reveal the hidden abuses? Shall we denounce the traitors? If we do, we shall be told that we are shaking the constituted authorities, that we want to acquire influence for ourselves at their expense. What shall we do then? Our *Duty*. What can be objected against him who wishes to speak the truth, and who consents to die for it (the truth). Let us declare then that there exists a conspiracy against public liberty; that it owes its force to a criminal coalition, which intrigues in the very bosom of the Convention; that this coalition has accomplices in the Committee on General Security, and in the offices of this Committee, which they control; that the enemies of the Republic have opposed this Committee to the Committee of Public Safety, and thus constituted two governments; that members of the Committee of Public Safety have entered into this complot; that the coalition thus formed seeks to destroy the Patriots and the country. What is the remedy for this evil? To punish the traitors, to renovate the offices of the Committee on General Security, to purify this Committee itself, and make it subordinate to the Committee of Public Safety; to purify the Committee of Public Safety itself; to constitute the unity of the Government under the supreme authority of the National Convention, which is the centre and the judge, and thus crush all factions under the weight of the National Authority, in order to raise upon their ruins the power of justice and Liberty. Such are the principles. If 'tis impossible to reclaim them without passing for an ambitious man, then must I conclude that principles are proscribed, and that Tyranny reigns amongst us, but not that I ought to be silent on the fact; for what can be objected to a man who has reason on his side, and who is ready to die for his country? I am made to combat crime, not to govern it. The time is not yet arrived for honest men to serve the country with impunity; the defenders of liberty will be no better than proscribed so long as the hordes of cheats and traitors shall be in the ascendant."

Press Report

Robespierre delivered a long discourse on the villainous factions, heirs of the Héberts, the Chaumettes, *etc.,* that strain in every way to sow division among the representatives of the people. He uttered some strong truths on the present state of things and frankly unmasked the leaders of this new plot: we shall return to this interesting article. His discourse was loudly applauded and the majority of the assembly demanded that it be printed.

Journal de la Montagne, 9 Thermidor.

National Convention

8 Thermidor [26 July]

Collot d'Herbois presiding:

Robespierre, who has not appeared in the assembly for a long time, mounts the tribune and begins to speak.

He reads a long discourse in which he begins by vaunting his virtue. He complains of being slandered and singles out as enemies of the people all those who seem to him to be opposed to his projects. He then runs down all the government's operations; he declaims successively against the committees on Public Safety, on General Security, and on Finance. Without complaining specifically of the civic opposition raised by this last committee against his projects, he tries to include it in the proscription by accusing it of having "counter-revolutionized" the finances of the Republic.

He then claims that the patriots are oppressed. "Why these discourses," he says, "which are made to you about the success of the Armies? Dumouriez's system is followed in Belgium; sterile trees of liberty are planted; the gunners are being taken further away from Paris, a camp has been formed which could become dangerous," etc.

He adds that people have been trying to deceive us about the situation of the Republic; finally he adds that he will propose the only measures suitable for saving the fatherland.

LECOINTRE DE VERSAILLES: I ask that the speech be printed.

BOURDON DE L'OISE: I oppose printing it. The speech contains matters serious enough to warrant being examined; there may be errors as well as truth in it and it would be prudent for the Convention to send it up to be examined by the two committees of Public Safety and General Security before ordering the printing.

BARÈRE: And I also esteem above all the quality of man and that of the French citizen; I speak here as an individual and not as a member of the Committee; I insist on the printing of the discourse because in a free country there is no truth which ought to be hidden; the light should not be placed under a bushel and there is no assertion which cannot be attacked and examined; it is for this reason that you are the National Convention, and I do not doubt that all our colleagues will insist on the printing.

COUTHON: I add to the proposal for the printing an amendment which seems very unimportant but which I think is very important; all of France, down to the tiniest commune, must know that there are

Le Moniteur universel, XXI, 329-31 (Edition of 11 Thermidor).

men here who have the courage to tell the entire truth; France must know that the great majority of the Convention knows how to listen to it and take it into consideration. I demand not only that this discourse be printed but that it also be sent to all the communes of the Republic; and when someone asked that it be sent to be examined by the two committees, that was an outrage against the National Convention: for it knows how to feel and it knows how to judge.

I am very happy to find this opportunity to pour out my heart. For some time this abominable maneuver of spreading the rumor that several members of the Committee of Public Safety seek to hinder the revolution has been joined with the system of slandering the most faithful representatives of the cause of the people, the oldest servants of the revolution; I am one of those who have spoken against several men because I have regarded them as immoral and unworthy of sitting in this hall. I will repeat here what I said then; if I thought that I had contributed to the loss of a single person, I would immolate myself out of sorrow.

The Convention adopts Couthon's proposal.

VADIER: I have heard with sorrow Robespierre saying that the report concerning a girl named Catherine Théot [A religious visionary who expected to be the mother of a new Messiah, and whose prosecution before the Revolutionary Tribunal was pressed by Vadier and prevented by Robespierre, whom the Théotists had identified as a redeemer] seemed to be connected only with a ridiculous farce of mysticism, that she was a woman to be scorned.

ROBESPIERRE: I did not say that.

CAMBON: I demand to speak also . . . (*He dashes to the tribune.*) Before being dishonored, I will speak to France. . . .

THE PRESIDENT: Vadier has the floor.

VADIER: I will speak with the calm which accompanies virtue. Robespierre has said that this report, by airing a ridiculous travesty, could harm the Republic. This report has been made with the tone of ridicule which is proper for foiling fanaticism. I have since gathered new information, immense documents; you will see that this conspiracy is one of the most widespread; you will see that Pitt conspires here; you will see that this woman had intimate relations with the former Duchess of Bourbon, with Bergasse, and all the *illuminés*.

I will place this conspiracy in a more imposing framework; but this is a lengthy job because it is connected with all the plots; and we will see figuring there all the conspirators, old and new.

I have something else to say about Robespierre's speech. The operations of the Committee on General Security have always borne the stamp of the justice and severity necessary for repressing the aristocracy; justice and severity are contained in the decrees it has ordered, which can be printed and so judged. If we have had agents who were corrupt, who put terror into the souls of the patriots, the Committee has punished them in the measure which was proper, and the heads of several have fallen under the blade of the law.

This is what our conduct has been, and here is the proof of it: the popular commissions, established in concert with the two Committees, have already judged seven to eight hundred affairs; how many of those do you think involved patriots? They are in proportion of one to eighty. That is indeed the proof that it is not patriotism which has been oppressed but aristocracy which has been justly prosecuted.

That is what I ought to say for the justification of the Committee on General Security, which has never been at odds with the Committee of Public Safety. There may have been some explanations made, but never have they diminished in any way the esteem and mutual confidence which the two committees bear each other.

CAMBON: And I also ask to speak. I present myself in the lists: although I have never tried to form a party around me, Robespierre has just said that the last decree on finances had been calculated in such a way as to augment the number of malcontents. It would perhaps be easy to make him admit that he has done nothing to become acquainted with these calculations, but I will content myself with repulsing an attack from which my conduct, known since the beginning of the revolution, ought perhaps to preserve me.

I will not come armed with polemic writings: the truth is clear; I will answer with the facts.

The last decree on annuities respects independent incomes from 1,500 to 10,500 livres, depending on age; it does not in the least deprive anyone of the income necessary at any age; we therefore limited ourselves to reforming abuses.

I know that the speculators have an interest in attacking this operation. It is proved by a table which I will put under the eyes of the assembly, that the stockjobbers are interested in this matter of *22 millions worth of annuities* and it is they only whom we wanted to attack. It is therefore not surprising that they have hunted for support to avoid the reform; the stockjobbers would be able even to furnish the materials to make speeches; but firm at my post, I will always have the courage to denounce all that seems contrary to the national interest.

If I had wished to serve intrigues, it would perhaps have been easy for me, under critical circumstances, to stir up dissatisfied persons who would be useful to the party which I could have embraced; but, foreign to all factions, I have denounced them each in turn, when they have tried to attack the public weal: completely devoted to my country, I have known only my duty, and I will serve only liberty. Also all the parties have always found me in their way, opposing to their ambition the barrier of surveillance, and finally, no one has neglected to try to discover just how far my firmness goes, and to shake it. I have scorned all attacks; I have carried everything to the Convention. It is time to tell the whole truth: a single man has paralyzed the will of the National Convention; it is the man who has just made the speech; it is Robespierre, judge for yourselves. (*Applause.*)

ROBESPIERRE: I ask permission to answer one word only to this indictment which seems to me as unintelligible as extraordinary. Cambon claims that I paralyze the will of the Convention in financial matters. If there is something which does not lie within my powers, it is to paralyze the Convention, above all in financial matters. Never have I been involved with that issue: but by general considerations of principle, I have thought I saw that Cambon's ideas on finance are not as favorable to the success of the revolution as he thinks. That is my opinion; I have dared to express it; I do not think that that is a crime.

Cambon says that his decree has been attacked by the stockjobbers; that may be true; I do not know what advantage they can draw from it; I don't concern myself with it. But without attacking Cambon's intentions, I persist in saying that the result of his decree is to desolate poor citizens.

CAMBON: That is false. *We have already received 65,000 bonds, and they have paid 25 millions worth of income in a month and a half.*

BILLAUD-VARENNE: The day has come to bring to light all the truth. The more Robespierre's speech inculpates the Committee, the more scrupulously the Convention ought to examine it before decreeing that it be sent to the communes. I ask that the two Committees make public their conduct. It is said that Paris has been stripped of cannons and gunners; if Robespierre had not abandoned the Committee for the past six weeks, he would know. . . .

ROBESPIERRE: It is not the Committee as a whole that I attack. To avoid these discussions, I demand from the Convention the liberty to state my opinion (*A number of members rising simultaneously:* We all demand it!)

BILLAUD-VARENNE: I declare that the Convention and public opinion have been taken advantage of about the gunners; there exists a decree which orders that of the forty-eight companies of gunners of Paris, half will always be in this commune. Well, at this moment there are thirty-three. It is with such ideas that they deceive the people and that they decree, as happened several days ago, that the powder supplies of the army of the North were extremely short. Robespierre was right: we must tear the mask off whatever face it happens to cover; and if it is true that we do not enjoy freedom of opinion, I prefer my corpse to serve as a throne for some ambitious man than to become by my silence the accomplice of his crimes. I demand referral to the two committees.

PANIS: I reproach Robespierre for having expelled whatever Jacobins he liked. I wish that he had no more influence than anyone else; I wish that he would tell if he has proscribed our heads, whether mine is on the list which he has drawn up. I wish that Couthon would explain about the six members whom he is prosecuting.

It is time that I pour out my broken heart: I have been overwhelmed with slanders. I have not earned enough during the revolution to give my son a saber with which to fight on the frontiers, or a skirt for my daughters, and yet I am described as a scoundrel, as a plunderer, as a man dripping with the blood of the prisons, I who have such a sensitive and tender soul.

Here is another fact which proves how necessary the explanation which I am demanding of Robespierre is. A man approaches me at the Jacobin club and says to me, "You are a good man; you have saved the fatherland." "I do not have the honor of knowing you." "I know you well, you are in the first batch." "What?" "Your head has been demanded." "My head! I who am one of the best patriots!" He did not want to tell me any more. Since then I have learned from all sides that the fact is true and that it was Robespierre who made the list. I demand that he explain himself with regard to this as well as on Fouché's account. (*Applause.*)

ROBESPIERRE: I ask the floor. My views are independent, a retraction which is not in my heart will never be extracted from me; throwing down my shield I have presented myself unarmed to my enemies; I have flattered no one, I do not fear anyone. I have slandered no one.

PANIS: And Fouché?

ROBESPIERRE: People talk to me of Fouché, I do not wish to concern myself with him right now; I am setting all that aside; I will listen only to my duty; I do not wish the support of the friendship of anyone;

I am not trying in the least to form a party about me; it is therefore not a question of asking me to exonerate this or that. I have done my duty; it is up to others to do theirs.

BENTABOLE: To send Robespierre's speech out seems very dangerous to me: The Convention would appear, in decreeing this dispatch, to approve its principles, and would make itself responsible for movements which the frenzy into which it will throw the people might occasion.

COUTHON: In asking for the dispatch to the communes, I wanted the National Convention, which has already decreed the printing of the speech, to make the entire Republic the judge of it, not just one section of the people.

CHARLIER: I insist on delaying the dispatch of the speech; it contains principles which it seems to me merit the most careful examination by the Committees. I demand that it be sent to them.

ROBESPIERRE: What! I have the courage to come depose in the bosom of the Convention truths which I believe necessary to the welfare of the fatherland, and you would send my speech to be examined by the members whom I accuse! *(Murmuring.)*

CHARLIER: When one boasts of having the courage of virtue, one must have the courage of truth. Name those whom you accuse! (*Applause.*)

SEVERAL VOICES: Yes, yes, name them!

ROBESPIERRE: I persist in what I have said, and I declare that I do not take any part in any decision which might prevent the dispatch of my speech.

AMAR: The speech of Robespierre indicts the two committees. Either the opinion which he has about several members has a bearing on public affairs or it is a private opinion. If it bears on public affairs he must give the names; the public interest will not stand for any circumspection; but if these are only private sentiments, a man must not put himself in the place of every man; the National Convention should not be troubled by the interests of a man's wounded vanity. If he has some reproaches to make, let him make them; let our political life be examined, it is without reproach; let the record be consulted, one will see that we have always voted in the sense of liberty; let people remember our opinions and they will be convinced that we have never spoken except in support of the rights of the people. It is in those terms that we ask to be judged.

THIRION: Robespierre's speech presents to you accusers and accused, all of whom are our colleagues, and to whom you owe equal justice. If you send the accusing speech to the communes, you are not exercising an impartial justice, for you prejudge by that very act in favor of the accusation. *(Applause.)* I do not know how Robespierre alone can claim to be right against many. The presumption must be in favor of the Committees. *(New applause.)* I ask therefore a decree which so shocks your conscience be referred [back to the Committees].

BARÈRE: It is time to end this discussion which can only benefit Pitt and the Duke of York. I have proposed the printing of Robespierre's speech because my opinion is that in a free country one should publish everything. It is not at all dangerous to liberty, especially when one knows the French people. If for forty days Robespierre had followed the activities of the Committee, he would have suppressed his speech. The word accused must be erased from all of your thoughts. It is not up to us to appear in the area. We will answer to this declamation by the victories of the armies, by the measures which we will take against the conspirators, by those which we will take in favor of patriots, and finally by polemic writings if it is necessary.

BRÉARD: If the Convention in decreeing the dispatch of this speech, attaches itself to it, it will give it an influence which might become dangerous. It is a great trial to be judged by the Convention itself. I ask therefore that the Convention refer the decree of the dispatch.

The referral of the decree is pronounced. [The Convention voted to print the speech but to distribute it only to its members.]

Jacobin Club

8 Thermidor, Evening [26 July]

At the beginning of the meeting, the Society was disturbed by a very violent tumult: Billaud-Varenne, Collot d'Herbois, and Robespierre all demanded the right to speak; a great number of voices forcefully took the side of Collot d'Herbois; they said that Robespierre had no right at all to preference. But those who sided with Collot d'Herbois found themselves in a *very small* minority, and, lacking the favor of the majority and hearing the murmuring, they were forced to bow. Robespierre rose to speak:

This report on the meeting of the Jacobin club on 8 Thermidor is taken from *Correspondence politique de Paris et des départements,* No. 90, which was printed in *Annales historiques de la Révolution française* (1924), pp. 498-501.

"From the turmoil of this assembly it is easy to perceive that it is not unaware of what happened this morning at the Convention; it is easy to see that factious persons among us fear to be unveiled in the presence of the people."

Javogues cried: "We are neither factious individuals nor conspirators, but we do not want the Jacobins to be dominated by one man."

"For that," continued Robespierre, "I thank you—for revealing yourself in such a pronounced manner and for permitting me to better know my enemies and those of the fatherland."

After this preamble, Robespierre read the speech he had delivered that morning at the Convention. It had a prodigious effect. The truth of the facts it presented were beyond doubt. It was interrupted often and crowned by universal applause, general enthusiasm, and repeated acclamations. The galleries especially expressed their indignation at that portion of the assembly which seemed not to welcome the speech.

In the middle of this expression of favor and indignation on the part of the people, Dumas, president of the Revolutionary Tribunal, climbed to the rostrum. He said that there was no doubt a conspiracy existed, that the government was counter-revolutionary and then, addressing himself to those who at the beginning of the meeting had disputed Robespierre's right to speak, he said: "It is strange that men who for several months now have kept their silence demand today the right to speak, in order no doubt to oppose the exposure of some startling truths which Robespierre has held back. It is easy to recognize in these people the heirs of Hébert and Danton; they will also, I prophesy, inherit the fate of these conspirators."

Collot d'Herbois followed next to the rostrum where he was greeted by jeers and shouts of disfavor and hostility. In vain, he reminded the audience of the services he had rendered the revolution; in vain he recalled the dangers he had run, but the more he talked the more the storm of popular indignation thundered around him.

Billaud-Varenne shuddered: "I no longer recognize Jacobins," he cried, "who insult a representative of the people that reminds them how close he had come to perishing as a result of his patriotism."

The threats, cries, and tumult of the audience prevented him from speaking further. Collot d'Herbois began to speak with great energy; he needed the full force of his lungs to make heard his suspicions about Robespierre's intentions, arguing that the latter should have communicated the denunciations in his speech to the government before delivering it to the people, that such an action would have been called for only if the two committees had resisted correcting their error, and that, finally, Robespierre would have deleted many things from his speech if he had not been absent from the Committee of Public Safety for the last six weeks. He finished by urging that Robespierre's speech be placed before the Society for discussion, close examination, and debate.

This proposal was very badly received. Collot d'Herbois was obliged to descend from the rostrum. His emotion, his look, his gestures all revealed the most profound grief and the most pervasive despair. In vain Billaud-Varenne energetically demanded the right to speak; in vain he faced the cries of the galleries and the murmuring of the Society, gazing at them with a look of defiance and fury. He could only speak with the aid of brusque and menacing gestures. Some of his words, nevertheless, succeeded in being heard above the cries and the fracas of "To the guillotine, to the guillotine!" coming from the crowd. He spoke of new Jacobins, of the errors into which Robespierre had led them, and he seconded the motion of Collot d'Herbois.

A horrible noise erupted throughout the hall, but when the voice of Couthon was heard asking for the right to speak, a deep silence mixed with applause and cries of approval followed the noise. "Citizens," he said, "I am convinced of the truth of the facts enunciated by Robespierre."—"And we also!" replied a thousand voices. "But," continued Couthon, "I do not believe that it is possible to throw enough light on the subject, for this is the greatest conspiracy that has taken place up to the present." "Yes! Yes," shouted the crowd. "Without a doubt," said Couthon, "there are some pure men on the Committees, but it is also certain that there are some rotten ones on the same committees. Well then! I too demand a discussion, not of Robespierre's speech, however, but of the conspiracy. We have seen them appear at the rostrum, these conspirators; we will examine them, we will watch their embarrassment, we will listen to their vacillating replies, they will turn pale in the presence of the people, they will be convicted and they will perish."

Expressions of general agreement burst forth throughout the hall. Couthon's motion was put to a vote and adopted. The applause redoubled, hats were waved in the air, everyone in the hall and in the galleries was standing and a single cry resounded from all parts of the hall: "Conspirators to the guillotine!" However, a part of the Society remained still in the middle of this demonstration of enthusiasm. Their immobility reanimated the indignation of the people, who threatened, who thundered, and who renewed their threats with fury. A part of the Society cried out that the people had become fanatical, that oppression had reached its height.

A few members and Sijas among others finished the session by giving new details on the conspiracy.

Voulland's Correspondence

Paris, this 9th Thermidor, Year II of
the One and Indivisible Republic

Voulland, Citizen of the Commune of Uzès, Representative of the People to the National Convention
To his fellow-citizens, the members of the administration of the District of Uzès

It was in very good faith, brothers and friends, that I believed I could write you yesterday that all the clouds malevolence had for several days been trying to pile up around the two government committees had finally been dissipated. I believed it as sincerely as I wished it. I felt all the more pleasure in telling you because I thought it would never be necessary to go into detail about the cause and development of this unfortunate event. Robespierre's speech, thrown into the midst of the Convention yesterday, made a most painful impression. I shall not undertake to describe it. I have neither the courage nor the means. The two committees spent the night working out a just and legitimate defense. I shall not anticipate it here, but will confine myself to telling you that what I see in everything that is happening in the two committees adds up to petty wounded vanities that have grown bitter with time, and whose explosion was terrible. Robespierre, to borrow his own words, threw down the gauntlet to the two committees and attacked them cruelly. The injuries and complaints he imputes to them have been referred back to be answered. I think the response will be easy and peremptory: no one on either of the two committees has ever conspired against the Republic, nor against any individual devoted to its interests. Robespierre was singularly deceived when he let himself be persuaded that a plan to ruin him or to accuse him had been conceived and that the moment was approaching to execute it.

I ask you, brothers and friends, you who have known me since birth, do you think me capable of joining in any plot to disturb the state or to deprive it of any athlete useful to its defense? No, I swear to you that I have never had even the idea of any kind of conspiracy. I am con-

Annales historiques de la Révolution française, IV (1927), 66–77.

vinced that it never crossed the mind of any of my colleagues either. I want this day to serve a useful purpose to Liberty; it will not have been in vain if it can enlighten us and bring about a meeting of minds.

I close with this desire in my heart and I limit myself to urging you, in the name of the nation, to follow calmly the debates that will take place within the Convention. Do not miss any relevant fact and do not take sides until you are able to make out where truth and justice lie.

I embrace you, if not with the same pleasure at least with the same confidence and tranquility as yesterday, because my conscience is clear. Whatever may happen to me, I shall be, as I believe I have never ceased to be, worthy of your esteem and of the position with which your choice has honored me.

Adieu, I embrace you from the bottom of my heart, as pure as the light of the day that shines on us.

Salut et Fraternité,

Voulland

V
THE NINTH OF THERMIDOR

Introduction

The problem presented by the documents in this section is a straightforward one. The reader is given the opportunity to reconstruct the course of events from the meeting of the National Convention on the morning of 9 Thermidor to Robespierre's recapture at the Hôtel de Ville sometime after midnight on the 10th. The documents reprinted here will obviously not permit a detailed reconstruction. There will be some contradictions and ambiguities, as well as some misrepresentations and errors. The reader should nevertheless be able to arrive at a reasonably accurate account of the events of the 9th and 10th. He should, moreover, be in a position to advance tentative explanations for Robespierre's failure.

Throughout the revolution, the crucial factor in determining the outcome of life-and-death struggles between political factions had often been the violent intervention of the sans-culottes. On 9 Thermidor the people of Paris did not rise up to support Robespierre in numbers sufficient to overwhelm the Convention. In the selection from his study of the Paris commune, Sainte-Claire Deville offers an explanation for the attitude of the people.

The arrest of the police official Daucour by the Section des Arcis, and the encounter described in Citizen Bouillette's interrogation are particular episodes in the city-wide struggle of the night of the ninth of Thermidor. The success of the deputy Peniaire should be noted, for it suggests that the political attitudes of the *sectionnaires* had changed in the months preceding Thermidor.

One final explanation of the passive attitude of much of the populace not contained in our documentary evidence should be mentioned. Marxist historians like Albert Soboul and George Rudé have interpreted Thermidor in the light of what they consider to be the basic contradiction between the bourgeois and the popular revolutionary movements. Following the researches of Mathiez, they have pointed to the fact that the economic plight of the poor in Paris worsened steadily during the spring of 1794. At the same time, the Committee of Public Safety, never sincerely in favor of economic controls, turned an increasingly deaf ear to popular cries for higher wages to offset inflation. On 5 Thermidor the commune of Paris posted the "*maximum des salaires,*" a wage schedule which fixed wages at a level below that which most workers were then receiving. This impolitic move, these historians argue, completed the alienation of the popular movement from the Committee of Public Safety.

National Convention

9 Thermidor, Year II [27 July 1794]

Collot d'Herbois presiding:

Saint-Just mounts the rostrum; he starts the same kind of discourse as the one read by Robespierre yesterday; he declares that he belongs to no party, no faction; and that though this tribunal may be for him, as it has been for many others, the Tarpeian cliff, he will nonetheless speak his opinion on the causes and the reasons for the divisions that have appeared, etc.

He is interrupted by Tallien, who asks the floor for a point of order.

TALLIEN: I ask the floor for a point of order. The speaker began by saying he belonged to no faction. I say the same thing. I belong only to myself, to liberty. It is for that reason that I am going to make the truth clear. No good citizen can restrain his tears at the sad fate to which the public weal has been abandoned. Everywhere there are divisions. Yesterday a member of the government was left quite isolated, and made a speech in his own name; today another has done the same thing. They are coming to attack one another, to aggravate the ills of the fatherland, to hurl it into the abyss. I demand that the veil be entirely torn away. (*Very lively applause, repeated in three successive waves.*)

BILLAUD-VARENNE: I ask the floor for a point of order. Yesterday the Jacobin Society was packed with planted agents; none of them had membership cards; and yesterday there was deployed in that Society a plan for strangling the National Convention. (*A movement of horror.*) Yesterday I saw men openly vomit out the most terrible slanders against those who have never deviated from the revolution.

On the Mountain I see one of those men who threatened the representatives of the people. There he is. . . . (*Cries from everywhere:* Arrest him! Arrest him! *The individual is seized and carried out of the room amidst the liveliest applause.*)

The time has come to speak the truth. . . . I am amazed to see Saint-Just at the rostrum after what has happened. He had promised the two committees to submit his speech to them before reading it and even to suppress it if it seemed dangerous to them. The assembly will ill judge events and its circumstances if it blinds itself to the fact that it is between two kinds of butchery. If it is weak it will perish. (No, no! *cry all the members, rising together and brandishing their hats. The*

Le Moniteur universel, XXI, 331-43 (Editions of 11 and 12 Thermidor).

gallery responds with applause and cries of Long live the Convention! Long live the Committee of Public Safety!)

Le Bas asks for the floor; he is told it belongs to Billaud-Varenne; he insists, and causes trouble.

DELMAS: I move that Le Bas be called to order.

The motion is adopted.

Le Bas again insists.

ALL THE MEMBERS: Either he obeys, or off to the scaffold with him.

BILLAUD-VARENNE: I myself ask that all men explain themselves before this assembly. One is strong when he has justice, probity, and the rights of the people on his side. You will shudder with horror when you learn what situation you are in; when you learn that the armed forces are in the hands of murderers; when you learn that the chief of the National Guard has been denounced to the Committee of Public Safety as an accomplice of Hébert and an infamous conspirator. You will shudder with horror when you learn that they who accuse the government of putting nobles and conspirators at the head of the armed forces are the very individuals who pressured us to put in the few nobles who are there; and Lavallette, the conspirator of Lille, is one proof of it. You will shudder with horror when you learn that there is a man who, when the question came up of sending representatives of the people to the *départements,* was unable to find twenty members of the Convention who were worthy of that mission on the list presented to him. *(The assembly murmurs with indignation.)* Let me say more: there have been complaints of the oppression of patriots. For sure, you will have a strange impression of this complaint when you learn that he who made it has caused the arrest of the best revolutionary committee in Paris, that of the Indivisibility *section,* even though only two of its members had been denounced. *(Renewed murmurs.)*

When Robespierre tells you that he left the Committee because he was suppressed there, he must avoid telling you everything; he does not tell you that after he had had his way in the Committee for six months, he came up against resistance at the moment when he, alone, wanted to revive the decree of 22 Prairial—that decree which in the impure hands which he had chosen could be so fatal for patriots. *(Indignant murmurs continue.)* Know, citizens, that yesterday the president of the Revolutionary Tribunal openly proposed to the Jacobins that they should drive all impure men from the Convention, which is to say all those whom they wanted as sacrifices; but the people exist, and patriots will know how to die to save liberty (Yes! Yes! *cry all the members.—Lively applause.*)

I repeat: we shall die with honor, all of us; for I do not believe that there can be a single representative here who would live under a tyrant. (No! No! *cries from all parts of the hall;* death to the tyrants!—*Prolonged applause.*) The men who talk endlessly to the Convention or to the Jacobins of Justice and of virtue are the very ones who trample them beneath their feet when they can do it; here is proof. A secretary to the Committee of Public Safety had stolen 114,000 livres. I demanded his arrest; and Robespierre, who talks incessantly of justice and of virtue, is the one person who prevented his arrest. *(Renewed movements of indignation.)*

There are, citizens, a thousand other facts I could cite; and it is us that he accuses! What! men who are isolated, who know nobody, who spend their nights and days in the Committee of Public Safety, who organize our victories, these men are supposed to be conspirators! And those who did not abandon Hébert until it was no longer possible for them to back him, they are supposed to be men of virtue! The first time I denounced Danton in the Committee Robespierre rose up like a wild man, saying he knew my intentions, saying I wanted to ruin the best patriots. All this made me see the abyss that was dug beneath our feet. There is no need to hesitate between filling it with our bodies and triumphing over traitors. We must not hesitate to fill it with our bodies, or [else?] triumph over traitors.

They meant to destroy, to mutilate the Convention; and that intention was so concrete that they had organized a spy system among the representatives of the people whom they wanted to destroy. It is infamous to talk of justice and virtue when you defy them, and when you speak out only when you have been arrested or contradicted.

Robespierre rushes toward the rostrum.

A GREAT MANY VOICES: Down, down with the tyrant!

TALLIEN: Just now I demanded that the veil be torn away. Now I have seen this done, completely—seen the conspirators unmasked, seen that they will soon be destroyed, and that liberty will triumph. *(Lively applause.)* Everything points to the fall of the enemy of the national representation, under its blows. We are giving proof of our republican loyalty to our infant Republic. Heretofore I have imposed silence upon myself because I knew that the man who was close to becoming the tyrant of France had made a list of proscribed persons. I wanted no recriminations; but yesterday I observed the session at the Jacobins; I trembled for the fatherland; I saw the army of the new Cromwell forming; and I armed myself with a dagger to pierce him to the heart if the National Convention should not have the courage to accuse him.

Republicans, let us accuse him with the loyalty of courage, in the presence of the French people. It is well to enlighten the citizens and those who frequent the Jacobin tribunes are no more attached to Robespierre than to any other individual, but to liberty. *(Applause.)* I am not going to make my attacks in particular anymore; I am calling the attention of the Convention to this vast conspiracy.* I have no doubt that it will take energetic and immediate steps; that it will remain here permanently to save the people; and whatever the partisans of the man I denounce may have said, there will be no proscriptions; national justice alone will strike the villains down. (*Lively applause.*) And as it is of the utmost importance that the citizens be not misled amidst the dangers which surround the fatherland, and that the chiefs of the armed forces be unable to do harm, I ask for the arrest of Hanriot and his staff. Then we will take up the decree which was rendered on the sole authority of the man we are dealing with. We are not moderates, but we do not want innocence to be oppressed. We want the president of the Revolutionary Tribunal to treat accused men with decency and justice. (*Renewed applause.*) That is true virtue; that is true probity.

Yesterday a member of the Revolutionary Tribunal tried to incite the citizenry to insult a representative of the people who has always been in the vanguard of revolution. He was slandered at a society; and in his person the national representation was reviled. Those who fought Lafayette and all the succeeding factions will unite to save the Republic. Let the patriotic writers awake. I call upon all the old friends of liberty, all the old Jacobins, all the patriotic journalists. Let them join with us to save liberty. They will keep faith; and that guarantees me their patriotism. Eyes had been cast upon me. I should have borne my head to the scaffold with courage, because I should have said to myself: a day will come when my ashes are resurrected with the honors due a patriot persecuted by a tyrant. The man at the rostrum is a new Catiline. Those with whom he had surrounded himself were new Verreses.† No one can say that the members of the two committees are my partisans, for I do not know them, and since my mission, I have been greeted only with disgust. Robespierre tried to attack us by turns, to isolate us; and finally he would have been left without rivals one day, with those vicious and debauched men who serve him. I

*[Translator's note: The language seems especially uneven and garbled here and in the following pages; presumably either the speakers or the stenographer, or both, are suffering from the strain and from the fast pace of events.]

†[Verres was a tyrannical Roman provincial governor, creature of Sulla, attacked by Cicero.]

move that we declare ourselves in permanent session until the blade of the law has made the revolution secure, and that we order the arrest of his creatures.

The two proposals of Tallien are adopted amidst the liveliest applause and cries of Vive la république!

BILLAUD-VARENNE: The men whom the Convention has just struck down do not include the one who merits its greatest indignation. He is called Boulanger, conspirator with Hébert, who was publicly sentenced, at the time of the latter's conspiracy, to the Cordeliers [prison]. This man also conspired with Dumouriez; he was the friend of Danton; and it was Dumas who injected him into the Jacobins yesterday to keep Collot d'Herbois from speaking. It was this Dumas who, after he had rallied counter-revolutionaries together, tried to picture Collot as a conspirator, so that he could not tear aside the veil; this Dumas, whose whole family are *émigrés,* who is accused of having dined with his brother on the eve of his emigration, and against whom there are at the Jacobins proofs of the most atrocious perfidy! I therefore move the arrest of Dumas, of Boulanger, and of Dufraisse.

The arrests are decreed. (Applause.)

DELMAS: In light of the facts which have just been proclaimed, it is impossible not to believe that Hanriot was cunning enough to surround himself with conspirators. His adjutants and his aides-de-camp must be infinitely suspect. I move arrest.

This proposal is decreed. (Applause.)

Robespierre insists on getting the floor.

Down! Down with the tyrant! *all the members shout at him.*

SEVERAL VOICES: Barère! Barère!

ROBESPIERRE: I call for the floor.

THE SAME MEMBERS: No, down with the tyrant!

The Convention decrees that Barère will be heard.

BARÈRE, *in the name of the Committee of Public Safety:* Citizens, one of my colleagues, recently returned from the Army of the North, has reported to the Committee that an enemy officer, made prisoner in the recent action which gave us Belgium, had said: "All your successes amount to nothing; we expect in any case to arrange peace with some party, whatever it may be, with a fraction of the Convention, and to change the government soon."

Saint-Just brought us this instructive news.

Would not this moment predicted by the Austrian officer have arrived, for the party abroad and the enemies within, if you had not taken rigorous measures?

The two committees can no longer avoid this truth: the government is under attack; its members have been heaped with slanders and injuries; its connections are broken off, public confidence has ceased; and those who are calling tyranny to account have themselves been called to account.

There is talk of the persecution of patriots; but cannot the committees complain of the same oppression? And then in a few days the citizenry gets all stirred up, and they are egged on against the government: could the English or the Austrians ask anything better?

There are efforts to produce popular movements, there are efforts to seize national power in the midst of a manufactured crisis; and it is well known that every free state in which great crises have not been foreseen is in danger of perishing with every storm.

In these same crises it is only you, citizens, who have been able to find new means of maintaining revolutionary government. The same opportunity for your civic courage has been presented to you to-day; and you have grasped it. Have no doubt of it: without the united committees, the revolutionary government and the Republic would long since have been overturned.

Cast your eyes over what has happened in the last eighteen months: without centralized government, France would have been subjugated by the kings; liberty would have been forever destroyed, and the true patriots strangled.

Who here then would wish to deprive the Republic of the resources and the institutions which have so often saved it? Oh! do not suppose that by getting rid of a few ardent and pure patriots, a few men can control public affairs: it is not by speeches that one governs; it is not by constant complaints that one builds a republic.

The committees are the shield, the asylum, the sanctuary of the central government, the unitary government, the revolutionary government; as long as they survive, it is impossible for royalism to revive, for aristocracy to breathe, for crime to rule, for the Republic not to triumph.

Attempts are made to destroy everybody who has energy or intelligence; attempts are made to annihilate everything that is republican pure and simple; and these proposals come not from the Revolutionary Tribunal, which is doing its duty, but from certain members of that tribunal, on whose patriotism you must today make judgment.

You must make judgment on several individuals who exercise important functions; only violent events make it necessary to reveal so many truths to you; for then the government has no privileged activity other than the salvation of the Republic, and that role belongs to the people. Established forms are altered; governmental processes are suspended; the liberty of citizens is compromised; public safety is shaken; public opinion is reeling.

Unitary governments and free peoples are antitheses, and absolute opposites; great reputations and human equality cannot coexist for long; artificial unrest and real work cannot go together; we must humbly serve the fatherland for its sake, and not for our own.

While the two committees were preparing to refute, with as much wisdom as energy, the statements concerning them in the speech of Robespierre, they considered the measures which the public peace requires, in the circumstances into which personal passions have cast them. First they directed their attention to the means which the aristocracy, delighted by the present events, can employ in Paris; that aristocracy which all our efforts seem unable to expunge, and which hides in the muck when it is not in the blood; aristocracy has been bubbling up since yesterday with a vigor which can only indicate a counter-revolutionary movement.

Who then sought to raise its murderous hopes? Whom could it base its efforts on? On certain nobles located in the armed forces; on certain unpunished Hébertists; on certain military counter-revolutionaries. Yes, citizens, you have sensed where their resources lay, and you have just seized them; you have just done justice to those ambitious military men.

The committees asked themselves why there still existed a military regime in the midst of Paris, comparable to the one that existed in the days of kings; why all these permanent commanders, with staffs, and immense armed forces. The popular system of the National Guard had established rotating legion chiefs. The committees have thought it best to restore to the National Guard its democratic organization: accordingly they propose the suppression by decree of the general command, and that legion chiefs serve by turn.

The mayor of Paris and the national representative of the commune must at this moment fulfill their duty, their loyalty, and their obligations to the people; let us hope they do fulfill them. They must take upon their shoulders the responsibility for the security of the representatives of the people and for the troubles which the aristocratic parties would like to stir up, whenever they see any perversion of the will of the National Convention.

The committees have believed that in the present state of public opinion, and in the crisis in which we are, it was necessary to address a proclamation to the citizenry. In a free country it takes only a few rays of light, and the people's reason immediately seizes upon them, defends its own true defenders, and sustains its own rights.

This is the proposed decree:

"The National Convention, having heard the report of the committees of Public Safety and on General Security, decrees:

"Article I. All ranks higher than that of chief of legion are abolished.

"The National Guard will resume its original organization; accordingly, each chief of legion will command in turn.

"II. The mayor of Paris, the national representative, and whoever shall be taking his turn as commander of the National Guard will see to the security of the national representation; they will take responsibility for any troubles that may arise in Paris.

"This decree will be sent forthwith to the mayor of Paris."

The decree is adopted.

Then Barère, in the name of the two committees, reads the following proclamation [published in the Moniteur *of 10 Thermidor]:*

"Citizens, in the midst of the most signal victories, a new danger menaces the Republic; it is all the greater as impressions are confused, and as a part of the citizenry is letting itself be led to the precipice by force of certain reputations.

"The labors of the Convention are made sterile, and the courage of the armies made null, if the citizens of France put a few men into the balance against the fatherland.

"Personal passions have usurped the place of the public weal; certain chiefs of the armed forces seemed to menace the national authority.

"The revolutionary government, object of the hatred of the enemies of France, has been attacked in our very midst; the institutions of republican strength are close to their ruin; aristocracy seems triumphant, and the royalists are ready to reappear.

"Citizens, would you lose in a day six years of revolution, of sacrifices and of courage? Would you go back under the yoke you have broken? No, unquestionably. The Convention will not cease for a moment to watch over the rights of public liberty. Therefore it invites the citizens of Paris to help with their solidarity, their wisdom, and their patriotism in the preservation of that precious body entrusted to them by the people of France. Let them especially watch military authority, ever ambitious and ever usurpatious. Liberty is nothing in a country where the military commands the civil.

"If you do not rally to the national representation, the constituted authorities will be without subordinates and the armies without direction; victories will turn into oppression, and the French people will be delivered over to the furies of internal divisions and all the vengeances of tyrants. Hear the voice of the fatherland rather than mingling your cries with those of the malevolent, of aristocrats, and of enemies of the people; and the fatherland will be saved once more."

The National Convention decrees that this proclamation be printed forthwith and sent to all the Paris sections, *to all the communes, and to the armies of the Republic.*

[*The* Moniteur *of 11 Thermidor resumes:*]

Debate is resumed.

VADIER: Up to the 22nd Prairial my eyes were not open regarding the cunning individual who has been able to assume every mask, and who, when he was unable to save his creatures, himself sent them to the guillotine. Let no one ignore how he openly defended Bazire, Chabot, and Camille Desmoulins, and how he diverted the dishonor to the account of the Committee on General Security.

On the 22nd Prairial, the tyrant (that's the name *I* give to him) (*lively applause*) himself issued a law instituting the Revolutionary Tribunal; he composed it in his own hand; he instructed the vigilant Couthon to bring this decree to the Convention and get it passed, without even reading it. He complains that patriots are oppressed. But on the contrary it is against him that this reproach applies, against him who had imprisoned the purest revolutionary committee in Paris; against him who, to carry out the arrests he wanted, instituted his general police.

The government committee which directs the armies has done its duty, and the victories won by the Republic are also the fruit of the suppression of internal enemies, and that suppression is the work of the Committee on General Security. Do you know why he slandered it? that was to divide the two committees, to suffocate opinion, to make sure that no patriot spoke out or rose up against tyranny. If this tyrant addresses himself particularly to me, that is because I made a report on fanaticism which has never pleased him; there you have the reason. There was under the Mother of God's * mattress a letter addressed to Robespierre. This letter announced to him that his mission had been prophesied in Ezekiel; that the re-establishment of religion, freed of priests, was owing to him. He was done the honor of a new cult. Among the documents I later received there is a letter from a certain

*[Catherine Théot; see above, pp. 160, 176.]

Chénon, notary of Geneva, who is at the head of the Illuminati. He proposes to Robespierre a supernatural constitution. (*Laughter.*)

Would you believe that after the decree you issued subsequent upon my report, it pleased Robespierre, with his full power and authority, to say to the public prosecutor: you shall not judge that trash.

There came back to me with the trial materials a dossier of other materials which said that this woman is an old nut who was shut up in the Saltpeter Asylum, for always having done the same thing; so this woman, who was looked upon as a nothing, was always around the ex-Duchess of Bourbon; and to prove to you how much this man tyrannized the public prosecutor, it is enough for me to tell you that the latter came to see me to tell me that he could not manage to get a trial of this affair.

BOURDON DE L'OISE: Robespierre prevented, after the 20th Frimaire, the promulgation of the decree of indictment against Lavalette; and he sacrificed six patriots of Lille.

VADIER: To hear Robespierre, he is the only defender of liberty; he is giving it up for lost, he is going to quit everything; he is a man of rare modesty (*laughter*), and he has a perpetual refrain: "I am oppressed; they won't give me the floor"; and he is the only one with anything useful to say, for his will is always done. He says: "So-and-so conspires against me, I who am the best friend of the Republic; therefore he conspires against the Republic." That is novel.

He had still another way of frustrating patriots. He set spies on several deputies. To me he attached a certain Taschereau, who devoted rare attention and good nature to me. He followed me everywhere, even when I was asked out to dinner and he was not invited. This Taschereau knew all the speeches of Robespierre by heart and recited them to me incessantly. After I found out that the relatives of prisoners were hanging around him, I forbade him my house; to get revenge for that he denounced a man who wanted to do me a favor. That is how these good patriots operate. (*Laughter.*)

TALLIEN: I ask the floor to get the discussion back to the real point.

ROBESPIERRE: I'll know how to get it back there. (*Murmurs.*)

The Convention grants the floor to Tallien.

TALLIEN: Citizens, it is not to any particular facts that I wish to direct the Convention's attention in this moment. The facts which have been stated are doubtless important, but there is no member of this assembly who could not make comparable allegations, who could not complain of some tyrannical act.

It is to the speech made yesterday in the Convention, and repeated at the Jacobins, that I call all your attention. That is where I meet the tyrant; that is where I find all the conspiracy; it is in that speech that, with the aid of truth, justice, and the Convention, I hope to find the weapons to defeat him, to defeat this man whose virtue and patriotism have been so vaunted, but who, at the memorable time of the 10th of August, did not emerge until three days after the Revolution; this man who when he was supposed to be the defender of the oppressed in the Committee of Public Safety, who was supposed to be at his post, abandoned it forty days [*quatre décades*] ago; and at what time was that? when the Army of the North was causing all his colleagues serious anxiety. He abandoned it to come and slander the committees, and all [*tous* (*sic*)=*vous?*] saved the fatherland. (*Lively applause.*) Of course, if I wanted to trace the particular acts of oppression which have taken place, I should point out that it was during the time when Robespierre was in charge of the general police that they were committed, and that the patriots of the revolutionary committee of the Indivisibility *section* were arrested.

Robespierre interrupts with cries. (*There are violent murmurs.*)

LOUCHET: I move the decree of arrest against Robespierre.

LOSEAU: It is an established fact that Robespierre has dominated; I move the decree of arrest for that single reason.

LOUCHET: My motion is seconded; vote on the arrest.

ROBESPIERRE THE YOUNGER: I am as guilty as my brother is; I share his virtues. I ask the decree of accusation against myself as well.

Robespierre abuses the president and the members of the assemly in the most insulting terms.

CHARLES DUVAL: Mr. President, is one man to be master of the Convention?

LOSEAU: Vote on the arrest of the two brothers!

BILLAUD-VARENNE: I have some positive facts which Robespierre will not dare deny. I shall first cite the reproach he addressed to the Committee for wishing to disarm the citizenry.

ROBESPIERRE: I said there were some villains. . . . (*Murmurs.*)

BILLAUD-VARENNE: I said he reproached the Committee for wishing to disarm the citizenry. Well, it was he alone that issued that order. He accused the government of having had all the monuments to the Supreme Being removed; well, know that it was by Couthon. . . .

COUTHON: Yes, I co-operated there. (*Renewed murmurs.*)

SEVERAL MEMBERS: Vote on the arrest!

It is unanimously decreed.

All the members rise and make the hall resound with cries of Vive la liberté! Vive la république!

LOUCHET: What we meant by the vote was the arrest of the two Robespierres, Saint-Just, and Couthon.

LE BAS: I do not want to share the blame for that decree; I demand to be arrested too.

ÉLIE LACOSTE: I move the arrest of Robespierre the younger; he is one of the ones who sounded the tocsin against the committees at the Jacobins. He finished his speech with these memorable words: "They say the committees are not corrupt; but if their agents are, then they are too."

The arrest of Robespierre the younger is decreed. (Lively applause.)

FRÉRON: Citizen colleagues, on this day the fatherland and liberty shall emerge from their ruins.

ROBESPIERRE: Yes, for the brigands are winning out.

FRÉRON: They meant to form a triumvirate which recalls the bloody proscriptions of Sulla; they meant to raise themselves on the ruins of the Republic, and the men who tried it are Robespierre, Couthon, and Saint-Just.

SEVERAL VOICES: And Le Bas.

FRÉRON: Couthon is a tiger thirsting for the blood of the national representation. He has dared, as a royal pastime, to talk in the Jacobins of five or six heads at the Convention (Yes! Yes! *cries from everywhere.)* That was only the beginning; and he wanted to make of our corpses so many steps toward the throne.

COUTHON: I wanted to get to the throne, yes!

FRÉRON: I move the decree of arrest also against Saint-Just, Le Bas, and Couthon.

ÉLIE LACOSTE: I support that proposal. It was I who first told the Committee of Public Safety that Couthon, Saint-Just, and Robespierre were forming a triumvirate. Saint-Just turned pale and became ill. When he returned from the Army of the North, after he had told us about the position and condition of the army, he reported to us that a Swiss officer made prisoner had told him that we could take no account of our successes, that the enemy was informed as to our resources, and that they expected a schism in the government, to aid which they would treat for peace with any faction whatever. It is they, the villains, who wanted to produce the schism. For some time we had been tranquil; intrigues were frustrated; those who had formed them had perished under the blade of the law, and the armies had made victory the order of the day, when these perfidious men sought to strangle liberty. I urge the decree of arrest against Couthon, Saint-Just, and Le Bas.

This proposal is decreed amidst the liveliest applause.

Colombel puts through the following decree:

"The National Convention, after hearing the report of its Committee on Public Aid on the petition of Citizen Larcole, captain in the light cavalry regiment of the Montagne, decrees:

"Article I. There will be paid from the national treasury a sum of five hundred livres for the purpose of the relief of Citizen Larcade.

"II. The present decree will be inserted only in the Bulletin of Correspondence."[1]

(Continuation of the session to be printed tomorrow.)

[*The* Moniteur *of 11 Thermidor appends the following report:*] N.B. During the permanent session of the night of the 9th to the 10th, the Convention was informed that a seditious crowd had invaded the Committee on General Security, surrounded it by force, and wrested away from it the conspirators who had been placed under arrest; that from there they were taken to the town hall, where the General Council had raised the standard of rebellion, so as to free them of the authority of the national representation, notifying the *sections* of Paris that they were to communicate only with them, to arm, and to march against the Convention, and arresting the commandant and officers named by it. The Convention placed outside the law all those who resisted or opposed the execution of its decree, and chose twelve from among its members to go and carry out among the National Guard of Paris the functions which the representatives of the people exercise among the armies. "Go," it said to them, "and let the sun not rise before the rebels and conspirators are turned over to the hands of the national justice."

At three in the morning, the twelve representatives came to announce that the town hall was in their power, together with the traitors it contained; and that they had seized a seal, quite recently engraved, bearing a fleur-de-lis.

The administration of the Paris *département* came to present the following address: "It is at the moment of the new day that dawns for the welfare and the liberty of the French people that the Paris *département* hastens to congratulate you on the wise and vigorous measures by which you have once more saved the fatherland and frustrated the plots of traitors who, using the bait of liberty, were readying us for chains.

These murderers, thirsting for the blood of their fellow citizens, hoped to mislead the people; they were aided in their horrible plot by perfidious magistrates; but how they deceived themselves! the Paris *sections,* faithful to the Republic, were wise enough to hear the voices of their representatives.

"Your immortal decrees will transmit to posterity both our dangers and your courage. May our submission to the laws, and our indefatigable zeal in carrying out our duties, forever prove to our fellow citizens our firm resolve to co-operate with you in the annihilation of all conspiracies, and to die at our post. The Paris *département* asks the Convention for the orders it may see fit to give in the present circumstances."

During the night the *sections* appeared in succession at the bar, and assured the Convention that it would always find them rallied around it, and ready to shed their blood to defend it. Thus the rebellion of a usurping municipality served only to provide new proof of the atrociousness of the plots concocted by the faction whose instrument it was.

Vivier, president of a seditious meeting held at the Jacobins; Taschereau, confidant of Robespierre, and several other emmisaries, guards, and confederates of this new Cromwell, were put outside the law.

Le Bas killed himself; the two Robespierres and Couthon tried by the same means to escape the vengeance of the people; but they were only wounded, and were unable to escape the more terrible and more infamous punishment reserved for traitors.

On the evening of the 10th, their heads fell on the scaffold, amidst the acclamations of an immense crowd and cries, repeated a thousand times, of *Vive la république! Vive la Convention!* A memorable example for anyone who may hereafter dare attempt to usurp the national sovereignty! Glorious day! which has seen the instantaneous disappearance of the hopes of the despot coalition! They counted on coming to terms with a dictator! The French people will be their own dictator; and from them [the French people] they can hope for no peace, no truce. What a sublime spectacle was the energetic humanity of the National Convention! how the firm posture of the people of Paris and the spontaneous rallying of all citizens around the Convention must dismay agitators! This revolution, by giving a new countenance to the national representation, will be the death sentence to all those who would strive to divide and degrade it.

In vain would the slanderers of the people seek to profit from these events by accusing the people of fickleness. The people are always right in their judgments. They want liberty, and have no love for those who forbid it. The less they idolize individuals, the more steady will be their love for the fatherland. The more precarious individual reputations are, the more public liberty will be affirmed. Anyone who has made himself powerful enough to seek to rise above the law must find his Brutus in his fellow citizens. The excessive influence of a single man is the most dangerous scourge of a republic.

[*Continuation of the permanent session of 9 Thermidor, printed in the* Moniteur *issue of 12 Thermidor. Collot d'Herbois still presiding.*]

COLLOT D'HERBOIS: There is one measure which I believe essential: that is to decree that Saint-Just must deposit on the bench the speech he was to make to help bring about the counter-revolution.

This proposal is adopted.

COLLOT D'HERBOIS: Citizens, it is true to say that you have saved the fatherland. The suffocating fatherland, its heart lacerated and torn, has not spoken to you in vain. Your enemies said that another insurrection of 31 May was in order.

ROBESPIERRE THE ELDER: He lied. . . .

(*The assembly explodes with the liveliest indignation.*)

CLAUSEL: I move that the bailiffs carry out the decree of arrest.

THE PRESIDENT: I have already given the order; and when the bailiffs presented themselves, [the accused] refused to obey.

(To the bar! To the bar! *cries from all parts of the hall.*)

LOSEAU: I remind the Convention that when it places a number of its members under arrest it makes them go to the bar. I move that there be no special privilege for these, and that they descend.

SEVERAL VOICES: Yes, yes, to the bar!

The Convention decrees this proposal.

The individuals whose arrest was decreed descend to the bar. (*Repeated applause.*)

COLLOT D'HERBOIS: The fatherland smiles at your energy; its enemies said a 31st of May insurrection was needed. No, it was not an insurrection that was called for, because ten thousand counter-revolutionaries were ready to seize upon the first movement to strangle liberty. They were already glowing, the partisans of counter-revolution, but it will be a dark day for them. (*Applause.*) It was not an insurrection after their fashion that was called for; it was an insurrection against tyranny; and you have made it. (*Lively applause.*) It too will have its place in history, this insurrection which has saved the fatherland. (*Renewed applause.*) Look, citizens, upon the fugitive hordes of your enemies; see their armies scatter in consternation into the distance; their final resource was civil war in the heart of the Convention, to force us to accept a tyrant. But all the French will perish before they compromise with tyranny. Never, no, never will the French people have a tyrant. (No! No! *cries from all parts of the hall.—Members of the assembly and spectators rise simultaneously crying:* Vive la république!)

They had to try to dissolve the national representation, break up the government, bring on civil war. Good; an instrument had to be made ready, under cover. Do you know what the instrument was? It was the speech of Robespierre. (*Applause.*)

(*A secretary notifies the members of the Committee on General Security that they are needed at their ordinary place of meeting.—They cross the hall to the sound of repeated applause.*)

COLLOT D'HERBOIS: Citizens, those of you who heard this speech, I ask you: was anything better calculated to rupture the threads of confidence, more cunningly designed to dissolve the National Convention? In short, was there any more inflammatory way of igniting civil war?

That was by no means enough; they still had to corrupt the public mind, undermine morale, confuse opinion. All right, that was done; for in a celebrated Society, which has so far resisted aristocracy, which was misled for a moment but which will doubtless soon recover its luster and its energy; in this Society which always manifested its profound veneration for the national representation, which always recognized the beneficence of its decrees, where brother always reached out to brother—I spoke there yesterday about the inquietudes of the fatherland: I was silenced by hostile murmurs.

I spoke of the sweet fountains of amity; I was answered only with threats. I said I had escaped both barrels from Ladmiral [*sic*]; and they smiled ironically. *(Movement of indignation.)* Clearly I was not with Jacobins there *(applause);* but I am today *(renewed applause).* When the true Jacobins, who were absent yesterday, reappear there; when they see the great work you have completed, what great criminals you have punished, those good citizens who did not dare take their places there will return; they were disheartened yesterday; they foresaw the dangers which threatened the fatherland; their souls, the souls of these athletes of liberty, were palpitating; their hearts were oppressed; but now there is no more oppression. (*Lively applause.*—Yes, yes; there is no more oppression!) Yet [the conspirators] still feared the return of those faithful athletes even for today; they feared that energetic sentiment which necessarily would arouse the friends of the fatherland in every corner of Paris; yes, they feared it, they the traitors whom you have struck down; that is why the speech of Saint-Just had to be made today; the motion which Couthon made yesterday at the

Jacobins was bound to make a stir; Couthon had demanded a new vote of purge in the Society; he did not disguise the intent that those members of the two committees whom that conspirator dared call traitor must be excluded. That is why Saint-Just came, contrary to his promise to the two committees, to read the speech you have interrupted. It is well in that connection to make a few details known: Saint-Just was at the Committee; I arrived there from underneath knife points, for a number of those who escorted me along the passage managed to repeat in my ears several times, "In a couple of days you won't talk so much; you'll be past that;" somebody said to Dubarran, "His cackle will have to be cut;" these propositions were made by ordinary hirelings, by Robespierre's bodyguards.

Anyway, I arrived at the Committee; I turned to Saint-Just; I energetically conveyed what had happened; he saw how upset I was; he was like stone. He coolly presented the Committee with that report, in which he did not hide the fact that several members were accused, yet without daring propose decrees of accusation against them, for he held that much back. Do you know what that report was based upon? On all that came in from Robespierre's spies. There was something remarkable in my case. He claimed that I had made such and such a proposal in a café; and everybody knows that I never set foot in a café; another reported that I had told Fouché to prepare a decree of accusation against Robespierre; that Fouché had said to somebody that if Robespierre would agree to change his conduct toward him, he would uncover the whole intrigue; but I have not seen Fouché for two months, while public opinion has been in abeyance on his count. We told Saint-Just that these facts must be told to the Convention, if they were true, but beforehand they had to be examined, so as not to cause trouble. We decided with him that we would send someone to look for Fouché, so that it could be cleared up in his presence.

We let Saint-Just go at five in the morning; he was to return at eleven. He did not keep his word. The two committees were assembled. Fouché was summoned; Rühl questioned him; he said he had not seen me for two months, and that he felt I had treated him severely. There are a good many other infamies in that report. That is why I have asked that it be deposited upon the bench. This second volume of the speech of Robespierre was to have been read this evening at the Jacobins, and we do not know what would have happened at the festival tomorrow. That might have been, perhaps, a day of mourning; it will be, on the contrary, a day of triumph. (*Applause.*)

Your committees will make you a detailed report on this conspiracy, and it will not be difficult to convince you that there was in the making here something favorable to the overthrown despots. It will not be difficult to prove that they were joined together in conspiracy.

Notice, citizens, that those who come and call upon the law are those who violate it readily. Notice that the brother of Robespierre, in contempt of the decree which directed him to join the army in Italy, has remained here despite the arrangements for that campaign.

Saint-Just was twice summoned from the Army of the North by Robespierre, to prepare a document of accusation against the courageous men who opposed the despotism of these new tyrants.

I tell you, these were the veritable proscriptions of a new Sulla; for it was not a question here of friends or enemies of the people; it was a question of proscribing those unwilling to obey this or that individual. I am going to cite a fact which will prove that Robespierre, who for some time has talked only of Marat, has always detested this friend of the people. At the funeral ceremonies of Marat, Robespierre talked at length from the rostrum that had been set up in front of the Luxembourg, and the name of Marat did not once come from his mouth. Can the people believe that anyone loves Marat who declares humorously that he does not want to be compared to him? No; in vain these hypocrites talked incessantly of Marat, of Chalier; they loved neither Marat nor Chalier: Chalier, whose conduct I observed, whose virtues I cherished, admired, and respected! The people know it well; it is in the virtues of private life that one recognizes public virtues. (*Applause.*)

FAYAU: I ask the floor so as to give information. A *section* commissioner asked the director of a shop for guns to arm the young people of that *section* tomorrow at the festival. The guns were refused. (*Applause.*)

The session is suspended.

9 Thermidor, Seven P.M.

BOURDON DE L'OISE: Citizens, this morning the Convention took security measures necessitated by the circumstances; all good citizens applauded. Nevertheless, a rumor is spreading this evening to which I call your full attention. It is claimed that the Paris commune is in league with the Jacobins to bring off an insurrection. (*Movements of indignation.*) Such a fusion would doubtless be dangerous with any other than the people of Paris: with them it can cause you no uneasiness. I remind the Convention that in a similar circumstance it fraternized with the people, and calmed the excitement of the people with its presence. Not that I think this action is necessary; yet it is useful to be sure of the truth; I move therefore that the commune be summoned to the bar to make you an account of the facts.

This proposition is sustained.

MERLIN DE THIONVILLE: Because I spoke neither for nor against in this morning's discussion, I have not been suspect during the day. I am going to tell you (*slight murmurs*) I am going to give you an account of a fact. If there was any good citizen who could still doubt the existence of the conspiracy being concocted, or the imminent danger which liberty and the national representation were running, this fact will easily convince them.

I was leaving my house to go to my post when Hanriot, at the head of forty wild men, came in view. To see me, pounce upon me, put a pistol to my breast, and cover my head with their sabers—all that was a matter of a moment.

I was unarmed; I could not defend myself; I bared my breast to them, saying *Fire!* They seized me, then took me to the guardhouse at the Palace of Equality. There, recovering my character as representative of the people, I harangued the armed citizens who were present. True to principles, and imbued with respect for the national representation, they set me free on the spot. (*Lively applause.*)

I announce to the Convention that these citizens were from the Mountain* *section*. A memorandum has been prepared on my arrest and my liberation; it has been filed with the Committee on General Security. Still Hanriot continued his wild march, bringing trouble and terror to all the different quarters of Paris where the truth regarding this day's events had not yet penetrated. Five policemen bravely resolved to arrest this villain and carry out your decree. They set out, pounced on Hanriot and his satellites, pistol to breast, and made the villains prisoner. (*Applause.—All the citizens cry:* Vive la république!) That, citizens, is the fact I had to communicate to you; now that I have given you an account of it, I am going to suggest an amendment to the proposal of Bourdon (de l'Oise). He moved that the Paris commune be summoned to the bar; I move that the *département* be summoned too, and come to receive the orders of the Convention.

These two proposals are decreed.

LEGENDRE: What does it matter to the Convention, what does it matter to the Republic if a General Council of the commune does de-

*[Butte des Moulins]

clare itself in insurrection? Be careful not to confuse the people of Paris with a council nominated perhaps by the conspirators. Every time a decree comes from you, count on the people, count on the Montagnards; for the Mountain exists wherever the desire for the Republic does. (*Applause.*) It is not easy to bring an enlightened people to insurrection; today you have given them a great lesson; from today forward liberty is consolidated. (*Lively applause.*) The people, drawing upon the instinct it had at the beginning of the revolution to rebel now against tyrants, will attach itself to you alone; but it will never again adore a personality.

When an individual does his duty it will say to him: "I was in the audience, I saw you on the stage, you did well, I applauded; but I shall see what you do tomorrow." (*Lively applause.*) The people will remember that it was once said: "No constitution without Pétion, Pétion or death; no patriotism without Robespierre;" today it will say: "No patriotism without principles." (*Applause.*) I move that the president say to each petitioner who comes to congratulate the Mountain that the whole Convention is but one Mountain; the Convention includes as many Montagnards as there are men of good will; and the proof that the Convention is composed of men of good will is that the decree of arrest against traitors was voted unanimously. (*Renewed applause.*)

POULTIER: A municipal officer met me and tried to arrest me; I myself seized him and brought him to the Committee on General Security. (*Applause.*)

ROVÈRE: There is in the commune one of the agents of Robespierre; it is this Payan. . . .

SEVERAL VOICES: He has been arrested. (*Applause.*)

ROVÈRE: Observe the villainy of Robespierre; this Payan has been elected by the Drôme *département* to federate with the Midi.

BRIVAL: Citizens, the president of the pretended Jacobins, at the demand and after the arrest of the counter-revolutionaries who had slipped into that Society, invited me to make a report on the Convention session. When I reached the rostrum I spoke in these terms:

"Intriguers, counter-revolutionaries, clad in the mantle of patriotism, sought to murder liberty; the Convention decreed that they would be put under arrest; these representatives are Robespierre, Saint-Just, Couthon, Le Bas, Robespierre the younger."

"What was your opinion?" the president asked me. I replied: "He who always voted with the Mountain, in the Legislative Assembly and in the Assembly of the Convention, voted for the arrest; he did more; he is one of the ones who instigated it, and in his capacity as secretary he worked to expedite and validate the decrees." At these words I was buried under boos, and I was ejected from the pretended Society; they took away my card. I went out saying to them, "I was not made to associate with members who drive out those who seek to save liberty."

I have just learned that the pretended Society has recalled its decree, and that it has named an emissary to give me back my card. I shall not take it until after the regeneration of the Society.

GOUPILLEAU THE ELDER: I was at the Committee on General Security; when I was going out, what a surprise I got; I saw the antechamber filling with citizens bearing the tricolor ribbon; I asked them what they were doing there; one of them asked me in turn who I was: "A representative of the people," I replied. He said that he did not believe a word of it. I showed him my card. "All right," he said, "I despise you." This individual is the one who is presiding over the Revolutionary Tribunal in the absence of Dumas.

SEVERAL VOICES: That is Louvet.

GOUPILLEAU: Then I move the arrest of Louvet. I also move the arrest of Fleuriot-Lescot, mayor of Paris, he is another villain who must necessarily be in the conspiracy. (*Applause.*)

FRÉRON: I am told that Payan and Fleuriot are not under arrest. I move that the decree of arrest be carried out against them immediately.

BILLAUD-VARENNE: The graver the circumstances become, the more the committees felt it their duty to act energetically. Payan was arrested four hours ago. The mayor is still not under arrest; but within a few minutes the General Council of the commune, which has raised the standard of revolt, will be surrounded. *(Lively applause.)* The more public opinion was misled, the more the Convention and the friends of the fatherland must felicitate themselves on the counterrevolutionary movement which is unfolding at this time; this movement, organized for three months in the heart of the government, and intended to destroy it, is precisely what has saved the fatherland. (*Applause.*)

I ask you, citizens: if any other representative had been struck down by the decree of arrest, would the satellites of the villain Robespierre have run to save him? Certainly not. *(Applause.)* There are only two manners of existence: either on one's knees like a slave, or upright like a man. (*Applause.*) Nevertheless, citizens, would you believe that despite the decrees of the Convention, men wrapped in the mantle of the law have been put under arrest? Would you believe that despite the will of the people a man you have struck down with arrest, Sijas, that infernal conspirator, is at this moment at the Jacobins to provoke the people: but the people is calm, and desires liberty. (*Lively applause.*)

There is one fact of which I must not leave you in ignorance. A company of artillerymen, misled by the villain Hanriot, has tried to direct its cannon against the Convention. . . . (*Movement of indignation.*) The armed forces opposed it. (*Lively applause.*) One must know how to take vigorous steps; one must know how to die at his post. (Yes! Yes, *cry all the members,* we all know how!) The united committees want to place before you a report of measures designed to save liberty. They are immediate; for that impudent rebel, that cunning conspirator who for six months has hidden behind the mask of virtue so as to strangle republicans is now at the commune. You shall hear the report of the two committees.

Collot takes the rostrum.

THE PRESIDENT: Citizens, here is the moment to die at our posts; villains, armed men have surrounded the Committee on General Security and seized it.

(*The citizens who occupy one part of the hall and the galleries all cry:* Let's go! *They go out. Applause.*)

The département *of Paris presents itself at the bar.*

SPOKESMAN OF THE DÉPARTEMENT: We have written to the commune to ascertain what measures it has taken to assure public tranquillity. We are awaiting its report before taking a stand.

The Convention sends the département *to the committees on Public Safety and on General Security, to receive their orders.*

THURIOT: Could anyone doubt that there was a conspiracy, after what has happened? This morning, before nine o'clock, the muster was sounded, orders were given, and the armed forces raised against the Convention. What then was the plan, if not one of crime? If crime triumphs, do you believe that in twenty-four hours one virtuous man can exist within the walls of Paris? No, virtuous men must either stab themselves or bring the villains to the scaffold, these brigands who, had they succeeded, would have had hanging from their windows everyone who retained a degree of public reputation, and who would have finished by devouring the entrails of the mothers of families.

AIMÉ GOUPILLEAU: I announce to the Convention that Hanriot has just escaped and is being borne away in triumph. (*The Assembly shudders with horror.*)

ÉLIE LACOSTE: Several conspirators have just been set free. Robespierre, who contrary to the desire of the Committee on General Security had been taken to the Luxembourg, was refused by the police administration at that building, who had him taken to the commune. The municipal officers embraced him, treated him as a brother, and told him they would protect him. The municipal officers are in rebellion against the decrees of the Convention. I move that they be placed outside the law.

This proposal is decreed amidst applause.

A citizen announces at the bar that he has come from the Antoine suburb, which he found aroused and ready to fight for the Convention. (*Applause.*)

A member announces that Hanriot is at the square of the Palais National, and that he is issuing orders there.

THE WHOLE ASSEMBLY: Outside the law! Outside the law!

The Convention places Hanriot outside the law.

AMAR: I am back from the square; I saw Hanriot there trying to mislead all the citizenry, and especially the artillerymen. I cried out: "Artillerymen, will you dishonor your fatherland, which has always owed you so much?" The artillerymen immediately came over to my side. An aide of Hanriot threatened me with his sword; the artillerymen protected me against him. (*Applause.*) Explain to the people, and we shall brave every danger.

VOULLAND: Citizens, we need a chief of the National Guard; but that chief must be one of your men, and that means he must be chosen from among you. The two committees propose to you Citizen Barras, who will have the courage to accept.

The assembly, amidst applause, names Citizen Barras to direct the armed forces. At his motion the Convention attaches to him six members, which it invests with the powers given to the representatives of the people with the armies. These six members are Ferrand, Fréron, Rovère, Delmas, Bolleti, Léonard Bourdon, and Bourdon de l'Oise.

BARÈRE, *in the name of the Committee of Public Safety:* Citizens, there has then broken out this terrible conspiracy, hatched beneath the cloak of patriotism, and by usurpers of public opinion; it had numerous ramifications, which have emerged this evening with frightful rapidity; for the events of just a part of this day must open the eyes of the most skeptical citizens. All the preparations for this counter-revolution were made, and all the positions taken; and among those who co-operated there can be none but accomplices. While you were issuing salutary decrees, Hanriot loosed in the streets of Paris the rumor that Robespierre had just been assassinated. The most inflammatory news was spread about you. Ammunition was issued to the police to use against the representatives of the people; and the loyal soldiers have just deposited with the Committee this ammunition distributed by the crime.

During this time the administration of police, following an order from the mayor, from the national agent of the Paris commune, and from one of his deputies, issued an order to set free Citizens Lavalette and Boulanger, officers of the Parisian armed forces, and also Villate, member of the Revolutionary Tribunal. Thus the administration of police, the mayor, and the national agent have constituted themselves as superiors of the Committee on General Security, which had had Villate arrested, and brazenly usurped the national authority confided in the Convention.

At the same time Hanriot had taken to the [Prison de la] Force a policeman bearing a decree from the Convention, until such time as the *magistrates* of the people should have ordained otherwise.

Inasmuch as Hanriot created magistrates he insulted your authority, and arrested the sergeant-at-arms of the Convention; he had the call to arms drummed in one *section,* the general alarm in the other, and the tocsin sounded in all the *sections* surrounding the commune. The mayor of Paris sent out orders for all the gates to be closed. We ask you for a decree which again prohibits the closing of the gates and designates those disobeying this order as enemies of the people.

Boulanger took refuge in the Paris encampment; Hanriot went up and down the streets on horseback crying: "They are assassinating the patriots; to arms against the Convention!" and he stirred up the people, who never respond to these insolent provocations when they are calm.

Payan declaimed against the national representation at the commune, and the commune declared itself in open insurrection against the Convention.

The revolutionary committee of the Temple informs us that the Paris commune has closed the gates and summoned an immediate meeting of the *sections* to consider the dangers threatening the fatherland.

At the municipality, the order is not to let in anyone sent by the Convention. Nevertheless the bailiff was admitted. A municipal officer said in response to the decree which summoned the municipality to the bar: "O yes, we are coming, but with the people!" To this response he added a gesture which the people would not have avowed, for the people honors itself in honoring its representatives.

Here you see conspiracy at its most atrocious, military conspiracy, conspiracy plotted more broadly, skillfully, and coolly than were ever those of the Pisistratuses or the Catilines.

One group of the *sections* has already pronounced for the representatives of the people; another group is moving toward support of the law. If some few are misled or the victims of communal intrigues, do not believe that the delusion can last.

While waiting, declare outside the law all those who give orders to move the armed forces against the National Convention, or to ignore its decrees. It is necessary also to place outside the law individuals who, struck by decrees of arrest or of accusation, do not defer to the law, or who flee it. Courage must accompany public virtue, and virtue must characterize the representatives of the people: with courage and the people, you shall conquer.

The object of the efforts of the committees is that the citizens of Paris may recollect the republic to which they belong, that they may not go and swear allegiance to a commune disloyal to its duty, and accomplice to the most horrible of conspiracies. Certain ones of those whom the Convention has struck down have got away, and found asylum in the bosom of that commune; how have they dared thus to dirty the home of the citizens of Paris; and could they count on long impunity, if they believed themselves among Frenchmen, among republicans? The eyes of the fatherland are on Paris, and the National Convention will know how to tell the good citizens from the bad.

The *sections* are assembling; it is to them that we must address ourselves.

Barère proposes a decree which is adopted in this form:

"The National Convention, having heard the report of its committees of Public Safety and General Security, prohibits the closing of the gates, and any convocation of the *sections* without authorization from the committees of Public Safety and General Security.

"It places outside the law all public functionaries who give orders designed to move the armed forces against the National Convention, or to prevent the execution of decrees it has made.

"It also places outside the law individuals who, struck by decrees of arrest or accusation, do not defer to the law, or who flee it."

Barère presents the following proclamation:

"The National Convention to the French people."

[*Here reappears the proclamation given earlier in the debate, pages 196–7 above.*]

Citizen Devèze, municipal official, who was absent from the General Council of the commune, disavows everything done there, and declares he knew nothing about it.

Some artillerymen, led by representatives of the people, march into the hall to the sound of applause.

A member of the civil committee of the Unity section, *admitted to the bar, announces that that* section *recognizes no authority save that of the Convention, and that it has received from the municipality the order to assemble and to send it, every two hours, emissaries to communicate with it.*

An officer of the company of disabled soldiers, on guard outside the Convention, comes to ask for its orders to march against the traitors. (Applause)

VOULLAND: Hanriot is not the only one who has escaped the decree of arrest; Robespierre and all the others have escaped it too; I move that they be placed outside the law.

This proposal is decreed amidst the liveliest applause.

ÉLIE LACOSTE: The Sablons encampment is commanded by a creature of Dumouriez, Beurnonville, and Custine: by Bertèche. This villain was in Calvados, whence he came to Wimpfen.

BILLAUD-VARENNE: I announce to the Convention that Bertèche was arrested about four hours ago. Apart from his counter-revolutionary conduct in Belgium, he had given the Committee grounds for suspicion. Two weeks ago Le Bas came and demanded his dismissal; and when he saw that the Committee was inclined to agree to it, he opposed it and praised him.

I call the attention of the assembly to another matter. There is no doubt that the parade planned for tomorrow was a measure designed to surround the Convention and the committees, under the pretext of having the young people from the camp march before the Convention. It was requested that they carry arms, and bring along fifteen cannon. I have no wish to cast a shadow on the patriotism of the young people, nor on the virtue of the people; but I believe there must be no parade tomorrow. What we have to concern ourselves with is the destruction of villains. We will go to the Pantheon with more enthusiasm when we have purged the ground. (*Lively applause.*)

The Convention decrees the postponement of the festival.

TALLIEN: The villains we have struck down took many steps to pervert public opinion in that camp. One of them, I hear, has just taken refuge there. I move that two representatives be designated to go there.

The Convention decrees that Brival and Bentabole will be adjuncts to Pessard, people's representative at the camp.

A deputation from the revolutionary committee of the Mutius Scoevola [*Luxembourg*] section *appears to communicate a decree of the commune council, asking constituted authorities to come take their oaths to them. The deputation announces that the tocsin is being sounded at the commune. (Movement of indignation.)*

All the sections *of Paris come successively to the bar to swear to the Convention that they recognize no authority but that of the Convention, that they will rally to it alone, that they will build it a rampart of their bodies; they congratulate it on its energy, which once more is preserving liberty.*

The Convention gives them testimony of its satisfaction, and the president announces to each of them the decree which places the conspirators outside the law.

Barras enters the hall. The liveliest applause is heard. He takes the floor.

BARRAS: I have just traversed a major part of Paris; everywhere the people are primed with liberty; everywhere one hears cries of *vive la république! vive la Convention nationale!* The artillerymen of the Fontaine de Grenelle *section* accompanied us everywhere. (*Lively applause.*) The military dispositions have just been made; the Convention is surrounded by all the republicans of Paris. I have just had arrested a policeman who was sent by the commune to Bertèche. I am going to deposit with the two committees the letter that was taken from him.

FERRAND: I have been visiting the posts on the perimeter; everywhere I have found only true republicans; all have sworn to die in the defense of the Convention. (Yes, we'll all die! *cry the citizens in the galleries.*)

I have had arrested a policeman who came from Hanriot to order the armed force which surrounded the Palais National to retire. (*Applause.*)

FRÉRON: The Convention can count on the patriotism of the citizens of Paris. The criminal Hanriot and the Catiline, Robespierre had concerted their efforts so well that they had named the traitor Le Bas to inspect the Sablons camp; but that is all undone, and the Convention was perhaps never so sublime as in that moment when, stripped of force to oppose the conspirators, it imitated the senators of Rome who awaited the enemy on their chairs of office.

We sent to the town hall square five brave artillerymen to explain things to their comrades. As soon as the latter knew that Hanriot was outside the law, they said they only needed our orders to turn their cannon against the town hall.

Moments are precious; we must act; Barras has just returned to the Committee of Public Safety, to get in concert with them. The rest of us, we must march against the rebels. (*Lively applause.*) In the name of the Convention we shall call upon those perhaps misled men who may be in the town hall to deliver the traitors over to us; and if they refuse we shall reduce the building to powder. (Yes! Yes! *cries from all parts of the hall.—Lively applause.*)

Tallien takes the rostrum.

I must not forget to tell you that we have found at the Pont-Neuf [bridge] a body of fifteen hundred men who are guarding that important position with cannon. (*Applause.*)

THE PRESIDENT: I urge my colleagues to depart at once, that the sun may not rise before the heads of the conspirators have fallen. (*Applause.*)

RÜHL: I move that a force be sent which is sufficient to hold the imprisoned conspirators.

ÉLIE LACOSTE: The two committees have sent troops to the prisons, the Temple, and the treasury.

The chief of the constabulary of the tribunals, whose liberty has just been restored by the Committee on General Security after he had been robbed of it by Hanriot, takes this opportunity to assure the Convention of the loyalty of his corps.

The constabulary of the Convention send word that if they do not present themselves at the bar it is because they are more valuable at their posts, and that even though they lost half their number in the Vendée they would lose it all here in the defense of liberty and the Convention. (Applause.)

The president announces that he is holding in his hands the original of the convocation of the Paris sections, *by the commune, as well as the appointment of a general which it made despite the decree issued this morning.*

The Marat [Théâtre-Français] section *comes to announce that it has had arrested commune agitators which had come and made it insidious propositions. (Applause.)*

DUBOIS-CRANCÉ: I must give homage to the wisdom of Marat; at the time of the judgment of the tyrant Capet, he said to me, speaking of Robespierre: "See that rat over there?" "Rat? Why?" "Yes," he answered, "that man is a greater danger to liberty than the whole despot coalition."

BRIVAL: We have come from the camp; all the students cried out with one voice, when they heard about the conspiracy you have foiled: "Perish the traitors! *vive la liberté!*" We had immense trouble restraining their ardor; they all wanted to come to the Convention to make a rampart for it of their bodies. (*Applause.*)

BENTABOLE: There was near the camp an arsenal of five hundred three-mile guns; and because we were afraid they were not safe we put them under the care of the young students, who swore they would not be got away from them but at the cost of their lives. (*Applause.*)

BILLAUD-VARENNE: The Convention cannot but applaud the energy of the people of Paris; they are hurrying to arms; but also at this very moment the conspirators are galvanizing people's minds to act against the Convention; counter-revolution is being organized at the commune, and already several cannon have been prepared for the march against the Convention; it is time to finish this struggle between liberty and tyranny, between the Convention and those who would strangle it; and I move that it order the representatives which it has named to take all steps necessary for the seizure of the conspirators, so that their heads will fall within one hour. (*Applause.*)

A citizen announces that he has come from the town hall; that as he went through the square he saw that all the artillerymen were not for the commune but for the Convention.

BILLAUD-VARENNE: I have no doubt that the artillerymen, once things have been made clear to them, will turn their cannon against the commune; but we must not lose precious time talking. When you are sitting on a volcano you must do something. Robespierre has just said that within two hours he would march on the Convention; it is up to us to get ahead of him. We'll sleep as soon as the traitors have been destroyed. (*Applause.*)

The president asks the members of the two committees to meet together in a room nearby, the deputies to remain at their posts, and the citizens to fly to arms. All the citizens who are in a part of the hall and in the galleries go out; only women are left.

LEGENDRE: Hanriot's *section,* the Sans-Culottes [Jardin-des-Plantes] *section,* which he tried to mislead, is here en masse, armed in your defense. (*Armed citizens, conducting an individual whom they have arrested, are brought to the bar.*) But my soul, citizens, is torn. At the moment of the arrest of the municipal official whom you see at the bar,

I ran at him to stab him; I had the misfortune to wound a patriot. (*Legendre despairs; people cry to him that the patriot is only slightly wounded in the hand.*) I should never be consoled for his loss. The Sans-Culottes *section* has told me that Hanriot had strewn the place with money.

A member of the revolutionary committee of the Mountain [*Butte des Moulins*] section *congratulates himself at the bar for having saved a representative of the people from the hands of Hanriot, and announces that he is bringing in a municipal official. He announces at the same time that the town hall is taken, and that Robespierre the elder is being brought in a litter.*

Charlier takes the rostrum.

THE PRESIDENT: The dastard Robespierre is here. You don't want him to come in? (*Cries from all sides:* No! No!)

THURIOT: To bring into the bosom of the Convention a man covered with every crime would deprive this glorious day of all the splendor it deserves. The body of a tyrant can carry only disease; the place marked for him and his accomplices is the Square [*place*] of the Revolution, The two committees must take the necessary measures to see that the blade of the law strikes them down without delay.

The Convention decrees this proposal. (Applause.)

ESNARD, *commandant of the armed forces, at the bar*: As soon as I had in my hands the decree naming me provisional commander of the National Guard, I went to the mayor, who read my credentials. Payan also got notice of it, and had me put under arrest with my adjutant. Half an hour ago, as soon as I heard the representative of the people, at the town hall, cry out *vive la Convention! vive la liberté!* I summoned the jailer to open up the door for me; he refused; I beat it down with a stick and hurled myself into the arms of the representative of the people. (*Applause.*)

There are requests for the president to give the fraternal embrace to Esnard.

Esnard mounts to the rostrum and receives the accolade amidst the liveliest applause.

Léonard Bourdon enters the hall amidst applause. He is accompanied by a policeman, and asks permission for the latter to mount to the rostrum with him.

This request is granted.

LÉONARD BOURDON: This brave policeman whom you see did not leave me; he killed two of the conspirators. (*Lively applause.*) When

I left here I looked for forces in the Lombards, Arcis, and Gravilliers *sections,* to lay siege to the town hall; we moved into the square in several columns. At our approach the misled citizens opened their eyes, and the dastards fled. We found Robespierre the elder armed with a knife, which this brave policeman snatched from him. He also struck Couthon, who was also armed with a knife; Saint-Just and Le Bas have been taken, and Dumas and fifteen or twenty others are shut in a well-guarded room in the town hall.

We have given three citizens tasks: one to bring the prisoners here, another to watch at the treasury, and a third to make a search to uncover other conspirators who may be hidden there. It seems likely that Hanriot has escaped, for some citizens told me they saw him flee; but as they did not know about your decree they did not fall upon him. In short, citizens, liberty triumphs and the conspirators will soon appear before you at the bar. (No! No! *cries from all sides.*)

Here is a notebook and papers seized on Robespierre. Here too is a letter found on Couthon, signed Robespierre and Saint-Just; it is framed in these terms:

"Couthon, the patriots are all proscribed, the whole people had risen, it would be treason not to come to the town hall, where we are."

I ask that the president give the fraternal accolade to this brave policeman.

The president does so amidst applause.

THE PRESIDENT: I must tell the Convention what this brave policeman has just said to me; "I have no love for blood; still I should have liked to shed that of the Prussians and the Austrians; but I do not regret not being in the army, for today I have shed the blood of traitors." This citizen is called Charles-André Médal.

The Convention decrees that honorable mention shall be made of the civic devotion of this citizen, and instructs the Committee of Public Safety to give him a promotion.

LEGENDRE: When I left this rostrum I spoke to ten determined citizens whom I took with me; my intention was to go blow out the brains of the man who presided at the Jacobins yesterday and today. With my pistol loaded in both barrels I entered the hall; but bad luck had it that the villain had mixed with the crowd, and I stopped myself out of fear of hitting the innocent; he is named Vivier. I said to the women in the galleries: "You have been misled; go; the Convention punishes crime and not error." I locked the doors of the Jacobins; here are the keys. (*Applause.*) As it is the Convention en masse which has saved the fatherland, tomorrow the National Convention en masse will be Jacobin. (*Renewed and lively applause.*) It will be virtue that goes to open the doors of that Society.

THIRION: I move that measures be taken against the villain Vivier. This man, devoted to Robespierre, who has presided at the Jacobins this night, was in rebellion against the Convention; for he presided in support of people who were in rebellion.

The Convention places Vivier outside the law. (Lively applause.)
The session is adjourned at six o'clock in the morning.

Revolutionary Committee, Section des Arcis

20 Thermidor, Year II [7 August 1794]

Deposition:

The said Daucour, police officer, residing at no. [ ], quai de Gèvre, was arrested during the night of the 9th to the 10th Thermidor in the General Assembly [of the section] and, according to his statement, there preaching revolt against the Convention, seeking to draw the General Assembly into the party of the commune, showing the ropes and straps that had been used to bind Hanriot at the Committee on General Security and boasting of having himself released Hanriot, and stipulates and affirms all these facts, stating that he was astonished that only the Section des Arcis was in rebellion against the commune while the other forty-seven were on its side as well as the neighboring communes.

P.C.C. Auguis (Secretary)

This document has been published in *Annales historiques de la Révolution française,* XXXVII (1965), 90-91.

Vigilance Committee, Ninth Arrondissement

8 Vendémiaire, Year III [29 September, 1794]

Interrogation of Citizen Bouillette:

Having appeared, citizen Jean Bouillette, sheathmaker, residing at no. 20, rue Jean de l'Épine, twenty-five years of age sergeant-major of the 14th cy of the armed Arcis *section* states to us that, being on the quai de Gèvres on the night of the 9th to the 10th Thermidor, at one

Ibid., 91-2.

in the morning, the superintendent of police named Freine of the Section des Arcis, proclaiming, being mounted on a pillar near the Pont de la Raison, formerly Notre-Dame, the Convention's decree that outlawed the municipal government as well as Robespierre, who was given more prominence than the others in the same decree, which appeared instantly to create a great sensation among those who heard it; that then a citizen in the crowd, claiming to be a representative of the people, who in fact was invested with power and had his representative's identity card which he showed to all those around him, climbed onto the same pillar and embraced Freine, the aforesaid superintendent of police, and beginning to speak, harangued the people saying that Robespierre was a scoundrel as well as the officers of the commune, and having pointed out that the aforesaid and the others were outlawed by decree of the Convention which had just been read by citizen Freine, invited the armed force which was around to hear the aforesaid proclamation, to support it in order to upset the liberticide plans of the commune officials and the other scoundrels, and carry out the decree of the Convention.

To which the major part of the citizens replied that they should go to the commune in a body, which took place at once, but that arriving at the entrance to the [Place de la] Grève, at the end of Quai Pelletier, a gunner about five feet, four inches tall, seeing a crowd moving in the direction of the commune, called for a drumroll and blocked the passage of the deputy as well as the accompanying citizens.

The aforesaid gunner occupying the parapet approached us with drawn saber and learning from the shouts of some citizen (observing that at the sound of the drumroll the great crowd melted) that this was a representative of the people, told his gunner comrades as well as those who were accompanying the deputy that the aforesaid deputy had to be arrested and brought to the commune, seeing that he was a false deputy and that he demanded a king; that at the same moment, seeing the same gunner was about to use force, citizens Bouillette and Girardin, who had not for a moment ceased to hold the aforesaid deputy by his arms, opposed him with all their strength.

The said Bouillette and Girardin, not wishing that a national representative be injured and seeing the aforesaid deputy was running the imminent risk of a saber blow which the said Bouillette and Girardin warded off above the head of the aforesaid deputy and which the pernicious gunner intended to land, the aforesaid Bouillette and Girardin, without letting go of the aforesaid deputy, went to the respective Section des Arcis and to the Vigilance Committee of that *section*.

Upon which, the representative of the people having said that his name was Peniaire and having shown his representative's identity card, the Comité des Arcis ordered citizens Bouillette and Girardin (at their own request) to remain with the representative and immediately take him back to the National Convention, which was done at once, and after this important mission which was the fondest desire of citizens Bouillette and Girardin, they returned to the aforesaid *comité* to report the safe delivery of aforesaid deputy to the National Convention and took up their weapons and returned to their post.

Paris Commune

9 Thermidor, Year II [27 July 1794]

Executive Committee

Courage, patriots of the Section des Piques, liberty triumphs! Already those whose steadfastness rendered them formidable to traitors are at liberty; Everywhere the people are showing themselves worthy of their reputation.

The meeting place is at the commune where the brave Hanriot will carry out the orders of the Executive Committee which has been established to save the country.

[signed] Louvet, Payan, Legrand, Lerebours, Ro

This letter to Robespierre's own *section* has been reproduced several times. The bottom of the page has several brownish stains, the largest of which measures about an inch across. See note, pp. 225–6.

Memoirs of Joseph Barras

. . . A decree of indictment is pronounced against both Robespierres, Le Bas, Saint-Just, and Couthon. Thereupon great becomes the noise; the accused men protest, while cries of "To the bar!" are repeated a thousand times over. The president commands the ushers to bring the accused to the bar of the house; the ushers hesitate. The armed force is called upon; it also hesitates. Robespierre and his adherents are dragged to gaol.

The terror inspired by Robespierre is such that at the two prisons to which he is brought, the Luxembourg and the Conciergerie, the gaolers

Memoirs of Barras, I, 236-48. The notes following are by G. Duruy, editor of the French edition.

refuse to open the doors to admit him; he insists on being received, and like Socrates bows to the law; such behaviour on his part was undoubtedly most wise, and threatened to place the National Convention in a very embarrassing position. How, indeed, could it place on his trial a man against whom it could bring no other charge than that of having uttered from the tribune words it listened to approvingly, subsequently converting them into decrees.

Fortunately, Robespierre is shortly to find himself disobeying the Convention, nay, in insurrection against it. He is led in triumph to the commune. . . .

. . . Hanriot was body and soul devoted to Robespierre. On hearing of the catastrophe which had happened to his master, the bravo rushed to the commune to his rescue, caused every honour to be shown to him, and declared that the whole of the population belonged to Robespierre, and that he considered it his first duty to take the orders of the august persecuted one. The commune, without even Robespierre preferring the request, but by an act of anticipatory obligingness, and that devotion of which the Terror was the principle, ordered General Hanriot, who had under him some 15,000 men, to surround the Convention, keep it in private confinement, and prevent all debate.

Hanriot, armed with this order, marched on the Assembly and took possession of the room wherein were held the sittings of the Committee of General Security.

Its members, as well as those of the Committee of Public Safety, who should have remained at their posts and taken such measures as the circumstances demanded, fled to the Convention. Hanriot thence wended his way to the courtyard of the Tuileries, seized the cannon of honour, and trained them on the Convention, which, in so desperate an emergency, recovered its energy.

Dissatisfied with all the resolutions of which I was a witness, I at first refused the request preferred by the committees that I should take command of the troops in Paris. "You have generals enough," I had said; "let them mount their horses; do so yourselves, for the purpose of defending the country you have compromised." And, abandoning there and then these men, only a short while ago so insolent and cruel in the prosperity of their power, but now cowards in the hour of peril, I had returned to my place in the Convention, where its members, seated on their curule chairs, awaited an almost certain death. I was at once surrounded and questioned as to the measures taken by the committees, for it was known that I had been summoned by them. My reply was: "They are dead even before a blow has been struck." This was at the very moment that their members were entering the hall of the Convention. After giving expression to their fears for the safety of the national representation, they proposed my appointment as general-in-chief of the Army of the Interior, and to the command of the Paris troops, which I had just declined. The National Convention, rising to its feet as one body, pronounced the decree, which was rendered unanimously.

There were at my disposal only the poorest resources for putting down the rebellion; they held possession of our guns and blocked up every exit from the Tuileries. This was not the time for discussion; it was necessary to act; but in order to act there was required, for want of the means taken from us, a double confidence on the part of that portion of the citizens and deputies determined not to bow to Robespierre's supremacy. The Convention, once more rising to its feet *en masse,* gave me proof of the most generous confidence. All my colleagues, some shaking me by the hand, others embracing me, told me that they reckoned on this fresh proof of my devotion to the country. . . .

Hanriot, arrested temporarily by Merlin de Thionville, had been restored to liberty by the maddened and drunken soldiers led by Coffinhal, whereupon the Convention at once decreed the outlawry of the rebellious general. I left the Assembly, bearing the decree. "I am going to my post; remain at yours!" Such was the whole of my speech. Hanriot was outside with his gunners. I called out to them in a loud voice, "Away with you, you wretches! Hanriot is an outlaw!" The very few soldiers and citizens who were accompanying me exclaimed in their turn, "Obey Barras! He is general-in-chief." On hearing this, the insurgents and their vile commander were seized with fright, and fled helter-skelter to the Commune.

The cowardice of Hanriot and Lavalette, and the disappearance of their soldiery, gave rise to some uproar, followed by a numerous desertion on the part of his troops, which had remained stationed in the Place de Grève at the orders of the Commune, whose diminishing ardour seemed to be inclining to some little moderation.

I took in this state of affairs at a glance, and grasping all its details in an instant, I thought I saw I had sufficient time to make an appeal to the good citizens and prevent the meeting in the Carrousel of the troops then in Paris and those outside the gates at Meudon and at Saint-Germain. I gave orders to beat to arms and to fire the alarm gun.

As I had presumed from the hesitating and timorous character of Robespierre, he had not adopted any particular course on reaching the commune. The rhetor, no longer able to speechify, was passing his time discussing the minutiæ of an address to be drawn up. Couthon having proposed to issue an address to the troops, Robespierre asked, "In whose name?" "Why, in the name of the Convention," replied Couthon. "Is it not wherever we are? The rest are but a handful of factious men whom the armed force will scatter and make short work of." "My opinion," Robespierre went on to say, "is that we should write in the name of the people." In this way Robespierre refused to advance on the Convention and dissolve it. This hesitation, communicating itself to all about him, served to spread a state of fright by which I was to profit, and which I had reckoned upon. My agents went through the streets proclaiming loudly that large forces had rallied to me. I had about 4000 men under me. I was desirous of avoiding a fight, and dreaded being obliged to cannonade the Hôtel-de-Ville. The committees, on finding the scene of the battle transferred from the Tuileries to the Place de Grève, recovered from their fright, and, as a consequence, at once resumed their insolent tone and taste for cruelty. They would have had me sweep everything with fire and sword, and exterminate all the insurgents with one discharge of grape-shot. I was fortunate enough to be able to prove to them that it was possible to avoid both carnage and the use of flames. The positions I had taken could at all events protect the retreat of the National Convention to the heights of Meudon.

The display of the measures I had taken created so great an impression that I was not called upon to proceed to extremities. Fear was gaining the conspirators. The defection of their early accomplices soon became known to and shared by the outside Jacobins, as if by some electric current. From time to time I sent reassuring reports to the Convention, keeping, at the head of my little army, the road open by way of the quays to the Place de Grève, the rumbling of my artillery putting to flight the remnants of the insurrection. I wended my way to the Hôtel-de-Ville, which Merlin de Thionville had already entered. Robespierre had shattered his jaw* with one of the two pistols carried by Le

* The Thermidorians were interested in casting dishonour on the memory of their victim. The suicide story, showing as it does Robespierre in the light of a great criminal punishing himself in order to escape just chastisement for his misdeeds, is consequently the one they have seen fit to adopt. In spite of the assertions made by Barras in his memoirs, and of those of Courtois in his report of the 8th Thermidor, Year III., I am inclined to believe that by no means did Robespierre seek to kill himself, but that he was treacherously wounded at the very moment when, after prolonged wavering—the cause of his ruin—he had at last made up his mind to respond to the outlawry pronounced against him by an appeal to arms against his enemies in the Convention and in the committees. As I write these lines, there lies before me the original draft of this appeal to arms.

Bas, who had blown his brains out with the other. Couthon was hiding under a table, and Robespierre in a little room, by the door of which Le Bas lay. Saint-Just was ministering to Robespierre. Hanriot was crouching in a watercloset. I could not endure this melancholy spectacle, so I left, and had Robespierre carried into the *salon* of the Committee of Public Safety, where he was laid on a table. Medical men commissioned to examine and dress his wounds drew up a report confirming that Robespierre's condition was the result of an attempt to commit suicide, and the direction taken by the charge was that of a man who had shot himself. One of the surgeons having placed on the table the teeth which had fallen from Robespierre's mouth during his examination of it, one of the gunners on duty pounced on them, and addressing Robespierre, exclaimed, "You scoundrel, I will keep them as a monument of execration." In a report submitted to me on the circumstances connected with Robespierre's agony, I read that he had repeatedly asked for a pen in order to write, as he could no longer articulate, and that this request, again and again made in the hearing of the members of the Committee, had been by them denied. I have heard this fact, to which I declare not having been a witness, repeated, for I would not have refused a pen to this man in his agony; and, in view of his not being able to speak, he might therewith have given us information which the others might have had interest in suppressing. Was the refusal of the members of the Committee merely an expression of the hatred which might have been inspired by the man who had sought to have them all killed but a short while ago, and who had almost succeeded in carrying out his design, or, as it has also been stated, did they dread some divulgation? The sequel of events and an examination of

---

. . . I doubt whether there exists to-day in the world a document of more tragic aspect than this sheet of paper bearing the imprint of the Commune. The hurried, violent, convulsive handwriting is the expression of the feverish mental agitation of Robespierre's friends in this supreme contingency. The letters run, the words rush in their headlong course; it is indeed a cry, one of distress or of battle. Side by side with the nervous signatures of Lerebours, Legrand, Louvet, and Payan, the first two letters of Robespierre's name stand out in relief, calm in the midst of all the tumult, signs as cold and methodical as the inflexible will of the man who was deliberately tracing them when the shot was fired. The unfinished word, the name severed with a clean stroke, decapitated, and having as a paraph a wide splash of blood, irresistibly calls up the crimson vision of a head falling from its trunk under the knife of the guillotine. But not only do these two sinister letters flash lightning-wise before our eyes a vision of the drama, they also explain its *dénouement*. The truncated signature seems to prove the surprise, the sudden and thunder-like attempt on life, the bullet despatched by another hand than the one which was tracing those bold characters, so abruptly interrupted—in a word, murder, not suicide. [This interpretation, however moving, is wrong. The document in question was dispatched before Robespierre's recapture.]

his papers have not proved that Robespierre and his accomplices had anything to reveal they would not have said, and which was not already known. A week later, this table, round which the members of the Committee were deliberating, was still dyed with the blood of Robespierre. What carelessness and ferocious attention on the part of those dear colleagues of his!* All arrested were taken to prison; I was on the point of having Couthon transferred to an hospital, but the circumstances did not permit even the most sincere humanity to display any such particular attentions. What attentions could claim individuals on whom death had already laid its hand, and who were about to be delivered over to it?

On the 10th Thermidor, the Revolutionary Tribunal sentenced Robespierre and his accomplices to death, or rather fixed the date of their execution, for, as they were outlawed by the decree of the Convention, there was nothing left to do but establish their identity and hand them over to the executioner. . . .

Revolutionary Tribunal

10 Thermidor [28 July]

Maximilien Robespierre, aged 35 years, born at Arras, ex-deputy of the National Convention; G. Couthon, aged 38 years, born at Orsay, ex-deputy of the National Convention; L. J. B. T. Lavalette, aged 40 years, born in Paris, ex-noble, ex-commandant of a battalion of the section of the Gardes Françaises, ex-brigadier-general in the Army of the North; F. Hanriot, aged 33 years, born at Nanterre, ex-exciseman, ex-commander-general of the armed force of Paris; L. C. F. Dumas, aged 37 years, born at Lucy (Haute-Saône), lawyer at Lons-le-Saunier, ex-president of the Revolutionary Tribunal in Paris; A. Saint-Just, aged 26 years, born at Liser (Nièvre), ex-deputy of the Convention; C. F. Payan, aged 27 years, born at Paul-les-Fontaines, ex-juryman of the Revolutionary Tribunal, ex-national agent of the Commune of Paris; N. J. Vivier, aged 50 years, born in Paris, ex-judge of the criminal

* Robespierre was placed in a room which was not the one wherein the Committee held its sittings. None of its members can have even seen him. They had gone to take a rest immediately after Robespierre's arrest at the Hôtel-de-Ville. The Committee did not sit again till eight o'clock on the forenoon of the 10th, some three hours after Robespierre had been transported to the prison of La Conciergerie.—Note in the handwriting of M. Prieur de la Côte-d'Or.

Le Moniteur universal, XXI, 559-60 (Edition of 6 Fructidor, Year II [23 August 1794]).

tribunal of the department, ex-president of the so-called Jacobins on the night of the 9th Thermidor; A. N. Gobeau, aged 26 years, born at Vincennes, temporary ex-deputy of the public prosecutor near the tribunal of the department, municipal officer of the Commune of Paris of the 10th August; J. B. L. Fleuriot-Lescot, aged 39 years, temporary ex-deputy of the public prosecutor near the Revolutionary Tribunal, ex-mayor of Paris; A. P. J. Robespierre the Younger, ex-deputy of the Convention; J. C. Bernard, aged 34 years, born in Paris, ex-priest; A. Gency, aged 33 years, born at Reims, cooper; A. Simon, aged 58 years, shoemaker; D. L. Laurent, aged 33 years; J. L. F. Warmé, aged 29 years; J. L. Forestier, aged 47 years, metal-founder; N. Guérin, tax-collector; J. M. B. d'Hazard, hairdresser; C. Cochefer, ex-upholsterer; C. J. M. Bourgon; J. M. Quenet, wood-merchant—the last eleven ex-members of the Council General of the commune of Paris;—all outlawed pursuant to decrees of the Convention of the 9th and 10th Thermidor, and, their identity having been established by witnesses, they were handed over to the executor of criminal judgments to be put to death within twenty-four hours on the Place de la Révolution, and were executed.

Jacobin Club

9 Thermidor [27 July]

After the reading of correspondence, about eight o'clock in the evening, the crowd being very large and the galleries filled with citizens and citizenesses from all quarters of the city, someone asked that a member of the Convention report on its meeting that day. Chasles, a deputy of the *département* of Eure-et-Loire, wounded at the siege of Lille, climbed to the rostrum with the aid of his crutch. He began to give his report, but was interrupted after almost every word by a universal clamor condemning the decree that had been passed against the two Robespierres, Couthon, Saint-Just, and Le Bas. Chasles finally terminated his report and descended from the rostrum amid the murmurs and jeers of practically all the members of the Society and of the citizens in the galleries.

A Secretary of the Society proposed that each representative of the people present be called to the rostrum and questioned whether he

Conservateur décadaire, No. 13 (20 Fructidor), published in *Annales historiques de la Révolution française,* I (1924), 501-3.

voted for or against the decree of the day. The motion was adopted by the great majority of the Society and to the unanimous acclamation of the galleries. Brival presented himself first for interrogation. Vivier, interim president, acting according to the will of the assembly, asked Brival how he had voted on the decree of the day against Robespierre. Brival replied that he was astonished at the question put to him by the president; if the Society, he added, had listened quietly to Chasles report, it would not have acceded to the motion to question each deputy. Chasles came to tell you that the whole Convention rose up against Robespierre. If you rigorously follow your plan, you will have to expel from the body of the Society all the deputies that you have admitted, for they all voted against Robespierre. For myself, who has always voted according to the beliefs of the Mountain, in the Legislative Assembly and in the Convention, I confess that I voted for the arrest of Robespierre. I did more; I was one of those who provoked the measure, and as secretary, I rushed to expedite and sign the decree.

Brival's remarks and reply were badly received in the tumult which dominated the Society. "Down with him! Down with him! Chase him away! Send him away!" were the cries from every side. Brival descended from the rostrum, followed by jeers and insults. He left his card. He was pushed toward the door and he left. Shortly afterwards, a member made some judicious observations about the notion of interrogating representatives of the people about the day's decree against Robespierre. They were favorably listened to and his motion was carried unanimously. A commissioner was named to return Brival his entrance card.

However, the Society, uneasy about the fate of Robespierre, Saint-Just and Le Bas, declared itself to be in continous session.

The President read a letter which was addressed to him by the Committee of Public Safety and which demanded that the Jacobin Society send it immediately the manuscript copy of the speech which Robespierre read the evening before from the rostrum of the Society. Vivier consulted the Society as to the response it should make. Some of the members were of the opinion that the demand of the Committee of Public Safety should be rejected as the Committee had no right to demand papers of the Society or to have them communicated under threat of force. Others, and they represented the majority, thought that it was necessary to reply to the Committee that the Society did not have Robespierre's last speech. In fact, it had been left in the hands of the printer Nicholas. The Society decreed that the president reply to the Committee that it was no longer in possession of Robespierre's speech.

At nine thirty, a member rushed into the meeting, hurried to the front and said: "Citizens, I am going to announce some good news." A great silence fell upon the assembly. "Citizens, the cannoneers with their cannons at this moment surround the Committee of Public Safety; they are preceded by some magistrates and followed by a large crowd of people. The magistrates again demand from the Committee, in the name of the people and the law, the liberty of Robespierre, Couthon, Le Bas, and Saint-Just." At these words, cries of "Long live Liberty! Long live Liberty!" broke out throughout the hall and throughout all the galleries; hats were waved in the air, people applauded with their feet and their hands, and expressions of the liveliest and most intense joy were prolonged for several minutes.

It was then that commissioners were appointed to go fraternize with the Commune and other commissioners sent to the *sections* on the same mission.

The Sections of Paris

It is difficult, even with the aid of the documents which are closest to the events, to say what was the actual appearance of the streets of Paris during the afternoon and evening of the 9th of Thermidor.

Without doubt in what was then the center of the city, in the *sections* closest to the Hôtel de Ville [City Hall] and the Tuileries, spectators leaving the galleries of the Convention that day spread word about the extraordinary meeting and broadcast the stupefying news of Robespierre's arrest. From three o'clock onward, the call to arms was heard in some of the *sections,* and a number of citizens, interrupted during their dinner, appeared at their windows, napkins around their necks, then returned inside so as to get their equipment and hastily join the assembling of armed groups. But this would not have sufficed to alert and disturb very much of the mass of the population, which so many documents reveal as being inert and passive throughout the revolt.

A little later, nevertheless, a certain restlessness manifested itself when Hanriot and his escort were passing: the managers of the boulevard theaters could be seen closing their halls, and after the grotesque scuffle at the Place du Palais-Égalité, the merchants of the arcades at the garden hastily put up the shutters of their shops. But the immedi-

Paul Sainte-Claire Deville, *La Commune de l'an II: Vie et mort d'une assemblée révolutionnaire d'après de nombreux documents inédits* (Paris: Librairie Plon, 1946), pp. 266-8, 272-4, 278. Reprinted by permission of the publisher.

ate evidence agrees in showing that outside the *sections* of the center, no general trouble was visible among the population. If, here or there, people in the outlying districts heard it said that there was something afoot in Paris, this was due to a movement of workers, discontented because the Commune, according to Payan's newspaper, had just established and made public, in conformity with the law, the maximum rates for daily wages in various skills.

In the three adjacent *sections,* all remote from the center, of Bondy, Poissonnière, and Faubourg du Nord, an incident occurred, in itself quite insignificant and unrelated to the political drama of the day, which that evening excited the population and especially the active citizens. Certain people had found in the middle of a refuse heap at the rue des Vertus a rather large quantity of lard and of salted pork. These people, passing through the streets, brandishing these morsels, accused "the enemies of the people" of having thrown them there as part of "a most criminal scheme." Happily, the revolutionary committee of the Faubourg du Nord questioned the carrier who had upset the cart filled with lard and the whole thing explained itself: it was a simple question of a lot of stale, damaged merchandise, unfit for consumption, which the ministry of provisions had ordered thrown out.

The emotion caused by what had hastily been attributed to the criminal intrigues of Pitt and Cobourg ceased towards seven thirty, at the precise moment when the news of Robespierre's arrest and that of his colleagues was heard in the distant suburbs. At that hour also newspaper vendors began to spread through the streets. Their sheets, despite a modest format, had no need of signaling the public's attention by enormous headlines, because the vendors took every liberty to cry out the events of the day. And that evening their howlings proclaimed to every comer the great session of the Convention, the decrees of arrest for Hanriot, for Robespierre, and for four deputies. . . .

In many of the *sections,* at that moment, the call to arms had already been sounded; in others the citizens, advised by word of mouth, rushed towards the places of assembly. In this way the major part of the male population of active citizens was rather early concentrated at the central points of the *sections,* waiting orders; and we will shortly see what effect this concentration of people had on the composition and the attitude of the general assemblies which were just about to open.

The directors of the Commune all hoped for an uprising from the masses, for which they wanted to enlist the *sections;* and, following an insurrectionary tactical procedure, well-tried on the 10th of August and on the 31st of May 1793 alike, they counted upon the opening of the general assemblies in order to create one of those pretended outbursts of opinion by means of which they could intimidate the Convention and its Committees.

As it was, before the 9th of Thermidor the assemblies had long been deserted by the moderates who, in spite of everything, formed the immense majority of revolutionary Paris but who, by their abstention, tried to sidestep the propaganda which would incite them to action. The assemblies were normally frequented only by a few citizens who monopolized for themselves the name of "patriots," refusing this name to all others, making it easy for them to categorize them as "enemies of the people." These "patriots" were disciplined and fiery, vowing many times over their fidelity to the Commune, their adulation for Robespierre, and providing undisguised warnings to the Convention—so that one would think that they would furnish well-trained Jacobin orators.

However accurate this calculation might be for evenings in general, it was false for the night of the 9th of Thermidor. That particular evening a public very much more numerous and very different from the usual hard-core of militants invaded the assemblies and submerged the turbulent minority which ordinarily dominated them.

The call to arms, one will recall, had been sounded early in a number of the *sections;* in the others, citizens, alerted at home by their captains, had rejoined their companies at central military points. Thus, all these citizens, silently mounting guard, responded to the call; but having no great revolutionary ardor, they silently permitted the overthrow of Robespierre to take place, wanting only to see a bit of calm finally come. And these people dominated; no longer the pretended "patriots." And when the chiefs of the *sections* opened the general assemblies under these conditions, they appealed—most of their accounts reveal this—to those groups gathered at their central military points. The violent minority was drowned, that particular evening, in the crowd of moderates, men little inclined toward the measures sought by those normally in control. This was not one of the least factors in the refusal of the city to come to Robespierre's aid.

Just as rapidly as the Commune ordered the citizenry to meet in general assemblies, the Committees replied with a decree expressly forbidding the calling together of the *sections.*[1] But it is quite probable

[1] The committees of Public Safety and General Security decreed that it was expressly forbidden to man the barricades and to convoke the *sections.*

that upon reflection, they suspended the transmission of the order, because one finds no mention at all of the reception of the decree in question. Moreover, the opening of the assemblies did not take the shape of any enthusiastic adhesion to the cause of the Commune, or of any declaration of war on the Convention, as the people of the City Hall hoped.

Under these conditions, how did the diverse *sections* react to the order calling for general assemblies broadcast by the municipality?

In the first place, in nine *sections,* the civil committee, the body regularly in charge of the opening of assemblies, plainly refused to obey the General Council's decree, which it declared illegal, and no assemblies were held.[2]

Ten other *sections*[3] did have gatherings, but rather tardily, in order to declare immediately that they did not intend to obey the rebellious Commune and rapidly to vote an address of support for the Convention.

Thus there were already a substantial number of *sections* which, at the outset, rejected the General Council's invitation. The leadership of twenty-nine other civil committees and presidents of about fifteen of the assemblies opened the meetings and mentioned in their reports and in their official minutes that the meeting took place as a result of orders received from the General Council. But this obedience by the majority of the *sections,* which was purely nominal, fell far short of being accompanied by anything like an immediate mass rally to the Commune's cause. On the contrary, many of the *sections* rapidly expressed their faithfulness to the National Assembly and sent deputations to carry their assurances to the Convention.

In others, such a resolution was debated at greater length, and intervention was less rapid, but as it turned out, all the *section* assemblies ultimately declared themselves for the Convention, with the sole exception of the *section de l'Observatoire*.

Nearly everywhere, and apparently at the same hour,[4] in most of the assembled *sections*, an address of fidelity to the Convention was voted, and it was decided to communicate this decision to the forty-seven other *sections* in order to obtain their support. At that moment there was a great swarming of people throughout Paris, an intermingling of deputations which passed down the streets going from assembly

[2] Tuileries, Champs-Élysées, République, Muséum, Lombards, Réunion, Arsenal, Révolutionnaire, Pont-Neuf, Fontaine de Grenelle.
[3] Montagne, Butte des Moulins, Piques, Gardes-Françaises, Guillaume-Tell, Bonne-Nouvelle, Faubourg du Nord, Invalides, Unité, Bondy, Quinze-Vingts.
[4] From about eleven o'clock at night onward.

to assembly, between eleven o'clock at night and two or three in the morning, exhibiting their credentials, reading their addresses to the accompaniment of applause, giving and receiving everywhere the fraternal accolade.[5] The great mainspring of the mechanism of popular insurrection had broken into pieces in the very hands of the Commune, and part of it had fallen helplessly away.

Correspondence of Dyzez

Paris, 11 Thermidor, Year II

To Laffitte, executive officer of the
district administration at Saint-Sever

Robespierre has gone to join Camille Desmoulins. He was guillotined yesterday with Saint-Just, Le Bas, and Couthon, who will not be going to our *département,* you can tell Besselère.

The speeches Couthon made at the Jacobin club against certain members of the Convention had already antagonized people. For a month Robespierre had not attended the meetings of the Committee of Public Safety and this antagonized people more. Finally the speech he delivered against the two committees on the 8th [Thermidor] brought dissatisfaction to the most extreme degree. The evening session at the Jacobin club was the culmination. In it, Collot d'Herbois was mocked and Robespierree alone triumphed.

On the 9th, an attack on him was led by Tallien, whose head was almost touching the guillotine. Robespierre asked for the floor in order to reply; he called us all assassins because the floor was given to another first, for he was to have it next. His brother joined with him. The assembly, already very irritated, enacted the decree for his arrest. Here is what went wrong: the committees of Public Safety and General Security, charged with carrying it out, delivered the accused per-

[5] Of the 39 assemblies which held meetings during the night, 33 communicated their addresses of loyalty to the other *sections.* Of the remaining six, two (Halle au Blé and Marchés) had openly taken the side of the Convention from an early hour. The *section* of Sans-Culottes [Jardin-des-Plantes; Hanriot's *section*] hesitated, and only rallied rather tardily to the government; its neighbor, Finistère, did likewise, turning, however, sooner and more voluntarily to the Convention. The two *sections* of l'Observatoire and Chalier [Thermes] were the only ones clearly and persistently to have sided with the commune. Only at the last moment, when defeat was certain, did they with obvious reluctance side with the victors.

Jean Dyzez, "Lettres," *Revue de France,* VI (1926), 517-21.

sons to men who, having been unable to get the Luxembourg opened, took the prisoners to the Commune. All the friends and favorites of Robespierre were there. They embraced each other, sounded the tocsin; the people gathered; thirty cannon bristled in the avenues off the Place de Grève. All this was going on, and in the evening, at seven o'clock, when we went to the Convention, nobody knew anything about it. We had been saying trivial things from the rostrum for almost an hour, when suddenly we were told that the Committee on General Security had been forcibly entered and that [Hanriot] the chief of the National Guard and seventeen of his adjutants, who had been held there under arrest, were freed. If Hanriot had then moved against us, only two steps away, we would have been lost. If Robespierre, instead of having fun drawing up orders at the *hôtel de ville,* had marched at the head of the eight or ten thousand men who filled the Place de Grève, and if with Couthon's help he had aroused the people by his speeches, we would have been lost; but destiny decided otherwise. We finally had the sense to take some measures instead of declaiming to one another that we had to die at our post.

Robespierre was abandoned, and he is no more!

It is too bad, for the Republic, that this event can be counted among the great events. The death of one man in a free state ought to make no commotion. We shall now have to wait several days to know what course events will take. I very much wish it were clear that we knew how to take advantage of liberty and that passions would cool.

Salut et Fraternité.

VI
THE REACTION BEGINS

Introduction

The men who defeated Robespierre were united only in their opposition to him. The so-called Thermidorians were a coalition of disparate and basically antagonistic groups that were able to agree on only one immediate goal. Once Robespierre was gone, the conspirators fell out.

The divisions among the Thermidorians were evident from the beginning, but a decisive rupture did not immediately occur. Instead they tried to maintain a false and superficial harmony in the face of events that were leading in an unknown direction. The debates in the National Convention from 10 to 26 Thermidor introduce the period of reaction that followed Robespierre's death. The period is an extremely confused one. The reader should expect to be somewhat frustrated for he will learn that the close reading of a series of parliamentary debates does not always enable one to discover a distinct and consistent movement of events. He should, however, be able to discover the general mood of the Convention and determine how the different members of the coalition reacted to a Convention that suddenly rediscovered its voice.

The session of 11 Thermidor should be studied with special care because in it the opposing sides drew their battle lines. In the speech that he delivered in the name of the Committee of Public Safety, Barère presented the Committee's view of the meaning of

9 Thermidor. Does the subsequent debate indicate that the Committee's view was shared by the majority of deputies? The Convention's reply to what had become a routine request—the appointment or renewal of the Committee of Public Safety—is significant. Did the offensive launched against the Revolutionary Government on 11 Thermidor produce definitive results? Or did the organization of the Revolutionary Government remain intact?

National Convention

10 Thermidor, evening, Year II [28 July 1794]

Collot d'Herbois presiding:

On a motion by Lecointre, of Versailles, the National Convention decrees that the popular commissions, named in conformity with the decree 26 and 27 Germinal [15 and 16 April] to judge detained persons, will be sent back for examination by the committees of Public Safety and General Security, to be purified during the next ten days in order that when the list of their names, conditions, and domiciles is reported to the National Convention, it may ratify or reject the members who compose them.

THIBAUT: I move that the committees also examine jointly the organization and composition of the Revolutionary Tribunal of Paris, which was the work of Couthon and Robespierre.

TALLIEN: This is one of liberty's finest days: the conspirators' heads have just fallen on the scaffold. (*Loud applause.*) The Republic triumphs, and the same blow shakes the thrones of the tyrants of the world. This example will convince them, if they could still doubt it, that the French people will never be governed by a master. (*Renewed applause.*) Let us go and join our fellow citizens, let us go and share the general joy; the day of a tyrant's death is a festival for brotherhood.

I move that all proposals which may be made be sent to the Committees for examination, and that the session be suspended until tomorrow at ten o'clock in the morning.

This proposal is adopted, and the session rises amid applause and cries of joy.

11 Thermidor, Morning

ROGER-DUCOS *remarks to the Convention that an abuse has arisen which it is essential to destroy:* Our sessions are public, *he adds,* the galleries are open to all citizens, men and women; but I see a large number of them in the Convention itself.

I move, in the name of equality, that henceforth no female citizen, except those admitted in deputations, may sit in the Convention.

It is remarked that it is needless to enact a decree on this subject, which is in the jurisdiction of the inspectors of the hall.

In consequence, the observation of Roger-Ducos is sent to them, and the Convention passes to the order of the day. . . .

Le Moniteur universel, XXI, 353-6, 358-63.

LACOSTE, *in the name of the Committee on General Security:* Citizens, I declare to the Convention that various information received by the Committee shows that a large number of public functionaries took part in the rebellion of the Paris commune; I propose outlawing them. (*Applause.*)

(A MEMBER): Citizens, it would be to give too much latitude to the measure to generalize it thus; I ask that the individuals outlawed be named in the decree.

LACOSTE: I did not intend to generalize the measure. The Committee wanted to strike only the guilty individuals; I therefore do not insist on my first proposal. Citizens, another subject ought to attract your whole attention: some of the judges and jurors of the Revolutionary Tribunal were devoted to Robespierre; it is therefore essential to purify it; I propose to the Convention abolishing this tribunal composed as it is now, and creating a provisional commission which would fulfill its functions.

THURIOT: . . . As for what you have been told concerning the Revolutionary Tribunal, Robespierre felt how important it was for him to attach the jurors of this tribunal to himself; and so he peopled it with his creatures; and when his holiness, for it is thus that he was called by his partisans, when this Catholic, or rather sacreligious, king, indicated the individual, the juror pronounced, and the judgment was executed. (*Movement of indignation.*)

I move that henceforth the jurors be called from all the *départements* of the Republic and chosen among those men who do honor to the Republic and not among hypocritically patriotic intriguers like that man, who was so little, who wanted to be so big, and who, if he could, would have displaced the Eternal to put himself in His place. (*Laughter and applause.*)

BRÉARD: The National Convention ought not, at this moment, to limit itself to a particular measure; it ought to take general measures; it ought to prevent the men who belonged to the tyrant you have just struck down from using the short instants that remain to them to destroy the patriots. The operations of the Revolutionary Tribunal must be suspended, and a patriotic jury must be chosen by all the deputations that compose the Convention; the popular commissions, the work of the infamous Robespierre must be destroyed, and their judgments revised. I move that the Convention decree this proposal, and refer its execution to its two committees together.

MALLARMÉ: We have just learned great truths; each day we shall discover new ones. Citizens, adopt the calm which suits a great assembly; let your decrees be the result of sagacity and cold reason; consider that the aristocracy watches at the doors of the Convention, that it has its eyes fixed on you, and that your first rash movement it will use to destroy liberty. We have recovered the liberty of our opinions, I use it to ask you not to suspend the Revolutionary Tribunal hastily. (*Murmurs.*) I mean that if you decide to suspend the Revolutionary Tribunal you ought to decree at the same time that a provisional commission will immediately replace the Revolutionary Jury; for if you charge the various deputations with presenting to the Committee of Public Safety the list of jurors taken from all the *départements,* the considerable time required for this operation would be very prejudicial to the public good. I move that the committees of Public Safety and General Security together be charged with presenting to the Convention the organization of a commission which will instantly replace the Revolutionary Tribunal and Jury.

TURREAU: It is especially necessary to suspend immediately the operations of the Revolutionary Tribunal because Catiline Robespierre sealed with his approval the lists that were presented to him by the jurors. (*Movement of indignation.*)

LACOSTE: It is not possible that the National Convention can hesitate an instant over the suspension of this tribunal. (*Cries of* A vote on suspension!)

Suspension is decreed amid the loudest applause.

FAYAU: It seems to me that the president has just put to a vote the suspension of the Revolutionary Tribunal. This proposal is dangerous, it——

(*Several voices*): Lacoste has not finished!

LACOSTE: You have just enacted a decree which saves our country; the members of the Revolutionary Tribunal, struck down by public opinion, could no longer do any good. I move that the National Convention decree that a provisional commission will replace it.

This proposal is adopted.

TURREAU: I move that this commission bear the name of Provisional Revolutionary Tribunal.

This proposal is adopted.

TALLIEN: Citizens, I share with you the opinion you have just expressed on the Revolutionary Tribunal; you have abolished it; you owed this to your conscience, to your duty, to the people who asked for it.

The proposal has been made to abolish the popular commissions existing in all the parts of the Republic; I think that the Convention ought not to do anything hastily in this matter. Citizens, I repeat what I was saying yesterday: The aristocracy is watching and spying on us; let us guard against rash measures. . . .

At this moment, I move for referral to the Committee of Public Safety. The patriots were under the knife, they have emerged from this oppression, we owe them protection; but we are also obliged to watch the aristocrats, we are obliged to pursue the enemies of the Republic with energy and without respite. For this, harmony is necessary in the government; everything must be linked together and operate in concert.

It is now that we feel the happiness of our situation. Now we can express ourselves freely; four days ago we could not do so. (*Loud applause.*) Let us sanction this liberty by a worthy use of it. Hatred for rogues, villains, accomplices of the tyrant, satellites of Robespierre; but friendship, brotherhood for good citizens. (*Renewed applause.*)

There will without doubt be a report from your Committees on another subject. I mean the purging of the executive commissions; you know that they have been affected by the liberticide influence of the conspirators; . . .

It will be necessary, then, to purge these commissions, and the same will have to be done with the tribunals. You have seen them appear successively to applaud the triumph of liberty and the salvation of the national representation and the Republic; but these congratulations are not equally sincere in all mouths. It has been possible to observe those men who, under this cloak, had the appearance and the stamp of aristocracy. All those who are not attached in their hearts to the Republic, which is only equality among citizens; all those who weakly groveled before Robespierre, are unworthy of ruling republicans. . . . Certainly all this requires a reform. . . .

. . .

BILLAUD-VARENNE: I have just arrived at the session, I do not know what direction the discussion has taken; but I learn that the Convention has suspended the members of the Revolutionary Tribunal, and in this regard I observe that, although in great part this tribunal is composed of men named by Robespierre to achieve his purpose, yet there are pure men——

(*Several voices*): We know it, they'll be reappointed.

BILLAUD-VARENNE: I hear it said that they are only suspended; but you do not know, then, that at this very moment the infamous horde which conspired is at the bar of this tribunal; if the monsters' plan had been executed in its full scope, sixty thousand citizens would have been butchered yesterday; you will be acquainted with this report which will be made to you. It is therefore necessary that the infamous accomplices of Robespierre be struck down. Already several have accompanied him to the scaffold, the others ought to be quick to follow him. They are ready to be judged; we have appointed pure men to compose the tribunal before which they are going to appear; I move for withdrawal of the decree.

(*Several voices*): No, no!

BILLAUD-VARENNE: It appears that you have not fully grasped my object; when I moved withdrawal, it was in order that the functioning of the tribunal undergo no interruption. It is not my intent to conserve its present organization; for the Committees are occupied now in preparing for you a plan for purifying this tribunal. If the public safety is not compromised, if on the contrary the fall of the counter-revolutionaries is effected by the existence of the present Revolutionary Tribunal, until the report of your committees, which perhaps will occur before the end of this session, I do not see why my proposal would not be adopted. Yes, I repeat, before the end of the session perhaps you will hear a report of the committees to remove from the Revolutionary Tribunal the accomplices of Robespierre; but until then it ought not to remain without effectiveness, and I maintain that, according to your decree, the Revolutionary Tribunal is now powerless.

THURIOT: There is no divison in the assembly as to purpose, nor is there one in opinion. We are all in agreement on the necessity of naming new judges and new jurors, but we do not want to commit an injustice, and we are all persuaded that there are members of the Tribunal who merit confidence; that is why the Committee is occupied with a plan which it is shortly going to present to you; until its report, there is nothing urgent to be decided at this moment rather than in an hour; hence I move to table the matter until the report of this committee.

The motion to table was passed.

11 Thermidor, Evening

. . . *Tallien took the chair.*

THE MEMBER PRESIDING [TALLIEN]: The Jacobins who remained faithful to the people's cause and to the Convention, and who at the time when villains who had sold out to Robespierre occupied their meeting place, stayed in their respective *sections,* ask to be admitted to the bar.

(*Permission was granted. The deputation advanced to the bar.*)

THE SPEAKER FOR THE DEPUTATION [COLLOT]: Citizens, you see before you the true Jacobins, who have earned the esteem of the French nation and the hatred of tyrants; you see before you men who have taken up arms against treacherous officials, usurpers of the national authority. True Jacobins have no special meeting-place at the moment of crisis; their place is everywhere that force and watchfulness are needed to combat conspirators.

The monstrous assemblage of conspirators which has sullied our land was composed of men who had no membership cards and who were devoted only to their infamous chiefs; but we marched with our *sections,* to strike down the new tyrant.

The president, in his vigorous reply, recalled what this celebrated society has done for our country; it has sometimes been misled by villains, but the signal services it has rendered the Revolution will be inscribed on every page of our history.

The Convention ordered the deputation's address and speech and the president's reply to be inserted in the Bulletin.

BARÈRE, *in the name of the Committee of Public Safety:* Citizens, the national representation saved itself in one day from the plots of a year; the national representation saved itself by its republican energy, its stern justice, and by the forceful position it has just assumed in the eyes of Europe. As soon as our country was in danger, the hearts of republicans were united; let us also unite at one center our intentions, our plans, and our capabilities for the public good; let actions that are useful, but spread among the diverse objects of government, not be done in isolation; the strength of free men always lies in unity. Unanimity of opinions and co-ordination of efforts are also a power. I come today to declare to the Convention, in the name of the committee, that the sudden explosion of that atrocious conspiracy which the genius of liberty, joined with the power of the people, the energy of the Convention, and the patriotism of the Paris *sections* have stopped with such swift success—I come to declare that this conspiracy did not alter the social organization for an instant; that this partial disturbance leaves the government with its full integrity for political, administrative, and revolutionary actions, within and without.

The conspirators did nothing for the organization or working of government; this is a fact which too few citizens know. Though proud of their patriotic reputations they disdained hard-working men; they scorned their obscure functions; they had aristocratised even the right to serve our country. Saint-Just and Robespierre had removed themselves from the steady day-to-day work whereby a state is inconspicuously governed; they found it vulgar of us to save our country in particulars; they kept for themselves the trappings and the luxury of government; they exercised surveillance only over part of the general enforcement, which they organized especially for themselves, as will be proven in the full report on the conspiracy, which was as unbelievable as much for the men who concocted it as for the means they employed.

Even the revolutionary government and the work of the executive commissions were organized against their wishes; and when they saw we were determined to organize the republican government, the advantage they hoped to gain from this was reduced to filling these commissions with men who were secretely their strong disciples. Thus while we in good faith established executive commissions, Robespierre and Saint-Just, rejecting your choices, presented to the committee certain commissioners and assistants who were intended to become instruments of their abominable counter-revolution.

We were far from foreseeing that men attached to national commissions would go and join local projects, and that men called to the honor of serving the Republic would prostitute themselves to the ambitions of a municipality.

Meanwhile, everything was arranged in preparation for the explosion that would come; it was not like the days of Brissot, Guadet, Buzot, and Barbaroux, whose connections and counter-revolutionary organization existed only in the southern *départements* and in the Calvados. This time the plan was to take over the center of the Republic by force; then they would spread the counter-revolution into various *départements*. Hanriot had taken an oath to the new tyranny; he had said he would answer with his head for the success of the movement; that he was entirely confident that the plan would succeed. Ah! how badly he understood both the people and the armed forces! How he slandered the zeal of the Paris *sections* and the patriotism of the cannoneers, and the republicanism of the citizens of Paris! Traitors understand neither civic conduct nor the public mentality.

But that abortive promise of Hanriot aroused the reproaches of his accomplices. Coffinhal, a judge in the Revolutionary Tribunal, had a sharp quarrel with him and threw him out of the window into the gutter where he was found; thus the conspirators themselves avenged us, and even wallowed in the mire and in their own blood.

What I am reporting to you is a statement made yesterday before the Revolutionary Tribunal; and I may add that it has also emerged from statements communicated to the Committee by the public prosecutor that the executive committee presided over by Simon, in the city hall, had ordered the shooting of the mounted police, the Revolutionary Tribunal, and a certain number of deputies. Dumas encouraged this murder of national representatives; he who declared himself the great enemy of conspirators was himself the most evil of the traitors. We shall communicate the main facts to the Convention, as the proofs are laid before our eyes. The citizens must be informed.

Thus all was arranged to re-establish tyranny on a bloody throne; all was to serve an ambitious municipality, cruel leaders, and false counselors.

One was to rule Paris, the other the hills; and the Pyrenees, the Alps, and the Mediterranean were to be presents handed over to the fraternity; and the coolest and craftiest one would take over command of the Armies of the North and of the Rhine, already prepared by intriguers.

Saint-Just was commissar of the North; Couthon and the younger Robespierre were the pacification committee of the Midi; Robespierre the elder would rule over mountains of corpses in Paris. The death of republicans, the abasement of the Convention, and the usurpation of the Paris commune would assure their tyrannical domination.

But connections in the interior were needed for so execrable and so difficult a revolution; many agents were sent out into the *départements*. Only one crime was still lacking: that of poisoning the most precious of springs, public education. Commissioner Payan, entrusted with this part, spent several days making up circulars impregnated with counter-revolution and poisoning the *départements* with Robespierre's aims, which he believed could not fail. We obtained proof that night, at one in the morning, that the circulars went out, that several *départements* were momentarily bewildered by these infamous suggestions, and that Payan, who was responsible for the circulation of these counter-revolutionary writings, disappeared amidst the excitement of the 9th of this month, saying he was on his way to the Committee of Public Safety. . . .

He is not the only national executive commissioner who used the national authority for the ruin of the Republic. Another, whose honorable duty it was to distribute charity to the countryside, aid to the asylums, and care and supplies to the military hospitals; Lerebours, Commissioner of Public Assistance, abandoned his responsibilities toward the defenders of the Republic, the indigent, and the aged to pursue the destruction of his country. He preferred the service of hypocritical conspirators to distributing the national beneficence; he preferred faction to fatherland. . . .

Finally the villain became conscious of his crime; he had to flee the city hall. At two in the morning he went to the Ministry of Public Assistance, and soon thereafter he fled through the garden gate.

His assistant hastened to inform us, but it was too late for national justice; he missed the punishment of conspirators yesterday; it remains for the law to catch up with him and we propose that you make him, like Payan, an outlaw.

Having discussed these two most urgent matters, we can assure the Convention that the committee has taken all provisional measures the circumstances and the general security demand.

Seventeen couriers have left tonight for the armies; proclamations have been sent to the people's representatives on the frontiers; others are leaving for the *départements;* and the remedy for so many evils and calumnies will arrive there as soon as or soon after the poison distilled by the parricide.

No branch of the public administration has been suspended by these events. Let there be no anxiety; all that is still needed is co-ordination of public measures and matching of the Convention's operations with the requirements of government. Moves that are premature or inconsistent with the measures we are taking can do more harm than good. It is up to the good sense and the patriotism of the representatives to keep this in mind.

The Committee is collecting the documents, writings, and completed work; it will shortly report in order to make known the state of the Republic and of the government in the most definite way, so as to put the National Convention in a position to take all the great measures required by the present situation, the recent commotion, and the dangers which the aristocracy and the foreigners will surely bring upon us again if we are not watchful. For great measures must and can come only from you. The National Convention is the repository of authority formed by the people. The committees are only secondary organs, auxiliary arms, and means of supplementing the national authority and that of the Convention, which alone exercises that authority.

But beware above all of that fatal moderatism which by speaking of peace and mercy is able to turn everything to its account, even the most violent events. Let the aristocracy be sure that in this temple of laws it has only steadfast avengers and implacable judges. Let true patriotism not forget that here is its temple, its asylum, and its ministers. Let the people always find here equality in laws, and liberty in means, let the revolutionary movement not hesitate on its purifying course; and let the Convention still terrify traitors and kings, conspirators within and despotic governments without.

Then our efforts will continue, the secret triumphs of our armies' political enemies, steeped in conspiracy, will be brought to naught; and victory's triumphal chariot will roll over the corpses of our enemies and over soil which still knows slaves and masters.

The conspirators had not left the armies out of their plans. Measures which must be kept secret prevent us from talking on this point today in detail; but we shall show you sinister projects strongly urged by them to the Committee, and others they had secretly carried out themselves.

I shall speak today only of one; but it is important for the valor of our armies that these facts be known. French courage will prevent any dangerous consequences.

Robespierre said, in his seditious speech, that the situation in the Army of the North was like that of Dumouriez's time. Let us see to whom this terrible imputation is applicable.

The Committee ordered, by a vigorous and steady flow of correspondence, unrelenting pursuit of the enemy against the foreign hordes on all frontiers, especially on the North, where France's most vicious enemies are, the Austrians and the English. Richard and Choudieu carried out the committee's instructions with all their power; and they gained Belgium and West Flanders for the Republic. Well, Robespierre on several occasions attacked the zeal of Richard and Choudieu before the Committee; amidst their victories he was suspicious of their zeal; and it is well known that Robespierre did not like these victories, that he never shared in the enthusiasm and applause they aroused.

What did military successes matter to conspirators against their fatherland? These successes only consolidated the Republic which they did not want; it suited them better to paralyze victory and tell of defeats. That was how they developed and increased their power, out of every public misfortune, and built their success on the anxieties of citizens. It was only in the midst of defeats that a vast and profound conspiracy against the committees could succeed, for then conspiracy could get power more surely in its own hands after overthrowing them; it is by rumors of reverses of the armies and of lost battles that unrest is aroused by terrible fears and the flame of civil war is most successfully ignited.

But no; the armies by their constant triumphs wore out the patience of the conspirators; the courage of the soldiers would have to be enchained; their fury against the English would have to be chilled.

Letters came to the Committee, from the North, near Antwerp, telling us how poisonous rumors had appeared among these victorious legions, spread by agents come secretly from Paris; they declared falsely that a treaty had been signed between us and our enemies: a treaty with brigands and royalists! a treaty between assassins and republicans! and consequently several bodies of troops did not fire upon the enemy for three days. The shock and the terrible turmoil being readied for the national representation was skillfully prepared indeed: the stagnation of business, the suspension of arms, the letters about peace—all was to be put into play to assure the success of the planned counter-revolution. But soon the efforts of the Committee of Public Safety restored victory to the Army of the North. I come to announce to you a new success in the midst of these momentary impediments; it seems that the genius of liberty has seen fit to crown your latest revolutionary labors by embellishing them with new successes. Thus at the moment the conspirators against the Republic were going down to the tomb by the path of infamy, the Army of the North stormed up Lillo fortress and could not even catch the fleeing English, who covered their retreat by flooding, thus making their presence cursed in the very country for whose sake they claimed they had taken up arms.

Here is the news:

> A true Republican has as father and son only Virtue, the gods, the Law, and his Country.
>
> Richard, people's representative with the Army of the North, to his colleagues, the Committee on Public Safety
>
> Antwerp, 9 Thermidor, Year II
> of the French Republic
>
> I announce to you, citizen colleagues, the evacuation of Lillo fortress; the troops of the Republic entered it yesterday. The English in their retirement opened the dikes on the left bank and flooded a vast territory more than six leagues in circumference. They bore with them the hatred and execration of the inhabitants, which they had earned by their looting and their indiscipline; their hasty retreat is continuing. Our reconnaissances have gone more than ten leagues before coming up with their outposts. They appear to be taking refuge under the cannon of Breda and of Berg-op-Zoom. Thirty-eight cannon were left behind for us at Antwerp; we found considerable stores there, especially oats, which may amount to sixty thousand sacks. More than three hundred civilians took home with them things belonging to the armies of the coalition; and at this moment we with Laurent are going to have searches made, to return these things to the Republic. To this commercialism of the inhabitants of Antwerp I must contrast the unselfishness

> and devotion to the French nation which distinguishes Jacques Leemans, merchant of that town. After the retreat of Dumouriez, to save four hundred sacks of oats which had been deposited with him he declared to the enemy commissaries that he had bought them; and by this patriotic mendacity he preserved them for the republic, and has just returned them to us.
>
> RICHARD

It seems to have been the Republic's destiny to overcome all its enemies on the same day, the same moment—to defeat the tyrants within and exterminate those without; at the very moment of the struggle against the Robespierre faction we vanquished the tyrants of Vienna and London. Many battles were won for liberty on the 9th Thermidor.

This evening we have received by courier more good news connected with the 9th Thermidor. You too are the army of liberty, and your civic laurels were intertwined on that day with military laurels; Robespierre and his accomplices were cast into irons on the very day the Austrians were driven out of the country around Liège. Liberty made simultaneous revolutions at Liège and in Paris, and the cause of the people was defended in both these places.

The call for the charge was sounded at the same instant on the banks of the Seine and on the river Jaar; enemy outposts were vanquished before Liège just as they were in the Place de Grève; and the city of the tyrant-bishop was occupied by the troops of the Republic at the same time that the lair of the tyrant Robespierre was being occupied by the loyal *sections* of Paris. Here is the news that completes your republican labors. Thus the strengthened Republic's glory is complete.

Thus in two weeks we have had twenty-two victories; and it was during this period that Robespierre was no longer attending committee meetings; it was during this time that he denounced us to the assembly, that he prepared his counter-revolutionary speeches; one has to love one's country to delight in its success.

> Ernouf, major-general, chief of the general staff of the Army of Sambre-et-Meuse, to the people's representatives on the Committee of Public Safety.
>
> General Headquarters at Warem, 9 Thermidor, Year II
> of the French Republic, one and indivisible
>
> The Army of Sambre-et-Meuse made a movement this morning whose principal object was to press the enemy more

> and more toward Maestricht and to force him to cross the Meuse, by taking the city of Liège. Our advance guard moved toward the river Jaar; the left wing was based on Wontrenge, the right on Saint-Nicolas; attacks were made on the enemy outposts before Liège. The enemy withstood an artillery bombardment of some duration; but the republican charge soon obliged him to take flight. Our troops have entered Liège, where they had been eagerly and impatiently awaited. The enemy army retired to the heights of Chartreux, and dug in there; he directed the fire of several batteries against the city of Liège, which caused a very violent conflagration and much inconvenience to the inhabitants. Jourdan is at this time occupied with setting up batteries on the citadel, where the position is very favorable, in order to silence the enemy's fire. It has grown too late to attack today; but Jourdan promises that tomorrow the soldiers of the Republic will occupy the enemy positions.
>
> ERNOUF
>
> *P.S.* We have taken many prisoners; I cannot tell you the exact number.

I cannot fulfill the duty imposed on me by the Committee without speaking to you of the Revolutionary Tribunal, that salutary institution which destroys the enemies of the Republic and purifies the soil of liberty; it crushes aristocrats, bars the way to the ambitious, sweeps away intriguers, and strikes down counter-revolutionaries; it wrecks the hopes of tyranny. We must have great respect for this institution; but the men who compose it ought to have been criticized and watched by the Convention.

Among duties was that of revising the organization of the tribunal, but with that wisdom which perfects without weakening, and rebuilds without destroying. It is far from our minds to take unconsidered action, even inspired by useful motives; they are apt to stir up the plots of villains and the sinister projects of conspirators. But while the national assembly was devoting its just solicitude to the men who had been planted in that establishment to serve perfidious ends, the two committees jointly revised its composition, purified its membership, and sought to give to good citizens the guarantees that justice assures to civil liberty, and the rights which the revolution must guarantee to good citizens. This is a difficult task; it is hard to know men thoroughly, especially amid the tumult of so profound a revolution.

I come to present for your nomination the names of the judges and jurors who seem to us to merit the confidence of the Convention and of good citizens; may it be comparable to your purposes in favor of justice and the revolution!

I conclude this report by notifying the National Convention of an urgent need of the Committee of Public Safety. The law's blade has struck down three ambitious men, three tyrants who had usurped public confidence, who had sought to overthrow that revolutionary government which is so fatal to the kings of Europe and so necessary to the defense of liberty. These three parricides were members of the Committee, and by their rash conduct belied the Committee's beneficent and modest name; the Committee asks you to add to it, until the 21st of this month when the [existing] Committee will be replaced or continued, three members able to bear the weight of its daily labors and carry out the operations now under way. To nominate provisionally these three members to serve until the 20th of this month, when you must hold elections to the Committee, would reaffirm the public confidence you have shown it; to re-confirm your appointments and fill up the Committee would assure new triumphs for the Republic; and what the Republic needs is loyal, co-operative workers and modest republicans. Men should not enter the national government who think more of their personal glory than the salvation of their country, who take high place as though mounting a brilliant stage, whose only patriotism is ostentation, and whose only republic is power. The revolutionary government must not contain either the egotists or the indifferent; nor those cold hearts to whom authority is only a plaything, for whom great affairs have no goal, and who because they are more occupied with holding onto power than serving our country are neither zealous republicans nor good public administrators. We have passed the time when a nation was sacrificed to a man, and posterity's happiness to the satisfaction of ambition.

This report was frequently interrupted by applause. Barère then proposed for membership on the Committee on Public Safety, to replace the three conspirators whose heads had just fallen under the blade of the law, Bernard de Saintes, Duval, and Eschassériaux.

Vote! vote! *called several members.*

MERLIN DE THIONVILLE: I am against putting the committee's proposal to a vote; the proposed members have my confidence; do they have that of the whole convention? They are going to be invested with great power. (*Murmurs.*) They are going to be charged with great and important functions; they will hold the reins of government; they must appear to the people, for whom they are going to work, invested with the confidence of the whole national representation. I move the previous question on Barère's proposal, and the postponement until tomorrow of the nomination of members of the Committee of Public Safety; and that those nominations be made like those of presiding officers and secretaries.

(AN UNIDENTIFIED MEMBER): The Committee of Public Safety ought to be composed of twelve members, in conformity with its original organization; Hérault has long been absent; no doubt there have been reasons why he has not been replaced. I move that the members of the Committee of Public Safety be named tomorrow by ballot. (*Applause.*)

TURREAU: I move they be named by a call of the roll and voice vote; that is how free men ought to utter their thoughts.

BILLAUD-VARENNE: I move that precedence be given to the motion for a roll call. If the Committee took the liberty of presenting a list of members it thinks appropriate for the work of the Committee of Public Safety, it is because an explicit decree prescribed that it do so. But since opposition has arisen, I insist on a roll call; this is the way the people have known their true friends.

It was just said that there were reasons for not replacing Hérault; yes, we had reasons; we did not want to add to the number of conspirators already on the Committee. (*Violent murmurs in the assembly.*)

(SEVERAL MEMBERS): Mr. President, call Billaud to order; he is insulting the Convention.

THE PRESIDENT: It was no doubt an inadvertent error of Billaud's; there is no need to call him to order.

BILLAUD-VARENNE: I am astonished that it is already forgotten under what oppression the National Convention once groaned. (*Several members:* We shall never forget it!) I maintain that that state of oppression must constantly be kept in mind, so that the Convention will not fall back again into such an abased condition. (*Applause.*) I am told that at this moment the assembly is free; yes, it is; but was it free before the law's blade struck down the tyrant? Was it free when the law on the Revolutionary Tribunal was put before it? No; and if these are established facts, how can they have been forgotten after the tyrant's death? I insist that the nomination of the members of the two committees be made by roll call.

The Convention decreed that it will name tomorrow, by a call of the roll, the members needed to fill the two committees of Public Safety and General Security.

FRÉRON: After what Billaud has just said, it is evident that if the

Committee of Public Safety had been complete, it would have blocked the tyranny of Robespierre; it is clear that by denouncing the traitor the members of the Committee would have covered themselves with glory; and that once the blindfolds had fallen the bloody law on the Revolutionary Tribunal would never have been adopted.

I conclude that the Committee of Public Safety must always be complete; Jeanbon Saint-André and Prieur are absent from it now. I move for their recall, and that the Committee never be empowered to send its members on missions.

BARÈRE: It is necessary to reply to what Fréron has just said. While we had a majority of five against the conspirators, we did not know whether, if we asked for a new member, the reputation for patriotism Robespierre had made for himself would not have enabled him to influence the nomination, and thus add to the number of the villain's partisans; whereas we were sure of ourselves; we could confer with one another by glances.

It has been said that if the Committee had been complete we would have come to denounce Robespierre; it is only a few days ago that the mask fell; it is only a few days ago that we evaluated his hypocrisy; and as long as it was still necessary to undeceive a great Society whose support he had usurped, as long as brave men had not even dared attack him, a certain maneuverability had to be maintained, the more surely to pull him down. Yet who first attacked the tyrant in this assembly? Billaud. Who first ripped off the patriotic mask with which he had disguised himself? Billaud, a member of the government.

(SEVERAL MEMBERS): It was Tallien.

BARÈRE: I shall always render the same justice to members of the Convention; they all concurred in the demasking of the tyrant; but the fact I have cited is true.

As for Fréron's second proposal, I think the Convention ought to consider whether the Committee may not employ certain of its members for major transactions. Carnot was very useful at Maubeuge, because, knowing the Committee's intentions and later plans, he was able to take appropriate measures. Jeanbon Saint-André likewise served the republic during our most recent naval expedition.

DUBOIS-CRANCÉ: It is in liberty's interest that the Committee of Public Safety always be complete. The more numerous its members, the better its functions are performed and the fewer dangers liberty runs. Surely if Robespierre had been able to send the members of the Committee on missions, his triumvirate would have triumphed and the Republic would no longer exist. You have defeated Robespierre and his accomplices; but cannot the habit of power give rise to new ambitious men? One who has drunk from the cup of power finds it hard to return to the rank of citizen. You have vanquished the tyrant; now suspect those men who identify themselves constantly with the government and maintain that they cannot be criticized without attacking the government itself. I move that no member of the Committee of Public Safety be allowed to be on mission for more than two weeks. (*Several voices:* Never!)

I add another proposal. We have seen the danger of leaving power too long in the same hands; I do not ask that the Committee of Public Safety be reconstituted every two weeks, but I maintain that each month three members should leave it and be replaced by new ones. In this way liberty will run no dangers; besides, there is not a member among us who does not know that the body and the spirit are worn out by continuous labor. I am persuaded that the members of the Committee think as I do. I ask that my proposal be put to a vote.

CAMBON: The question you are discussing merits examination in a wider perspective. I think it would be proper to turn to the organization of the government, and to consider whether the Convention cannot make use of its members in the surveillance of the general administration of the Republic.

Since the revolutionary government was organized, its executive functions have been assigned to commissions which replaced the old ministries; these commissions give daily accounts of their operations to the Committee of Public Safety, which was organized in sections to divide up the work, with one member at the head of each section.

Some members had as many as three commissions under their surveillance; and because they were overloaded with work they subdivided their sections into bureaus and appointed a chief for each bureau.

The commissions present to them their plans, their reports, and the orders they think necessary for the execution of the laws; and in their reports the committee member finds information and opinions useful for legislation.

The people's representative at the head of the section examines, modifies or adopts the projects submitted to him, and reports on them to the committee. But as business has greatly increased, sometimes he sends to the several bureaus and their chiefs make the reports.

It could happen that the people's representatives, overloaded with work or overconfident in the commissions, might adopt projects presented to them without thorough examination.

It can result from this scheme of things that the legislative and surveillance functions which the Convention ought to reserve to itself may pass into the hands of bureau chiefs of executive commissions.

I can cite, without fear of compromising anybody, one of our colleagues in the Committee of Public Safety who is charged with the surveillance of three or four very important branches of administration, among them that of commerce and food supply; everyone knows that he examines all the projects submitted to him himself and not through the medium of the bureau chiefs; but everybody knows too that he is obliged to spend days and nights at it. Anyone who replaces him, and does not have his health and his energy, would certainly be obliged either to slow these operations or to hand them over to bureau chiefs.

One thing that is sure is that gradually all the committees of the Convention will find themselves with nothing to do, or else will find themselves competing with the Committee of Public Safety.

We should find proofs of this hypothesis in the formation of the section for general police which the tyrant Robespierre organized, from which he sent out letters of proscription that contradicted the actions of the Committee on General Security, by removing patriots who often had important responsibilities.

The best remedy would be to concern ourselves with the internal organization of the Convention, to eliminate all existing committees, and to replace them by as many committees as there are executive commissions; each committee would oversee the operations of one commission, and require daily reports from it. The committees would meet, in part or all of them together, by invitation of a commissioner, at a common center, which would be the Committee of Public Safety for all executive matters and the Convention for legislative matters. The Convention would thenceforth be the center of government; its sessions would become more important because of the work of the committees; all the members of the Convention would be employed in overseeing the government, and would carry out the work which at present may be left in the hands of the chiefs of bureaus.

This idea was suggested to me by my experience on the Finance Committee, which, charged with a necessary surveillance, under the Legislative Assembly and the Convention required the commissioners of the treasury to give daily accounts of their activities; and the local information which the Committee procured must be attributed to this scheme.

This idea needs to be worked out and thought over; if the assembly permits, I shall lay before it or the Committee of Public Safety the study which I have begun. I move that you confine yourselves to replacing the Committee of Public Safety, and concern yourselves with the organization of that committee.

THURIOT: There is no question of deciding at this moment whether a certain number of the members of the Committee of Public Safety are to be replaced each month; we shall concern ourselves with that when it comes to the definitive organization of the Committee. At this time we must decree that members of the Committee shall never go on mission. We should be in sorry condition if when it came to an important mission nobody could be found to carry it out but members of the Committee of Public Safety.

I move that the members needed to fill out the Committee of Public Safety be named tomorrow, and that that Committee be charged with presenting its own plan for its reorganization.

There was a motion to postpone the discussion.

TALLIEN: The question being discussed at this time is of the greatest importance; and a few moments more will be useful to our country. The National Convention has made a revolution in three days. It did it by its energy; it did it for the people and not for a few individuals. We have struck down triumvirs; let us not raise decemvirs in their place; we want liberty, liberty whole and entire. You must not break up without decreeing the [partial] replacement of the Committee of Public Safety as proposed by Dubois-Crancé.

I move that you sanction at this time the principle that a quarter of each committee be replaced every month. (*Applause.*)

There was a motion that this proposal be put to a vote.

BOURDON DE L'OISE: In the style of the deliberations this evening I see the consequences of the infamous plot of Robespierre. (*Murmurs.*) His secret partisans have infiltrated within these walls, which he and his accomplices attacked only because there was a desire to put someone else in his place. Doubtless very little understanding of the human heart is needed to know that a certain exaltation of ideas follows upon a long period of suppression; but I ask the Convention not to dishonor its victory by a haste which can only be fatal to the public good.

For goodness' sake let us postpone this discussion; remember we have fourteen armies in action, directed by a strong and vigorous government; let us not disorganize it by a hasty decision.

Citizens, among the vigorous athletes who personally combatted machiavellism, it must be agreed that the two committees of Public Safety and General Security have honorably distinguished themselves. I demand postponement.

Lecointre de Versailles moved that the discussion be postponed for three days.

TALLIEN: I confess I find it difficult to imagine how there can be motions for postponement when it is a matter of establishing a principle that safeguards public liberty. We spent the other night striking down the tyrant; let us spend tonight assuring the triumph of liberty. Will what is true tonight be less true tomorrow, or in two or three days? Will it be less true tomorrow than it is today that the same men must not exercise power too long, if you do not want them to abuse it? Questions of the detailed means of carrying it out can be postponed; but I maintain that the principle must receive its sanction here and now.

BARÈRE: I cannot imagine why there is any difference of opinion, when it has been seen what great evils can come from the habit of power. Besides, the present members of the Committee of Public Safety need rest. We have more than once lamented not being able to keep up with your actions. After long labors one must be allowed to return to the body of the Convention, to rest. I oppose postponement.

There was a motion to close the debate. The assembly closed the debate. Several members insisted on postponement.

MERLIN DE THIONVILLE: I move that precedence be given to Barère's proposal. The opposition to it that I see makes me feel all the stronger about it. Vote on the proposal of Barère!

The President put it to a vote, and the Convention decreed the principle of replacing a quarter of each committee every month. (From all parts of the hall came repeated applause, with cries of vive la république!*)*

DELMAS: You have just dried up the source of men's ambition. To complete your action, I move that you decree that no member can return to a committee less than one month after he has left it. (*Applause.*) I ask this rule in the name of the people's happiness.

The proposal of Delmas was decreed amid applause. Barère presented the list of members proposed by the two committees to make up the new Revolutionary Tribunal.

(UNIDENTIFIED MEMBER): I move that these be printed and tabled until information is available concerning each of the individuals proposed.

Adopted. The session recessed at midnight.

Correspondence of Dyzez

Paris, 13 Thermidor, Year II [31 July 1794]

To Dubosc, executive officer of the administration of the *département* of the Landes

What shall I tell you about the night of the 9th Thermidor that hasn't already been said? From eight o'clock in the evening until eleven, we were constantly hovering between life and death. If Robespierre and his agents had had a little more presence of mind, only those he would have chosen to spare would be alive today. It is fortunate that he lost his head; otherwise we should have lost ours. If he had not been disconcerted in the morning session of the Convention when Tallien attacked him, it is a good bet that this attack would have turned against Tallien himself. But the Spirit of France struck him blind, his reason abandoned him, and he was no longer capable of anything but excesses of fury.

As this event cannot have effected any change in the *département,* always invincibly attached to the Convention, I have not written in detail. The papers tell it all. A truthful report is all that is needed.

Salut et Fraternité.

"Lettres," p. 519.

National Convention

13 Thermidor, Evening

Collot d'Herbois presiding:

DUMONT: Citizens, with the majestic and imposing attitude that you have taken, with that sublime energy of which you have given so striking an example, will you tolerate a traitor, an accomplice of Catiline, still sitting on your Committee on General Security? Will you tolerate David, that usurper, that tyrant of the arts, as weak as he is villainous, will you tolerate, I say, that despicable personage, who did not appear here during the memorable night of the 9th, still going with impunity into the places where he meditated carrying out the crimes of his master, the tyrant Robespierre? The moment has come, citizens; those shades of the villain whom France has just gotten rid of must be made to disappear; that energy, safeguard of liberty, and that heroism, savior of our country, must be maintained.

Le Moniteur universel, XXI, 366–72, 384–8, 401–2, 410–12, 413.

David is not the only one who sold himself to Robespierre; that Cromwell's court is not yet annihilated; his ministers, crime written on their faces, will soon be unmasked; I swear here and now to pursue them until death; but at this moment I limit myself to moving that the traitor David be ejected from the Committee, and that you proceed to replace him.

[*Similar motions were made concerning Lavicomterie and Jagot*].

BENTABOLE: The decree which allowed the two committees to cause representatives of the people to be arrested without a preliminary report was obtained by surprise from the Convention by the men who were accustomed to deceive its justice. This decree almost ruined the Republic by stifling the liberty of opinions; for, I ask you, what deputy could say what he thought? What deputy could share the suspicions he felt? What deputy could combat measures which seemed to him contrary to the interest of the Republic, when he was sure of being arrested immediately without being able to make himself heard by the Convention? I move for withdrawal of this decree, and that the Convention add that none of its members can be arrested without having been heard.

LEGENDRE: When the decree, whose withdrawal has been moved, was passed, the principles, which forbid arresting the representatives of the people without their having been heard by the National Convention, were violated; they would be violated a second time if the addition proposed by Bentabole were decreed. I move that we limit ourselves purely and simply to the withdrawal of the decree.

The proposal of Legendre is adopted amid the loudest applause. . . .

The president recalls the various proposals which have been made, and the Convention decrees that David, Lavicomterie, and Jagot will be replaced. (Applause.) . . .

David enters the hall. The Convention decrees that he will be heard.

DAVID: I do not know the denunciations which have been made against me; but no one can accuse me more than I myself. One cannot conceive to what point that wretch deceived me; he abused me by his hypocritical sentiments; and, citizens, he could not have succeeded otherwise. I have sometimes merited your esteem by my frankness; well, citizens, I beg you to believe that death is preferable to what I feel at this moment. Henceforth, I swear, and I believe I am fulfilling the oath even in this unfortunate circumstance,

I shall attach myself no longer to men, but only to principles.

(*A member*): David embraced Robespierre at the Jacobins, and he went there preaching insurrection.

GOUPILLEAU DE FONTENAY: I call upon David to declare whether at the moment when Robespierre descended from the speaker's platform, after having pronounced his speech, or rather his indictment, he, David, did not go up and embrace him, saying, "If you drink the hemlock, I'll drink it with you!"

DAVID: It was not to come and welcome Robespierre that I approached him, it was to go up on the platform and ask that the hour of the festival of the 10th be advanced. I did not embrace Robespierre, I did not even touch him, for he repelled everyone. It is true that, when Couthon spoke to him of sending his speech to the communes, I said it could cause trouble in the whole Republic. Robespierre then cried out that there no longer remained for him anything but to drink the hemlock; I told him: "I'll drink it with you." I am not the only one who was deceived about him; many citizens thought him virtuous as well as I.

THIBAUDEAU: I move for referral to the two committees.

TALLIEN: If a member of the Convention had not been accused here in a direct way, if he had not appeared on the platform to repel the accusation, I should move also for referral to the Committees; but as we ought to be careful not to attack lightly the national representation in any of us, so, when it is attacked, ought we to require an authentic reparation.

None but pure men ought to sit in this enclosure; no reputation ought any longer to blind us. We are at the moment when men, whatever talent they have, are no longer anything; virtue and liberty are everything. David has been charged with not being present here in the moment of crisis; I shall say more: on the night of the 9th, Coffinhal, that traitor whom the Lord's sword will soon strike, said that he was very sure that David's signature on the bottom of a proclamation was not his, because he was the friend of Robespierre. Doubtless this would not be the subject of an indictment, if there were not other accusations to make against David; but to the oscillations of his conduct in the Committee on General Security one can add other charges. I declare that no representative can sit beside David until he has exculpated himself.

DAVID: I had been ill for a week, and on the 9th I took an emetic which made me suffer a great deal, and forced me to remain at my house the whole day and night; I did not come to the assembly until the morning after.

FRESSINE: David was here on the morning of the 9th.

(*A member*): I ask David why in the plan for the festival that he presented to us, he proposed to begin at three o'clock. I noticed that this proposal was closely related to Robespierre's plan, and could have held the greatest dangers.

DAVID: In all the festivals for which I have given the program, I have been reproached with making them last too long. It is for this reason that I proposed making that of the 10th Thermidor begin at three o'clock. The Committee of Public Safety later pointed out to me that this could be dangerous, and I came to ask that it begin at nine o'clock.

LECOINTRE: I move that it be decreed that David cannot be on any committee.

DAVID: The two committees of Public Safety and General Security were assembled; Robespierre read us a speech in which I heard my name pronounced; I thought that it was a joke, and I admit to you that I was not a little surprised when the day after I heard him proffer my name from this platform. Finally, citizens, I assure you that he courted me rather than I courted him.

GOUPILLEAU: David heard Robespierre read his speech here; he heard him repeat it at the Jacobins, and I maintain that, if he had merely been deceived, he would not have said to Robespierre, after having twice heard his indictment: "If you drink the hemlock, I'll drink it with you."

LEGENDRE: I went to the Committee of Public Safety yesterday to ask whether it did not have some complaints against David, for I suspected him. Billaud answered me that there were great ones. I think then that, since the Committees have complaints against David, we ought to send them the ones that have been made here, so that they combine them and report to us as soon as possible.

This proposal was adopted.

The session was recessed at 11 o'clock.

14 Thermidor, Morning

LECOINTRE: I move for the repeal of the law of 22 Prairial concerning the new organization of the Revolutionary Tribunal. It is a veritable martial law.

The Convention withdrew this law unanimously and amid the loudest applause. . . .

Charlier presented several observations on the repeal of the law of 22 Prairial, and moved that the laws abrogated by it be put in force again.

COCHON: To conciliate all opinions, I think the law of 22 Prairial must simply be repealed, and it must be decreed that the judges and jurors who have remained in the tribunal will continue under the old laws to examine the cases pending there, until the definitive organization of that tribunal.

MERLIN DE DOUAI: If you adopt this proposal, you totally disorganize the Revolutionary Tribunal: under what law are the judges in that tribunal performing their duties? Under the law of 22 Prairial. Now, if you repeal that law, you no longer have judges. I move that the Committees present tomorrow the organization of the Revolutionary Tribunal.

BENTABOLE: I think it is necessary to repeal the law of 22 Prairial and its murderous principles of judgment. As for the judges and jurors, there has not been time to examine thoroughly the conduct of each of them. I think there are patriots among them; but there are doubts concerning a large number. Can life and death be left in the hands of men concerning whom there are doubts? Yet, as it is necessary not to interrupt the operations of this tribunal, which is terrible for conspirators, by repealing the law of 22 Prairial, I think the committees of Public Safety, on General Security, and on Legislation, must be enjoined to present tomorrow the list of the members who are to compose the new Revolutionary Tribunal.

BRIVAL: I am going to cite a fact to the assembly which will make it shudder with horror. A man to whom Robespierre caused a superb apartment to be given in the pavillon of Flore, and who used the furnishings there that belonged to the Republic, told me, a few days ago, that Robespierre had told him several jurors of the Revolutionary Tribunal were not voting for death in all cases and he was going to have them replaced. From this fact, you can see that the composition of the juries is altogether bad. I move that they all be changed.

BOURDON DE L'OISE: We are all convinced of the weakness of the accomplices of Robespierre who composed the majority of the jurors of the Revolutionary Tribunal; but, citizens, let us not stab the patriots who resisted the orders given them by the tyrant; let us recall that in the case of Gossin four of these estimable citizens voted for acquittal although they were surrounded by assassins.

The Convention withdrew the law of 22 Prairial and decreed that its committees on Public Safety, on General Security, and on Legislation will present tomorrow the organization of the Revolutionary Tribunal.

BARÈRE: Citizens, three days ago everything around us fortunately changed. A terrible storm suddenly lighted the political horizon of France. The tyrant overthrown revealed to us all the threads of that infernal conspiracy against the national representation and the rights of the people. . . .

Terror was always the arm of despotism; justice is the arm of liberty. Superstition was the instrument of all men ambitious to reign; morality is the means that is employed by the true republican. Tyranny over opinion, censorship of writings, usurped and excessive reputations have been in all epochs the symptoms that heralded the loss of liberty; the unlimited right to think, to write, and to believe what one wanted, the modesty of public functionaries, and the mutual confidence of representatives and citizens are the signs by which it will be recognized that there exists a popular representation which has twice struck down tyrants and several times destroyed all factions.

The committees, deliberating together on the happy change which has been effected and on the salutary influence that it must exercise on the happiness of the people and on the dignity of the national representation, have thought they were performing a sacred duty in presenting to you the means of better organizing the committees.

Citizens, the piece of work that I am charged with presenting to you in the name of the Committee of Public Safety has for its object a new delegation of the powers that the National Convention ought not to relinquish, for the sake of its authority and for the sake of the people. . . .

Centralization is indeed a means of government; but total centralization is monarchy or despotism. Robespierre dried up all the branches of the administration that he could not bend to his will or cut off entirely; he diverted into a common pool all the sources of power, all the derivations of public authority, in order to seize them more easily. . . .

Today all power must return to its legitimate source; the National Convention must take back at a stroke what the counterrevolution gradually robbed it of. If we have had the policy of not informing the assembly of this sooner, it is in order not to lead to inevitable discord which would hardly have been tolerated when public opinion was entirely misled or rather monopolized exclusively by Robespierre, and because we had not yet won so many victories. But at this moment we propose to you to free the Committee of Public Safety of legislative tasks, which do not naturally belong to it; to take from it the obligation to prepare the legislation for each executive commission, and to divide among the twelve committees the tasks and operations relative to each of those commissions. . . .

We have come, by the experience of the revolution, to bind ourselves no longer to enormous reputations for patriotism, nor to those men who mistake a rough and tough manner for republicanism, ignoble clothing and appearance for the costume of the free man, and a splendid display of civic words for the love of our country.

We have come, by the experience of the revolution, to remain attached to principles, instead of drifting with political or false considerations.

We have come to pay small esteem to brilliant qualities and individual talents, which are more dangerous than all the others if they are not joined with that sure, unchanging probity which, as one of the ancients said, can sometimes make up for all the qualities but can never be made up for by any.

The fate of Robespierre will teach us to do our work as representatives with no other hope than the pleasure of having fulfilled a duty; this example will doubtless make each of us henceforth know no other power than that of the people, no other authority than that of the National Convention, no other means than those that the law gives to the constituted authorities. He who wants the good of his country knows neither intrigues nor coalitions; he who has pure intentions does not fear to be isolated, or rather he never is so because the wishes of all good citizens follow him and defend him. Tyrants form coalitions; intriguers need to rally one another; thieves go in packs; the true citizen is naturally bound to the laws, to the public powers, to the constituted authorities; and still better, he is tacitly in coalition with all the honest citizens, with all the faithful public servants, and this civic joining together is surely equal to all the other bizarre gatherings of little ambitious men and great aristocrats. . . .

Who can answer that another ambitious man, a new little tyrant would not again give rise to the same abuses, and revive the wreckage of so many conspiracies, if you did not pursue them today? Power corrupts; it has destroyed the best principles and misled the best citizens; you owe it to your members to take from them this subtle poison.

You will do even more; by exercising a right of the Convention, you exercise it publicly; and your roll call, which alone is suitable for republicans, is at the same time the guarantee you give the people that your choices are good, your plans are good, and your intentions are pure. . . .

The Committee of Public Safety will be the point where thought concerning operations will be centralized, to unify the tasks of legislation and harmonize executive actions.

The Committee will continue, in accordance with the law of 12 Germinal [1 April], its immediate surveillance over the twelve executive commissions, which are the arms given by the Convention to the national government.

You want to establish the unity of the Republic; a spirit of unity is therefore needed in laws and in executive measures; the work does not need to be performed exclusively by the Committee, it will do only the work of government; but there must be a means of knowing what is being done in all the various parts of the Republic; otherwise we should have twelve governments, twelve legislations, and a moral federalism in place of republican unity. . . .

The Committee on General Security, which Saint-Just and Robespierre despoiled of part of its jurisdiction on the pretext of establishing a police agency, was almost destroyed or at least paralyzed; contradicted in some of its measures, it was almost overthrown. Today its whole jurisdiction must be restored and assured; its attributions are clearly indicated by the good it has done in the form of the security it has given to the Republic, in the punishment of the aristocracy which it has had arrested in the middle of its plots; but they are positively traced in the law of 14 Frimaire. . . .

Foreign relations have long appeared to the Convention not to merit operations separate from those of Government, to which they are very naturally attached.

You know, citizens, that since the coalition of the tyrants, since the war that the Republic has been waging against them with such success, our ambassadors are armies and our diplomatic means have been cannon, bayonets, and powder. Consular agencies can easily be carried on by an executive chief. Relations with neutral nations are more economic and commercial than political. Republican bravery has changed the diplomacy of Europe. The lying and brilliant art of plenipotentiaries can suit only monarchies; and the priests of diplomacy can no more exist among us than the priests of fanaticism.

National opinion decrees liberty and equality. The French revolution in its impetuous and terrible progress will bring in its train the revolution of all Europe. The old equilibrium of forces and alliances, that famous balance of power, that political charlatanism, is broken. A new order of relations and interests is going to be formed by the successes of the war. . . .

You will assuredly not forget, in reorganizing the government, that it is, by your decrees, revolutionary until the peace. The people see in it their salvation, the citizens the end of their troubles, and the armies the guarantee of their triumphs; they will not be able to forget the existence of this government which is intermediate between the revolution and the constitution and which assures us the enjoyment of all the benefits that ought to derive from it.

In vain some malevolent persons from abroad would like to cause the progress of the revolutionary government to turn back or stop or slow down; the people, like the Convention, would see in this inevitable misfortunes and dangers for liberty; in vain would some like to destroy the principle of its activity by modifying it. The revolution can be compared to a plant whose growth cannot be stopped without causing it to die; and we have all sworn that liberty is imperishable in France.

Here is the proposed decree:

"The National Convention, after having heard the report of the committees of Public Safety and General Security, decrees:

"I. There will be twelve committees of the National Convention, whose work will be related to the operations of the executive commissions and of which the names follow:

1. Committee on civil administration, police, and tribunals
2. On public education
3. On agriculture and the arts
4. On commerce and food supply
5. On public works
6. On transport, postal, and stage-coach service
7. On the organization and movement of the armies
8. On maritime affairs and the colonies
9. On arms, powders and the exploitation of mines
10. On finance
11. On archives, decrees and proceedings
12. On inspectors of the Palais National.

"II. Each of these committees will occupy itself particularly with the legislation, with the completion and improvement of the laws relative to the duties of each of the commissions.

"III. Government measures will continue to be taken by the Committee of Public Safety.

Those which concern police matters and the general security will pertain to the Committee on General Security, in accordance with the law of 14 Frimaire.

"IV. All the members of the committees of the Convention will be named by it, and renewed by quarters each month, counting from the day of their nomination.

"V. Each committee will be composed of twelve members; except that the committee on finance will be composed of thirty-five members.

"VI. The commission on the national revenues, the national treasury, the bureau of liquidation, and the bureau of accounts will correspond with the same committee, which will bear the name of committee on finance. There will be a sub-committee for the assignats and coinage.

"VII. The Convention will proceed successively to nominate the members of the twelve committees as well as to nominate the commissioners and adjuncts of all the national executive commissions."

The Convention ordered the report to be printed and the proposed decree tabled. . . .

15 Thermidor

. . . A discussion arose concerning the proposal by Montmayaut to exclude former nobles and priests of all religions from public office. After some debate, the Convention decided on exclusion and repealed the decree which gave the Committee of Public Safety the right to commandeer nobles, priests, and foreigners.

The session ended at four o'clock.

16 Thermidor

MERLIN DE THIONVILLE: I do not appear on this platform to plead the cause of the priests and the nobles; I asked for their expulsion from office before any one else, and my sentiments on this subject are known by my colleagues, but I come to speak in favor of the public good, which yesterday's decree on the former priests and nobles may compromise; I shall not discuss the reasons for this, all my colleagues can guess them; I shall rely upon a general reason: it is equality that I want to bring back, and only this do the malevolent not have the right to invoke; I move then that the National Convention decree that the execution of yesterday's decree against former priests and nobles is suspended and that the Committee of Public Safety is charged with presenting to the National Convention the list of the citizens in these categories who can be useful.

This proposal was adopted after some debates over the drafting.

VILLERS: I ask for the floor for an additional article. Courage is needed to speak against a proposal which has several times been accepted here enthusiastically; but the time of tyranny is past. Every one can, every one ought to, say what he thinks. It is not a question of individuals here so much as of principles. It is not a question of men but of the people's rights. Several of the men under discussion at this moment have rendered great services to our country. Why this stubborn insistence on taking us ceaselessly back to two castes, of which there should long ago have been no further question? Why ceaselessly bring our attention back to the individuals prescribed by the brigands of the Vendée and all the tyrants? I know of only two kinds of men in the Republic, good and bad; punish the latter, make the others happy. There is another class of men which has caused the revolution as much evil as the two castes under discussion, and these are the men of law. God grant me not to want to throw suspicion on citizens who have rendered, who still render, great services to the revolution; but I wanted to make the Convention sense how far it would be led if it once turned aside.

This motion had no sequel.

A deputation was admitted which in the name of the section *of the Montmartre suburb, demanded the liberty of five citizens arrested five months ago, and whose patriotism the* section *attests.*

A motion was made for honorable mention of the petition and referral to the Committee on General Security, which will rule on this matter.

GOUPILLEAU DE FONTENAY: In supporting the proposal which has been made, I ask to add a remark to it. You did not expect that the events of the 9th, events which have saved our country, would become an occasion for the aristocrats to repress the revolutionary movement. Their relatives have assembled in the *sections,* and there they have declaimed, not against the members of the revolutionary committees who may have erred and whom we shall find, but against the salutary institution of these committees. This agitation has reached the point of causing several *sections* to name commissioners charged with receiving denunciations against the revolutionary committees. The Committee on General Security will make it a duty to set at liberty all citizens whose patriotism and innocence are proven to it.

Honorable mention and referral of the petition were decreed.

The section *of the Champs-Elysées also came to demand liberty for several citizens arrested on the perfidious suggestions of one of Robespierre's men, the traitor Lubin, former assistant executive officer of the commune of Paris.*

MERLIN DE THIONVILLE: I move for referral to the Committee on General Security, and I seize this occasion to add to what has been said by my colleague that the committee is continuing to examine all matters of this kind in order to hold the aristocrats under a rod of iron and restore liberty to the patriots. (*Applause.*)

Referral was decreed. . . .

BARÈRE, *in the name of the Committee of Public Safety:* Citizens, six days ago I announced, in the name of the two committees on General Security and on Public Safety, that they were going to join to break the chains of all the oppressed patriots and all the good citizens whom abuse of authority or individual passions had crowded into the houses of detention. At that time, a political storm, occurring within the assembly, turned all attention and our time and our effort were consumed in delivering us from a too long tyranny.

Today, when justice is truly the order of the day in fact and not as a maxim; today, when you want to apply it beneficently, as much for our country as for the citizen, we are occupying ourselves with this important object, so closely related to civil and political liberty.

Already the most obvious claims, the most urgent demands, have been heard, and several citizens are enjoying the benefit of that happy revolution.

I am charged with announcing to you that the two committees are constantly acting together to put an end to the detention of patriots, of good citizens, of those whom personal passions and not the interest of the republic have caused to be arrested; of those who have been pursued by individual hatred and ugly revenge rather than by the laws. We are going to put the decree on suspects back in force, by proscribing all the odious and injust extensions, effected with impunity through intrigues, counter-revolutionary means, and impolitic measures; finally, we are going to follow the intentions of the National Convention, by reconciling morality and policy, by executing the revolutionary laws with justice, without forgetting that this national equity does not cease to be justice although it is placed between our country's salvation and its ardent enemies' crimes.

This policy on the part of your committees will doubtless have your approval at the moment when you are about to draw up with greater precision the laws on the Revolutionary Tribunal, laws that are terrible, but clear and positive; distinct with reason and terrible with justice.

Doubtless no member of the Convention wants to show mercy or come to terms with the vindictive and rebellious aristocracy; but we all desire that crimes against our country and counter-revolutionary offenses be punished; if some citizens, who are guilty or properly suspect to the Republic, inspire concern or pity, if unhappy families excite generous human sentiments, let the citizen remember that there is also our country which demands not to be torn apart and that there is a common family which ought to inspire a great concern; let the legislator not forget that he is charged with making and perfecting a revolution; let him not lose sight of the fact that moderatism is lying in wait at the door of this assembly and that the horrible specter of aristocracy can reappear to seek to frighten the liberty. Let the recognized enemies of the republic not hope for success; this revolution is entirely for liberty; one does not reverse a new tyrant in order to sustain the friends of the old tyranny. It is not the revolutionary institutions which are erroneous or vindictive or guilty; it is individuals, it is the instruments, whose operations and movements must be watched; good patriots speak out with an enlightened wisdom against the abuses of power; but aristocrats speak out with a hot fury against the institutions. The patriots want to put an end to the injustices, but the counter-revolutionaries want to break the instruments of national power. Grant the aristocracy the destruction of a republican institution, and tomorrow they will demand the suppression of the word "republic"; you are strong, you are wise; the people owe you their salvation in this latest crisis; do not lose from view the people and their gratitude for having struck down their enemies. . . .

18 Thermidor

GOSSUIN: In all the *départements* where Saint-Just and Le Bas were sent on mission, they ordered many arbitrary arrests. Everywhere these agents of the villainous Robespierre caused a mass of patriots to be incarcerated. I move that the National Convention decree that the constituted authorities and generally all the public functionaries, civil and military, will be required to send to the Committee of Public Safety, during the ten days following the promulgation of the present decree, copies of the various decisions taken up to this date by the representatives of the people who have been or are on mission.

This proposal was adopted.

BOURDON DE L'OISE: Justice must be made the continuing order of the day. Nothing is easier as to detained persons; the law of 17 September defines all that is meant by "suspect persons." The reasons for the arrests are left to the Committee on General Security; this work has been done well, it is classified by *département* and by *section;* it is therefore simply a matter of comparing the reasons for arrest with the law and setting at liberty all those whose arrest was for causes not enunciated in that law. In this way the Convention will prove to the people that it wants justice; in this way it will reap universal blessings. (*Applause.*)

I make still another proposal: that the revolutionary committees be required to give the relatives of the detained persons the reasons for their arrest. (*Renewed applause.*) I shall cite a fact which I was reluctant to believe, but I have the proof of it. In a *section,* some citizens had asked for the renewal of the revolutionary committee; this committee had them arrested and since that time they have remained in the committee's lock-up without having been transferred into a house of detention.

BENTABOLE: There are detained persons who have no relatives: I therefore move that the reasons for arrest be communicated to the detained persons and to their relatives.

The proposals by Bourdon were adopted with the amendment by Bentabole.

BASSAL: It is not only the revolutionary committees which have committed errors; there are also some citizens who were incarcerated by order of representatives of the people, whose good faith was taken advantage of. I therefore move that the representatives of the people sent on mission, and the Committee on General Security, likewise give the reasons for the arrests that they order.

This proposal was adopted. . . .

A clerk reads the draft of the decree to the effect that the motives of arrest of a citizen will be communicated to his relatives.

FAYAU: The National Convention ought not to forget the great principles of liberty. It doubtless does not believe that all the aristocrats have been punished and that all the detained persons are innocent. What is the plan, then, of those who at this moment want the reasons for arrest to be communicated to the relatives of the detained persons? (*Murmurs.*) No doubt patriots have been harassed, and it is the Convention's duty to investigate this. As for the detained persons, there exists a decree to the effect that they will be required to give proofs of their civic conduct since July 1789. It is therefore needless to communicate to them the reasons for their arrest, since it will suffice to execute your decree. (*Violent murmurs arise in all parts of the hall.* "A vote on the draft of the decree! *cry several members.*)

You didn't understand: it is clear that if your decree is executed, it is needless to communicate to the relatives of the detained persons the reasons for their arrest. (*Renewed murmurs.*)

A motion was made for the order of the day. . . .

BOURDON DE L'OISE: In order that all the people know that this proposal, worthy of the Spanish inquisition, has been punished as it merits, it is good to say that it was supported by no one. (*Applause.*)

The Convention passes to the order of the day.

CAMBON: Infatuation for one man has put the Republic two fingers from its loss: your courage and your unity have once more saved liberty; your wisdom will know how to preserve it from the return of a similar danger.

Already you have recognized the necessity of making notable changes in your internal organization, in order to concentrate in the Convention the operation of the revolutionary government, and the Committee of Public Safety has hastened to present to you a proposed decree drawn up with this in view. The basis of this proposal is in accord with the principles of the opinion I expressed in the session of the 11th of this month; it restores to the committees of the Convention a great part of the activity they had lost; but I still do not think it gives them all they are susceptible of and which the public good seems to me to demand imperiously. . . .

Instructive experience has warned us of the danger of removing the general administration from the direct surveillance of the Convention; it proves how important it is that the representation as a whole take part in the government as much as it can, without slowing the progress of operations; now this double purpose appears to me possible to attain, by entrusting to the various committees the direct surveillance of the executive commissions, and by establishing these same intermediary committees between the commissions and the central committee of the government.

It is in this principal point that my project differs from that of the Committee of Public Safety. . . .

Finally, the Committee proposes that you change the various legislative committees and distinguish their task from execution in order to entrust the latter exclusively to the Committee of Public Safety, to which all the commissions would make daily reports of their operations.

I would remark on this subject that the distinction to be established between legislation and execution appears destined to be a source of ceaseless difficulties; it could give rise to a struggle between the various committees and the Committee of Public Safety, a struggle necessarily prejudicial to the public good. Finally, . . . it is to this distinction, so difficult to grasp clearly and thereby so favorable to the extension of power, that I attribute the near nullity into which the Convention fell and from which your energy has so gloriously pulled it.

It is because of these considerations that I propose to decree that each of the executive commissions will make a daily report of its operations to the committee charged with its surveillance. It will submit to it the difficulties to be resolved and will propose to it the measures of execution. If these measures concern legislation the committee will communicate them to the Committee of Public Safety and report them to the Convention. If they are only relative to executive action the committee will draft the order which will be taken by a member to the Committee of Public Safety charged with ordering all measures of execution.

By this means, legislation and execution will all be examined at a central point, and all the members of the Convention will be enabled to take part, in turn, in the acts of government. . . .

Barère has told you that the Committee of Public Safety ought to have to do the thinking for the government; I am of his opinion, and it is to give this committee the time necessary to think that I propose to unburden it of some of the executive work; this is, moreover, a means of stopping the progress of bureaucracy, from which a government cannot escape when its principal agents are overburdened with details that they cannot all follow up in person.

The Committee of Public Safety sensed this truth when it proposed that you establish under its orders executive commissions as intermediaries charged with the surveillance of the agencies. These commissions consequently perform the same functions that I propose to attribute to the committees of the Convention; in this way, we restore to the national representation the direct surveillance which belongs to it.

This proposal will lead us naturally to examine whether it is useful to conserve the commissions, for nothing would appear to be in the way of the agencies corresponding directly with your committees. . . .

This question is important and can be decided separately; I limit myself to presenting it to you for reflection; it ought not to impede the organization of your committees, which is urgent.

I also propose changing the name of the Committee of Public Safety and calling it the Central Committee of the Revolutionary Government. This change may appear fussy; but I thought it would fittingly show that the public safety is a matter for the whole Convention; that the government of the republic is in its hands, and that it exercises surveillance over the agents of the entire general administration, through some of its members gathered in a central committee.

Such are the fundamentals of the organization which I have proposed to you and which contains certain details of execution; it appeared to me fit to prevent the dangers we were on the point of succumbing to. All the representatives of the people, I repeat, would thus be called on to participate in the government; knowledge of public business would no longer be concentrated in a small number of men whom, moreover, it is not fair to charge solely with the weight of an immense responsibility. The Convention would know all, and individual ambitions, the scourge of republics, would be no longer to be feared.

The assembly ordered Cambon's speech to be printed.

The session ended at three o'clock.

19 Thermidor

(A MEMBER): I ask for the floor to point out errors which have crept into the account that the papers have given of my opinion on the colonists held in detention.

(SEVERAL VOICES): Freedom of the press! Freedom of the press! (*Applause.*)

(ANOTHER MEMBER): If you have complaints, address yourself to the tribunals: freedom of the press! (*Renewed applause.*) . . .

Police Report

19 Thermidor, Year II [6 August 1794]

Yesterday all citizens ran to see the traitor Coffinhal guillotined. He launched bloody reproaches against everyone all the way from the prison to the place of execution. "You don't have the right to speak!" shouted one of the crowd. "Down with the tyrant!" shouted another. All these shouts ended with repeated cries of "Long live the Republic!" The people impatiently await activity from the new Revolutionary Tribunal. Everywhere citizens are seen rejoicing at the return to freedom of their brothers, their friends, and this joy seems to express the triumph of patriotism over tyranny.

Tranquillity reigns everywhere, even in the prisons. A great joy became manifest in the prison of Lazare when it was learned that ten deserters had been set free. Hope reigns presently in the soul of these prisoners, men crushed by the hasty judgments of the Revolutionary Tribunal.

Prostitutes are appearing on the streets with their usual audacity; they rely on the fact that the Commune no longer exists.

The armed militia who were requisitioned to maintain order at the charcoal distribution, at the Tournelle gate, instead only added to the trouble by demanding preferences for themselves (*sic*). Citizens who were in the ranks were obliged to restore order.

The shovel workers demand that the gates of the charcoal yard open no earlier than seven o'clock and close at six in the evening. When they were told that they could not refuse to work, they announced that if their demands were not met they would all quit.

The markets of the different quarters of Paris were all found very empty, and the little merchandise that did arrive was so high in price that it could not be approached.

Some distributions of butter to different grocers have taken place with order and tranquillity.

In the faubourgs Jacques and Marceau, the grocers sell butter above the maximum. A great deal of order, a great deal of tranquillity in these deliveries.

GÉRÔME, HIVERT

Alphonse Aulard has published a great number of police reports and extracts from newspapers in five volumes entitled *Paris pendant la réaction thermidorienne et sous le directoire* (Paris, 1898-1902). See I, 20-21, for this report.

National Convention

22 Thermidor [9 August]

BARÈRE: The committees of Public Safety and General Security have been busy carrying out the decree you enacted to limit the causes of detention to those indicated by the decree of 17 September 1793 (old style) and counter-revolutionary actions or violations.

If there was a time when our country had to be severe without exception, the recent victories have inaugurated a period when our country can be indulgent without danger, and regard faults of civic conduct as wiped out by a certain period of detention.

The committees are continuing to rule on petitions for release and to remedy errors or injustices. Soon all traces of personal vengeance will disappear from the soil of the Republic.

But the thronging of citizens of both sexes to the doors of the Committee on General Security only slows this work, so useful to the citizens.

We do justice to the natural impatience of families, to the solicitude of wives and mothers; but why slow up, by solicitations that are insulting to the legislators and by assemblies that are too numerous, the rapid progress that national justice ought to make at this time?

We therefore ask the citizens to rely on the civic zeal of the people's representatives for the judgment of the detained persons, and for the giving of warrants for release, which can now be safely granted to so many citizens, to fathers of families and to men who can attach themselves to and render themselves useful to the Republic. This is a matter neither of amnesty nor of clemency; it is a matter of justice, and of a justice equal for all.

In certain *section*s [of Paris], movements which were too violent to be natural to civic conduct have led to acts dangerous in these circumstances, needless in the eyes of a committee that continues to work for the cause of the detained persons and in the eyes of a convention that has shown all its beneficent justice in this happy revolution, which was never destined to serve incorrigible aristocrats nor to raise their guilty hopes. For them we have only chains or death; let them therefore cease to raise their insolent heads and hope that some fortuitous event of the revolution may be favorable to them, as long as there exist here representatives of the people.

That ridiculous aristocracy seeks nevertheless to get hold of the

Le Moniteur universel, XXI, 438-9, 447-8, 472-6, 484-8.

civic movement; it seeks to corrupt the national justice and to stir up the citizens against revolutionary institutions; but the public mind is sound and strong; the people watch the progress of events and the sudden changes of the revolution and it will be enough for the National Convention to warn good citizens of the measures that the two committees are taking at this moment: they are sending into the prisons two commissioners who twice a day bring back numerous reports to the Committee on General Security, which grants warrants for release; and they are busy day and night judging all the detentions; informing good citizens of the carrying out of these measures will be enough to stop this needless crowding, which is an obstacle to the committees and which, in the hands of the always scheming aristocracy, could damage or disturb liberty.

The National Convention ordered the report of the Committee of Public Safety to be printed and inserted in the Bulletin *of the Convention.*

TALLIEN: The remarks which have just been made in the name of the two committees, spread by means of the *Bulletin,* will be of the greatest utility; they will teach the aristocracy that at the same time as the committees render justice to harassed patriots they are busy repressing it [the aristocracy].

Already it has sought to raise its head in several *sections;* it sought, two days ago, to break a revolutionary instrument, but the progress it would like to make will be stopped.

Another fact that is no less important and that must be known is that there has been an effort to isolate some members of this assembly; some papers have told them they had ghosts to avenge.

Yes, there is no doubt, we have ghosts to avenge; but they are those of two hundred thousand of our brothers who died fighting the enemy; they are those of the patriots butchered by the aristocracy and the factions. The commissioners who visit the prisons, at the same time as they are busy taking information in order to free the patriots, are also busy tearing off the hypocritical mask with which the aristocrats cover themselves; for there is not a single man now in the houses of detention who does not call himself an ardent patriot and an enemy of Robespierre.

I have still another remark to make: disorder reigns in the appeals that are made. Many of our colleagues take it upon themselves to ask for the release of several persons, and they think that in doing this they serve justice and liberty; but I ask them to be wary of the traps that are being laid for them. It is especially the deputies who are strangers to the city of Paris who are addressed by schemers, counter-revolutionaries, men who are known by the deputies of this *département* for having followed the banner of Robespierre and for having been his most ardent sectaries, because they hope to achieve their purpose by deceiving persons who do not know them.

I give this brotherly advice to my colleagues, so that they will avoid involuntarily giving the aristocracy the opportunity for a momentary triumph. (*Applause.*)

23 Thermidor

Merlin read the final draft of the definitive law on the organization of the Revolutionary Tribunal.

CHARLIER: I notice that the law establishes no time limit on the proceedings; the jurors have only to answer the chief judge's request for a verdict by saying they have not enough information to prolong a case indefinitely, for six years, let us say. (*Protests against the decree in part of the hall; several voices moved that it be withdrawn.*)

BENTABOLE: The decree was enacted after having been discussed during several sessions; I have just heard it said with great petulance that this decree is worthless: Well, let those who disapprove of it ascend to the platform, let them speak, and we shall judge whether their tardy observations ought to destroy a decree that the Convention has passed in its mature wisdom. (*Some agitation in the assembly.*)

DUHEM: There is no surprise in the kind of perverseness that is to be seen in the opinions of——(*Noise.*) I declare, gentlemen, that I am not of your opinion, and I say that there is no surprise, after a revolution such as that which has just taken place, in seeing aristocracy and moderatism attempt to turn it to their advantage. And so, for several days, the only persons set at liberty to be encountered have been aristocrats. Yes, the decree is vicious; I move for its withdrawal, and I am going to give reasons.

Before the disastrous law proposed by Couthon [on 22 Prairial] for a new organization of the Revolutionary Tribunal, that tribunal proceeded vigorously in the path of justice. (*Applause.*) In fact, it had been formed according to the true principles of such an institution, after fifty-four hours of discussion and debate with the Brissotin faction around us. Well, citizens, because a villain, because a dictator has gone beyond the limits of this salutary institution, must it now be entirely deformed? What need do you have for a voluminous code which will supply weapons for chicanery and will assure means of impunity to the guilty?

Let us restore the tribunal to its original purity and this is enough; let us remember good effects it has produced, and let us not deprive it of its vigor.

I have just traveled through the North, and all the way here I saw the patriots obliged to enter into a difficult struggle with moderatism. I saw the patriots obliged to use all their strength to resist its efforts. Why? Because the aristocracy is triumphing, even while you are making the mask of false patriotism fall; it wants to take advantage of this to cause the truest and strongest patriots to be confused with those hypocritical villains.

Hence I should move, if you like, not immediate withdrawal, but at least a new discussion, which would return to the old organization of the Revolutionary Tribunal and bring us back to the pure principles that dictated it, because of the experience of the advantages which have resulted from it.

MERLIN DE DOUAI: The members who are protesting certainly have no knowledge of the manner in which the decree was enacted; it was discussed by the entire Convention during two sessions, and it was the fruit of the joint deliberations of the three committees of Public Safety, General Security, and Legislation, during a day and three nights. One cannot say that it is a law which was smuggled through.

Besides, I defy anyone to cite in this new law anything which is not either quoted directly or rephrased from the laws on the Revolutionary Tribunal as it existed before the law of 22 Prairial. We have brought back those laws and gathered them into a code, in order to prevent the abuses which have been introduced since their enactment. There is not a word in the decree which is not in this spirit. I call upon the testimony of all those who observed the Revolutionary Tribunal more than four months ago, at a time when it was fulfilling entirely the wishes of national justice; it then followed the same principles, the same procedure, that you have just adopted in its new organization.

Several voices move for returning to the order of the day.

Charlier goes back to his preceding remark; he moves that the assembly rule on it and fix a time limit beyond which argument cannot be prolonged.

DUHEM: Before deciding on this particular proposal, I move that the general proposal that I have made be put to a vote. Merlin has said that the new law was drawn word for word, and its provisions copied, from the spirit of the old one; in that case, let us re-enact that law itself. But here they have come and blocked the revolutionary movement by a multitude of formalities which have to do with the institution of juries and which are acceptable only in the ordinary criminal courts. The organization of the former Revolutionary Tribunal had reached the point of perfection which, without exceeding what was required by the interest of accused innocence, did not fall short of the energy made necessary by the safety of the Republic. I move, then, that the Convention, in repealing the decree of 22 Prairial relative to the Revolutionary Tribunal, decree that this tribunal will judge in conformity with the previous laws.

Several members: The order of the day!

The motion for proceeding to the order of the day was tabled.

Lacoste reproduced Duhem's proposal. He moved that the new judges and jurors named by the Revolutionary Tribunal take up their duties immediately, and follow the laws enacted for that tribunal previous to the law of 22 Prairial.

This proposal was decreed.

GRANET DE MARSEILLE: It is necessary that France know promptly the names of the oppressed patriots to whom the Convention has restored their liberty. I move that their names be printed, and that beside each of them be put the names of the persons who have attested their patriotism.

This proposal was adopted.

(UNIDENTIFIED MEMBER): I notify the Convention that four days ago the deputation from the Sarthe was advised that the nucleus of rebels is growing every instant, and especially since the tyrant Robespierre has been struck down, because the aristocrats are seeking to take advantage of the patriots' victory.

The draft of Granet's proposal was read.

MALLARMÉ: I move as an additional article that the committees of Public Safety and General Security cause to be printed, every five days, the list of citizens whom they release.

This proposal was decreed.

The draft of Lacoste's proposal was read.

SERGENT: I move that the judges and jurors of the Revolutionary Tribunal be commandeered and required to report immediately to their post.

This proposal was adopted.

BOURDON DE L'OISE: The laws under which the Revolutionary Tribunal is going to judge do not say explicitly that the jurors will decide on the question of intent; this is the only way to judge that is worthy of justice. I move that this provision be inserted in the law on the organization of the Revolutionary Tribunal.

This proposal was adopted.

The assembly proceeded to discuss the new organization of the committees.

24 Thermidor

CAMBACÉRÈS: The victory that the people and their representatives have just won is a new proof that, if all conspiracies seek support in the National Convention, they all find in it their tomb.

It is the part of wisdom, however, to remove the possibility of a return to the spirit of faction, and to guarantee liberty from all danger. It is for this purpose that you have decided to concern yourselves with the reorganization of your committees.

At first glance, this operation appears to be of slight importance; but when one examines what it may have to do with the conservation of the State, it ought to inspire interest in those who think that the government is the great means of achieving the establishment of the Republic.

It is not your intention to reduce the functions of your committees to the sterile consideration of a few proposals for laws; you also want to turn over to them a part of your work, and make them, so to speak, the first instruments of the government of which you alone must be the center.

It is therefore the revolutionary constitution of the National Convention that you are going to create.

We are placed between two hazards: misuse of power, and slackening of effort. The one is no less dangerous than the other; let us prevent the return of that state of oppression from which we have just emerged; let us also fear the catastrophic effects of a too hasty relaxation of tension.

If you cast your eye over our past situation, you will see liberty betrayed on every hand, the laws without vigor, our frontiers attacked, the Republic and its founders on the brink of the abyss.

Such was our situation last year, when the constitution came to terrify all our enemies and crush federalism.

It was not enough to establish liberty.

The revolutionary government appeared, and this salutary conception, unknown to all the peoples who have previously attempted to be free, soon gave everything a new look.

The revolutionary government can therefore be considered as the palladium of the Republic. Let us guard ourselves above all against slowing its course and let us not forget that on its strength and continued existence may depend our country's salvation and our individual existence.

We have said that the organization of your committees was the establishment of the revolutionary constitution of the National Convention; it remains to indicate the elements which ought to compose it.

The Convention alone is the center of government; it alone has merited the confidence of the people; there were traitors among its members, but in the national representation were to be found only fidelity and the ruin of all the conspirators.

The Convention alone ought to have the legislative power; this is a right that the sovereign people has entrusted only to it and that it is not free to delegate.

Let no authority interpret the laws; to interpret the laws is almost always to change them and often to destroy them; and hence the need to forbid the committees to issue orders not relative to matters of purely executive action.

Orders are to laws as laws are to principles. Laws are the consequences of principles; orders ought to be only the consequences of laws.

The government and the laws, that is the responsibility of the National Convention. But the laws must be prepared and presented with reasons which justify their utility, and the government must act quickly and consistently. Hence the need to establish committees charged with preparing the laws, and the need to entrust government to a few men chosen among you.

To give the authority charged with carrying on government all the power necessary to attain its purpose; to mark precisely the limits it must have; to create ways to contain it within the limits, this is the problem to resolve.

The plan presented by Cambon largely provides the solution of this problem; but I am going to express a few ideas which, without changing anything fundamental in that plan, may serve to complete it. . . .

It all consists, then, in excluding the governing committee from legislation, security measures, and control of public funds, and in entrusting to special committees the direction or surveillance of each of these branches. . . .

I should move that the plan to abolish the executive commissions be carried out; from the moment when you call the members of your committees into the administration, mere executive agents suffice;

the commissions then become a fifth wheel. By their suppression the machinery would be simplified, and the costs of administration reduced.

But there are a few points in Cambon's plan on which I am not in agreement with him. . . .

Cambon proposes to establish harmony between the central committee and the other committees through one member of each.

This operation involves complication and delays; it is needless in all that has to do with general security, finance, civil and criminal legislation. The committees to which the surveillance and the direction of these matters are entrusted ought to take the measures, for carrying out the laws, that they judge appropriate, subject to making reports on them to the National Convention.

For everything else, would it not be simpler to distinguish the responsibility of the central committee from those of the other committees in the following way?

When an order pertained only to the matter which forms one committee's assignment, this committee would decide on it alone; but when the order, being connected to other matters by its object or its consequences was an act of general administration, it could be issued only by the central governing committee alone.

It all comes down to defining clearly the cases in which executive orders would have to be decided on by the central committee and those in which they could be the work of the special committees.

This definition demands certain practical knowledge, which each of us could give for the branch in which he has been employed; and if this proposal were adopted, before drawing it up, there would be preparatory work to be done which could be promptly terminated. . . .

You will not attain the salutary purpose that you have in mind if several committees continue to meet jointly either to prepare proposed laws or to agree upon executive measures. The effect of these joint meetings is to place all power in the hands of some of your members.

There is still another effect. Discussion is no longer carried on within the assembly, and on this point we have the lessons of experience. For how can one debate, when all those who are currently informed about business remain in agreement on one plan which is brought before you, and present to their colleagues the authority of their unanimity and the power of opinion, so often favorable to influential men?

In the second place, it is not enough to have withdrawn the decree by which the representatives of the people could be brought to judgment without having been heard.

No committee ought to count in the list of its assignments the painful burden of preparing indictments against colleagues; if one of us should have the misfortune to be accused, the indictment of him must be drawn up by a commission named by a roll call.

Because of the fine institution of juries there is no man of whom another may say: "There is the one who will decide on my life." In the same way it must be impossible for any representative of the people to say of some committee: "Those are the ones who can accuse me.". . .

Limited duration of power is as necessary as the limit upon power itself. But don't frequent replacements have great disadvantages? And won't the interval required between re-elections, generally accepted for the committees of Government and on General Security, be injurious to the other committees in all that has to do with the systematic part of the laws? . . .

Citizens, great movement will be given the revolution if after having destroyed the chiefs of the most criminal and the most atrocious of conspiracies we steadily keep in view a few principles which ought to guide us in the mission which has been entrusted to us.

Let us attach ourselves to our country and not to individuals; to the Republic and not to persons; to principles and not to men. Let us not forget that the salvation of the Republic is essentially linked to the conservation of the National Convention, and that the National Convention can respond to the confidence of the people only by keeping a firm hand on the reins of government, by setting aside everything that can divide authority, by diminishing as much as possible the number of intermediaries between itself and the people, by carrying on itself or through its members all branches of government.

Consequently, I move that precedence be given to the plan presented by Cambon, that it be put to a vote article by article, and I reserve to myself to propose amendments to each of them, in accordance with the views in the speech I have just made to you.

Several members move for precedence for Cambon's plan.

A motion is made for precedence for Berlier's plan.

A MEMBER: I move for postponement of this discussion and that the speakers who have presented plans join to present to the Convention a proposed decree which can reconcile all opinions.

DELMAS: A question of this importance seems to me to require a very thorough discussion. I move that a commission be formed of one or two members of each committee, to consider all the plans presented and agree on a definitive plan which will be submitted to the Convention in three days.

BOURDON DE L'OISE: The procedural motion that has just been made changes the question. It was only a matter of deciding whether precedence would be given to Cambon's plan. I move that the discussion be continued; I think the assembly sufficiently enlightened to establish a few fundamentals itself; it is perhaps to be feared that prejudices may too easily become fixed for Cambon's plan, which I regard as infinitely useful in time of peace but which could have sorry consequences before the complete achievement of the revolution. Long experience has sufficiently enlightened you on the causes which have compromised the future of liberty up to now: first, a government created contrary to principle and to the revolution, and then an inactive government; the royal government wanted to ruin us by a frontal attack, the ministerial government, the extraordinary commission, in coalition with Dumouiez, by paralyzing everything.

For these two perfidious governments you have substituted a rapid and active government; because of it our victories began, because of it internal enemies have been vigorously repressed, and external enemies obliged to defend themselves on their own territory. Will you say that this government no longer suits us because monsters have conspired even within it to destroy public liberty? But what has been the terrible effect of these conspiracies, concocted by a small-time lawyer and a hypocritical cripple? A single day sufficed to stamp out the conspiracy and destroy the conspirators. (*Applause.*) Where are your most redoubtable enemies? Where are the dictators who must be feared? They are in your armies, at the head of the armies. It is by military force that all republics have been gradually subjugated; now if you deprive the government of its strength, if you weaken its effectiveness by dividing it, do you not have to fear making military authority prevail? The revolutionary government which was established had great vices, no doubt, and they must be corrected; it misused its power, and it must be brought within limits it cannot exceed. I move that the discussion open on the plan presented by the Committee of Public Safety.

CAMBON: The plans presented by my colleagues doubtless should lead to perfecting the plan I proposed. But the ideas I submitted are appropriate to the revolutionary government; I may cite, among other proofs, the right that I give to the committee on general police action to arrest suspect citizens, a right that it could not keep if the republic were firmly established and if the government were no longer revolutionary.

GOUPILLEAU DE FONTENAY: Citizens, it seems to me that, to obtain a good result, we must adopt the proposal made by Delmas, that one or two members of each committee assemble starting this evening and put together a plan that they will present tomorrow, if possible, for discussion by the assembly.

SEVERAL MEMBERS: Vote on the proposition of Delmas!

BOURDON DE L'OISE: Although it has been said that we have done nothing but wander in this discussion, I am convinced, myself, that it has greatly enlightened the assembly. It has proven that we all want a strong government, not in bad faith and against the Convention but to direct our armies abroad, to repress our internal enemies within. Well, it will be a happy idea that we owe to Cambon, that of giving one committee the internal surveillance and the Committee of Public Safety the direction of external operations and the movements of the armies.

I move that the three members who have presented plans join with the Committee of Public Safety, to combine them in a single plan.

BRÉARD: I really think, like Bourdon, that the discussion has enlightened the opinion of the National Convention. Yes, we all want a revolutionary government, a government which is the people's friend and which makes the enemies of the revolution tremble. I did not see what we are looking for in any of the plans presented; but together they appear to me to fulfill our purposes. I therefore join with Delmas and Goupilleau in asking for a commission composed of a member of each committee, which would present a proposed decree the day after tomorrow at the latest.

DUHEM: I move for precedence for Bourdon's proposal. The enlightenment of the members of the Committee of Public Safety suffices, with that of the members who have presented plans, to propose a plan such as we desire.

MERLIN DE THIONVILLE: It is doubtless not the opinion of my colleague Duhem that there is enlightenment only in the Committee of Public Safety. I was glad to make this remark before moving for precedence for Delmas's proposal.

TALLIEN: The Committee of Public Safety has been invested with great authority. It is even in a way, at this moment, the government itself. One of the greatest questions that we have to treat is whether the government still ought to have the same intensity. To illuminate this question, it seems to me that we shall find much more enlightenment in a meeting of members of all the committees than in that on Public Safety alone, several members of which have not yet been on any committee. It must be repeated, we want a government which is just to all citizens but which no longer weighs on them with an iron rod. We want the same energy, the same vigor, the same unity in the operations of the government; but we no longer want in the government a Robespierre, a Saint-Just, and a Couthon. I declare that if I were destined to be a member of a committee which was obliged to have the same powers, I should instantly resign. I insist on Delmas's proposal.

A vote gave precedence to this proposal.

BOURDON DE L'OISE: A roll call!

A FEW MEMBERS: A roll call!

THURIOT: It is possible to reconcile all opinions. It has been proposed, on the one hand, to form a commission composed of a member of each committee; and on the other hand, to refer the matter to the Committee of Public Safety, to which would be joined the three members who have presented the most luminous views on the organization of the government. The first proposal has been decreed; let this decree stand; but at the same time why do you not also adopt the other proposal? These two sentiments are not mutually exclusive; in fact, you cannot prevent three of your members, individually or together, or with the Committee of Public Safety, from also presenting to you a proposed decree; and there will be a certain advantage in this; for if your commission is slow to present a plan to you, or if that which it presents is not such as it ought to be, you will have provided yourselves with a resource; you will have the advantage of having created two means of action. Therefore, I move that Bourdon's motion also be adopted.

BARÈRE: The question must be met frankly. You have asked for great enlightenment, in order to have what? A just government; but is this just in the manner of the aristocrats? No, certainly not. (*Applause.*) We have been saved by the revolutionary government; the rascals, the schemers fear only the revolutionary government; it is then on this single foundation, on this government which accelerates the movements of the armies, which conserves victory, that everything must be based.

TURREAU: I ask Barère which of us opposes revolutionary government?

BARÈRE: I did not say that there is a single member of the Convention who does not want the revolutionary government. I speak to the assembly and not to men's passions. I asked that before pressing on with our researches a foundation be put in place first. Well, let us all agree, let us all declare that we want revolutionary government. ("Yes, yes!" *cried all the members, rising and waving their hats simultaneously;* "yes, yes, we all want it!" *Applause several times renewed.*) I do not know anyone who does not want a just government. The revolutionary government is the people's justice.

There can be abuses everywhere there are humans; but it is those members who have silently fought, during a month and a half, to unmask the traitor Robespierre—

(*It was observed that the speaker was departing from the question and it was moved that the discussion be closed.*)

BARÈRE: I conclude that precedence be given to Bourdon's proposal.

The discussion was closed.

The Convention adopted Delmas's proposal.

GRANET: I move that the definitive plan be presented tomorrow at the latest.

This proposal was adopted.

The session ended at five o'clock.

26 Thermidor

GRANET: You have enacted a salutary decree which ordains the printing of the names of the persons set at liberty and of those who have solicited these releases; it is possible that the respondents will not appear; I move that in that case the individuals released be put under arrest again (*murmurs*), unless the committee has in its hands the documents which attest the patriotism of the person released.

MERLIN DE THIONVILLE: I am against Granet's proposal; our conduct is outlined in the law of 17 September. If you adopt the measure presented to you, you are going to sanction the greatest injustice. We have set at liberty citizens detained for six, eight, and ten months with no reasons for their arrest. Can you without injustice have these citizens put back in prison? It is time, citizens, it is more than time, that no faction—(*vigorous applause rises from all parts of the hall*) that no faction make use of the steps of Robespierre's throne. (*Renewed applause.*) . . . Since we have been placed on the Committee on General Security to oppose tyrants——(*Applause several times renewed.*) Yes, we declare, we will, though not as Robespierre did, lay our heads on the scaffold——("No, no!" *cry a mass of members*) or we shall take all means necessary to prevent the tyrants from succeeding through perfidy. (*Applause.*) We must do nothing by halves, and, we must admit, the Convention has done several things by halves. If tyrants still exist among us, at least they should be silent.

The Committee on General Security, in the mass of business which overwhelms it, may have mechanically and unintentionally set a few aristocrats at liberty whom it can readily find again. In addition, to avoid errors and deceptions, it decided yesterday that any detained person who is rich enough to wait, even if he is innocent, will not be set at liberty until there are no more *sans-culottes,* no more true patriots under arrest. (*Applause.*) And that is why, since yesterday, more than fifty very simple claims on which one could decide immediately have been set aside for later. I therefore move that we proceed to the order of the day [ignoring] Granet's proposal; I move in addition that our colleagues, instead of harboring acrimony against us and appearing to want to destroy what the Convention has done since the fall of the last tyrant, come to us and say frankly and honestly: 'You have set at liberty such and such aristocrat;' then we shall take measures to have them incarcerated again. There must be no reason to fear that the lists that are being requested may one day become proscription lists.—(*Murmurs.*) Yes, proscription—And if, at the last festival, it was observed that some of the citizens did not bring the same gaiety to it as all the others, it is because this morning's motion had spread terror in all minds.

I repeat, the committee will always oppose whoever wants to put himself or his partisans in Robespierre's place. I insist upon the order of the day.

LEGENDRE: Do you want to know the motive that is behind the motion which has been made? I am going to tell you without passion and without any partiality. It comes from the fact that sometimes there is a member in the deputation from one *département* who opposes the release asked for by his colleagues for certain persons; the opposing member then comes to you to propose printing the names of the persons released and of those who put in claims for them. The Committee on General Security has seen clearly that the release of certain aristocrats was obtained from it by trickery; but the number is not large; I know of only two, the ex-dukes of Aumont and of Valentinois, and they have both been arrested again. If one of our colleagues comes to prove to us that there are others whom we have unintentionally set at large, we shall have them incarcerated again right away; and if the suspect individuals succeed in escaping our surveillance, our plan is to come and ask you to outlaw them until they have been arrested again. We want to accelerate the revolution; let us not be guided by passions ourselves; let none of us regard his colleague as an enemy of the public good because he differs in opinion. Did we not recently hear Couthon tell Bourdon de l'Oise, because he was arguing against his opinion, that he was reasoning like Pitt and Coburg? This example has been repeated often since then. Yet we all want the general good. I repeat, let us not regard one another as enemies when the same cause units us, when our intentions bring us together. . . .

I therefore move the repeal of the decree of the 23rd, of that decree which has cast terror into the people's souls at a moment when they need all their capacities, all their energy.

TALLIEN: I regard this session as one of the most important that we have had since the tyrant's end. Yes, yes, the Convention must finally be told the whole truth; it must be told that it is being led to the brink of the precipice; it must be told that there are those who want to annihilate it, and I am going to prove it.

For some days you must have observed with astonishment, and all good citizens with grief, that some are seeking to oppose individuals to one another, to cause private quarrels to spring up, to revive hatreds and passions which should all be buried in Robespierre's tomb. As I was coming in I was handed a note in which I was notified that several members were to be attacked at this session. No doubt it is the aristocracy which circulates these rumors; it is not a man whom they want to stab; it is not a few men whom they want to strike down; it is the Convention, which makes the tyrants tremble, that they want to destroy.

Let us not aid our enemies by our own divisions; let Europe know that we are forbidding ourselves all favoritism, that we are not listening to any passion. Let us show that we have been sent here to bring about the people's happiness, and not to quarrel and dispute with one another. (*Applause.*)

Continuators of Robespierre, do not hope for any success, the mass of the Convention is determined to perish here——("Yes, yes!" *shout all the members, rising simultaneously*) or to annihilate all the tyrants, whatever mask they cover themselves with. (*The same movement is repeated.*)

Yes, they have tried to destroy the Convention; they have tried to spread it about that it did not want the government to be revolutionary, or that it wanted it to be just in the aristocrats' fashion. No, the Convention does not want a government that is just in the style of the aristocrats . . . it wants a government that is just in the style of the people. (*Vigorous applause.*) . . .

It is possible that a few patriots have been deceived as to certain individuals; we do not believe in the infallibility of men. If some member has been deceived, let him climb up on this platform; it is a fine thing to recognize one's own error. (*Applause.*) If some other member has knowledge that an aristocrat has been set free, let him denounce him; let him turn in a list of them, and they will all be arrested immediately. But be on guard against the maneuvers of the the aristocracy; it insinuates itself into groups, it sows terror; it spreads it about that the Convention is divided, and that this division will gradually lead us to slaughter one another; it adds, to confirm these rumors, that we want to prevent the patriots from coming out of the prisons by intimidating those who would solicit their release. Well, I shall make a sincere admission, I should prefer to see twenty aristocrats set at liberty today, who will be arrested again tomorrow, than to see one patriot remain in irons. What! The republic with its million and two hundred citizens under arms should fear a few aristocrats! No, it is too great; it will always know how to discover and strike down its enemies.

Yes, there have been errors committed. I shall myself indicate some to the Committee on General Security and the Revolutionary Tribunal will do justice to the enemies of the people. But let us not sow discouragement among the citizens and division in the Convention. If the condition we are in lasts a few days more, if men are unable to esteem one another, if we are not united among ourselves, it remains only to bury us here; for without unity liberty is destroyed. But I envision a more cheerful future; liberty will triumph, the Convention will declare to all those who would imitate the tyrant we have struck down that it is here to strike them; that it wants a revolutionary government, just but firm; severe, but which does not make the citizens tremble; for terror is the weapon of tyranny; severe only for the enemies of the people, reassuring for the fathers of families, for the respectable man. . . .

I repeat, unity must reign here, those who have suspicions must explain them, so that the aristocracy does not profit from our divisions. As for me, I declare that I shall do so, and all the patriots will imitate me. I ask that impartiality and justice reign here. If that is a moderate idea, I declare that I am a moderate, and no doubt the whole Convention is, too. ("Yes! Yes!" *members shout.*) I move the repeal of the preceding decree, and the order of the day as to the new proposal.

BERNARD DE SAINTES: What I have just heard is astonishing. . . . It has just been said that the Convention was on the brink of the precipice, that it was divided; and what was the reason for this speech? Because there was a motion which aims at punishing the aristocrats. (*Murmurs.*) It was a matter of a motion to repress the aristocrats. (*Renewed murmurs.*)

It was not long ago that you learned, almost to your cost, how dangerous are those speeches in which people talk of factions; remember that Robespierre and his accomplices used to tell you constantly from this platform that people wanted to degrade the Convention, that they wanted to divide it. No one should come with speeches and flowery eloquence to sow a false discord here. If anyone knows men who want to follow in Robespierre's steps, he must have the strength to denounce them. You ought to fear being seduced by grand phrases. . . . You ought to oblige each member to keep to the subject of debate, and not to make attacks that are foreign to the subject.

There have been outcries against the decree of 23 Thermidor; it has been said that it cast terror among the people.

SEVERAL VOICES: It's true!

BERNARD: Reason alone ought to tell you that that cannot be. Examine your own heart, and ask yourself what respectable man would not make it a duty to declare what he has done; as for me, I declare that I should be honored to have caused a good man to be set at liberty. It is therefore only the villains who can fear your law, and our intention is not to favor them. I add that, if you repeal the decree you have enacted, you are going to thwart the Committee's operations, for people are going to come in crowds to solicit it, and the more they surround it, the more slowly it will act.

BENTABOLE: It is established that the National Convention is not in an absolutely tranquil condition; it is established that some want to cast doubt on the committees.

I know that the proposal to have the lists prepared is in conformity with all the principles. (*Applause.*) But we must know whether this proposal was not dictated by other reasons; we must know what proposals will follow it. Such a list will sanction proscriptions. It will result in a multitude of accusations by deputies against deputies. These accusations may be brought forward in good faith against colleagues who have been deceived; but how are you going to judge whether they have been deceived? Suspicions, anxieties, will still hover over us. I adjure you, in our country's name, to beware that division does not slip into our midst. It is unity that has saved us; why depart from it? I maintain that the printing of the lists will form parties and will have the most fatal effects. I propose a means of reassuring the people, who are watching you, and who are examining whether you truly want to save them. It is certain that the Committee on General Security has committed errors; it has itself told you that it was deceived; but despite this it still has your confidence. ("Yes, yes," *is shouted on all sides.*) Well, why not depend on it to repair these errors, to pursue the aristocracy? If it does not have your confidence, name another committee.

MERLIN DE THIONVILLE: . . . What has already happened can happen again, and the detained persons who owe their liberty to the beneficence of the Convention would be the first victims of a new faction which could arise. (*Murmurs.*)

I know that the Committee is supposed to account to the Convention for its operations, and it does not refuse to do so; its offices are not its own, they are those of the Convention; let our colleagues come and obtain there all the information they desire. They will be refused nothing; they can obtain knowledge of the names of all the persons set at liberty. . . .

TALLIEN: Since you want to have printed the list of those who have been set at liberty, I move that we have printed also the names of those who have had them incarcerated; the people must know their real enemies, those who have denounced patriots and have had them incarcerated.

Tallien's proposal, supported by several members, is quickly put to a vote and adopted.

Certain members protest. Several voices are heard to say, "It's civil war!"

TALLIEN: I declare to the Convention that my proposal had no other purpose than to make it see how dangerous is the decree that it enacted previously. I did not want to have it adopted. If you repeal the first decree, I move also the repeal of the one which the Convention has just enacted on my motion.

SEVERAL VOICES: Repeal both decrees!

[*After a short period of further debate, this proposal was adopted.*]

Correspondence of Dyzez

Paris, 27 Thermidor, Year II [14 August 1794]

To an unidentified correspondent

I'm no longer telling you about our victories, Citizen. They are so frequent that nobody pays attention to them any more. They are like

"Lettres," p. 520.

the sun that one enjoys without being impressed by the brilliant spectacle. People no longer think about anything much but watching the first moves of the Convention after the events of the 9th and 10th. People are stirring and the repercussions are rather strong. The subject of concern presently is the release of prisoners. A decree was passed to prevent the deputies from having influence. This decree was withdrawn after a violent struggle. As it was put to a vote in the midst of the greatest tumult, and no one heard the chairman, and the mass of the assembly adjourned without waiting to hear anything, I do not know whether the debate will be resumed today. If there are no protests, this is the new direction that public opinion will take. Tallien, opposed to the summit of the Mountain, based himself on this axiom: I would prefer to save twenty aristocrats accidentally than to expose one patriot to unjust oppression. With this maxim, you can see the turn things must take if it is maintained.

VII
THE COALITION ENDS

Introduction

The preceding section concluded with the debate in the National Convention on 26 Thermidor. That meeting was a watershed in the course of the Thermidorian reaction because it was then that the coalition fell to pieces. During Fructidor the Convention began to move more swiftly and openly against the principles—and the former leaders—of the Revolutionary Government. The debate of 2 Fructidor is especially significant. The Convention's spontaneous reaction to Louchet's proposal and Tallien's bold stroke indicates that a new mood reigned among the deputies.

Events after 2 Fructidor show that the situation was still complex. There was a strong desire to end the terror but it was clear that the immediate past could not be completely disowned. Too many members of the Convention had been too deeply involved in the task of saving the revolution. The reactionary elements in the Convention were not able to achieve total victory. The reception of Lecointre's attack suggests that he had miscalculated.

The second part of the section consists of retrospective analyses of 9 Thermidor and the justificatory memoirs of Billaud-Varenne, Collot d'Herbois, and Vadier. In their attempts to exculpate themselves, the three ex-terrorists cast additional light on the causes of Robespierre's defeat and on the events leading to 9 Thermidor. Do these men successfully answer the charge that they were the accomplices of Robespierre? Was it in fact possible for them to dissociate themselves from the work of the Revolutionary Government?

Finally, the selections from the memoirs of Levasseur and Thibaudeau are useful in analyzing the confusing events that followed Robespierre's death. And, conversely, the memoirs can be judged in the light of the other sources. For example, do the debates in the Convention substantiate Levasseur's description of the parties that combined to overthrow Robespierre?

National Convention

1 Fructidor, Year II [18 August 1794]

GOUPILLEAU DE FONTENAY, *in the name of the committees of Public Safety and General Security:* Citizens, the first duty of the founders of a republic is to direct all the movements of the revolution towards the purpose they intend; enlightened by experience, they ought to use the present to gain control of the future, and master it if possible. In casting our glance on the past, we shall distinguish the special character of our revolution: the events prepared by our internal enemies to slow its progress have always accelerated it, and everything has turned to the advantage of liberty.

It is thus that the infamous plans of an inevitably corrupt court hastened the fall of the last of the Capetians; it is thus that the conspiracy and death of the new Catiline and his accomplices tightened the bonds that attach the people to their representatives. But there is also a truth that we cannot conceal from ourselves: the aristocracy, which will never change, while applauding the just punishment of the last conspirators, still keeps its attachment to the former tyrants; while speaking of the abuses by a few men of a terrible but necessary power, the malevolent take the opportunity to decry the revolutionary government and to cast upon the most salutary institution the faults of individuals.

What! Because a few patriots have momentarily been the victims of hatreds and private vengeance, because the Convention is taking measures to repair partial injustices, does it follow that the career of evil ought to be reopened for those who have never known how to do good? Must the dagger be put into their hands to assassinate our country, which they detest and will always detest?

No, it is not for you, incorrigible men, you for whom the Republic's name alone is a punishment, it is not for you that the National Convention has made its revolution; but it is for you that the revolutionary government has been made, it is to contain you, repress you, punish you, that the machinery of that government is going to be tightened.

If we go into the assemblies of the *sections* of Paris, we shall see that since the memorable time when you showed yourselves more than ever to be worthy of representing a free people, a few schemers have sought to mislead public opinion by instigating deliberations destructive of the authorities established by the National Convention.

Le Moniteur universel, XXI, 525-7, 531-5, 548-50, 591, 620-21, 641-2.

Do not doubt, citizens, that is the reaction after the political crisis from which we are emerging, it is the aristocracy which is sending its emissaries to turn to the detriment of the public good an event which the friends of liberty will continue to applaud. It is the shade of the chiefs of the factions that you have struck down, who, hiding like them behind the mask of patriotism, are walking about in the *sections* of Paris, soon to go through all the *départements* of the Republic.

But the people, who want the revolution, and who are good judges of men, the people are there observing the small number of schemers; their patriotism will soon unmask them and, in concert with the revolutionary government which is following them, they will reduce them to inability to thwart the revolution's progress. . . .

The present state of the Republic, considered in relation to general police administration, therefore imposes on the National Convention the obligation to occupy itself with two measures.

The first is the preservation of the revolutionary government, without which the Republic cannot be consolidated.

The second is to utilize, to regularize the movements that the latest events have necessarily impressed upon all the *départements*. . . .

A committee of the Convention must, then, be specially charged with supervising the general police administration, and that is one of the most important branches of the revolutionary government.

But you would have done nothing yet if you had limited yourselves to that institution alone; there is another which exists and against which the aristocracy's efforts seem to be redoubled, an institution which the National Convention ought not only to preserve but which it ought to improve by simplifying its organization, by abolishing needless machinery, and by giving it a more rapid and better directed means of action: I mean the revolutionary committees.

Here I am touching upon a great question, whether we ought to keep one revolutionary committee for each commune, or whether the number of these committees ought to be reduced to one in each district.

With the first system, is it not to be feared that personal hatreds and private animosities would have too much influence on the decisions of these committees? The moment there exists a germ of division between men whom circumstances place close to one another, passions act with greater strength; they are ceaselessly stirring, and often prejudices, the spirit of self-interest or of revenge replace impartiality and the love of country which alone ought to guide discussion.

Besides what means will you employ to be sure that in some forty thousand communes these important duties will devolve only upon men who are fit for them? For it is there that you must have men who are either revolutionary or at least capable of being revolutionary. . . .

By reducing the number of revolutionary committees to one for each district, you will have, on the one hand, the advantage of giving the general police administration, that essential part of the revolutionary government, a procedure that is more rapid, an effectiveness that is more definite. On the other hand, you will extirpate the germ of passion which has often been substituted for the love of the public good; you will be sure of a better choice in the individuals who are to exercise this important magistracy; finally you will simplify, you will improve, an institution which could be perfected only by experience. . . .

We also thought that in the communes which are not seats of a district administration but have a population of eight thousand or more, there should be a revolutionary committee for the area of the commune alone.

Finally, the commune of Paris, which with respect to its immense population can be compared to no other commune in the Republic, appeared to us to contain an excessive number of revolutionary committees. It is principally in the assemblies of the *sections* that passions develop and act with great power; it is there that a peaceful citizen, who performs zealously the duties entrusted to him, often finds himself denounced by two or three schemers who are ambitious for his place. They succeed in getting him considered suspect, because instead of attending regularly the assemblies of his *section* he will have devoted himself more scrupulously to the activities required by his position.

Twelve revolutionary committees, each of which will include four *sections* in its jurisdiction, appeared to us sufficient in Paris.

As for the manner of naming the members of these committees, we began with the principle I established earlier, that the legislators charged with guiding the revolution to its end should themselves choose but the elements which are to join in it. It would be absurd, no doubt, to propose that the National Convention itself choose the individuals who are to make up these revolutionary authorities; but, unable to do this itself, it ought to charge some of its members with this task.

It is to achieve this purpose that we propose that you give an express commission to the people's representatives sent into the *départe-*

ments to reorganize the revolutionary committees in the principal place of each district and in the communes which contain a population of eight thousand individuals or more. . . .

With respect to the formation of the twelve committees in Paris, perhaps you will think it suitable to charge your Committee on General Security with doing this; it will have printed and distributed to all the members of the Convention the list of the individuals who compose these committees. . . .

We thought that the public interest required that the revolutionary committees be able to assure themselves as promptly as possible of the individuals against whom they thought they were obliged to take measures; thus three members of one of these committees will be able to issue a summons and order the seals to be applied [to a person's effects]; through this first operation, the public interest is protected; the law seizes and holds in its hand the man who may have or who could harm society.

But when it is a matter of deciding on the issuance of a warrant for arrest, do you not think, as we do, that then the majority of the committee is necessary? . . . You ought to consider the twelve members of the committee as a revolutionary jury, and I do not see what other mode of decision one could give it. . . .

Such is the plan that your committees have charged me with putting before you; it appeared to us to contain all the advantages of which such an institution is capable. . . .

Goupilleau read a proposed decree in conformity with the ideas he expounded in his report. The assembly ordered them to be printed and tabled.

2 Fructidor

LOUCHET: Representatives of the French people: . . . when, after so much courage, one sees the Convention compromised, degraded and almost destroyed by the terror which was inspired in it by one of its own members under the protection of a long and immense popularity, and suddenly, as if awakening from a deep sleep, rise up and break with a crash the yoke of iron which weighed on its head, and at the same instant send the new Catiline and his accomplices to the scaffold, without this great victory costing a single drop of the patriots' blood; when one reflects on these various events, which history will set down in ineffacable letters, one congratulates oneself, after so many storms and dangers, on having arrived at a time when nothing remains for the people's representatives, conquerors of all the factions, but to master themselves in order to do everything demanded of them by the safety, happiness, and glory of the Republic.

Citizens, how enviable is our political situation! . . . The internal factions have been struck down; everywhere the slaves of the tyrants' coalition are fleeing before the bayonets of republican soldiers; everywhere they are abandoning their arms, immense stores, vast regions. The free peoples recognize our Republic.

We have won, let us make use of the victory. The indomitable courage of the French people, their active, ingenious, fertile industriousness, their sacrifices of every kind, their heroic patience, their virtue, and their reason enable us to make them soon enjoy a happy domestic calm and all the benefits of liberty. . . .

Citizens, let our revolutionary energy continue to guarantee our responsibility!

To take pity on the fate of the ex-privileged is a crime; to punish their criminal attempts, and to punish them promptly and severely, is a duty. Your courage has risen proudly to the demands of the circumstances; let a false humanity not make it fall away.

Let us not lose sight of the policy of the ex-nobles; most of those who were able to bear arms have stolen away to serve under the flags of the universal crusade of kings against the French Republic or under the banners of the rebels of the Vendée; the others have remained in their homes to correspond with them and foment disturbances in the interior. Well, among the latter a large number have not been deprived of their liberty for an instant; there are also many, even fathers and mothers of *émigrés,* to whom a false interpretation of the law of 21 Messidor has just restored it. . . .

You want to give more energy to the revolutionary government by suppressing everything that the perfidy of the despot had imagined to make it unjust, barbarous, odious; but you do not want to paralyze the action of the national vengeance against the most dangerous enemies of liberty, against the scoundrels who appear to obey the laws but who really conspire against them. . . .

You want to break, and break immediately, the chains of useful artisans, of valuable workmen, of precious cultivators who have let themselves be led astray by seditious and hypocritical priests; but you do not want to extend these benefits to corrupt beings, to those foolish, proud creatures who see liberty only in their pocketbooks, only in their old parchments, and who pale at the word equality; to artistocratic millionaires who hire agents to instigate disturbances, to monopolize the people's food supply, to organize famine in the midst of abundance.

You want to repress with more force than ever the audacious acts of the aristocracy; you want to uproot from the soil of liberty that parasitic and harmful plant which is the mother of vice and crime, that corrupting and liberticidal plant which is the death of virtue and morality; but you do not want to make clemency the order of the day in favor of the people's natural enemies, you do not want the impure horde of aristocrats, royalists, moderates, fanatics, to go in red bonnet and carmagnole into the popular societies and make a false abjuration of their principles, and there to attack as "Robespierre's agents" the men who have faithfully and severely carried out your revolutionary decrees and who have rendered the most important services to liberty, to divide the best patriots into two parties, use one of these parties to drive out the other, then wipe out the former and remain masters of the battlefield. . . .

Citizens, let the experience of six years of betrayals, crimes and miseries proscribe the fatal system of indulgence.

Let us hang on to the revolutionary principles with the same strength as the sailor in a shipwreck hangs on to the plank which saves him from the depths of the sea, or we shall perish. . . .

Faithful representatives, the French people have entrusted the revolutionary sledgehammer to the vigor of your arms; they have entrusted it to us to avenge patriotism and crush aristocracy: do not put it down before you have annihilated all the enemies of the French people, or at least before you have made them unable to conspire and do harm.

Deeply impressed with the immensity of the perils which still threaten the public liberty and with the necessity to eliminate as soon as possible the source of our domestic disturbances; persuaded that for this there exists no other means than to maintain terror everywhere as the order of the day—(*Violent murmurs interrupt the speaker; from all parts of the hall burst out the words* Justice! Justice!) By the word "terror," I mean the severest justice.

CHARLIER: Justice for the patriots, terror for the aristocrats.

MANY VOICES: Justice for everyone. (*Applause.*) It is justice that will terrify the aristocrats and guarantee the patriots.

LOUCHET: It never entered my heart to make terror the order of the day. I move that the severest justice repress the infamous aristocracy and the slack moderatism, which everywhere are raising their insolent heads. (*A few murmurs.*)

Finally, convinced that we owe vengeance, we are obliged to avenge the incarcerated patriots, I am going to submit to the National Convention a decree which appears to me to lead toward this goal.

. . .

TALLIEN: . . . I shall content myself with remarking that the Convention did not approve all the principles contained in this speech, that it did not approve the statement that terror must be made the order of the day. I shall express myself with the frankness I have already shown; I repeat what I have already said: Terror is the weapon of tyranny. (*Applause.*)

The severest justice must be used against all our country's enemies. (*Applause.*) Robespierre also used to say constantly that terror must be made the order of the day; and while with the aid of these words he had patriots incarcerated and led to the scaffold, he protected the rascals who were serving him. Yes, the Convention must strike them down; it is against these robbers of the public that it must wage eternal war. I no longer recognize castes in the republic; I see in it only good and bad citizens. (*Applause.*) What does it matter to me that a man was born noble, if his conduct is good. What difference does the rank of a plebeian make, if he is a rascal! If the one disturbs the social order, he must be incarcerated; is the other robs the Republic, the law's blade must strike him; we must look for the people's enemies in official positions, in the administration, wherever they are; for, I repeat, in France there are only republicans, or anti-republicans who are rogues.

It has been moved that the speech you have just heard be printed; I, too, am of that opinion. All ideas must be published; everything must be known. The Convention must immediately occupy itself with a discussion which, I hope, will not last long, on the freedom of the press. (*Applause.*) The right to speak must not be reserved to a few individuals; on this platform, in the popular societies, in the theaters, one must be able to say anything except what is contrary to public order, to good morals and to morality; we must have freedom of the press or death. (*Vigorous applause.*) It is freedom of the press that will terrify and pulverize the rascals; it is with the aid of freedom of the press that we will tear the mask off those men who still feign patriotism, who declaim against Robespierre only because he has been struck down, and who, two days before his fall, were still weakly prostrated at his knees. (*Applause.*)

I also think that unity must reign within these walls, but among the men who want the public good, among those who want the revolution. It will reign steadily when we have sanctioned freedom of the press.

Severe justice against the enemies of the people; severe justice for the innocent; repression of the aristocracy's maneuvers; surveillance of the false patriots and schemers; those are our obligations. I therefore move the printing of the speech, referral to the Committee of Public Safety, and that we proceed to the discussion on the organization of the committees.

3 Fructidor

Goupilleau de Fontenay, in the name of the Committee on General Security, reads aloud for discussion the proposed decree on the organization of the revolutionary committees. . . . [Adoption of the first nine articles.]

The reporter reads Article 10.

UNIDENTIFIED MEMBER: I move to substitute for the words "immediately upon the reorganization," and words "before the reorganization."

This proposal is decreed as part of Article 10:

"Before the reorganization of the twelve revolutionary committees of the commune of Paris, the list of citizens who will compose them will be printed and distributed to all the members of the Convention."

DUBOIS-CRANCÉ: As the abuse of power arises nearly always from long enjoyment of it, without claiming to accuse the members of the present revolutionary committees, I move that they not be eligible for the new committees; they have performed these duties long enough.

DELMAS: I ask to refute Dubois-Crancé's proposal. It is against all the principles of justice. If there are members of these committees who have shown themselves to be good patriots, why exclude them? The Committee on General Security will purify the committees; it will give us the list of those who are to remain, and they will be maintained in office.

GOUPILLEAU: In the reorganization of the Revolutionary Tribunal you kept the members who had proved themselves; why depart from this arrangement for the revolutionary committees?

. . .

POULTIER: I move that the members know how to read and write.

GOUPILLEAU: If, when the revolutionary committees were first organized, they had been appointed by the people's representatives, it is not to be supposed that they would have appointed a man who could neither read nor write.

TURREAU: I think we ought to concern ourselves with this proposal, which is most essential. The Convention has decreed that soldiers who can neither read nor write cannot be commissioned. The same decree ought to be adopted for the committee members.

THURIOT: I support the motion of Poultier and Turreau. Those on whom the general security rests must have the necessary skills. A man can be very virtuous and not have this ability. The committee members are often obliged to travel, to express themselves, to prepare reports and interrogatories; they must therefore know how to read and write, otherwise could they not be led into errors? Nothing must be left to chance, when it is a matter of the liberty of the citizens. I move that this provision be inserted into the law.

This proposal is decreed. (Applause.) . . .

CLAUSEL: You want probity to remain constantly the order of the day. Too often in the administrations and in the constituted authorities we have seen immoral creatures who had their creditors arrested. I move that no bankrupt person be eligible to be a member of a revolutionary committee. (*Applause.*)

This proposal is decreed. (The applause recommences.)

UNIDENTIFIED MEMBER: I move that father and son, and two relatives within the fourth degree, not be eligible as members of the same revolutionary committee.

This proposal is adopted. . . .

The reporter reads Article 14; it is adopted as follows:

"The revolutionary committees can, with the concurrence of three members, issue summonses and have the seals applied provisionally; but they can issue arrest warrants only by a majority of seven votes."

MARET: I move as an additional article that the presence of the members who concur in issuing an arrest warrant be certified. I move in the second place that you oblige the revolutionary committees to keep registers of their operations. Several of them have been unable to state reasons for the arrest of citizens whom they had had incarcerated.

It is moved that the registers of the revolutionary committees be inspected by the district judges.

All these proposals are adopted.

The reporter reads Article 15.

"The revolutionary committees are required to send to the Convention's Committee on General Security within twenty-four hours after an arrest, the reasons for their arrest warrant as well as the documents and information they have obtained with respect to the individuals arrested."

RUELLE: I move that the revolutionary committees be required to deliver within twenty-four hours the reasons upon which they have decided to arrest a citizen.

UNIDENTIFIED MEMBER: I move that the time limit be fixed at three days, because there will be time to make sure of the detained persons accomplices, if any.

The latter proposal is adopted.

THIRION: I move that a citizen placed under arrest not be detained more than twenty-four hours without being interrogated.

This proposal is adopted. . . .

. . . The president suggests . . . that the Convention hear the Jacobin Society, which has appeared at the bar. The Convention decrees that it will be admitted.

8 Fructidor

RAISSON, *spokesman*: Representatives of the people, the regenerated Society of Jacobins of Paris, freed from the corrupt men who had slipped into its midst, restored to its original energy, has come to tell you certain necessary truths and to ask you for measures which the public safety demands. After each of the crises that have taken place since the revolution, a reaction has made itself felt; these dangers have only been indefinite and momentary, and until now the people have always made up for lost time; but this reaction has never made itself felt in so terrible a way as in the present situation.

We are very far from suspecting the sentiments and the intentions of the Committee on General Security; but it will agree itself that, among the mass of discharges it has ordered, a considerable number have let determined aristocrats out of the houses of detention, and they will use the liberty so imprudently restored to them only to conspire anew against the Republic.

We have come to ask you for the printing of a list of these men— (*Murmurs.*)

TALLIEN: I ask that the speaker be heard to the end; I shall ask for the floor afterward to answer him.

RAISSON: Crime alone can fear the publication of this list. Let it not be said that this will be a proscription list; the imitators of Sulla are dead, and the people will never tolerate new ones. Apply yourselves next to establishing a revolutionary government which is neither in the style of moderates nor in that of Robespierre's successors, but which represses and frightens the scoundrels, the corrupt men, all the people's enemies, and protects innocence!

THE PRESIDENT: The Republic will never forget what it owes to the

Society so honored by the slanders of kings; the Jacobins contributed powerfully to the fall of the throne, and at this moment many of these generous friends of liberty are sealing with their blood the people's rights, which they have defended with their eloquent and courageous energy. Above all they are not the friends of a few men; they love, they have eyes for, nothing but our country. They did not take an oath to the criminal commune [of Paris] while the National Convention, alone, abandoned, strong in its principles and in its great love both for the people and for liberty, was attacking, indicting, and overthrowing in an instant the tyrant who was still being defended by perverse men on your platform. You have disavowed those monsters, you have proscribed them; they will soon fall under the law's blade. Do even more today: prove that you want the revolutionary government, which alone can lead to peace and happiness, by giving the example of your submissiveness to the laws and by leading the opponents of the enemies of the people and the national representation. (*Vigorous applause.*)

The order of the day is loudly called for. The Convention decides to proceed to it, amid applause. There is a motion for printing the Jacobins' address and the president's reply. The Convention again decides to proceed to the order of the day.

12 Fructidor

LECOINTRE DE VERSAILLES: Citizens and colleagues, I undertake to demonstrate to the National Convention, both by authentic documents and by witnesses, that our colleagues, Citizens Billaud-Varenne, Collot d'Herbois, and Barère, members of the Committee on Public Safety; Vadier, Amar, Voulland, and David, members of the Committee on General Security, are guilty of:

1. Having repressed, by terror, all the citizens of the Republic, by signing and having carried out arbitrary orders for imprisonment, without, against a great number of them, any denunciation, any reason for suspicion, any proof of offenses mentioned in the law of 17 September 1793;

2. Having extended this system of oppression and terror to the members of the National Convention, by tolerating and supporting by a deliberate silence the rumor that the Committee of Public Safety had a list of thirty members of the National Convention designated to be incarcerated and then victimized;

3. Having never proposed the replacement of the members who were lacking on the Committee of Public Safety and having exclusively

perpetuated themselves in their positions by the repression under which they kept the Convention; Barère, reporting for the Committee, never failing, after the announcement of a few victories or successes, to propose as imperative the continuation of the committees' powers;

4. Having, in concert with Robespierre, destroyed freedom of opinion within the National Convention itself, by not permitting debate on any of the laws presented by the Committee of Public Safety;

5. Having instigated the repeal of all the laws favorable to liberty and repressive of the arbitrary acts which were being performed in the name of these committees unjustly and inhumanely;

6. Having surrounded themselves with a mass of agents, some with ruined reputations, others submerged in crime; having given them indefinitely extended powers; having repressed none of their persecutions and on the contrary having supported them;

7. Having rejected and left unanswered an infinite number of complaints and memorials which had been sent in against their oppressive agents; having taken their defense, notably that of Héron, Sénard and others; having, from the very platform of the National Convention, praised them, obtained the repeal of decrees justly hurled against them and having thereby delivered to the vengeance of these monsters the citizens who had had the courage to denounce them;

8. Having covered France with prisons, with a thousand Bastilles; having filled the entire Republic with mourning by the incarceration, unjustly and even without reasons, of more than a hundred thousand citizens, some infirm, others octogenarians, still others fathers of families and even defenders of our country;

9. Having led their colleagues into error by spreading the rumor, after the cruel law of 22 Prairial was enacted, that this law had been the work of Robespierre alone, who had communicated it only to Couthon, whereas they had been advised, even before it was passed, by members of the Revolutionary Tribunal, of the serious disadvantages which would result from it;

10. Having opposed, at the time this law was presented, the printing and tabling of it which had been moved; some having supported it strongly, others having indicated by their presence that it was the work and the fruit of thoughtful reflection by the two committees in whose names it was presented. . . .

11. Having, in the matter of Hébert, Vincent, and others, denied effect to a warrant for the arrest of Pache, who was to be named minister of justice by that faction; having notified Fouquier, public prosecutor, of the order not only to refrain from carrying out the arrest

warrant but even not to permit Pache to be talked about, whence it resulted that the opportunity to testify was denied to the witnesses who wanted to speak of Pache, and even to the accused when they asked that he appear;

12. Having, with the same unjust intentions and in order to save the guilty, prevented arrest warrants from being issued against General Hanriot, his aide-de-camp, Mathieu; Lubin, judge in the court of the first *arrondissement;* and Gobaut, assistant prosecutor of Paris, all implicated in the Hébert case, and who have since been guillotined as conspirators, and this although there were serious charges against them which were communicated in writing to the Committee of Public Safety, where they remained; in consequence, the opportunity to testify was likewise denied to the accused as to the witnesses when they wanted to talk about these individuals;

13. Having not informed the National Convention of the letter written by Fouquier on 15 Germinal, a letter in which he explained to the Convention that the accused were asking to introduce testimony by sixteen deputies whose depositions would prove the falseness of the facts of which they were accused, and that they were appealing to the people, in case of refusal; and having substituted for this letter a lying report, from which the committees obtained the conclusion that the accused had placed themselves in a state of rebellion against the law, which resulted in the decree declaring that anyone accused of conspiracy who resists or insults the tribunal's justice will be excluded from the arguments and judged immediately;

14. Having (Amar and Voulland), themselves brought the decree and, turning it over to Fouquier, said: "Here's something that will make it easy for you and make those mutineers listen to reason."

15. Having, when important cases were called, permitted and even ordered a selection of jurors from *sections* other than those whose turn it was, in order to obtain those who were known as the most docile;

16. Having (Amar, Voulland, David, and Vadier), when these jurors were in the jury room, and the rumor was spreading in the courtroom that the majority was for acquittal, passed into a small room next to the jury room, and having gotten Herman to persuade them, by all kinds of means, to impose the death sentence; which the latter, going into the jury room carried out by talking against the accused and by instigating those jurors who had voted for death to threaten the others with the committees' resentment.

17. Having several times ordered trials of fifty to sixty persons at a time for offenses that were different;

18. Having ordered the public prosecutor to have judgment rendered in twenty-four hours on those accused of the prison conspiracy, so that 155 persons named in the indictment of 18 Messidor were to be judged and put to death the same day; but the fear of public opinion having given rise to a few reflections, it was decided that they would be disposed of on three occasions;

19. Having tolerated that the same witnesses, receiving upkeep and nourishment in the prisons and commonly known as "sheep," gave depositions against the accused; and among these witnesses were to be identified Ferrières, Sauve-Boeuf, ex-noble, and Leymerie, private secretary to Amar;

20. Having formally denied the denunciations made to the Convention against Joseph Lebon, representative; having made a false report on his conduct, and having disguised his cruelties under the denomination "harsh procedures."

21. Having not notified the Convention of Robespierre's absence from the Committee for forty days; having tolerated that, despite and notwithstanding his absence, he continued to sign documents; having hidden the maneuvers which that conspirator had employed with the purpose of disorganizing everything, making partisans for himself, and ruining public affairs.

22. Having permitted General Lavalette, Dufresse, and so many other traitors or conspirators denounced long ago to the committees or indicted by decrees of the Convention, to remain in Paris, obtain employment here, having thus given them opportunity to commit new heinous crimes;

23. Having failed to take, on the night of 8 Thermidor and during the following day, any of the measures which could ensure the public tranquillity and the security of the Convention, obviously compromised by the tyrant's speech, delivered on the 8th from the Convention's platform and that night to the Jacobins, who promised him assistance, force, and protection;

24. Having failed to arrest, during the night of 8–9 Thermidor, General Hanriot, the mayor, and the national agent of Paris, Lavalette, and so many other principal accomplices of Robespierre, who had all been denounced by several colleagues;

25. Having failed to take, during the day of 9 Thermidor, any rigorous measure so that the decrees ordering the arrest of Robespierre and his accomplices would be carried out, and having, by this criminal negligence, exposed the national representation to being slaughtered, since the henchmen of the conspirators were able, the same day, under

the very eyes of the National Convention and its committees, to wrest away from the premises of the Committee on General Security, without any resistance, the traitor Hanriot, who had been kept in that Committee;

26. Having employed men recognized as counter-revolutionaries, ruined in reputation and debauchery; ill-famed and even within the terms of decrees of indictment, such as Beaumarchais, Espagnac, Haller, and others, and having entrusted to them immense treasure belonging to the Republic, treasure with which they emigrated.

I have finished. I move that a secretary read to you the documents which support my denunciation and which I am going to indicate one after the other. . . .

13 Fructidor

[*The accusation by Lecointre was debated article by article and at length. Among the concluding remarks in the debate were the following.*]

GOUPILLEAU DE FONTENAY: . . . One of us climbed up on this platform, a few days ago, and spoke to you indignantly of the system of terror that had been spread among us and among the French people; and yet today there has been an effort to establish it anew, and to cast divisions among you, by scrutinizing the conduct of men who have organized victories in the armies and who have constantly served the public good.

Citizens, after having examined each count in this indictment, you ought to be convinced that it was not these seven members but the revolution that Lecointre wanted to put on trial. You ought to be convinced that this indictment also had the motive of casting division among the members of the Convention. . . .

LEGENDRE: . . . A few days ago I went to find Lecointre, because I wanted to prevent him from delivering this speech and casting an apple of discord into the Convention. . . . I also remark that Merlin de Thionville, told him: "I declare that I shall not give you the floor until the assembly forces me to by a decree." . . . I limit myself to saying that this session must not be forgotten, for it has powerfully served the Republic. . . .

CAMBON: None of the National Convention's sessions ought to be useless to liberty. Yesterday you rejected indignantly, without having heard our colleagues, the denunciation against them; and the aristocracy, which was still in hiding, sought to raise the people against your decree; today, now that everything is clarified, now that no document worthy of belief has been presented to you, and now that you are convinced of the falsity of the accusation against several of your members, you ought, by a solemn decree, to declare it slanderous.

This proposal, put to a vote, is decreed unanimously and amid the most vigorous applause. The session ends at nine o'clock.

Correspondence of Dyzez

Paris, 13 Fructidor, Year II [30 August 1794]

To Dubosc, executive officer of the administration
of the *département* of the Landes

Yesterday's session is well worth noting, Citizen. Lecointre brought twenty-seven charges against seven members of the committees on Public Safety and General Security: Billaud-Varenne, Collot d'Herbois, Barère, Vadier, Amar, Voulland, and David. He did it in such a way that these members, who had been out of favor, suddenly regained it to the point that Lecointre, the accuser, barely escaped being arrested! Tallien is very much dissatisfied at the turn this affair has taken. I heard him say that he wanted to resign from the Committee of Public Safety, but if he thinks it over longer he may change his mind.

Batbédat does not need to be told to take note of this meeting, nevertheless I would be glad if you would tell him. The Mountain came out strongly against the Center. The program that was adopted appears suited only to perpetuate the quarrel, and I do not doubt that there will be important consequences. Every day the hall resounds with denunciations of deputies. If we are divided within the Convention it is impossible for France not to be divided. It would be better to lose twenty battles than to experience such a tragic schism. I have always feared that it is in our hearts that the evil lies. If they are sound the whole Republic will be so, and the foreign war will be mere child's play. Valenciennes is in our hands and Condé will soon follow. Bellegarde cannot fail to be reunited to the French Empire soon. With the possession of those places and the courage of our soldiers, we are safe abroad; let us try to be invulnerable at home.

We will follow up the matter with Laurens. Since I am one of those charged with examining the papers of Robespierre and all who were

"Lettres," p. 521.

guillotined or arrested with him, I can do nothing at the moment about your business myself. The activity of my colleagues will make up for it.

Salut et Fraternité

Paris, 15 Fructidor, Year II [1 September 1794]

To an unidentified correspondent

The papers will tell you everything that is going on in the Convention. The denunciation by Lecointre has put us in a painful situation. It was really the Convention that he was accusing. He has sown among us germs of division, by which we were already only too much infected. I shall abstain from all reflections. Everywhere there will be more than enough of them. To all this had to be added the explosion of a powder magazine located on the Rue de Grenelle. About 150 persons perished. Many are disabled. This event caused a good deal of talk. The preachers used to say that such events were caused by our sins and a divine punishment. Today people say that it is the aristocracy that does everything.

Salut et Fraternité

They now reckon at two or three hundred the number of deaths in the explosion. Tempers are rising among the people. The accident at the Abbaye, connected with this one, occasioned a thousand deaths.

THE TERRORISTS' DEFENSE

Billaud-Varenne's Defense

Year III

In attacking Robespierre, if one did not oppose his actions, usurpations of power, imprisonments ordered by him alone, nominations of traitors to the most important posts, legal projects presented without the assent of the two committees, the secret sending of agents to the *départements* and to the armies in order to fulfill his dictatorial projects, his well-known coalition with the military chiefs of Paris, the municipal heads, the Revolutionary Tribunal; the victims of his vengeance and of his liberty-killing designs whom one word from his mouth could with equal facility lose or save; how then could he not seem culpable? If he had not manifested the intention of striking blows, of spreading disorder, of exterminating the national assembly; if he had not reproached it until

Jean-Nicolas Billaud-Varenne, "Mémoire Inedit," *Revue historique de la révolution française,* I (1910), 7-43. This justificatory memoir is preserved in the National Archives under the title of *Défense de Billaud-Varenne.*

even his own popularity, insensibly eaten away by the affection of unceasingly getting evidence in order to fix upon himself alone the public regard, and finally soaring above everyone else with his trenchant and imperative tone of voice, in order to enslave all to his opinion; with his popularity so enormous, so frightening that it sufficed to render him suspect and dangerous for a free state; in a word, if he had not developed a monstrous power as totally independent of the Committee of Public Safety as of the National Convention itself, Robespierre would not have known how to display the odious traits of tyranny, and all friends of liberty would have retained their esteem for him, and he should no longer be remembered with horror today.

. . .

To better render palpable the bad faith of our accusers, it will suffice to remind you of the procedure followed by the committees which had to deal with a great flow of affairs, necessitated by the multiplicity of their operations. It is known that each part formed a particular division, whose direction and surveillance were attributed to one or several designated members, and that, outside the important objects which require a general deliberation, all the rest were done within each section, and were approved through mutual confidence, under the personal guarantee of those who were in charge; from which there resulted a particular responsibility for particular actions, and a common solidarity for all the general operations.

It was by means of this system that Robespierre, as you have been told, arrived at the point where he seemed able to venture almost anything, and, wishing as he did to disorganize the bureaus directed by Carnot, he would have hindered, if it had been possible, even military operations. We therefore approved, along with Carnot, the arrest of those of Carnot's assistants who had his greatest confidence; and we put into execution a mandate of arrest. In the midst of so much business, such surprises became so much the easier to realize. The task of collecting the signatures was confided to some assistants. One didn't even know from which bureau the papers one was presented with had come.

. . .

We are even reproached with the formation of the Bureau of General Police, although it had its origin in a decree passed under the direction of Saint-Just, and was legitimized by different decrees of referral to that bureau. Robespierre, abusing the confidence which he had, usurped and secretly perverted an institution which, in purer hands, would have conserved itself as intact as the other creations of the Committee of Public Safety. . . . It is the crime of a usurper always to employ the post of authority which he exercises to arrive at supreme power, while he takes the precaution of covering his tracks by hypocrisy, by sordid machinations, and by a pretended civic spirit which he maintains until the denouement.

Let us ask, as has already been done, why we allowed Robespierre to go so far. Not one single fact has been established, nor one single proof given, to justify the idea that that man's power was our work. Have we forgotten that, from the time of the Constituent Assembly, he already enjoyed an immense popularity, and that he obtained the title of the Incorruptible? Have we forgotten that, during the Legislative Assembly, his popularity only increased, with the help of a very widely known journal of which he was the editor, and through his frequent speeches to the Jacobins? Have we forgotten that, in the National Convention, Robespierre before long was the man who, fixing all regard upon his own person gained so much confidence that it rendered him preponderant, to such an extent that when he came to the Committee of Public Safety he was already the most important man in France? If someone asked me how he had succeeded in gaining so much ascendancy over public opinion, I would answer that it was by displaying the most austere virtues, the most absolute devotion, and the purest principles. . . . I would ask why those who today speak the most stridently against Robespierre were the first who fell at his feet then; they who then covered him with applause contributed more than anyone to propagating the general infatuation; they consecrated his supremacy, they who cooled their heels in the waiting room at his door in quest of his favors; they who, like cowardly courtesans, went him one better in the measures he pursued, to the point that one could hear them say, in that enclosure, that it was their wish to bring about the failure of the same measures which they carried to extremes. In a word, they had been rather knavish or rather stupid in consenting to forge the chain which bound their own hands, while appearing most complacent at the right moments, most "ultra" at others, they were, one could even say, the most wretched hired assassins of the tyrant.

. . .

For Robespierre, a scheming dictatorship and the aggrandizement of the powers of the Committee of Public Safety both facilitated his designs and served better to hide them. Though he had become, like another Pompey, the supreme arbiter of the Republic, he veiled from the eyes of the people his personal power, hiding it behind the mantle of government. But the more he worked to form a colossus above which he always soared, the more we ran the risk of being wiped out ourselves. In order to get rid of us, he would have turned the colossus upon our heads as the first step toward establishing his throne. What instruments, what arms did we fabricate in order to struggle against him? Did we have the kind of exclusive ascendance which permitted him, by one of his simple denunciations, to decide the ruin of whoever was its object? Did he not have under his orders the general chiefs of the municipality and of the Revolutionary Tribunal? Assuredly we could not oppose him in anything. It is not then so astonishing, when the disposition of minds and the direction of matters was such, no one sought to resist the superiority of means so extended, and that the members of the two former committees did little of what they wished to do. How can one ask that a few individuals should have been more capable than the National Convention itself to master the rule of circumstances?

I do not think that anyone can longer be accused of having ignored the conspirator within Robespierre, when his conduct, reprehensible as it was, attracted to him the confidence of men who, though they did not love him as an individual, held him in esteem as a patriot. Will anyone deny that it was only after the law of the 22nd Prairial that he visibly revealed his prefidious intentions? But, at that moment even, celebrated, proclaimed, idolized by all, was he not, so to speak, like an ark, to which, in public at least, one could only cling to to avoid being thrown to death at once? But one is bound to admit that from that moment, all the members of the old committees of Public Safety and General Security, with the exception of Couthon, Saint-Just, and Le Bas, Robespierre's accomplices, stopped going along with Robespierre. It is beginning with this period when that dictator wished to bring his last blows down upon the liberty of his country that he found an insurmountable resistance in the two committees. . . .

What trait of ambition besmirched our political and private conduct? . . . It will be recalled that Saint-Just accused us of having ceased to frequent and speak at the Jacobin Club. Are we reproached with having sought to find ourselves a following with naming our acquaintances to governmental positions, or with recommending them to others? Some of us perhaps have no posts to distribute, nor can we place a single public functionary. Are we denounced as infamous men? Few seek a more retired life than we do. We know a very small number of our colleagues; there are not two men to whom I am intimately tied. I have said elsewhere that I scarcely receive five or six people at my home, and I ordinarily go out only to go to the Convention. It is not that I attach any great merit to this kind of existence; it is just that my dominant taste has always been for solitude.

. . .

If we were asked why we did not denounce Robespierre more quickly, we could always reply that that objection ought to be addressed not to us but to our other colleagues. But, in any case, it would only be specious in the eyes of those who, after having escaped a peril, and content at finding themselves saved, forget, in order better to make themselves feel tranquil, the circumstances which had once threatened them. There is a distinction to be made between an ordinary conspirator and a man who sets out to be a dictator. The first works in the shadows and puts all his effort into remaining unknown. The other, on the contrary, arrives at his goal by appearing often at the right moment in order to attain an exclusive popularity. Catiline had only some obscure conspirators for accomplices. Pericles made all Athenians into instruments of his power. Rapid, sudden blows were necessary to overcome such men. With a usurper one is reduced to temporizing. Solon, who surely was not the accomplice of Pisistratus, was constrained by the blindness of his fellow citizens, to stoop so low as to play the role of a flatterer in the wake of perfidy; because an adroit usurper only begins to show his design after rendering himself master of public opinion, deceiving it from a distance with a simulated patriotism; because once wrapped in such a blind, general confidence, he is so to speak invulnerable; and if it happens that he can be struck down by the heroism of liberty, the idolatry which he has inspired immediately overwhelms the avengers of the country; and it is thus that Rome's slavery was cemented by the blood of even those who had delivered her from a tyrant.

. . .

It is claimed that we should have made public Robespierre's retreat from the Committee of Public Safety. But it is forgotten that this was precisely what Robespierre was waiting for. For, during this absence, he went every day to the Jacobins in order to denounce the two committees, without however designating any individual, while he persuaded the people that he was only moving aside because he had been maltreated there by his enemies, who were enemies of the state and who conspired against it in conspiring against him. When he had already brought matters to this point, there was little one could do. If one of his colleagues had asked for an extraordinary meeting so that Robespierre might expose his complaints in full daylight, Robespierre, immediately profiting from this misstep, would have cried out: "There they are, they whom I have denounced to you for the past five weeks! I would not have named them to you, but they identify themselves. They are not content to treat me in an unworthy manner and to separate me from the Committee; they now announce publicly the intention of dismissing from the government those whose love of liberty, whose devotion to the people perpetually keeps at bay the stabs of assassins." And I ask, in my turn, who would win in such a struggle, for in order to reply and confront the tyrant, in order to dispel the general illusion, we had at that time neither his discourse of the 8th Thermidor, nor the debates of the Jacobin meeting of the same day, nor the discourse that Saint-Just presented the following day, nor the rebellion of Hanriot and the municipality. Would it not have been useless to sacrifice oneself, and would not that sacrifice even have been to the detriment of the country, since each triumph scored by the usurper is a mortal blow against liberty?

. . .

Nor is it any better proof of our influence over the Revolutionary Tribunal to say it was our responsibility, for we had no control over that part of the work which might have given us some point of contact with that tribunal, nor with the Committee on General Security, nor the Bureau of General Police. Also it was in that section that the documents which concerned the Revolutionary Tribunal were drawn up. Elsewhere no one realized that Robespierre had for his principal accomplices Dumas and Coffinhal, the two presidents of that tribunal, with whom it is notorious that he schemingly conferred every day over the course of action which they would follow.

. . .

Finally, if during the absence of Robespierre, the operations of the general police took the same direction, it would hardly be astonishing, inasmuch as he had at his disposal the agents placed by him in that bureau. Besides, Saint-Just and Couthon, remaining on the Committee, were there to act as his deputies. People seem always to forget what an ascendancy these three conspirators had, and that elsewhere at that time emotions were so high-pitched that no one dared seem to wish to relax them, for fear of seeming a protector or an accomplice of counter-revolutionaries.

. . .

I can be reproached no more for a licentious life or for suspected liaisons. Nor can I be reproached for having ever been attached to some faction, nor for having defended counter-revolutionaries. What will my crime be, then? Analyze the charges which are addressed against me and you will see that they derive from my refusal to compromise either with the aristocracy or with factions, and that on the contrary, I acted in order to pursue them unsparingly, in order to forcefully denounce them to you and to reveal their crimes to you at the moment when they menaced the national representation and the liberty of the French people, they who, in ruining their enemies, finally rendered themselves so culpable in your eyes. . . . The citizen who withdraws is a cowardly egotist who, absenting himself from his first duty, renders himself worthy of the greatest contempt. The public functionary, depending on whether he has vigor or weakness, becomes either the saviour or the slayer of his country. At the time of Catiline's conspiracy, the firmness of Cicero saved liberty for his country, without the rending of flesh and without massacres. However criticised by Cato as having exceeded his bounds, that moment in Cicero's political life is the one which has brought him the greatest honor. And if his glory remains a bit tarnished, it is for having failed afterwards to show that vigor of character which makes Cassius deserve the title of the last of the Romans.

Barère's Defense

Year III

"You are the accomplices of Robespierre."

These are strange accomplices, those who were denounced ceaselessly at the Jacobin club by Robespierre as conspirators or defenders of a faction which he said existed in the National Convention!

Who were denounced at the National Convention even by Robespierre in his speech of 8 Thermidor and by his triumvir Saint-Just in the speech of the 9th.

These are strange accomplices, those who summoned Robespierre twice at the joint meeting of the committees. The first time on the 25th Prairial to answer about the reasons for arresting members of the revolutionary committee of the Indivisibility *section,* and on the reform of the decree of 22 Prairial; the second time to explain, on the 5th of Thermidor in the meeting of the joint committees, the conspiracies about which he endlessly talked in vague terms at the Jacobin club, on the reasons for his absence from the Committee for forty days, and about his intimate relations with the judges and jurors who speak only

Bertrand Barère, *The Reply of Barère, Billaud-Varenne, Collot d'Herbois and Vadier to the Imputations of Laurent Lecointre.* Originally published in *La Révolution française,* XXXIV (1893), 62-72.

of purifying the Convention and of guillotining deputies, judges, and jurors whom the Convention had arrested at once.

These are strange accomplices, those who boldly called Robespierre *dictator, counter-revolutionary, an ambitious man,* on several occasions in the Committee, and who, on several occasions, bravely opposed his criminal attempts against the national representation.

These are strange accomplices, those who on the reiterated entreaties of Saint-Just, at the end of Messidor and the beginning of Thermidor, refused to let Robespierre and Saint-Just pass a decree to ratify all the operations of the Bureau of General Police, and who refused to take upon themselves this work, in the last few days, when these scoundrels attempted to make us appear involved in their crimes.

These are strange accomplices, those who denounced him the 2nd Thermidor in a report to the National Convention* with all the zeal compatible at that time with the prudence which members of the government had to have when they were busy trying to stifle the germs of civil discord or the divisions which could lead the Republic to be torn apart, and who were close to being the victims of Robespierre's faction in the stormy and violent session held at the Jacobin club on the night of 8–9 Thermidor.

These are strange accomplices, those who, while Robespierre triumphed in the Jacobin club on the night of the 8–9 Thermidor and organized the counter-revolution, leading astray the people and joining with the heads of the armed force, these men prepared in the funereal silence of that night a report to the Convention to reorganize the public force, to have Hanriot, Lavalette, Dufresse, and other heads of the conspiracy removed from office and arrested, and drafted a proclamation of which the effect was to rally on the following night—the 9–10th—all the *sections* of Paris to the Convention.

These are strange accomplices of Robespierre, those who, against his wishes, made a political report on the religious troubles, sheltering

* *Extract from the report of 2 Thermidor by the Committees.*—"Since 1789 every faction has tried to govern, and this despotic and governing mania has not yet passed; since 1789 every faction has tried to monopolize the majority, either by seduction or by terror. It is by this sign that the committees have always recognized the factions and their insidious methods; it is by this sign that we will still recognize them.
"Political storms seem to have been gathering for several days. . . . The two committees will never forget all of the powers and functions which are confided to them; and this strong rock will throw back all the waves of royalism and will overcome all the storms incited by the aristocracy, which will be corrected only at the day of judgments, and all the storms incited by *overwhelming ambition, which can be corrected only by the scaffold.*" [Note from the original.]

from all investigations in this matter the representatives of the people sent on mission into the *départements,* who defended Tallien, Dubois-Crancé, Fouché, Bourdon de l'Oise, and other representatives whom Robespierre persecuted without cease.

These are strange accomplices of Robespierre, those who were denounced by Saint-Just, on 9th Thermidor, as *wishing to destroy the Revolutionary Tribunal.*

These are strange accomplices of Robespierre, those who upheld the representatives of the people on mission, against whom Robespierre did not cease to declaim and to make denunciations, and who several times told this tyrant who demanded the accusation of several deputies, that he would only be able to commit crimes against the national representation over the bloody corpses of six members of the Committee.

You corrupters of public opinion, who pretend to believe and who repeat ceaselessly that Robespierre governed the Committee to the point of having only accomplices, tell us why he himself was going to denounce and to have denounced ceaselessly by his brother, by Dumas and by Couthon, the committees on Public Safety and General Security and several other representatives. Tell us why he stayed away from the Committee for forty days; why the principal and charitable operations of the Committee were done without his participation and why the minutes of the decrees of the Committee for the constant and essential functions of the government were not written by his hand.

Tell us why he affected never to sign the military operations, the campaign plans and the letters to the generals; he refused in order to lay all the responsibility for the hazardous events of battle on us.

Very well, the majority of the Committee of Public Safety, forgetting the hazards of war and thinking only of the courage of the republicans, alone took the entire responsibility for the armies; Robespierre was opposed to all measures of this kind or did not vote on them. If the campaign plans succeed, he said, that will reflect on all the members of the Committee of which I am a member; if there are reverses, I will say that I signed nothing, and I will use the military disasters to make accusations of treason at my will, and to have members of the Committee proscribed. There! certain accomplices of Robespierre of an entirely new kind!

"If you are not his accomplices, you are his rivals."

We would never have had the courage and the prudence to prepare the means to undo the tyrant with a sure stroke and to work with the Convention to overthrow him, only to have the baseness and the madness to replace him. Can one aspire to a tyrannical power which one has denounced, abhorred, and punished? Can one believe that in an enlightened country, amongst a people involved in a revolution, idolatrous and jealous of liberty, amongst whom it is easier to make torrents flow back to their source than to re-establish royal or aristocratic power, that the idea of rebuilding with impunity the temple of revolt and treason could come for one moment into the thought of legislators, of reasonable men, after having destroyed it with their own hands?

We may be only very ordinary men, very little skilled at governing and very little versed in the administration of republics, but we have at least shown ourselves constantly attached to the Republic and tireless in serving her; at least we are not foolish nor scoundrels nor aristocrats; our justification lies in our constant work for the one and indivisible Republic and for the rights of the people from the month of August 1793 to this moment. Our justification is in the success of the armies prepared and organized by us; in the glory won by the Convention to which we have not ceased to report everything as to the only center of the government; in the accusation of rivalry with Robespierre; in our numerous works which you have seconded and in the useful decrees which you have rendered.

We are accused of being the rivals of Robespierre!

But what were our means? Where was the commune which conspired with us and in whose arms we were able to take refuge? What was the armed force whose chiefs were at our disposal? What was the Revolutionary Tribunal which could lend us its horrible help? What was the popular society which was our accomplice or our protection or our auxiliary? We do not know any center of government and of public authority except the National Convention; we have not made any campaign plans, activated any military operations, excited the resentment of all the traitors, and destroyed all obstacles except in the interest of the Republic and for its consolidation; we have not instigated the destruction of revolutionary armies and military commissions except in the interest of civil liberty.

But who will be persuaded that six individuals, always united in spirit for the public interest, but living obscure and separated outside the Committee; who will be persuaded that six isolated individuals who had support only in the Convention, able to act only through it, having influence only through the justice of their activities, having security only by the success of their works, managing public opinion only by the purity of their views and having means of action only by law, how could these six individuals set themselves up thus, without any ulterior motive, without any combined project, without any agreed-upon plan, as rivals of an atrocious tyrant, as the inheritors of a cruel oppressor against whom our indignant souls protested every day and in all the meetings of the joint committees?

If we were rivals of Robespierre, there would have been a project of rivalry, preconceived, organized, a thought-out plan of usurpation; how could it be that of the six of us, none had communicated, none prepared this system of succession to the tyranny which Laurent Lecointre has found organized only in his head?

"But," it is said, "why did a majority of five members, who had indications of Robespierre's conspiracy, permit his tyranny for six months without warning the Convention?"

The indications which we had were the same ones which were known by other members of the Convention; ha! let all citizens reflect on the despotic influence with which Robespierre wished to lead them! One should have been even better able to perceive his tyranny in the Convention and at the Jacobin club than in the Committee, where he disguised the motives of his complaints and presented proposals only under the pretense of patriotic solicitude. The proof of the resistance of the Committee is in the good which it did without him and often in spite of him.

If sometimes the Committee yielded to his proposals, it is because he colored his opinions with strong suggestions of the public good and that he rallied them in the interest of the most serious circumstances.

To fight him only in order to be opposed to him, that would have meant giving him the power to accuse our intentions, to decry our works and to diminish our resources for essential occasions.

Those who accuse us—did not they feel or experience the yoke of that colossal reputation, of that public opinion put to his own use by Robespierre? Did they not attend the meetings at the Jacobin club, where he even publicly commanded the newspapers not to publish any of his opinions without having consulted him?

Did not even the Convention come under the shadow of this tyrannic influence of Robespierre, or of the impression which he gave by his patriotic speeches?

Were not the people themselves, by their error or by a blind confidence, the most active agents of the despotism exercised by that man? And what would an earlier denunciation in the Convention by a majority of the six members of the Committee of Public Safety have accomplished?

He would have accused us at the tribune of the Convention of conspiring against him as he did several times at the Jacobin club during Messidor, he would have made us appear to be enemies of the Republic as Saint-Just and Robespierre did in their speeches of 8 and 9 Thermidor at the Convention; and we would have drawn from this untimely denunciation and this imprudent majority no other advantage but shame and death, with the enslavement of citizens and the total loss of liberty.

THIBAUDEAU, LEVASSEUR, AND BAUDOT: THE REACTION

Memoirs of Thibaudeau

During the first days which followed the 9th of Thermidor, all hearts were opened to the sweetest hopes. It was a touching sight to observe the eagerness of citizens seeking each other out, telling each other of their good or bad fortune during the terror, congratulating each other, consoling each other. The oppressors no longer carried a grim and menacing air; their features expressed only spite and shame. Some of them, through cowardice or in good faith, even shared in the common happiness. Among the victims, serenity and joy had replaced constraint and desolation. It was like venturing forth from a tomb and being reborn to life. All the broken social lines, all the interrupted political connections re-established themselves. France ceased to be for itself and for the foreigner an object of fear; stricken, so to speak, from the list of civilized nations, she took back her rightful position. . . .

. . . It was then that one had pride in being French, and one's pride was legitimate. At that time our glory was still [evident] in all its purity. We had taken arms for the noblest of all causes, liberty—for the holiest of all rights, independence. Our victories had never oppressed other peoples in the least, and their consent had consecrated our conquests.

The individuals and the families whom the terror had isolated began to reunite; societies formed themselves again. Dinners, balls, concerts were given. Wealth was no longer a crime. Luxury reappeared bit by bit, no longer with its monarchical profusion, but enough to [enable one] to procure the commodities and the enjoyments of life. In place of pomp and splendor there was neatness and elegance.

There were none of those obligatory displays attached to ranks,

Mémoires sur la Convention et le Directoire, I, Chapter 11.

places, and dignities, nor consequently of those salons open to all comers where the one who receives and those who are received compete in being bored. Wealth was not united to power. The representatives of the people, highest functionaries of the Republic, had only a mediocre salary; and the worst-paid employees of the state had scarcely enough for subsistence, because of the depreciation of the paper money.

Display was therefore at that time a taste and not a duty. It belonged to those who had the means to bear the cost of it, such as bankers, suppliers, and businessmen. Some noble families, who had not emigrated, also opened their salons alongside those of new persons. Here they might result from the taste for spending money, there it was the need for society, so imperious in France and above all in Paris. One man might seek to develop protectors for his enterprises, another to recover his confiscated fortune, or to obtain pardon for his relatives or his *émigré* friends. All sought that importance in society which is provided by relations with powerful persons or persons distinguished by their talents. The most perfect equality reigned in these meetings. The revolution having abased the nobles and raised the bourgeoisie, people were drawn together on a middle line where no one humiliated or was humiliated in turn, and where monarchical refinement and republican awkwardness tempered each other. A great many have declaimed against the ostentation of the nouveaux riches and joked about their clumsy, imitative manner, and upon the bad style which ruled in the salons of the Republic. It could seem so to the men of the old regime or to the factional spirit which denatures or exaggerates everything. The title of *citizen* was indeed as good as that of *monsieur,* and in spite of the critics, our former marchionesses or countesses did not find that our revolutionary officers had too bad manners and they did not disdain, in order to please them, to become "citizens."

Paris recaptured the empire of fashion and taste: two women celebrated for their beauty, Madame Tallien, and a little later Madame Récamier, set the style. It was at this time that the revolution in the usages of private life, which had commenced in 1789, was completed. The antique had already been introduced in the arts by the school of David; now in feminine costume, in the coiffures of both sexes, and even in household furniture, it replaced the gothic, the feudal, and those mixed and bizarre forms invented by the slaves of the courts. If convenience was sometimes sacrificed to purity of design and appearance in the case of furniture, both were united in women's costume. What was not fitting from the heritage of the Greeks and the Romans for our customs and climate has since disappeared, and from that imitation, too servile in principle, there remains only what was good and reasonable, and Europe has become accustomed to it as has France.

Madam Récamier owed her success to her personal charms. She had the beauty, the grace, and the simplicity of a virgin of Raphael.

Madame Tallien, no less beautiful, joined agreeable French vivacity with Spanish voluptuousness. Daughter of M. Cabarrus, a banker at Madrid, wife of a French gentleman, M. de Fontenay, arrested during the time of the terror, she owed her salvation to Tallien, and she paid him by giving him her hand. By that union she was associated with the revolution and thrown into politics. Here she enjoyed the only role which is fitting to her sex; she took over the department of favors. She was called Our Lady of Thermidor because she rendered service to the unfortunate of all factions. That did not prevent the royalists, by way of gratuitous insult and atrocious ingratitude, from calling her Our Lady of September, in an allusion to the massacres of 2 and 3 September 1792, during which Tallien was secretary of the commune of Paris. Madame Tallien was sought out and courted at the same time for herself and for her husband's influence on affairs. She was the ornament of all the festivals and the soul of all the pleasures; she reigned without having the embarrassment of a throne; her rule dried many tears, and, as far as I know, cost no one anything. I speak quite impartially of this, because I have only seen her in public, and I do not believe I have spoken with her a single time. I did not esteem her husband, indeed I attacked him openly on 1 Brumaire, Year IV [22 October 1796]. I shall admit, whatever judgment it deserves, that I was at that time so scrupulous over the maintenance of equality that all those who acquired political prominence gave me offense. The inflexibility of my character did not permit me to pay homage to the wife of a public man whom events had given a great importance, whose principles were suspect to me and whose ambition I feared. However some men who were very severe-minded in most respects set another example for me. On the eve of the anniversary of the 9th of Thermidor, Lanjuinais, with whom I was, left me in order to go to the home of Madame Tallien, for whom a party was being given.

A woman with other claims to fame, Madame de Staël, was also in Paris during those times. Sweden had recognized the Republic and sent M. de Staël as ambassador. He was a good man, little made for politics, more French than Swedish, and more occupied with keeping his post than with anything else. Originally from Geneva, the family of

Madame de Staël had become French. M. Necker, her father, financier, man of letters, man of state, had made a great fortune and played a great role in France, above all at the outbreak of the revolution. Madame Necker, a wit and authoress, had worthily sustained with her personal qualities the rank in the world where the responsibilities of her husband had placed them. Madame de Staël was born with happy gifts, then found herself in the most favorable situation for their development. In ordinary times, with the force of her spirit and the vivacity of her imagination, she would in any event have obtained success in the world of letters, but the revolution opened yet another career to her. She became a political and literary personage. She belonged to the aristocracy by virtue of her education and her social contacts, and to liberty by that of her sentiments and her reason. This situation explains the contradictions which her life more than once presented. She had known all the celebrated or famous personages of the court and of the national assemblies; she was witness to most of the events. She had shared the good and the bad fortune of her father; she had drunk of his triumphs and had accompanied him in his reverses. Her admiration for that man of state, exalted by filial piety, was a veritable cult; for her the principles of her father were oracles, his plans the pinnacle of wisdom, his virtues the ideal of beauty, his talents the ideal of genius. . . .

Madame de Staël, although of the school of M. Necker, did not have his candor. A woman, without political duties or responsibilities, she knew how to yield to circumstances. She was frankly republican, without disowning her father and without abandoning her royalist friends. Her salon was open to all parties. She was pardoned for this by virtue of her sex, her wit, her talent, her principles. There have been other women in Paris who have joined with them the elite of agreeable men, of men of letters and savants; but, since the Fronde [in the mid-seventeenth century], perhaps none has had so marked a political influence.

M. Devaines, student of Turgot and former receiver-general of finances, brought together a society of men small in numbers but therefore all the more agreeable. Far from having the ridiculous ways and failings which one ascribes to financiers of the old regime, he had simple and polite manners, a sweet and amiable character, marked by good-heartedness and finesse, and ornate wit and a delicate taste. He had lived in high society before the revolution; he knew its personages and anecdotes. He lent interest to trifles by the grace with which he talked about them, and he brought to serious things the gravity which suited them. He was in all an old man with whom one could get along excellently, and one of extremely good counsel.

Madame Devaines was in a great many ways the entire opposite of her husband. She had an ardent imagination, a lively style of speech. She loved discussion; she provoked and animated it by the warmth with which she sustained an opinion. Without possessing that profound knowledge which a special education and a sustained study can alone provide, she had general notions about most matters, which one can acquire with natural wit in the company of educated men, and which are adequate to let one play a role in conversation. She touched lightly on that about which she knew little; she abstained from that of which she was ignorant. Disagreements excited her without making her angry, and as the discussion, in spite of its vivacity, never degenerated into dispute, one never left less good friends, even though each person had stood by his own opinion. She loathed the revolution, but she was resigned to it, and her salon was filled with members of the National Assembly and of the Convention. Like all passionate persons, she had some antipathies; she was as constant to them as to her attachments. But she was incapable of hurting people whom she did not love, and capable of a rare devotion for her friends, above all during their misfortunes. Her entire ambition confined itself to being able to serve them at such times. This was the only profit she wished to reap from the influence which her political ties were able to give her. Her new acquaintances did not make her neglect her old ones in the least. She knew perfectly how to bring together friends of more than twenty years, such as Suard and the abbé Morellet, with friends of a few days, such as Boissy-d'Anglas, Siméon, and myself. In that house one could see old servants—always a good sign for the character of their masters. M. Devaines's friendship for me only passes away as he does.

My friendship with M. Lehoc was no less close. He had initially been commissioned by the navy and employed in the diplomatic corps; with a noble figure and manners, educated, witty, with a taste for the arts and letters, he was suited to business as well as to society. His soul was proud and generous. Although of a ripe age, he had the sensitivity and enthusiasm of a young man. Strong emotions made him cry like a child. He passionately loved liberty and detested its excesses. Injustice irritated him to the point of making him execrate the human species and of rendering it unjust to himself. He had few possessions and incurred many expenses. His defaults arose from his needs. For the conserving of his character he lacked only an independent fortune. He never had one; in a time when one could succeed with fewer qualities and powerful friends than he had, he was not well treated by destiny, and his old age was not a happy one.

We passed most of our evenings at his home. General Menou, Admiral Truguet, the Baron de Staël, Signeul, consul-general of Sweden, Maret, Bourgoing, General Faucher formed the habitual core of our society. Diplomatic figures also came there, some deputies and some men of the old regime, Talleyrand, when he had returned from the United States, his friend Sainte-Foix, and other men of that circle, men of good form and of the best society, who exploited the revolution to their profit.

It was after the 9th of Thermidor when I really made my entry into what is called "society" in Paris. It was, as in all the great capitals, a fortuitous gathering, a day-by-day movement and a rapid flow of individuals of all estates, all ranks, all countries, in contrast to provincial society, which only consists of the gatherings of [established] families or coteries. I was sought out like all the members of the Convention who had made a name for themselves. To accept one invitation was to draw ten others. Once started on the giddy round of dinners and parties, one did not know to whom to respond; it was impossible to satisfy the demand. I yielded to these attentions. The "gilded" salons —thus were called those of the former nobility—exercised an immense influence. It was not the personal merit of these noblemen, nor the pleasure which they procured which drew the revolutionaries there; the revolutionaries were not looked upon fondly, they were only entertained in order to gain their services or to corrupt their opinions. To their face they were overwhelmed with all kinds of seductions and behind their backs they were mocked. It was in the order of things. But there were many of them who did not see this; they believed they were augmenting their own importance and esteem by associating with men of the old régime, and they let themselves be caught by these deceptive baits. In front of them their tempters straightway ventured a few jokes about the revolution. How could one become angry? It was a pretty woman who allowed herself the liberty of joking. Their republican sentiments could not stand firm against the fear of offending or of seeming ridiculous. After having been won over by banter, they were gradually worked around to scorn the institutions. They justified the saying, One is known by the company he keeps. In fact, it is impossible, no matter how much strength of character one has, not to be influenced by the society one frequents. One yields initially out of politeness, thereafter a false shame prevents one from turning back, and one ends by espousing the opinions of others, in spite of oneself, so to speak. It was in this manner that the republican party sustained a great many defections, some of its members making concessions and others selling themselves entirely to royalism. I would not dare claim not to have been, without my being aware of it, affected by this contagion sometimes, but it never took away my independence; and, in serious circumstances, I always found the necessary vigor for attacking and combatting our enemies. It is true that, without being an unsociable savage, I could not accustom myself to the brilliance, noise, and agitation.

Memoirs of Levasseur

. . . It is time to sum up this excessively long chapter; I have, I think, proven that whatever the faults of the Committee of Public Safety, it at least had in view only the interests of our country and of liberty; I have proven that the accusations against us were destitute of proofs or were supported only by documents collected in bad faith. I have proven that these documents themselves often speak in our favor. . . . People thought they were serving liberty, by proving that the misfortunes that followed its noble outburst were all the work of its enemies. They have delighted in this idea, which as to the blighting excesses at least is completely true, and they have given it an exaggerated application. They have, I think, fallen into a strange error, for they have not sensed that a cause as noble as the one we defend needs nothing but the truth. The inquisitors' crimes never prevented regarding religious enthusiasm as sublime; the misfortunes inseparable from the sudden explosion of the need for liberty in a great people will never prevent regarding such a movement as one of humanity's finest hours.

We have arrived at the moment when the revolution, having reached its apogee, is going to turn back. It was time no doubt for the revolutionary régime to cease, but for the principles of the revolution to lose nothing thereby, it had to be stopped by its own children. . . . a Danton or a Robespierre. . . . It was not so. To consummate the revolution of 9 Thermidor, its authors addressed themselves to all the parties, even to the men who, after 31 May [1793], had become the enemies of the Republic: their fatal support made of 9 Thermidor a veritable reaction. . . .

We saw a coalition, composed of the most disparate elements, over-

Mémoires, III, 234-55.

turn Robespierre's party. It was impossible to foresee what would be the result of a victory won by such a coalition. Let us cast a glance at the various parties which composed the improvised alliance of 8 Thermidor, and let us see what were the relations which were established after Robespierre's fall, in order to understand better the great struggle which remains to us to describe, and the odious reactions which bloodied it.

The faction which showed itself in the front rank in the struggle of 9 Thermidor was formed of Mountaineers who had been attached to the party of Danton, and since the death of that celebrated man, fiery enemies of Robespierre, of the Committee of Public Safety, and of all those colleagues who, during the last months of the terror, had contributed to the movement of public affairs. Tallien, whose lucky audacity had begun the combat of 9 Thermidor; Barras, who had directed the military operations of that day; Fréron, friend of Tallien and evil genius of Barras, were the principal chiefs of this faction; in their following came Merlin de Thionville, Bourdon de l'Oise, Thuriot, and other old Mountaineers, who had associated with us only in hatred for the Gironde, whose talents were offensive to them. Legendre was the orator of this party; we saw the butcher argue vigorously against Lanjuinais, timidly defend Danton, and tremble before the Committee of Public Safety. . . . But this man was certainly the most honest in the party, which took the name of Thermidorian. The political faith of Tallien and Barras was more than suspect; they had several times been suspected of relations with the foreigners; they were compromised in all the intrigues, and a mass of letters seized on *émigrés* denounced them as hidden partisans of the anti-national cause; . . . besides, Barras and Tallien were men of pleasure, very accessible to the need for money. Tallien made his fortune several times. He led the life of a great lord, and died poor. Barras, until his last day, lived in luxury and riches; it is even said that he adopted an astounding cynicism to advertise the impure source of his opulence; the rest of this party was composed of subordinate intriguers and men of money: Courtois, later convicted of malversations, Merlin de Thionville, whose immorality I have already shown, Fréron, whose name sufficiently recalls his dismal renown. It was, however, to such men that the direction of affairs was turned over; it was they who daily accused the Mountain of alleged excesses.

What must be noticed above all is that the Thermidorians had placed themselves at the head of the warmest partisans of 31 May [1793]; that they had joined powerfully in the impulse to the anarchical movement which had carried us so far; that nearly all of them had taken an active part in the government of the terror; that most of them had been on missions in the *départements,* and there had given themselves over to reprehensible acts which they later wanted to cast on their adversaries. Thus Bordeaux was still terrified by the memory of Tallien's power, thus Marseille and Toulon were reeking of the blood spilled by Barras and Fréron. . . .

The Committee of Public Safety had joined with the Dantonists to effect 9 Thermidor, and in the first days which followed, Billaud, Collot and their friends seemed to move in accord with the Thermidorians; we shall soon see what causes divided them; around them were grouped those old proconsuls who, recalled by Robespierre because of their excesses, had joined the conspirators of 9 Thermidor for fear of seeing the anarchical movement stop; around them were grouped likewise the remnants of the Hébertist party, who thought they would find more support among them than among the friends of Danton. Yet, I repeat, the party of the Committee of Public Safety, long marched in accord with the Thermidorians, and if they divided later, it was only after circumstances that neither group had been able to foresee. Close to these men, already so little in agreement between them, began to appear the members of the old right wing, who, annihilated by the revolution of 31 May, had seen their salvation in the disagreements of the Mountain, and its resulting enfeeblement. These deputies were joined by old Mountaineers, like Thibaudeau, Cambacérès, Siéyès, who had at first rallied to us in the hope of seeing an energetic impulse given to the government of the Republic, and who had since become weary of the republican energy from seeing the excesses which had disfigured it.

There still existed, at that time, another party which had not been the last to wish for the fall of the decemvirs' tyranny, and which by its vigor, had powerfully served to limit the result of 9 Thermidor. This party was the true and constant Mountaineers. Lecointre of Versailles, Ruamps, Duhem had been the first to come out against Robespierre, and had contributed with all their might to strike down his sinister dictatorship; but it was to the advantage of liberty that they had wanted to turn the catastrophe of 9 Thermidor. They were not slow to perceive that they had been mistaken. As for me, who, like my colleagues, had been sorry to see the power delegated by us to the Committee of Public Safety degenerate into dictatorship, on learning at Namur, where I was then on mission, of the fall of the triumvirs, my first emotion was joy, but on learning which men had become influential in the Convention, my joy was quickly changed into grief. The deputies who had taken control were, for the most part, men without principles, ambitious mercenaries; with what sadness, good God, did I see my country's destiny entrusted to such hands!

I have used the term "parties" for the various nuances of opinion which divided the Convention after 9 Thermidor; but these various opinions were still far from forming what we call parties; they concealed within them seeds of discord which had not sprouted . . . . Each of the nuances of opinion that I have made known had a decided aim that it wanted to have triumph at any price: the Committee of Public Safety wanted to keep power and continue without Robespierre the system that Robespierre had made triumphant. The Thermidorians wanted to get power; the Girondins wanted to recall their proscribed colleagues, and substitute for the constitution of '93 the constitution contemplated by Gaudet and Vergniaud and their ilk. The moderate faction of the Mountain desired, at any price, order, calm, and peace. Finally, the pure Mountaineers, satisfied to have done justice to the dictatorship, desired to lose nothing of the revolutionary energy and, while restoring the forms of order and justice too long forgotten, to keep nevertheless the redoubtable stance towards our enemies that had already made us victorious so many times. . . . The Thermidorians had no fixed opinions, no settled doctrines. They studied public opinion in order to conform to it, and all their acts were the result of outside influence. Thus, when it was clear that moderation was the general desire, they paraded moderation; Fréron even preached clemency with the same impetuosity of character that he had used to maintain severity. . . . With such men a reaction was imminent. Yet their former political relations and the part they had taken in the bloody acts of the terror stopped them for some time on the counter-revolutionary descent which sooner or later was to sweep them along. But when the opinion of the middle classes was strongly manifested, when above all the advances of the old Girondins proved to them that in politics everything is forgiven to success, they put themselves at the head of the reaction; their speeches, their journals, their acts were no longer anything but a long series of accusations against their former acts and their former speeches. They condemned themselves in the person of their former friends. They dared even more, they organized battalions of young men who, on the pretext of avenging the memory of victims of the terror committed in their turn unpardonable excesses. Enrolled under the name of Fréron's gilded youth, dressed with a refined elegance that caused the people to call them *muscadins* [fops], these young men spread about in the streets and public squares, dominating by physical force, insulting the patriots, and finally making their atrocious vengeance the successor to the vengeance of the sans-culottes with pikes and wooden shoes, whom they had in some sort replaced.

In addition, with the era of the reaction began the era of corruption; to the fierce loyalty of the Mountaineers succeeded the Thermidorian frivolity which was only too reminiscent of the monarchical French character and the shameful customs which have forever blighted the regency period. The Mountaineers had professed simplicity in clothing, frugality, austere probity; the reactionaries on the contrary paraded a desire for dressiness, for a brazen luxury, and for pleasure-seeking, altogether opposed to the republican genius. Everywhere we saw sumptuous repasts, balls, private festivals reappear and there the enemies of the revolution hastened to go; intrigue reappeared everywhere, and with it, women's influence on public affairs; beauty again became a corrupting power, and Madame Tallien was, so to speak, associated in government on the new Committee of Public Safety. Little by little the former aristocracy, which had claimed to be ruined by the requisitions and the revolutionary taxes, advertised aloud its splendor and opulence; the Thermidorians and the Girondins accepted admission in the salons of the Saint-Germain suburb, and lost there that republican ruggedness which had once rendered them incorruptible: good style became fashionable, and more than one man sacrificed his conscience to the desire to see linked to his name the epithet "well-bred." It is deplorable no doubt to have to take account of such puerile facts; it is certain, however, that they had the greatest influence on the last acts of the revolution; I blush to recall that lamentable influence, but truth forces me to make it known.

I must also recall a truly shameful circumstance of the saturnalia which succeded the reign of the inflexible republicans. Amid those balls which seemed to have become the principal occupation of people once admirable for their virtues, there was one above all which was the rage, and which future generations will not be able to believe. They established in the Saint Germain suburb a dancing society which called itself the Victims' Ball. To be admitted to it, one had to prove membership in a family of which some member had perished on the scaffold. Such were the men who accused us of immorality! . . .

Baudot's Notes

I wanted to write about the persons whom I have known, about the things that I saw or in which I took part. Persecuted by the Convention, ignored under the Directory and the Empire, persecuted again under the Restoration, I was alert enough not to expose myself further; I have therefore left my notes to the disposition of time. Having reached an age when infirmities begin, I need repose; I've made my decision: I am going to be a posthumous author, I am giving up fame in life. The time has not come when one can live in peace and reveal every truth. To write colorless memoirs like those of Thibaudeau, that is in truth effort wasted; in the times we are living in, one must be dead to say everything one thinks; it is the fault of the century. Perhaps a better era will come; I hope so; meanwhile, reader, here in good faith is my testament concerning the National Convention.

. . .

Those who sat on the summit of the Mountain were in general hecklers; their grasp was prompt and accurate, they were always ready to fling an epigram. Those whose imaginations were slower, but with the same opinions, placed themselves on the slope, in order to have more time to think and consider; the methodical men occupied the Plain; finally came the Marsh, which, on the left and on the right, surrounded the bar [in front of the front row]. These men, without talent, without ability, found their share of self-esteem there at no cost. Guests given the honor of taking places in the session sat among them, in order not to have the inconvenience of crossing the hall, and ordinarily paid with a little compliment to their neighbor for the kindness of their reception. Originally all these nullities appeared gentle, peaceable and conciliatory; but after the misfortunes of the Mountain, all at once there surged forth from this Marsh a mass of reptiles who were not lacking in poison. They then rose up against the same opinions they had supported at first, and did not cease to shout for what people wanted.

Alas! people were wanting justice, virtue, good faith, and the Convention was then dominated by the most deplorable perversity.

Bonaparte, after his first abdication, cried out: "By what slime I was surrounded!" Ah, if he had been well acquainted with the Marsh and the reactionaries!

. . .

Marc-Antoine Baudot, *Notes historiques,* edited by Mme. Edgar Quinet (Paris, 1893).

The Marsh in the Convention

There was a great instinct for liberty in the National Convention, but also a great deal of ignorance; the ignorant members voted with the Mountain against the Girondins, and with the fragments of the Gironde in favor of the reaction. They always saw the strongest party as the wisest party. They were what was called the Marsh. In the assemblies which followed they were called the pot-bellies. But in the Convention and later that type has always been the worst of all the political ills.

. . .

The carmagnole was a kind of clothing in use during the revolution, but it was scarcely worn except by workmen and proletarians. Yet several members of the Convention adopted it, but they were a small number, I think no more than six. It is well known that Robespierre was always carefully dressed, in a suit of sky-blue color and with hair curled. Among the six members of the Convention who wore the carmagnole, I distinguished particularly Chabot, Thibaudeau, and Granet of Marseille. Later, they had in common only this kind of clothing, and their political fortunes were very different. The carmagnole consisted in a jacket of a round cut which came down a little below the waist, with no coat, and trousers of the same material. The members of the Convention who wore this singular costume had had it made of mattress cloth with blue and white lozenges.

. . .

The Convention, to defend itself within and without, had to take the way of force. The legislative line was forbidden it; hence that divergence of opinions within it; some wanted the written reasonableness of peacetime; others the thunderstrokes of wartime, and certainly nothing resembled peace less than the era of 1793. Hence the error of nearly all the writers on the Revolution; they treat the questions of the most terrible epoch quietly and impassively like a judicial tribunal.

. . .

The terror was a necessity of the time. Ought we to repent it? Not I, at least. Among those who blame us are to be found royalists of every stripe, their hatred is logical, it is in the nature of things. There are also a few feeble, illogical patriots; they do not understand us, with them all explanation would be useless; besides it is not our duty to supply intellect to all nature's moral disgraces.

. . .

After 9 Thermidor, they imprisoned many persons with this note: "Partisan of the conspirator Robespierre, partisan of the conspirator Saint-Just." There is not a shadow of truth in this accusation. Robespierre was speaking out openly in the National Convention, at the Jacobins, he took no precaution in coming to the Assembly on 9 Thermidor. He sounded out the Committee of Public Safety some time previously to learn whether he could hope for dictatorship; he got a refusal, he took no more precautions because of that. Seeing himself overwhelmed, he appealed to virtue: a conspirator appeals to arms. He was often enough surrounded by satellites, but satellites who proceeded with audacity, acted in the open, and never by ruse and in the shadows. Saint-Just was no more sly in his conduct; he several times forced the Convention to confirm his death sentences. On 9 Thermidor he came with a written speech, and he contented himself, that time, with one accusation: conspirators do not compromise.

Everything was done at the city hall by a spontaneous movement; General Hanriot knew so little what he ought to do that he lost his head, and it was well for the Convention that the armed force was not in more capable hands. If Robespierre had conspired and given instructions in case of events, there would have been order in the revolt, and [in fact] there was only confusion. There was a conspiracy, however, but in the opposite direction; Collot d'Herbois and Billaud-Varenne had been preparing people's minds for three days. Tallien and others communicated with the chiefs of the Gironde party; he was informed of all these moves and did not forestall them.

They agreed to attack the tyrant, they took away all his support and he found himself isolated, lost and intended for death, still believing in and appealing to his alleged virtue which was to defend and sustain him. He fell under the blow of a conspiracy, then, and did not conspire at all. Saint-Just and the other shared his fate.

The deserts and the consequences are another question. I have tried to demonstrate elsewhere, and I am convinced, that in the political situation of France before 9 Thermidor, whether truth or slander, the Republic could no longer maintain itself through Robespierre and with Robespierre.

. . .

The National Convention, after 9 Thermidor, was best and most surely placed to represent greatly the people's interests. There was in its position enough ability and power for the moral and political regeneration of the universe. Neither privilege nor king nor nobility nor the influence of the Catholic clergy nor foreign clerical power existed any longer; the *parlements* had been overthrown, the intermediate aristocracy shamed, the armies of the kings of Europe had been beaten and they remained without energy, we had for us ardent youth who were going to arms with the enthusiasm of liberty and especially of equality; we had only to close ranks among civilians and to have the will. Unfortunately, passions were exacerbated. The deputies who had perished in our dissensions left successors in opinion [who were] always ready to rush into every kind of action to avenge them. A few were at Coblentz, the greatest number auxiliaries of the domestic royalists.

Fréron accepted the title rather than the duties of a party chief, chief of the gilded youth; all the deputies full of hatred applauded the formation of the Companions of Jéhu and the Sun; they found avengers in those frantic assassins, thinking to cast on them the odium of massacres and revenge. Each reactionary deputy was thinking of the death of his enemy, without wielding a stiletto himself. As for those who armed themselves with that fatal instrument, there were plenty of them outside the hall; in the end, even members of the Convention, finding that vengeance was not going fast enough for their taste, supplemented it by decrees. The evil began with the killing of deputies, whatever their opinions, and finally everything was lost by the reaction.

. . .

The Committee on Legislation, like the governing committees, felt the influence of that dreadful reaction which eclipsed the fine day of our liberation and of our hopes [9 Thermidor]. All the agencies of authority, all the agencies of justice, made the cry for revenge heard and gave the signal for death. Whoever was not a victim was a persecutor, and the crowning scandal was that among the executioners, and under new colors, were former agents, accomplices of the triumvirate [Robespierre, Saint-Just, and Couthon].

What a harrowing spectacle was then presented to us by the Committee on Legislation invaded by tigers, setting itself up as a committee on investigations and indictments, putting to death representatives of the people every day without their being heard, and turning over to all the dangers of proscription those who, just before, had been exercising the power of the National Convention!

A dreadful change was decreed in the political, military, and administrative conduct of the people's representatives whom the Convention had sent either to the armies or into the *départements,* and the haste of a blind vengefulness confounded them and exposed them to the same dangers.

On what grounds were the recalls issued? On denunciation by royalists and enemies of the Republic!

The base jealousy of all the unnoticed members of the Convention, and their number was large, provided an immense majority for the decree, and the reactionaries declared themselves its executants.

These unknown members thought that by their indictment, they were assuming an importance that they had not been able to obtain otherwise.

To appreciate the justice of that Committee on Legislation, one must examine those whom it accused and those whom it did not submit to any investigation, whose missions were supposed to be approved by its silence.

Certainly, no mission had ever been more destructive, more murderous, bloodier than that of Barras and Fréron at Marseille and Toulon. Barras and Fréron were among the chiefs of the reaction, one was very careful not to attack them.

Tallien and another deputy, whom I do not want to name, had established the revolutionary committee of Bordeaux; they had authorized and caused to be carried out a mass of spoliations and murders. None of the accused men had gone so far, but Tallien had assumed the scepter of Thermidor; the other was a member of the Committee on General Security. Not only were they personally inviolable, but, in their reactionary power, they could send people to death without protest.

I could greatly extend this parallel, but this fully suffices to make it known what men composed the Committee on Legislation.

. . .

The reactionaries caused many more men to perish than did all the revolutionary tribunals together; but as the victims of the reaction were less noticeable in society, the philosophy of Sieyès takes no account of them. To stop that torrent of violence and assassination would have required the philanthropy of Chénier. If one takes account of the drownings in the Rhône and the Saône, the prisoners slaughtered in Fort Saint-Jean at Marseille, all the victims immolated later 1 Prairial, the assassinations ordered on Romme, Soubrany, and so many others, which were the result of that catastrophe, certainly this is no exaggeration.

I hold Robespierre and his horrible revolutionary tribunals in horror, but the reactionaries did not even trouble with that derisory and, if you like, atrocious legislation; they assassinated with no other formality than assassination.

The reason reckonings are not done is that few writers have had the courage to discuss it; none that I know of has listed the names, while the revolutionary tribunals had the stupid good faith to have the list of their victims printed. The reactionaries, more adroit, immolated in darkness in order to make it easy to deny at need.

. . .

The Republic

The Republic is in people's hearts and not on a written document. And so when the Thermidorians and the reactionaries had forced it out of people's hearts, there no longer remained anything but the writing which, from one moment to the next, could be torn up, as did not fail to occur. Other governments can do without it, the Republic cannot exist without conviction. The Republic is the sentiment of equality, the knowledge of the just and the unjust, innate in all men in society.

. . .

Thibaudeau, who at the beginning of the Convention was dressed as a sans-culotte, adopted an Albanian costume after 9 Thermidor: he had long moustaches, hair slicked down flat, pistols and a dagger in his belt; it is in this semi-Turkish costume that [in 1795] he had Romme, Soubrany, and others arrested and put to death.

. . .

Tallien made himself the sole hero of 9 Thermidor, although others, such as Cambacérès or Charles Duval, could have claimed a great part of his glory, if glory there was. Anyway, he profited from the error and the illusion of the times to marry a great lady, celebrated for her beauty, her mind, and her favors. He announced his marriage almost officially from the platform of the Convention. Returning from Quiberon on the eve of 9 Thermidor, Year III, he sought the triumph of a double ovation, and it was not refused him. Tallien, until then, had been a personage. After the session, Tallien, who had only a language of circumstance, fell into complete discredit. It was then a question of discussing written laws, and Tallien did not know a word of legislation. His antecedents had been questionable, the present reduced him to nothing. His wife perceived that she had married, instead of a hero, a man with nothing in the way of merit. The mask falls, the man remains, and the hero vanishes. He was no longer that violent Thermidorian who, after 12 Germinal, designated the victims; he was no longer that little Sulla who called out the names to be proscribed and imposed on the Assembly the obligation to sanction his hatreds and his vengeances. . . .

. . .

Merlin de Thionville at that time took over the country house of a prince [Raincy] to relax from his parliamentary work. He had a considerable pack of hounds, hunting carriages, equipages for the chase; he hunted the stag; there were coaches for his mistresses, splendid meals for his guests.

He was a new prince sprung up from the democratic mob; he had good reasons to want equality no longer. . . .

SUGGESTIONS FOR FURTHER READING

General

Students whose knowledge of pre-revolutionary France is slight could do no better than turn to the first volume of Alfred Cobban's *History of Modern France, 1715-1799* (1961). It is eminently readable and often witty. George Lefebvre's *Coming of the French Revolution* focuses on 1788-89 and still constitutes the best account of the origins of the revolution. The same author's study of the entire revolution in the *Peuples et Civilizations* series has been translated into English (in two volumes) as *The French Revolutio*n (1962-64). A difficult work for the beginning student, this study is the epitome of Lefebvre's years of work in a field of which he was the acknowledged master. Students who are studying the revolution for the first time should perhaps turn first to histories that do not take for granted as much knowledge as does Lefebvre's. Although somewhat dated in parts, J. M. Thompson's *French Revolution* (1943) is the best introduction to the revolution for English-speaking students. The book is rich in detail, and its narrative pace is comfortably unhurried. It is especially valuable for its glossary and for the pains that Professor Thompson took to describe revolutionary institutions and terminology. Crane Brinton's *Decade of Revolution, 1789-1799* is what one has come to expect from Professor Brinton. It is witty, urbane, and lucid. A more recent general history of the revolution to 1794 is J. M. Sydenham's *French Revolution* (1965). The author of a pioneering reassessment of the Girondins, Professor Sydenham manages to incorporate much of the work done recently by specialists. He includes a long and useful bibliography. An important general work from a particular point of view is Norman Hampson's *Social History of the French Revolution* (1963). It is the best introduction to that area of revolutionary studies which has advanced most rapidly in recent years. Unfortunately Albert Soboul's *Histoire de la révolution française* (1962) has not yet been translated. It is an exciting and persuasive Marxist interpretation of the revolution and an extremely useful manual for the serious student.

Robespierre and the Ninth of Thermidor

There are dozens of books in English on Robespierre and the period of the terror. The titles listed below are a sampling of the best of them. The terror as a whole and the work of the Committee of Public Safety from July 1793 to July 1794 are treated in R. R. Palmer's *Twelve Who Ruled* (1941). A rather discursive book, it remains the best single work in English on the period. Palmer's biographical sketches of the twelve members of the Committee are of special interest and value. Robespierre is the subject of a number of biographies in English. J. M. Thompson's two-volume *Robespierre* is by far the best. Two excellent biographies of other members of the Committee have been written in English. Leo Gershoy's *Bertrand Barère, A Reluctant Terrorist* (1962) was preceded by Geoffrey Bruun's shorter *Saint-Just, Apostle of the Terror* (1932). Of a somewhat different nature is George Rudé's *Robespierre* (1967), a collection of short texts by and about Robespierre. It provides an orientation for the student interested in following the vicissitudes of Robespierre studies.

A detailed study in English of the events of 9 Thermidor has not yet been produced. However, we are fortunate in having an English translation of several of Albert Mathiez's essays entitled *The Fall of Robespierre* (1927). Mathiez was a vehement defender of Robespierre. Although his intensely polemical style tends to become somewhat wearying, some of his essays—especially the study of 9 Thermidor—are models of incisive historical investigation. Also of interest is Mathiez's scathing account of the Thermidorian reaction published in English as *After Robespierre* (1929). For a general interpretation of the Year II the reader should turn to Soboul's *The Parisian Sans-Culottes* (1964). This is an English translation of Soboul's monumental *Les Sans-culottes parisiens en l'an II* (1958) minus the fascinating narrative chapters. The student who reads French might want to leaf through the final chapters to see how a brilliant historian constructs a narrative with data obtained through years of painstaking archival research. A more succinct statement of Soboul's view on Robespierre can be found in his article, "Robespierre and the Popular Movement," *Past and Present,* May 1954. George Rudé's *Crowd in the French Revolution* (1959) is concerned with the behavior, composition, and motives of revolutionary crowds throughout the revolution. It has an excellent short account of the events of 9 Thermidor.

BIOGRAPHICAL APPENDIX

Bertrand BARÈRE (1755-1841), son of an attorney in the small town of Tarbes, in the Pyrenees, earned a reputation for brilliance as a lawyer practicing before the Parlement of Toulouse and a member of provincial academies. Deputy to the Estates-General and National Assembly from 1789 to 1791, whose sessions he reported in his newspaper *Le Point du Jour;* judge in the Court of Cassation, 1791-92; prominent in the Convention from its beginning, member of the Committee of Public Safety from July 1793 onward, characterized as a "reluctant terrorist" by his most judicious biographer, Leo Gershoy. Escaped deportation in 1795, but his political career was ended; in exile at Brussels, 1816-30.

Paul BARRAS (1755-1829), son of a minor noble in Provence, served as an infantry lieutenant on two expeditions to India, resigned his commission in 1783, remained unoccupied until he was elected a member of the administration of his home *département,* the Var, in 1790. As a deputy in the Convention on missions to Toulon and Marseille, he displayed bravery and cruelty; he was later accused of keeping large sums confiscated from executed individuals. On bad terms with Robespierre, he became more prominent after the latter's death, and in 1795 returned to active service in the army with the rank of brigadier general, then was elected a member of the Directory, where he remained until 1800.

Théophile BERLIER (1761-1844) practiced law before the Parlement of Dijon, became, in 1790, a member of the administration of his *département,* the Côte-d'Or. In the Convention, he served on the Committee of Public Safety during June and July 1793, helped to draw up the Constitution of 1793; served on the Committee on Legislation in

1794, prepared treatises on the laws dealing with the rights of illegitimate children, the legal powers of fathers of families, and inheritances. Member of the 11-man commission that drew up the Constitution of the Year III. Elected to the Council of 500 in 1795, appointed Councillor of State in 1800; in exile at Brussels, 1816-30.

Jacques-Nicolas BILLAUD (1756-1819) was the son of a lawyer in La Rochelle. He was admitted to the bar there, wrote a comedy which failed, turned to teaching, and then in 1787 recommenced law practice in Paris, where he became acquainted with Danton. Active as a pamphleteer and member of the Jacobin club of Paris, he was a member of the revolutionary municipality of Paris on 10 August 1792 and was elected as a representative of Paris in the Convention. Member of the Committee of Public Safety with Robespierre. Deported to Guiana in May 1795, lived there until 1816 when he traveled to New York, then settled in Santo Domingo.

Jean COLLOT d'HERBOIS (1749-1796) was the son of a goldsmith in Paris. He became an actor, director, and playwright, and was director of the theater at Lyon in 1787. His *Famille Patriote* was immensely successful in Paris in 1790. He was active in the Jacobin club of Paris, and a member of the municipality after 10 August 1792. It was he who moved, in the first meeting of the Convention, for the abolition of the monarchy. On mission with Fouché in Lyon, in the fall of 1793, he ordered thousands of individuals shot by firing squads, and was finally recalled by the Committee of Public Safety, and was one of the small group who planned the arrest of Robespierre. He was deported to Guiana in May 1795, where he died.

François-Louis BOURDON (1758-1798) was the son of a tax collector in a village near Amiens. He practiced as an attorney in Paris, participated in mob action there in July 1789 and again in August 1792. When the electors of the *département* of the Oise chose as a representative in the Convention "Citizen Bourdon, one of the conquerors of the Bastille," he claimed a seat, in competition with Leonard Bourdon, deputy city attorney of Paris. The two men showered one another with invective. The quarrel was ended when the electors at Orleans chose the latter to represent the *département* of the Loiret. F-L Bourdon was generally drunk when he arrived for the Convention's evening sessions. He was well known as an adversary of Robespierre in the spring of 1794. A member of the Council of 500 until 1797, he was then accused of being a Royalist and deported to Guiana, where he died.

Jean-Jacques Régis de CAMBACÉRÈS (1753-1824) was mayor of the town of Mirepoix and judge in the Court of Accounts and Tax Appeals at Montpellier before 1789. The nobles of Montpellier chose him as an alternate deputy to the Estates-General, but he was never called upon to sit. He was elected chief judge of the criminal court of his *département,* the Hérault, in 1791. In the Convention, he sought to avoid taking part in factional strife, served as chairman of the Committee on Legislation in 1794, member of the Committee of Public lic Safety for three terms in the winter, spring, and summer of 1795. Member of the Council of 500 until the elections of 1797; appointed by the Directory as Minister of Justice in 1799 and by Napoleon as Second Consul in 1800, Arch-Chancellor of the Empire, 1804-15.

Pierre-Joseph CAMBON (1756-1820) succeeded his father in the textile business at Montpellier in 1785. He was elected an alternate deputy in 1789 by the third estate, went to Versailles expecting to be called on to sit, remained to observe the assembly until January 1790. Elected a municipal councillor in Montpellier, he founded the Jacobin club there. By the end of 1791 he had become a republican. He was elected a deputy from the Hérault to the Legistlative Assembly, in which he was chairman of the finance committee, a post he filled in the Convention as well. His relations with Robespierre were unfriendly.

Pierre-Joseph DUHEM (1758-1807), son of a master weaver in Lille, was a physician before 1789. He was elected justice of the peace in 1790, deputy to the Legislative Assembly in 1791. In the Convention, he was sharply criticized by Robespierre in December 1793, and ejected from the Jacobin club of Paris. Only after Robespierre's death did he become active again. Imprisoned from May to November 1795, he served as an army doctor until his death.

Joseph FOUCHÉ (1763-1820) was born near Nantes. He studied at the *collège* of the Oratorians in Nantes, took minor orders, and became a teacher. When the revolution broke out, he quickly emerged as a leading local radical and played a dominant role in the Jacobin club at Nantes. After his election to the National Convention, he moved steadily to the left, vehemently demanded the execution of the king. Because of his well-known revolutionary energy, he was sent to help put down the rebellion in the Vendée. Later, on mission to the Nièvre, he vigorously repressed counter-revolution, harassed aristocrats and the wealthy mercilessly. Together with Chaumette, Fouché directed and encouraged the anti-Christian movement in that area. He forbade religious ceremonies outside the churches, participated in grotesque parodies of religious ceremonies, and attempted to force all priests to marry or adopt a child. He proved himself to be extremely ruthless when he assisted Collot d'Herbois in the repression that followed the capture of Lyon. Robespierre urged the Committee of Public Safety to recall Fouché on several occasions. He succeeded in obtaining his recall in Germinal, Year II.

Jean François GOUPILLEAU (1753-1823) de Fontenay, was the son of a manorial court official. He served as a junior officer of dragoons, then became an attorney and notary in his home province of Poitou, where he was elected deputy to the Estates-General in 1789. In 1791-92 he was clerk of the criminal court of the *département* of the Vendée. In the Convention, he came into conflict with the Committee of Public Safety in the summer of 1793 over the measures to be taken in the Vendée. He was a member of the Council of Elders until May 1797, then was administrator of the Mont-de-Piété, 1797-1816.

Marc-Antoine HUGUET (1757-1796), son of a notary, was the parish priest of the small town of Bourganeuf in central France. He accepted the Civil Constitution of the Clergy, was elected bishop of the *département* of the Creuse, and in this capacity presided over the electoral assembly of the *département* in September 1791. He was himself elected to the Legislative Assembly, where he was noted for his violent denunciations of the royal ministers. Re-elected to the Convention, he continued to sit with the Mountain even after the death of Robespierre. He renounced the priesthood and married. In the end he was arrested during a civil disturbance in Paris in 1796 on a trumped up charge of robbery, and shot.

André JEANBON (1749-1813) known as Jeanbon-Saint-André, came from a Protestant family at Montauban. After several years in the merchant marine, during which he became captain of an ocean-going vessel, he turned to theology and became a minister with considerable reputation as a preacher. He was elected municipal councillor of Montauban in 1791. In the Convention, he was a member of the Committee of Public Safety during the Year II and was chiefly occupied with missions to the ports, serving in effect as civilian chief of the navy. Under the Directory, he was French consul at Algiers, then at Smyrna. Napoleon appointed him a prefect and special commissioner for the *départements* on the west bank of the Rhine, where he won popular esteem.

Élie LACOSTE (1745-1806) was a physician in the small southwestern town of Montignac until 1790, when he was elected a member of the administration of the *département* of the Dordogne. He was next elected to the Legislative Assembly and re-elected to the Convention, in which he served on the Committee on General Security from October 1793 through August 1794. His political career ended in 1795.

Laurent LECOINTRE (1742-1805), son of a Versailles cloth merchant, went into business on his own account. He began his revolutionary career as an officer in the national guard at Versailles, was elected to the Legislative Assembly where he became noted for denunciations against local administrations, ministers, and others. In the Convention, he was prominent because of his excitability, but never enjoyed great power. His political career came to an end in 1795.

Louis LEGENDRE (1752-1797), the son of a butcher-shop proprietor in Versailles, served as a sailor for ten years and then became a butcher in Paris. He was a powerful street orator, was one of the assailants of the Bastille on 14 July 1789. He commanded the armed force of the Luxembourg *section* on 10 August 1792. Elected to the Convention as a representative of Paris.

René LEVASSEUR (1747-1834), was born in a suburb of Le Mans, where before 1789 he practiced as an obstetrician. After serving as a member of the administration of the Le Mans *district,* he was elected to the Convention representing the surrounding *département,* the Sarthe. It was Levasseur who in March 1793 proposed the idea of the revolutionary tribunal to try traitors, conspirators, and counter-revolutionaries. He was relatively lenient in missions to Beauvais and Sedan but, accused of desiring a return to the terror, he was arrested on 5 April 1795. Released the following October, he resumed his medical practice.

Philippe-Antoine MERLIN (1754-1838) of Douai, was the son of a landowner in Flanders. He became a lawyer, bought an office as king's secretary. As a member of the Estates-General and National Assembly, he drafted much of the legislation that abolished feudal land law, concerned himself with the sale of nationalized church property, and suggested the law against emigration. During 1791-92 he was chief judge of the criminal court of the Nord *département*. In the Convention, he was a member of the Committee on Legislation, drafting, among others, the law of 17 September 1793, and the penal code of 1795. Under the Directory he was minister of justice, and under the Empire he was solicitor general in the court of cassation. In exile, 1815-30, he edited a multi-volumed encyclopedia of jurisprudence.

Claude-Antoine PRIEUR DUVERNOIS (1763-1832) was the son of a finance official and served as a brilliant officer of engineers in the army, until his election to the Legislative Assembly. In the Convention, he was known as Prieur of the Côte-d'Or to distinguish him from another deputy named Prieur (no relation). As a member of the Committee of Public Safety he was ceaselessly active with military matters and, with Carnot, was in effect one of the civilian chiefs of the army.

Maximilien François Marie Isadore ROBESPIERRE (1758-1794), was born in the northern town of Arras. Orphaned early in his childhood and reared by maternal aunts, Maximilien was forced to assume heavy emotional responsibilities as the eldest of four children. At an early age he acquired the traits that later distinguished him as the "incorruptible" revolutionary leader. He was earnest, serious, and hard-working even as a child. His intellectual ability won him a scholarship to the Jesuit Collège Louis-le-Grand in Paris, where he met Desmoulins. When he returned to Arras to practice law, he earned a reputation for his enlightened views and his willingness to defend poor subjects against old-regime injustice. He served as a deputy to the Estates-General and the National Assembly until 1791. During the period of the Legislative Assembly, he exercised a growing influence at the Jacobin club and in his newspaper, which he used to combat the war policy of the Brissotins. Although he did not actively participate in the insurrection which overthrew the constitutional monarchy, he was elected to the revolutionary Paris commune on 11 August 1792. When elections were held for the National Convention, he was the first choice of the voters of Paris.

Jean-Lambert TALLIEN (1767-1820) was the son of the Count of Bercy's maître d'hôtel. He began as an attorney's clerk, became secretary to a deputy in the Estates-General, was active in a political club in the east end of Paris. He acquired political importance only after 10 August 1792, when he became secretary of the municipality of Paris; he was later accused of complicity in the massacres of September 1792. As a member of the Convention he went on mission to Bordeaux, where he met Teresa Cabarrus, daughter of a Spanish banker and wife of an émigré French noble. She followed him to Paris in the spring of 1794 and was arrested. On 26 Thermidor Year II, Tallien, as a member of the Committee of Public Safety, obtained her release and five months later he married her. Tallien was a member of the Council of 500, but he was no longer influential. In 1798, he accompanied Bonaparte on the Egyptian expedition; he returned to France only in 1801, to discover that his wife had left him; he lived out his life ill and alone.

Antoine-Clair THIBAUDEAU (1765-1854), son of a lawyer in Poitiers who served as a deputy in the Estates-General and Constituent Assembly from 1789 to 1791, was himself a lawyer in Poitiers and executive officer of the municipality when he was elected to the Convention. Up to July 1794 most of his effort was devoted to the Committee on Public Education. On a mission in the West in 1793, he succeeded in getting the local authorities in Poitiers, who had adopted certain federalist resolutions, to withdraw them; but his father, father-in-law, and uncles were nevertheless imprisoned for their connection with them.

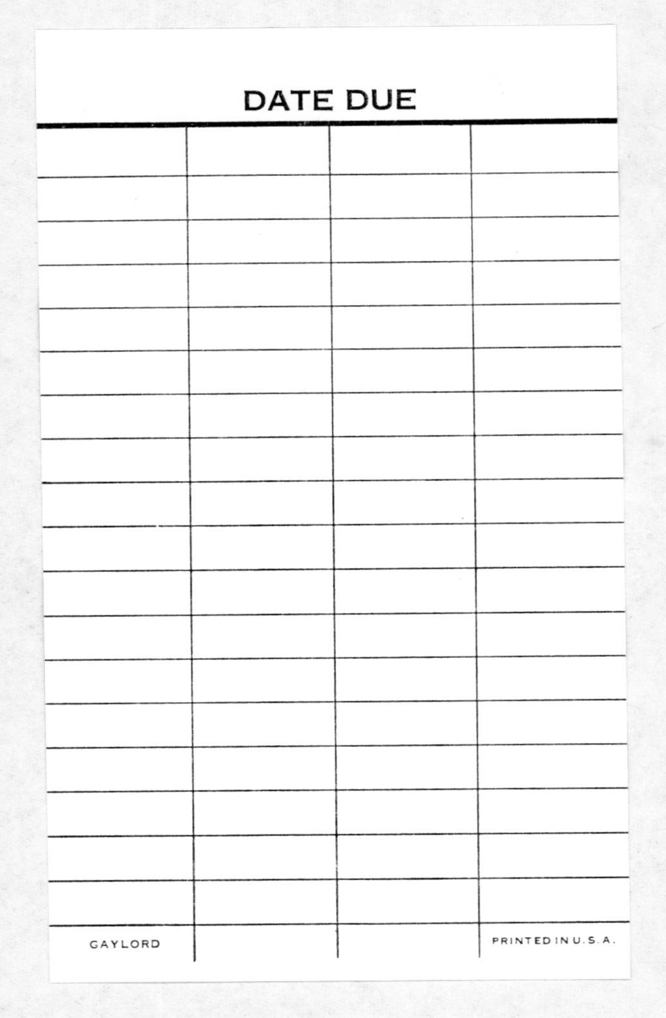
DATE DUE
GAYLORD
PRINTED IN U.S.A.